Voice Over!
Seiyu Academy

8

Vol.8
Story & Art by
Maki Minami

TECHNICAL ADVISORS
Yoichi Kato, Kaori Kagami, Ayumi Hashidate,
Ayako Harino and Touko Fujitani

Voice Over! Seiyu Academy

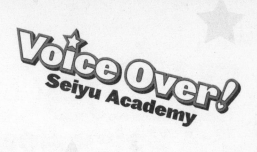

Vol. 8

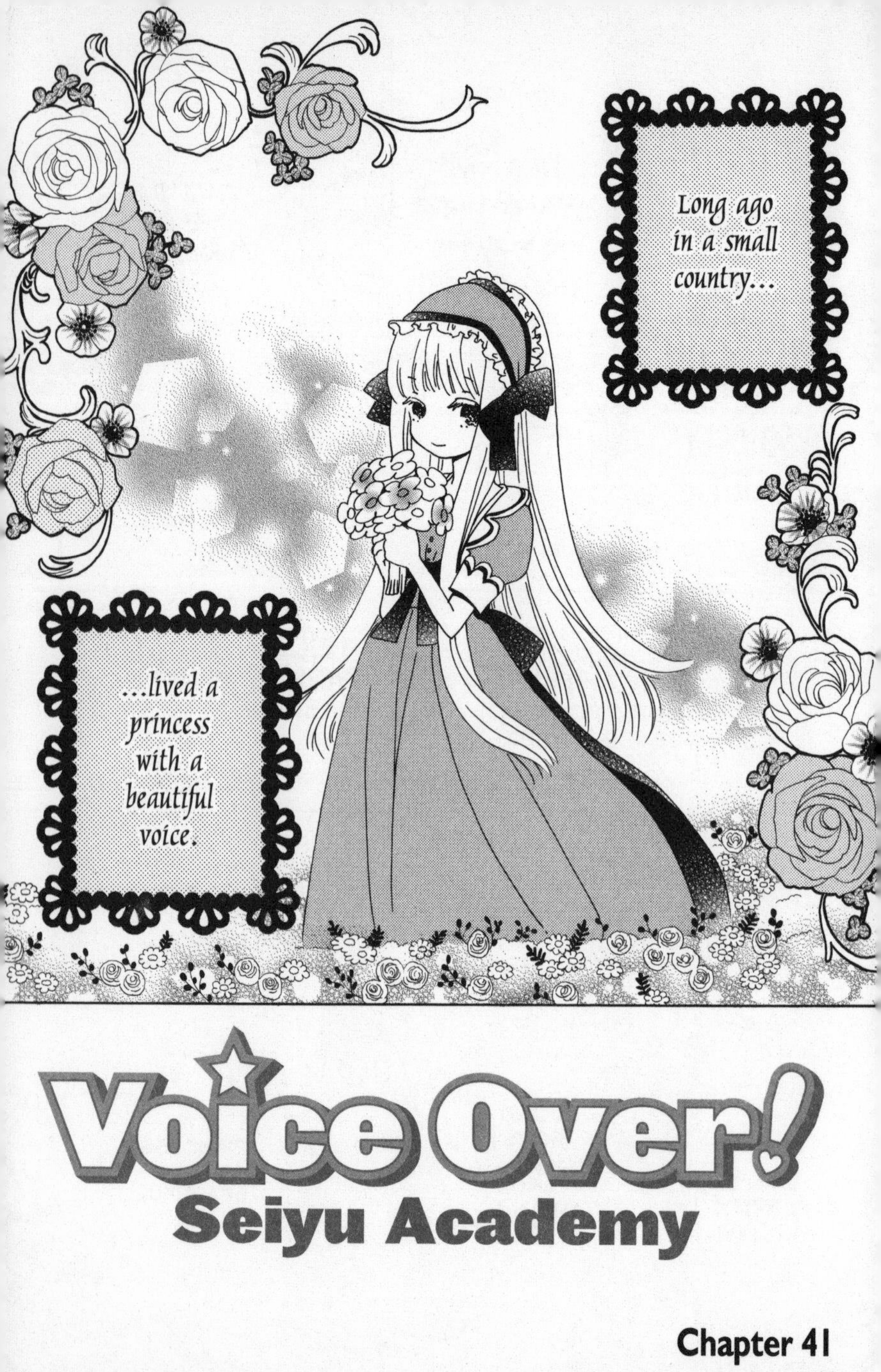
Long ago in a small country...
...lived a princess with a beautiful voice.

Voice Over! Seiyu Academy

Chapter 41

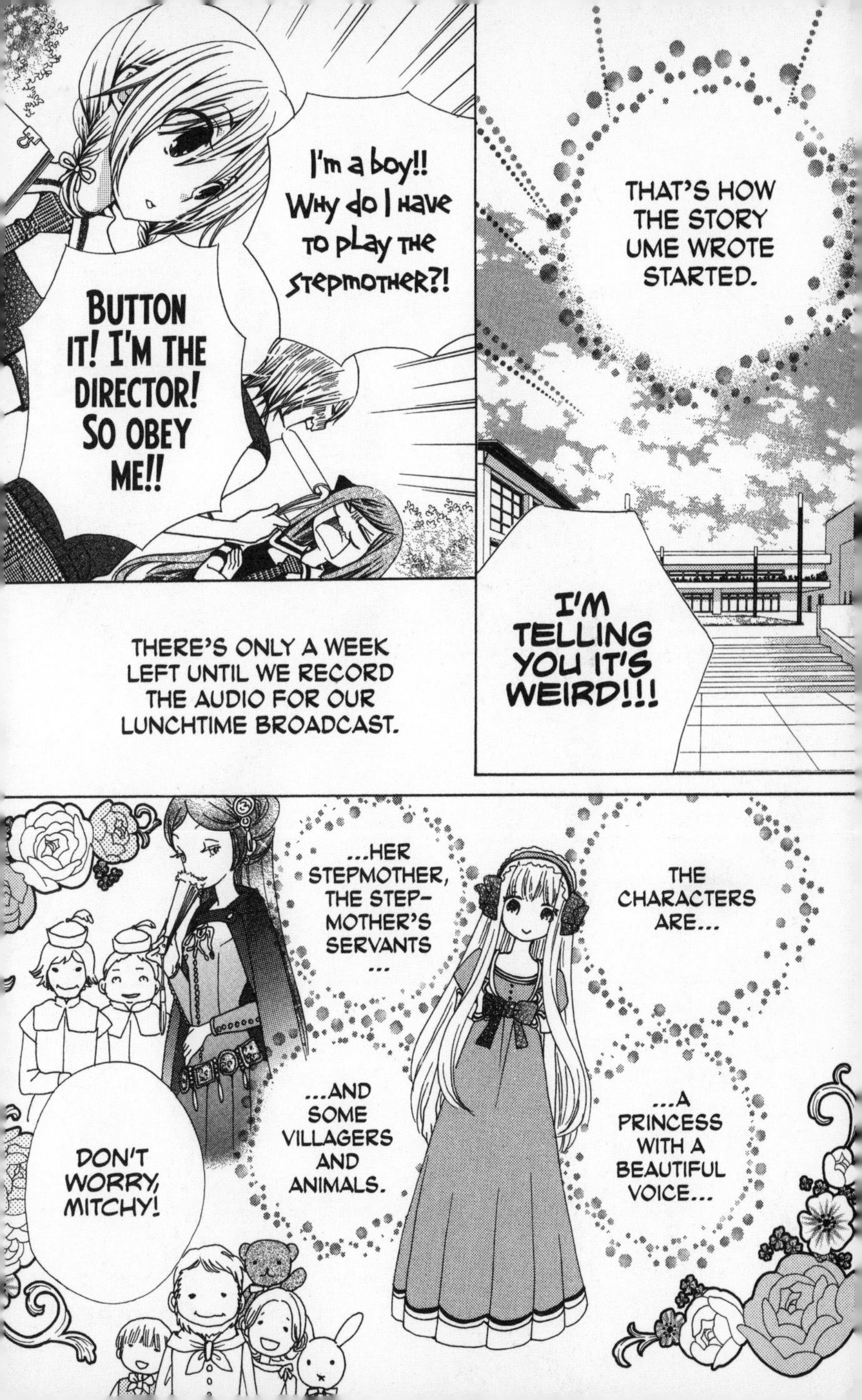
THAT'S HOW THE STORY UME WROTE STARTED.
I'm a boy!! Why do I have to play the stepmother?!
BUTTON IT! I'M THE DIRECTOR! SO OBEY ME!!
I'M TELLING YOU IT'S WEIRD!!!
THERE'S ONLY A WEEK LEFT UNTIL WE RECORD THE AUDIO FOR OUR LUNCHTIME BROADCAST.
THE CHARACTERS ARE...
...A PRINCESS WITH A BEAUTIFUL VOICE...
...HER STEPMOTHER, THE STEP-MOTHER'S SERVANTS...
...AND SOME VILLAGERS AND ANIMALS.
DON'T WORRY, MITCHY!

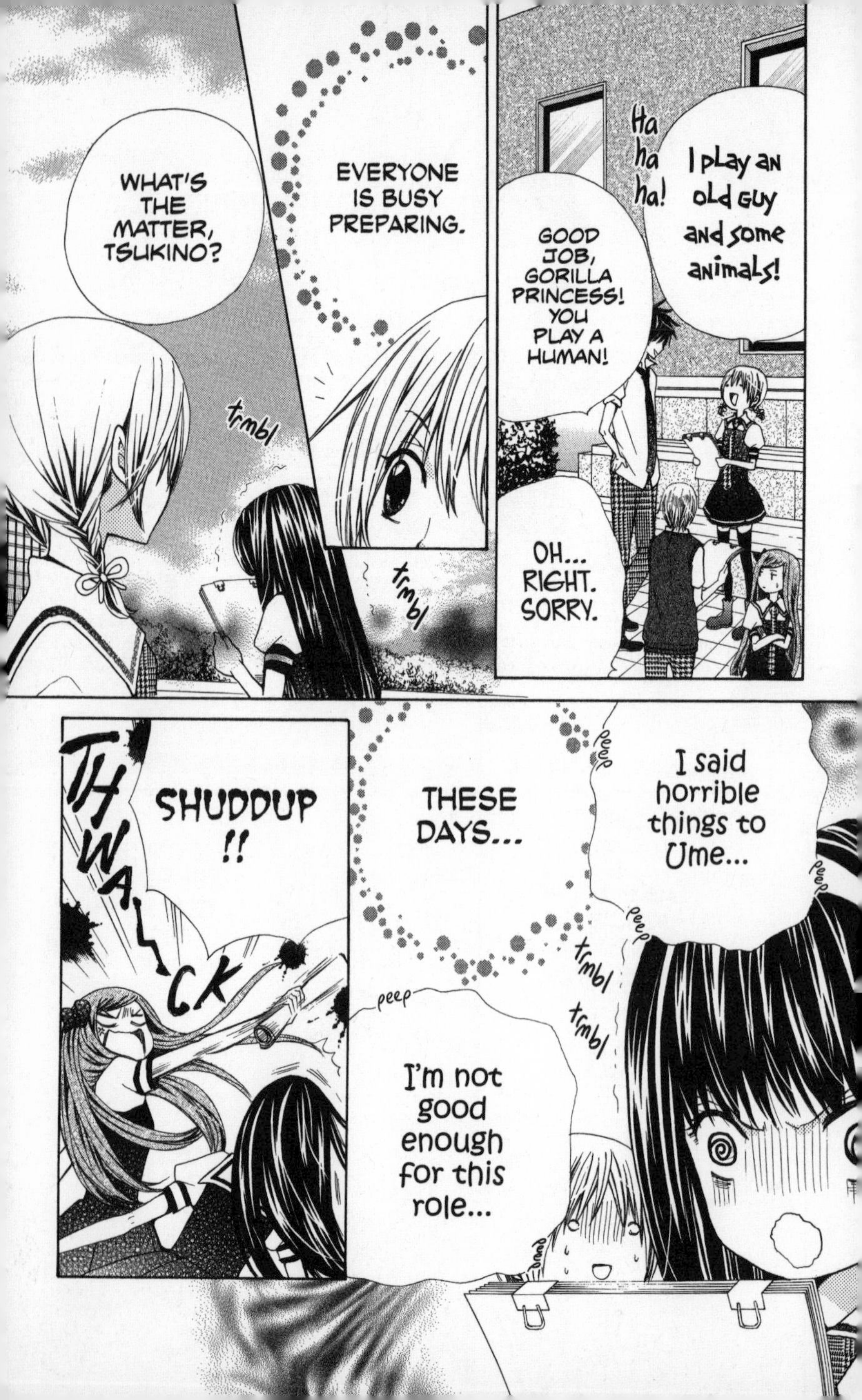
I play an old guy and some animals!
Ha ha ha!
GOOD JOB, GORILLA PRINCESS! YOU PLAY A HUMAN!
OH... RIGHT. SORRY.
EVERYONE IS BUSY PREPARING.
trmbl
WHAT'S THE MATTER, TSUKINO?
trmbl
I said horrible things to Ume...
peep
peep
peep
THESE DAYS...
trmbl
trmbl
peep
I'm not good enough for this role...
peep
SHUDDUP !!
THWALLCK

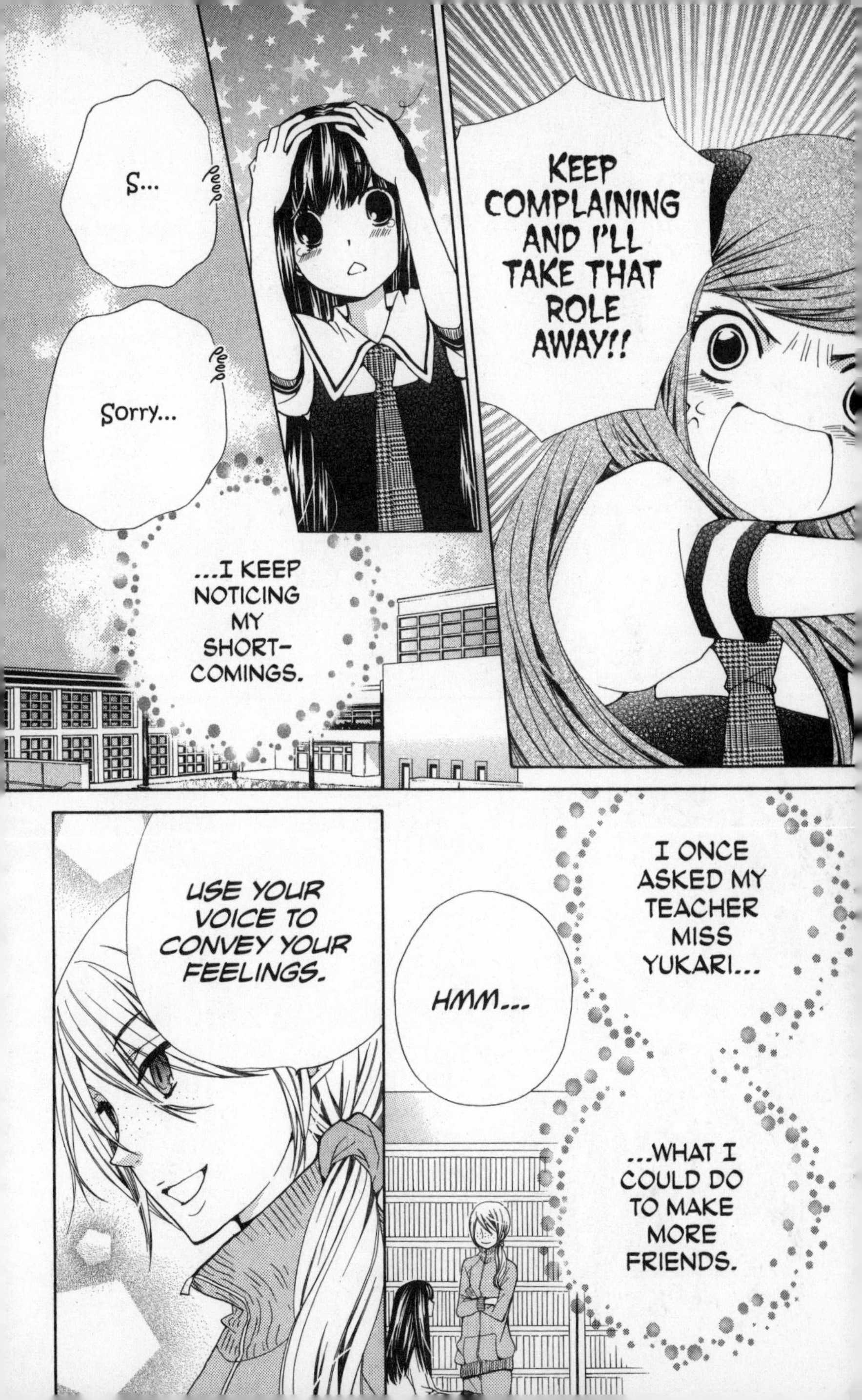
KEEP COMPLAINING AND I'LL TAKE THAT ROLE AWAY!!
S...
peep
Sorry...
peep
...I KEEP NOTICING MY SHORT-COMINGS.
I ONCE ASKED MY TEACHER MISS YUKARI...
...WHAT I COULD DO TO MAKE MORE FRIENDS.
HMM...
USE YOUR VOICE TO CONVEY YOUR FEELINGS.

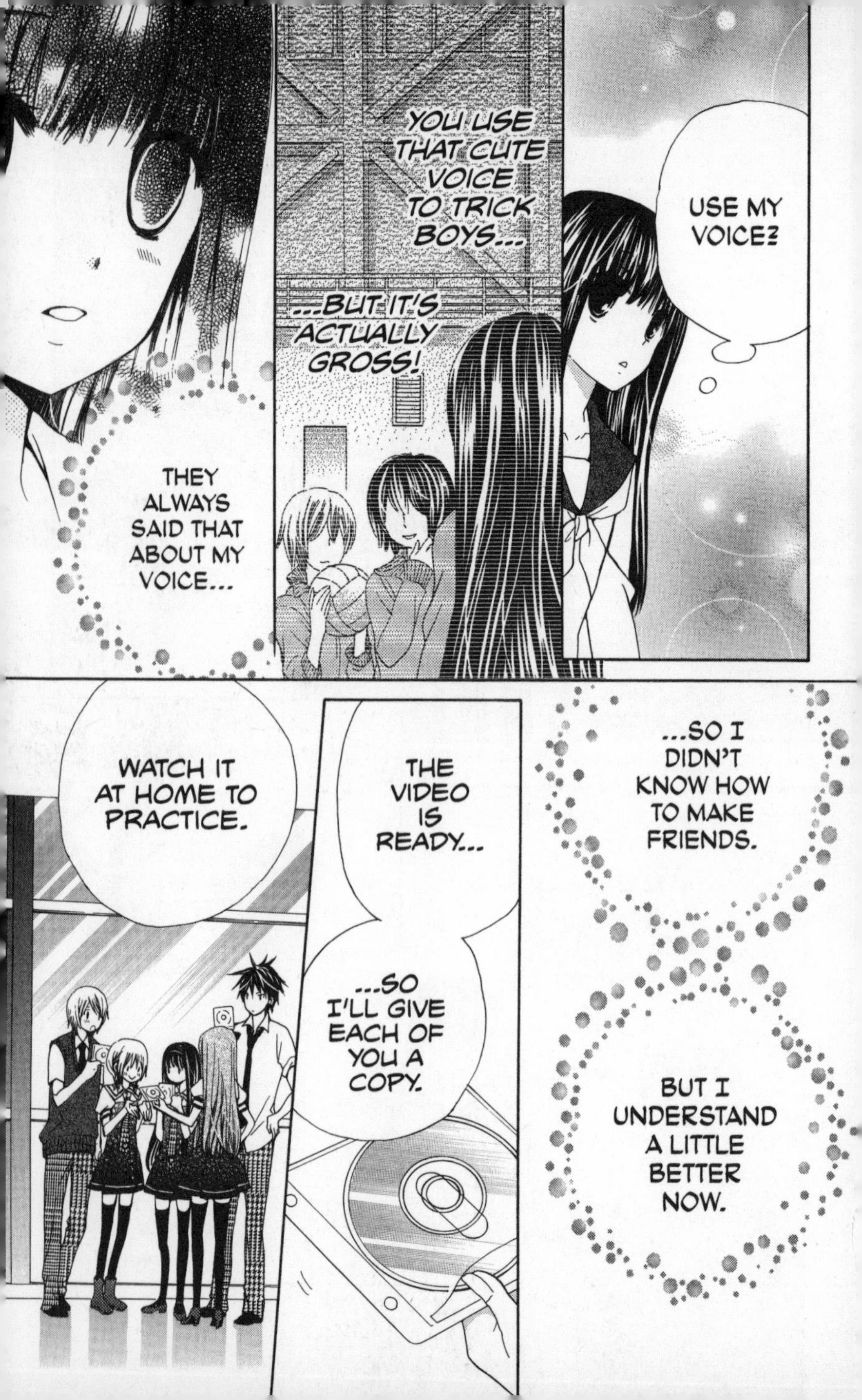
USE MY VOICE?
YOU USE THAT CUTE VOICE TO TRICK BOYS...
...BUT IT'S ACTUALLY GROSS!
THEY ALWAYS SAID THAT ABOUT MY VOICE...
...SO I DIDN'T KNOW HOW TO MAKE FRIENDS.
BUT I UNDERSTAND A LITTLE BETTER NOW.
THE VIDEO IS READY...
...SO I'LL GIVE EACH OF YOU A COPY.
WATCH IT AT HOME TO PRACTICE.

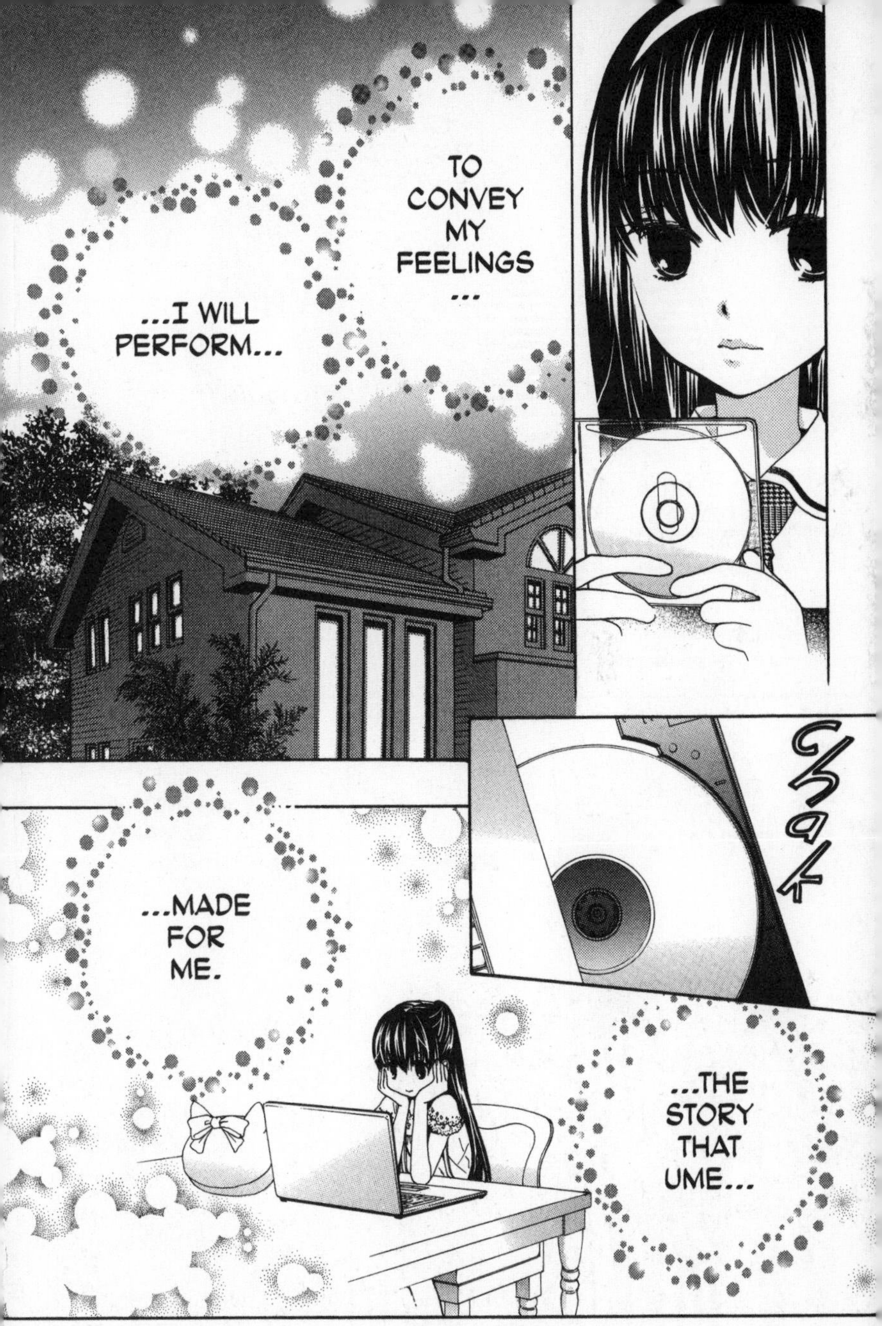
TO CONVEY MY FEELINGS...
...I WILL PERFORM...
Chak
...THE STORY THAT UME...
...MADE FOR ME.

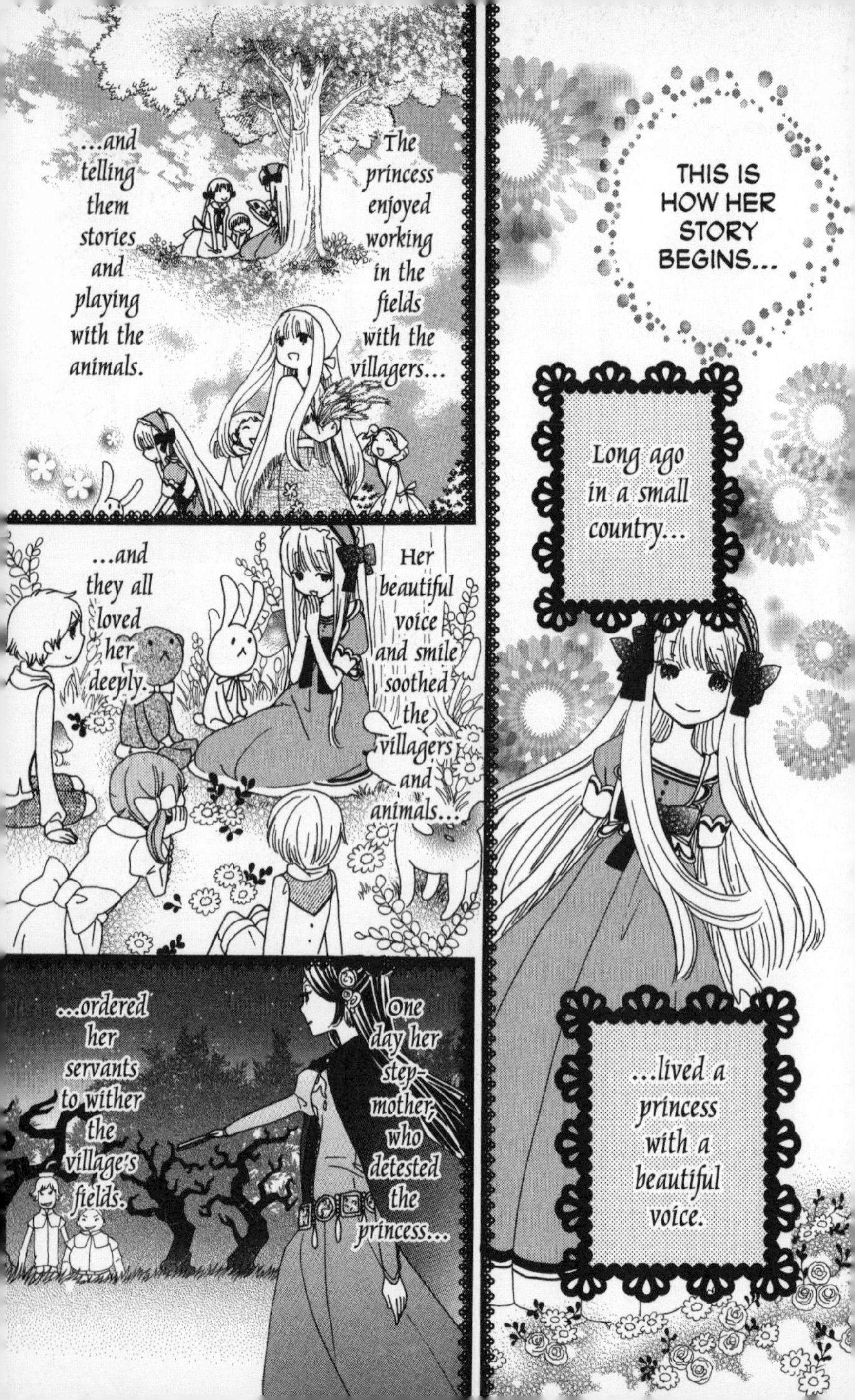
THIS IS HOW HER STORY BEGINS...
Long ago in a small country...
...lived a princess with a beautiful voice.
The princess enjoyed working in the fields with the villagers...
...and telling them stories and playing with the animals.
Her beautiful voice and smile soothed the villagers and animals...
...and they all loved her deeply.
One day her stepmother, who detested the princess...
...ordered her servants to wither the village's fields.

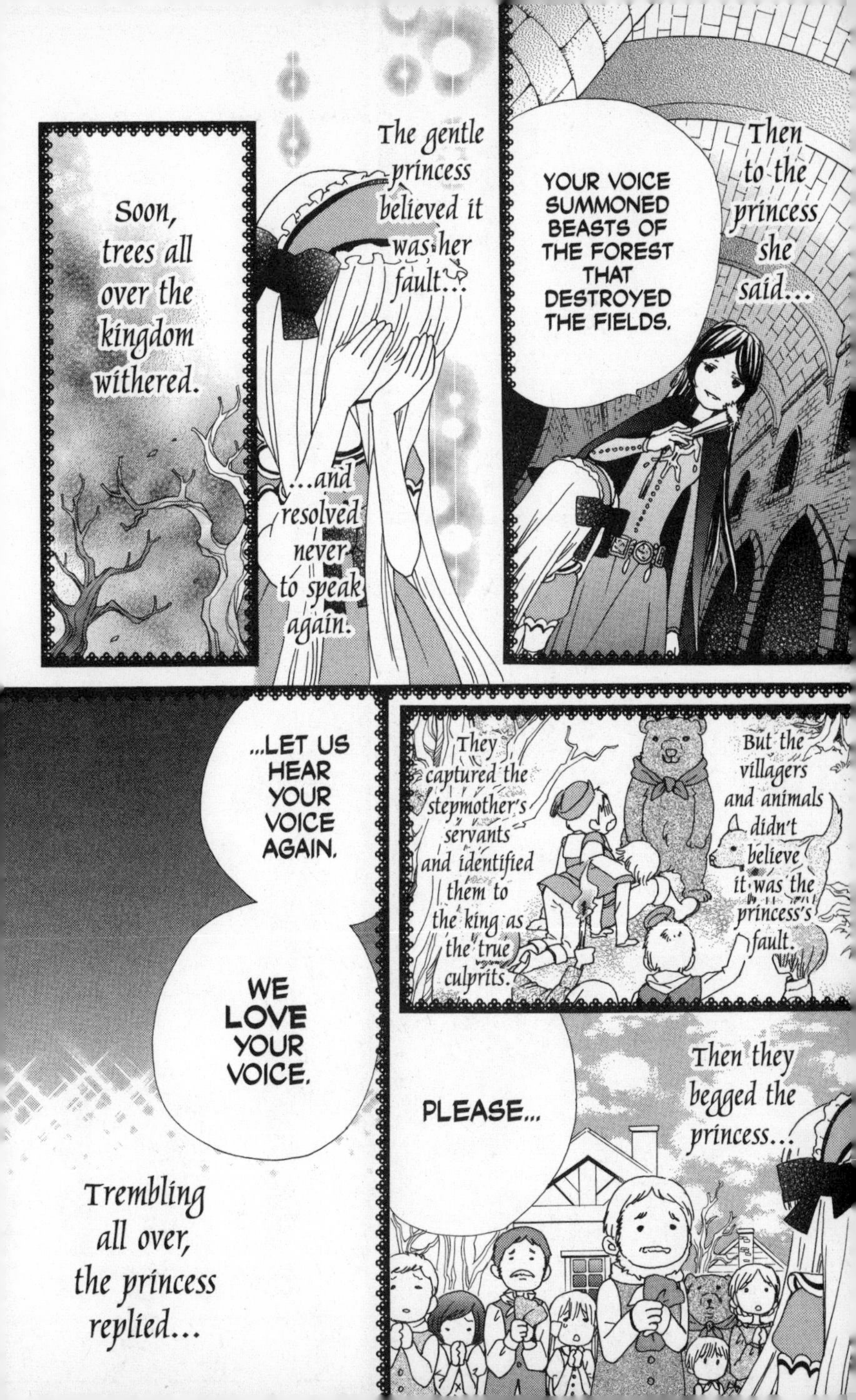
Then to the princess she said...
YOUR VOICE SUMMONED BEASTS OF THE FOREST THAT DESTROYED THE FIELDS.
The gentle princess believed it was her fault...
...and resolved never to speak again.
Soon, trees all over the kingdom withered.
But the villagers and animals didn't believe it was the princess's fault.
They captured the stepmother's servants and identified them to the king as the true culprits.
Then they begged the princess...
PLEASE...
...LET US HEAR YOUR VOICE AGAIN.
WE LOVE YOUR VOICE.
Trembling all over, the princess replied...

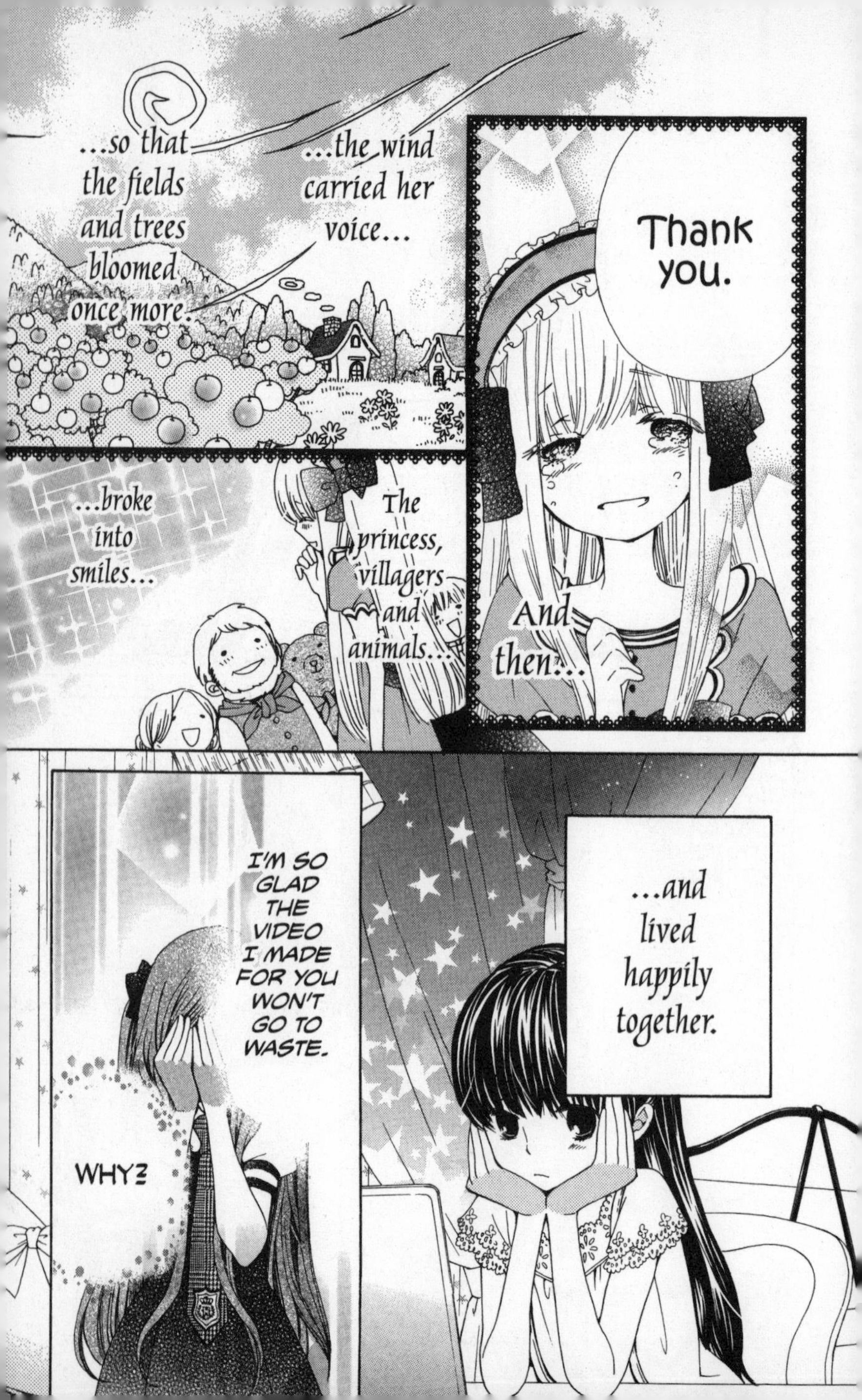
Thank you.
And then...
...the wind carried her voice...
...so that the fields and trees bloomed once more.
The princess, villagers and animals...
...broke into smiles...
...and lived happily together.
I'M SO GLAD THE VIDEO I MADE FOR YOU WON'T GO TO WASTE.
WHY?

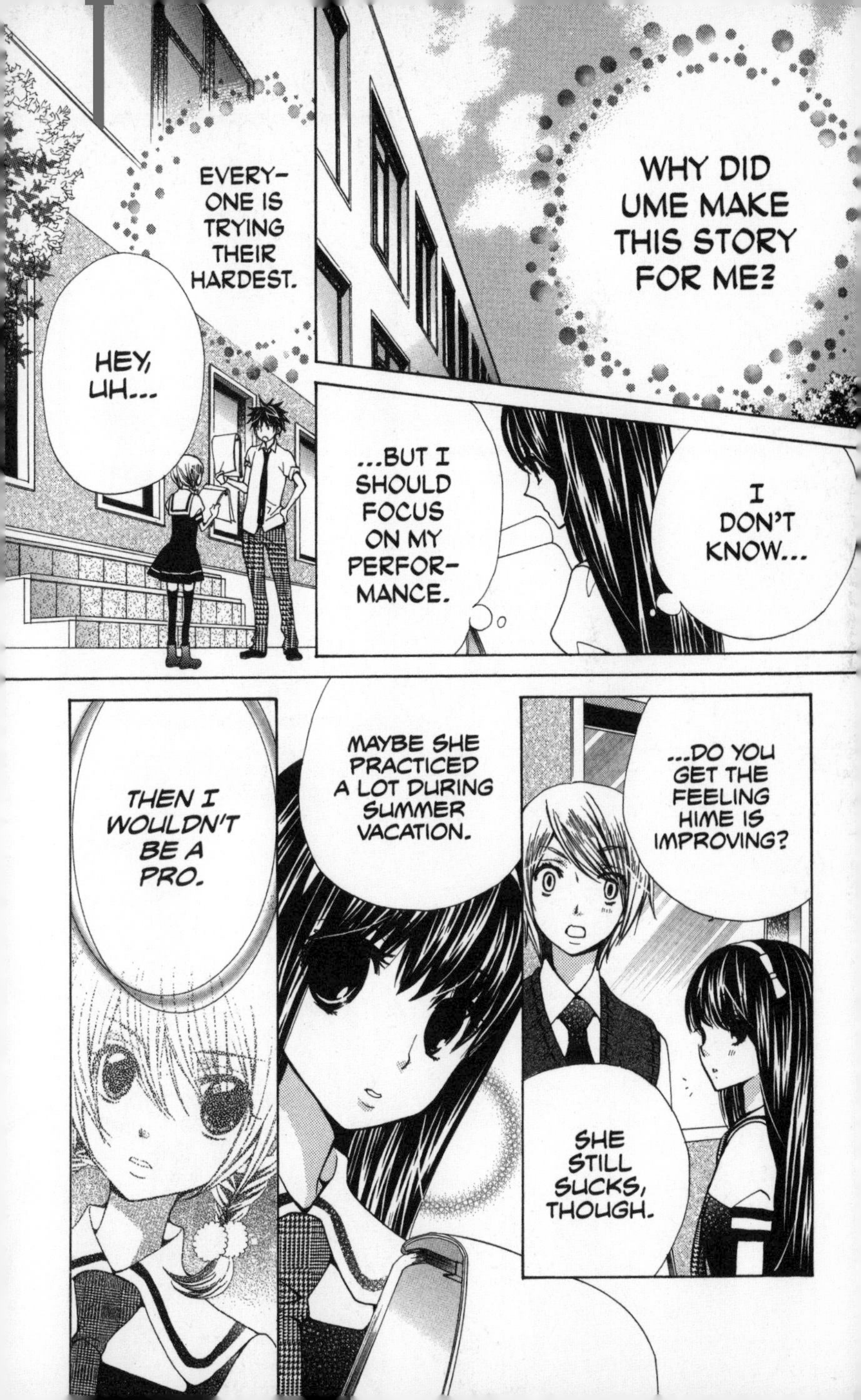
WHY DID UME MAKE THIS STORY FOR ME?
I DON'T KNOW...
...BUT I SHOULD FOCUS ON MY PERFORMANCE.
EVERY-ONE IS TRYING THEIR HARDEST.
HEY, UH...
...DO YOU GET THE FEELING HIME IS IMPROVING?
SHE STILL SUCKS, THOUGH.
MAYBE SHE PRACTICED A LOT DURING SUMMER VACATION.
THEN I WOULDN'T BE A PRO.

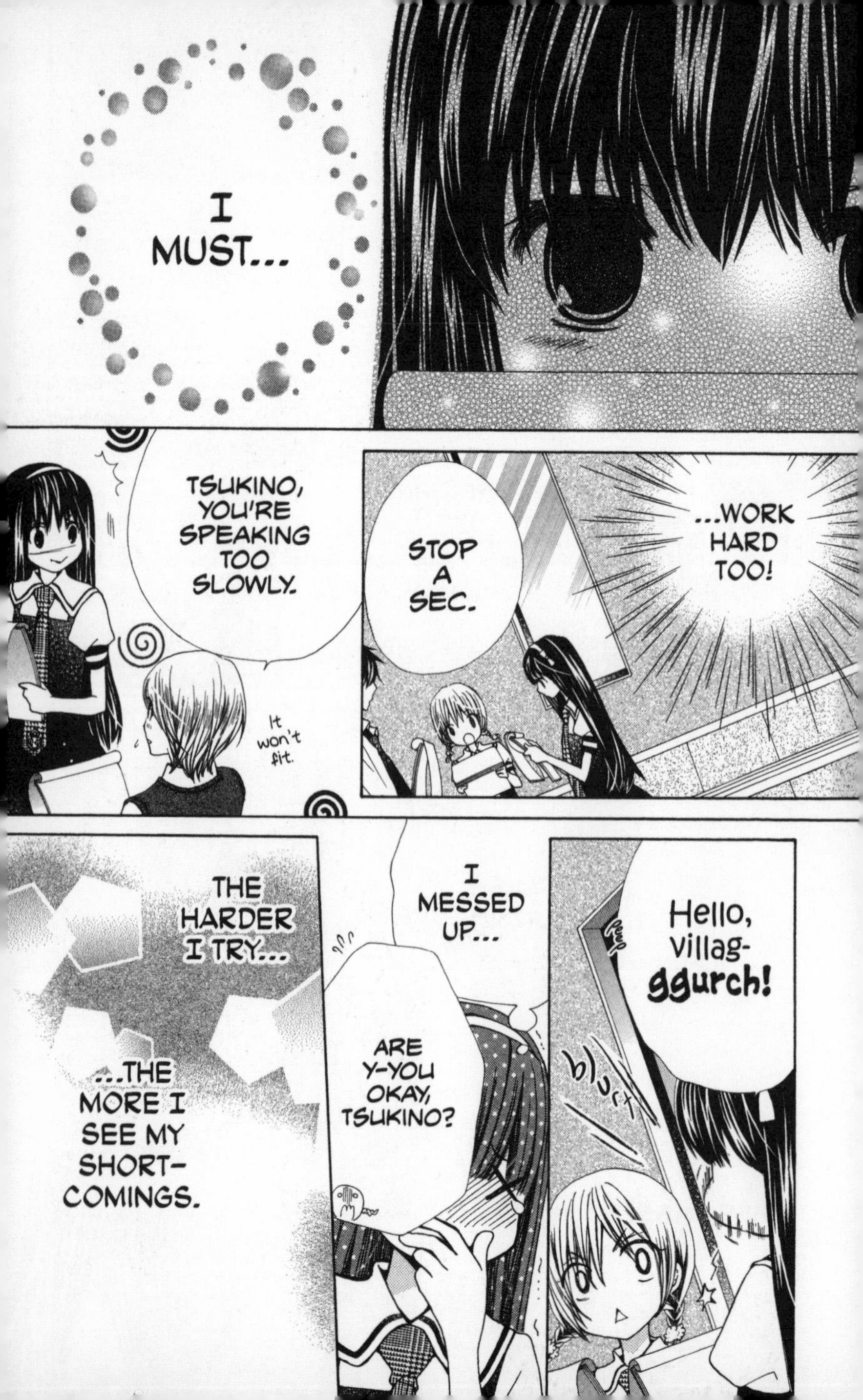
I MUST...
...WORK HARD TOO!
STOP A SEC.
TSUKINO, YOU'RE SPEAKING TOO SLOWLY.
It won't fit.
Hello, villag- ggurch!
blurt
I MESSED UP...
ARE Y-YOU OKAY, TSUKINO?
THE HARDER I TRY...
...THE MORE I SEE MY SHORT-COMINGS.

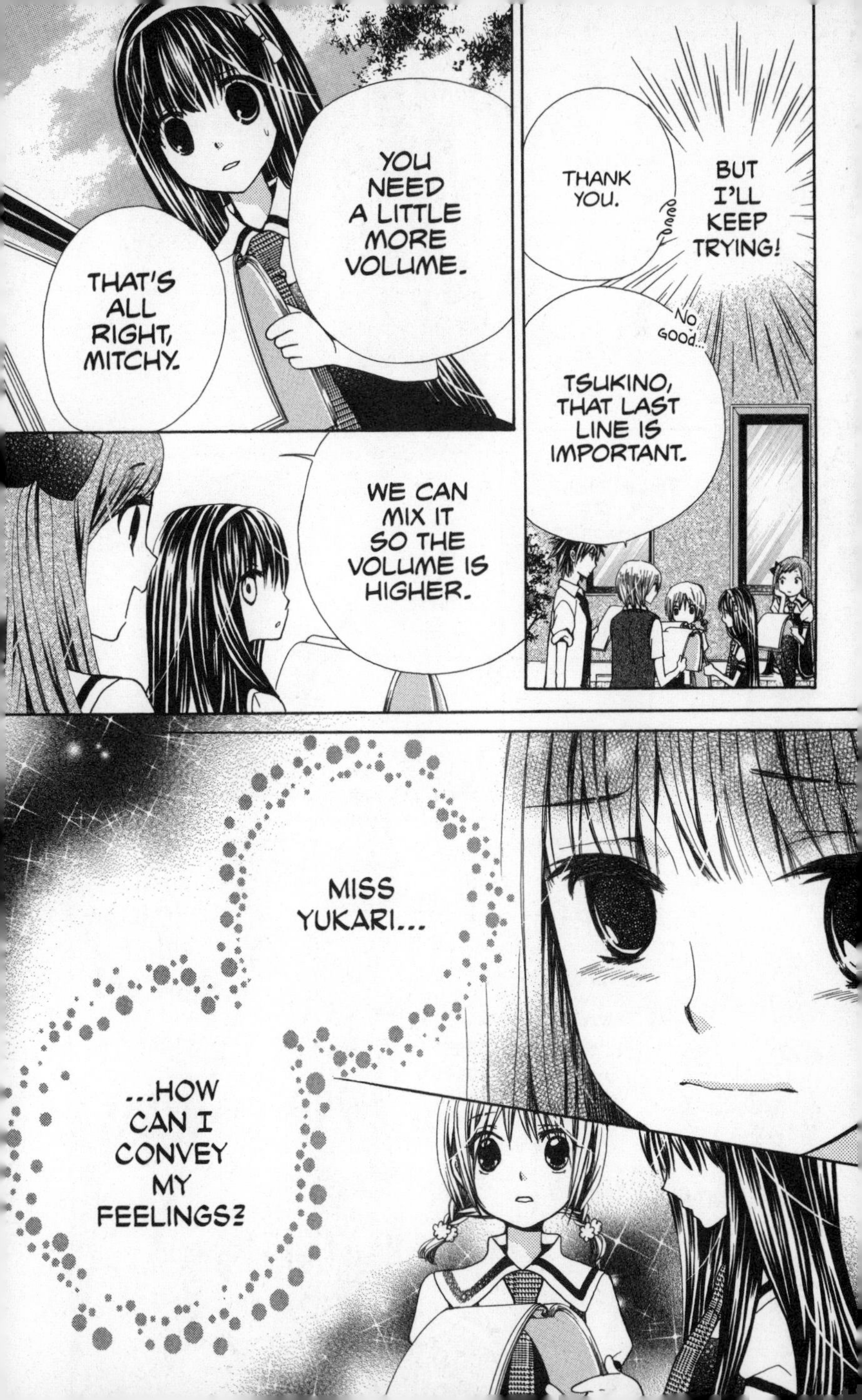
BUT I'LL KEEP TRYING!
THANK YOU.
No good...
TSUKINO, THAT LAST LINE IS IMPORTANT.
YOU NEED A LITTLE MORE VOLUME.
THAT'S ALL RIGHT, MITCHY.
WE CAN MIX IT SO THE VOLUME IS HIGHER.
MISS YUKARI...
...HOW CAN I CONVEY MY FEELINGS?

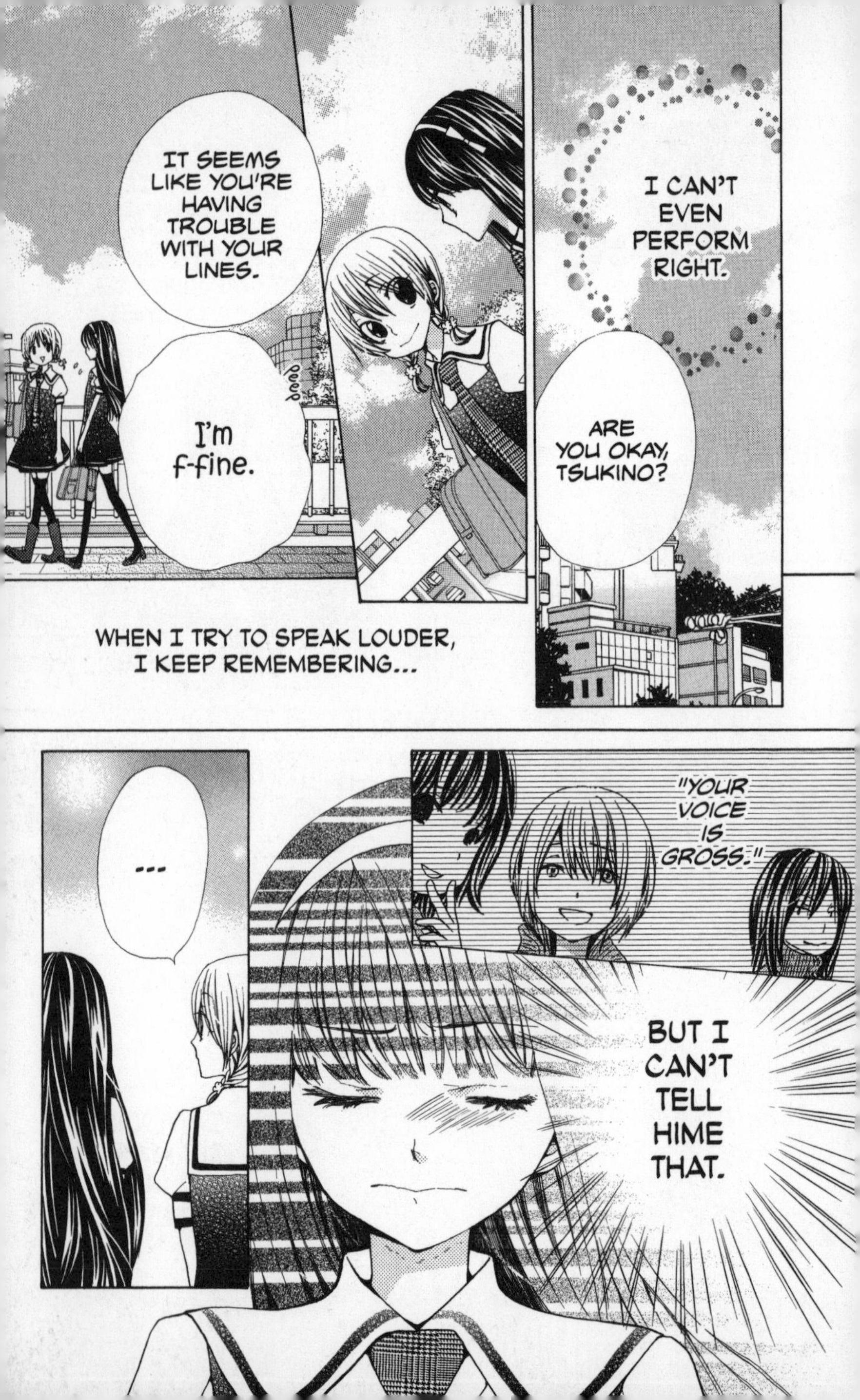
I CAN'T EVEN PERFORM RIGHT.
ARE YOU OKAY, TSUKINO?
PEEP
IT SEEMS LIKE YOU'RE HAVING TROUBLE WITH YOUR LINES.
I'm f-fine.
WHEN I TRY TO SPEAK LOUDER, I KEEP REMEMBERING...
"YOUR VOICE IS GROSS."
BUT I CAN'T TELL HIME THAT.
...

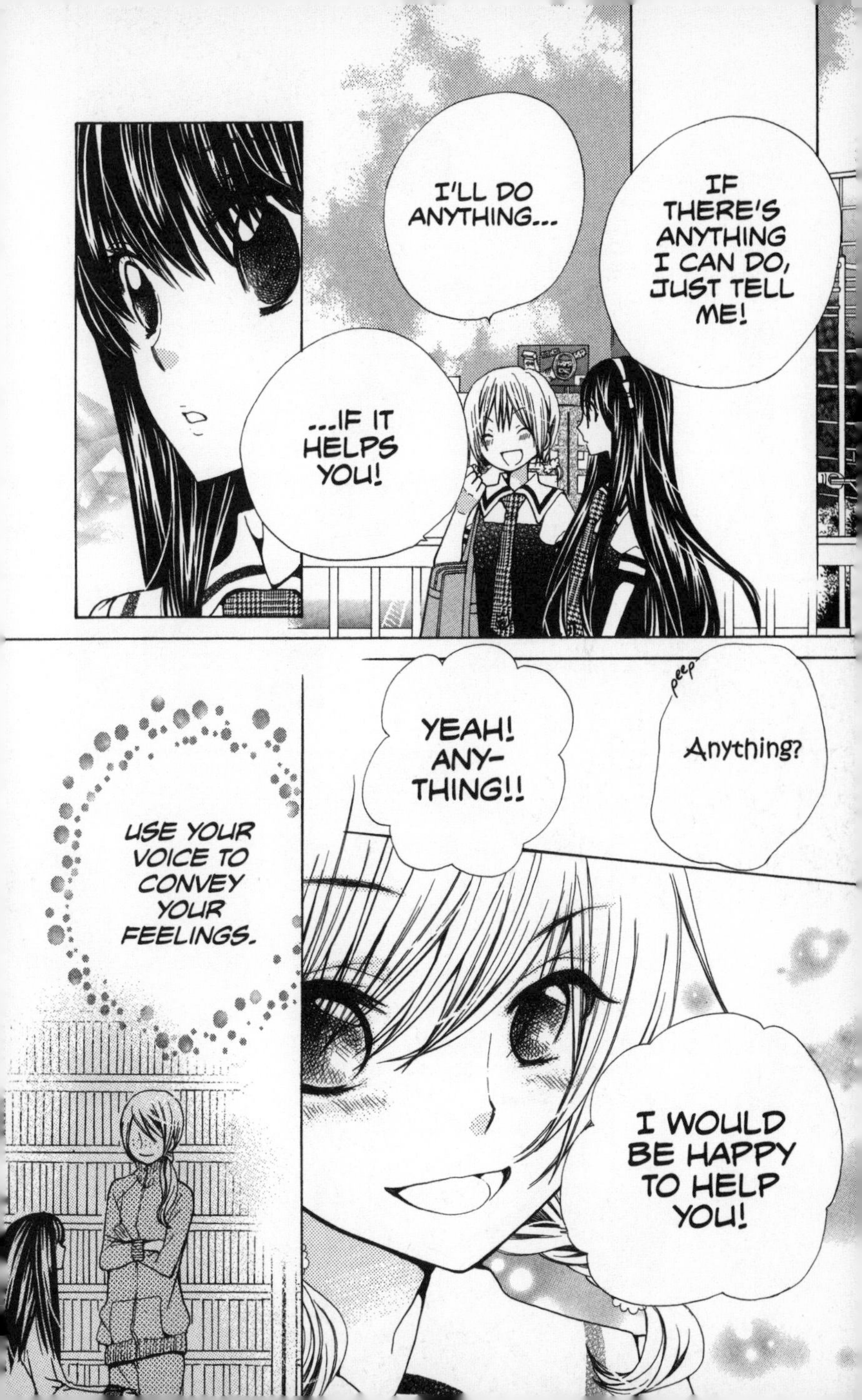
IF THERE'S ANYTHING I CAN DO, JUST TELL ME!
I'LL DO ANYTHING...
...IF IT HELPS YOU!
peep
Anything?
YEAH! ANYTHING!!
I WOULD BE HAPPY TO HELP YOU!
USE YOUR VOICE TO CONVEY YOUR FEELINGS.

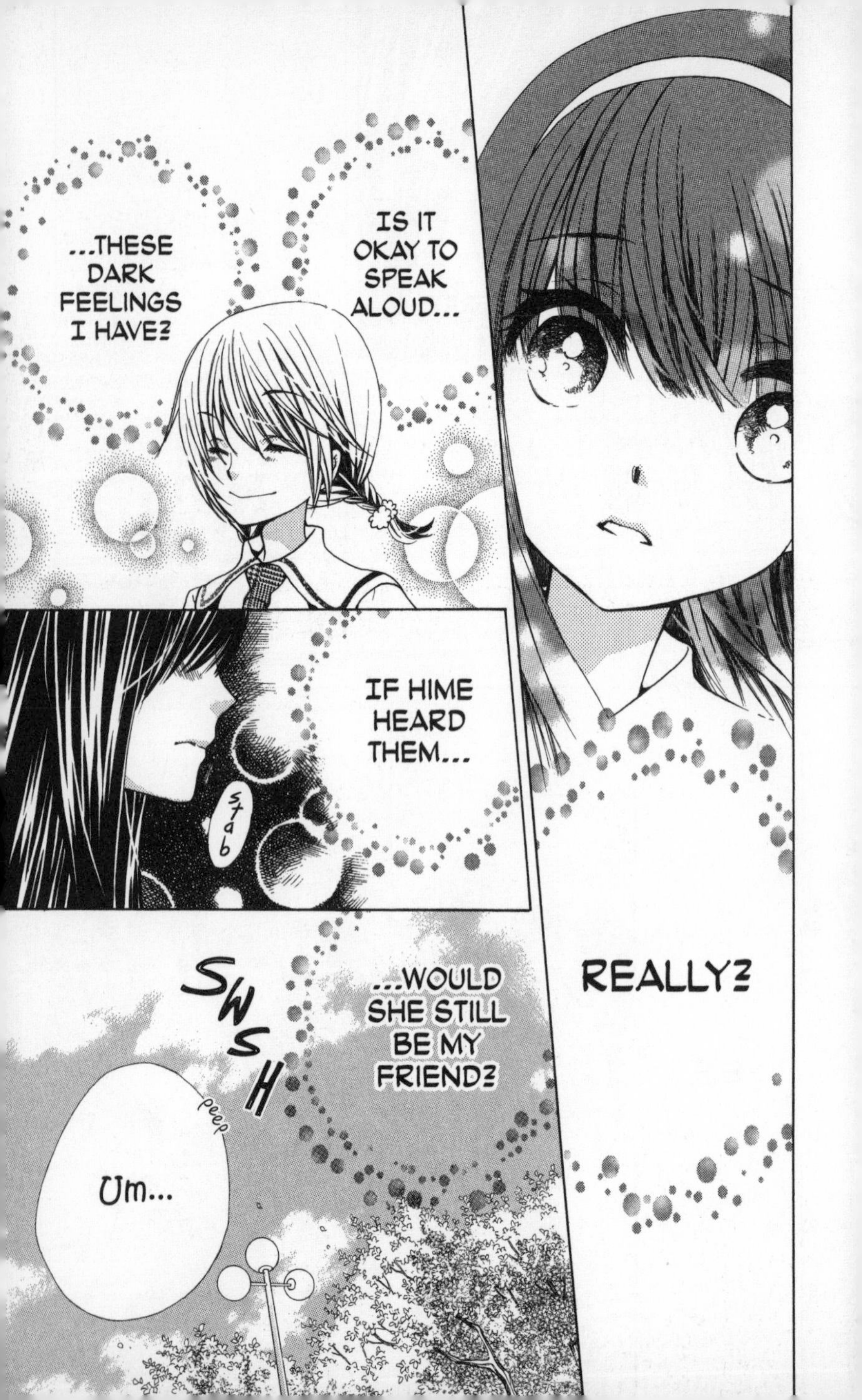
REALLY?
IS IT OKAY TO SPEAK ALOUD...
...THESE DARK FEELINGS I HAVE?
IF HIME HEARD THEM...
stab
...WOULD SHE STILL BE MY FRIEND?
SWSH
peep
Um...

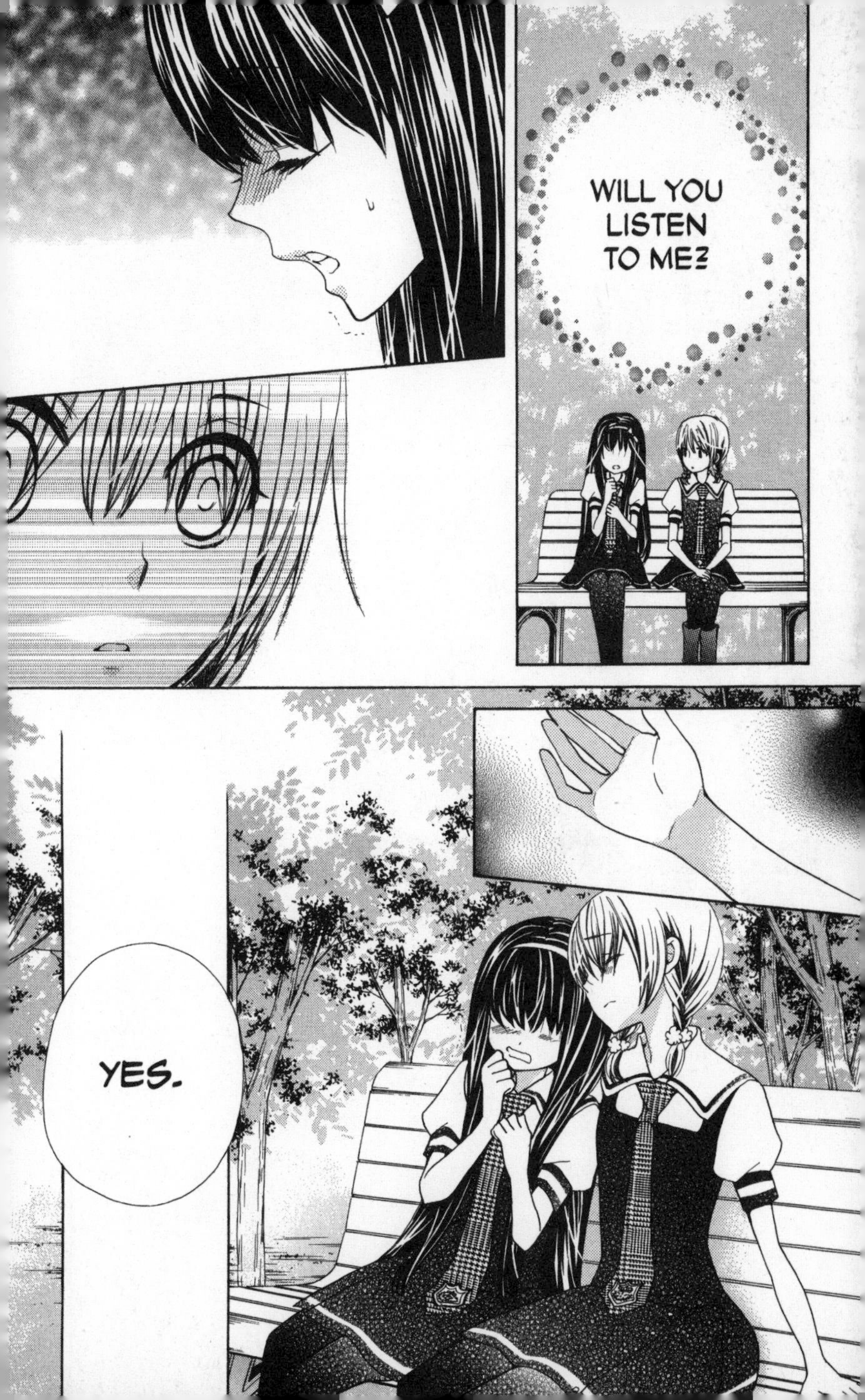
WILL YOU LISTEN TO ME?
YES.

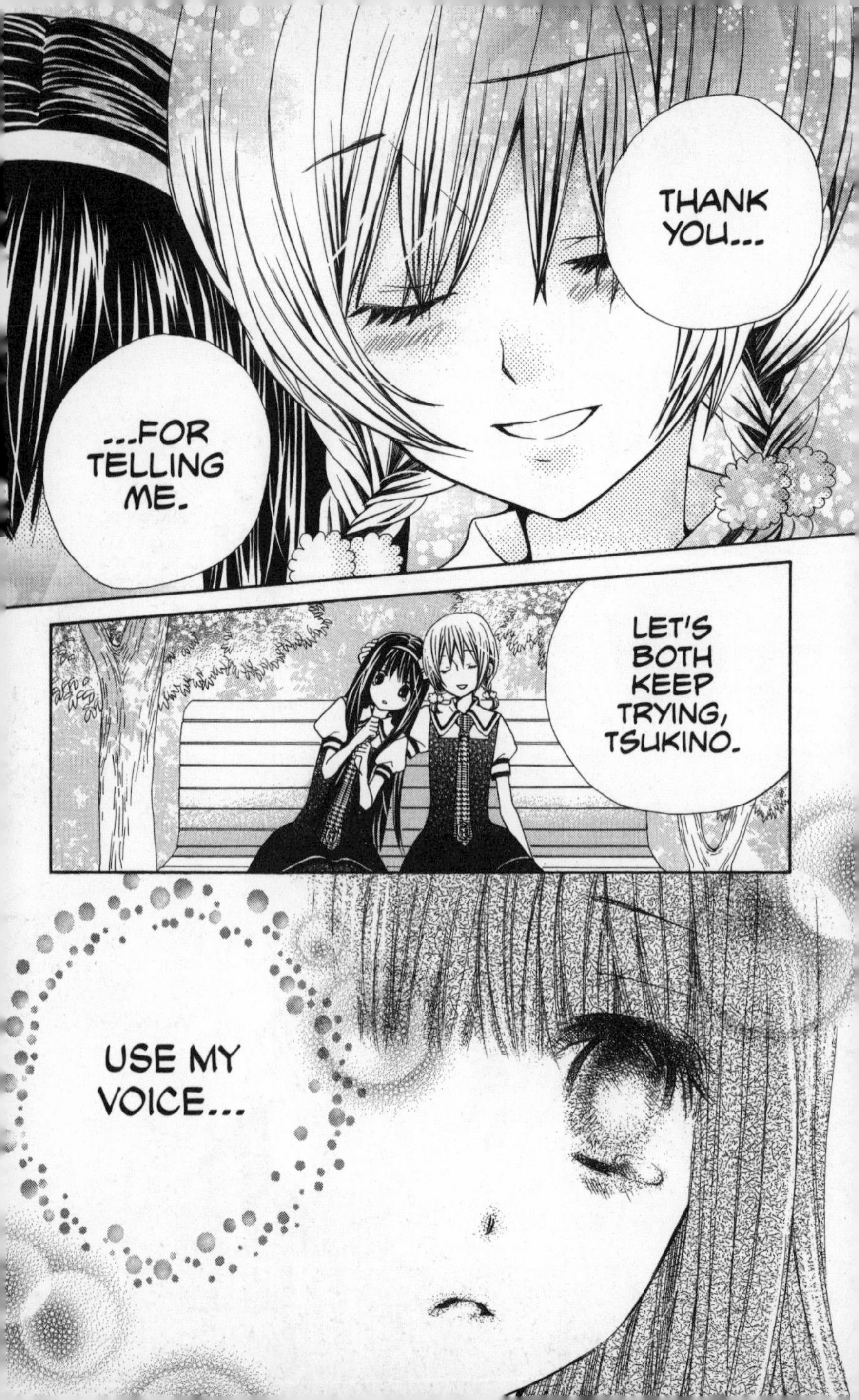
THANK YOU...
...FOR TELLING ME.
LET'S BOTH KEEP TRYING, TSUKINO.
USE MY VOICE...

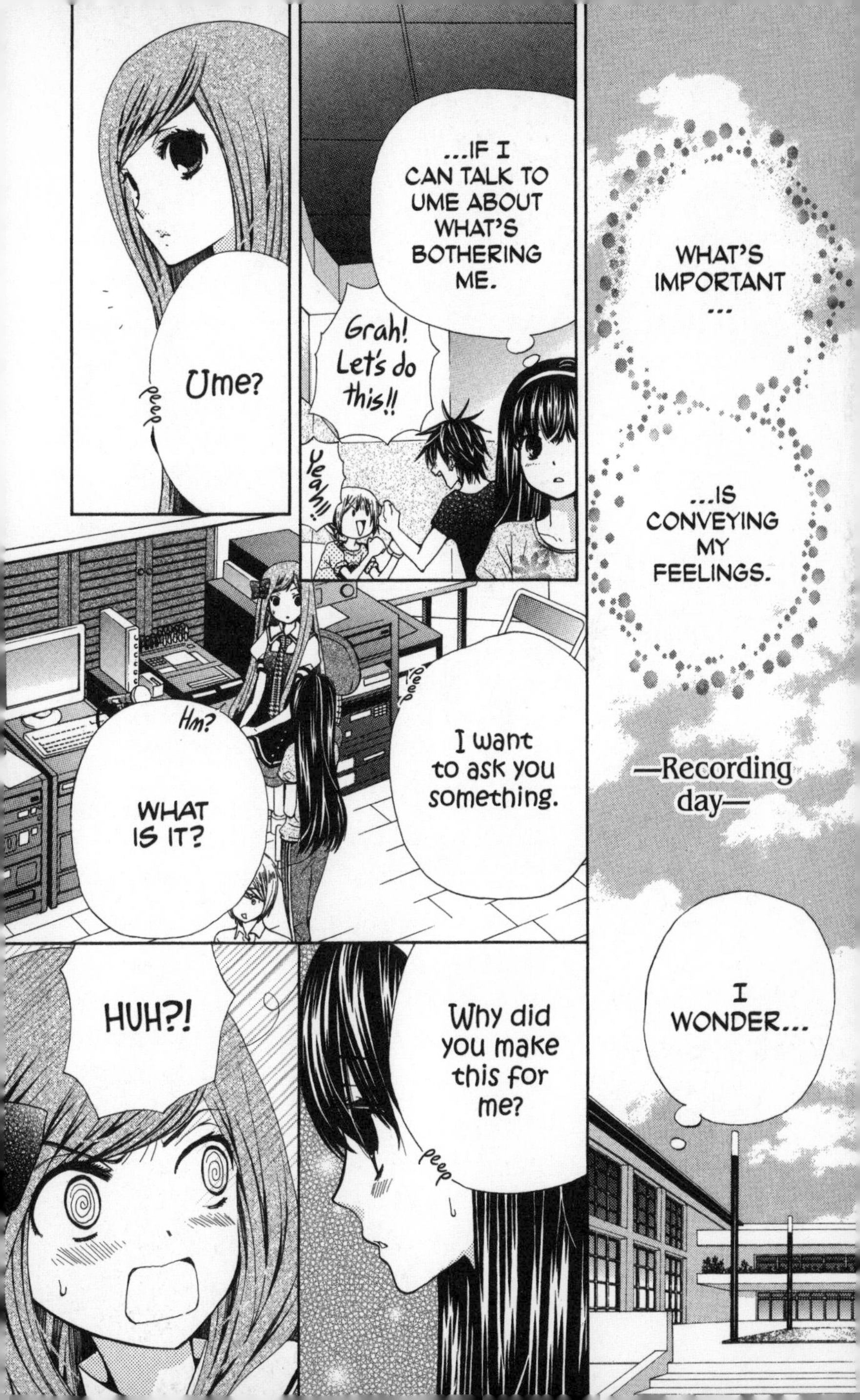
WHAT'S IMPORTANT ...
...IS CONVEYING MY FEELINGS.
—Recording day—
I WONDER...
...IF I CAN TALK TO UME ABOUT WHAT'S BOTHERING ME.
Grah! Let's do this!!
Yeah!!
Ume?
peep
peep
I want to ask you something.
Hm?
WHAT IS IT?
Why did you make this for me?
peep
HUH?!

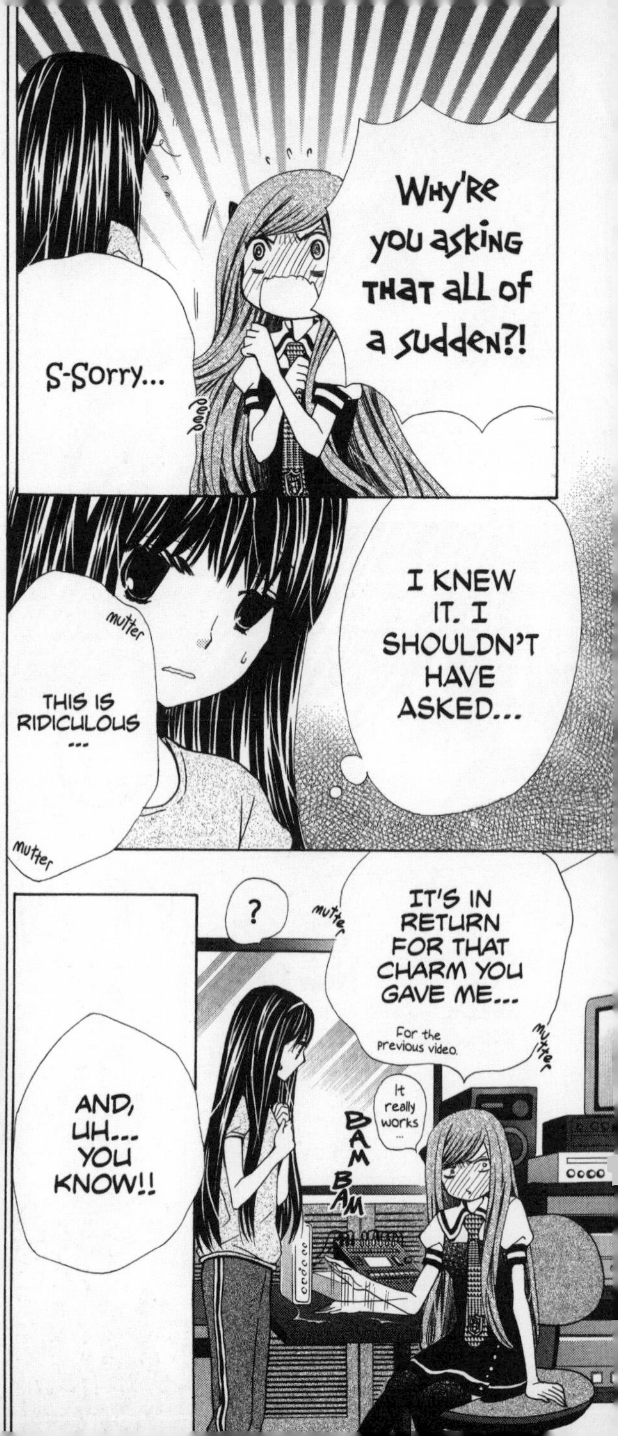
WHY'RE YOU ASKING THAT ALL OF A SUDDEN?!
S-SORRY...
peep
I KNEW IT. I SHOULDN'T HAVE ASKED...
mutter
THIS IS RIDICULOUS...
mutter
IT'S IN RETURN FOR THAT CHARM YOU GAVE ME...
mutter
For the previous video.
mutter
?
It really works...
BAM BAM
AND, UH... YOU KNOW!!

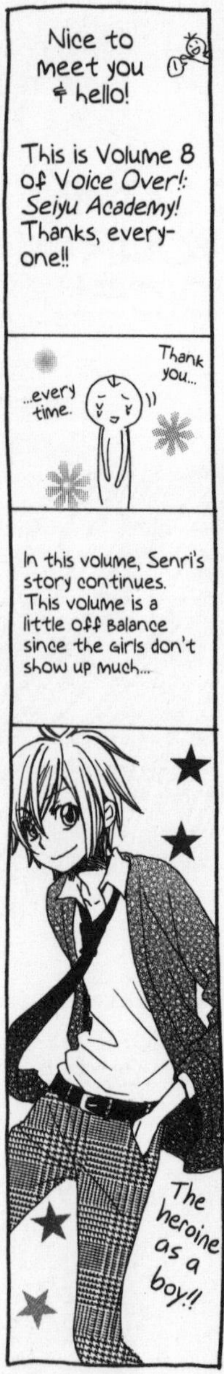
Nice to meet you & hello!
This is Volume 8 of Voice Over!: Seiyu Academy! Thanks, everyone!!
Thank you...
...every time.
In this volume, Senri's story continues. This volume is a little off balance since the girls don't show up much...
The heroine as a boy!!

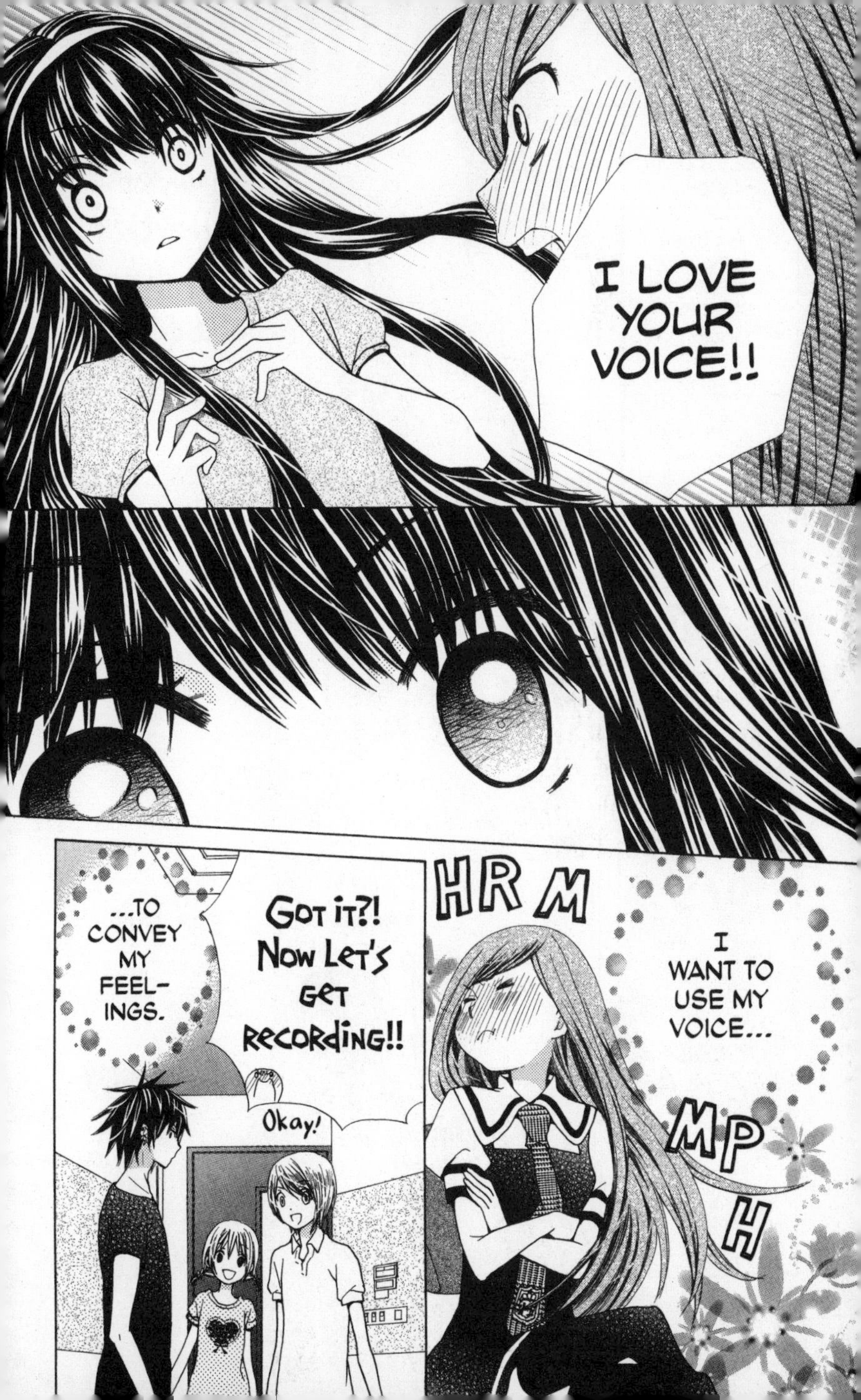
I LOVE YOUR VOICE!!
HRM
I WANT TO USE MY VOICE...
MPH
...TO CONVEY MY FEEL-INGS.
GOT IT?! NOW LET'S GET RECORDING!!
Okay!

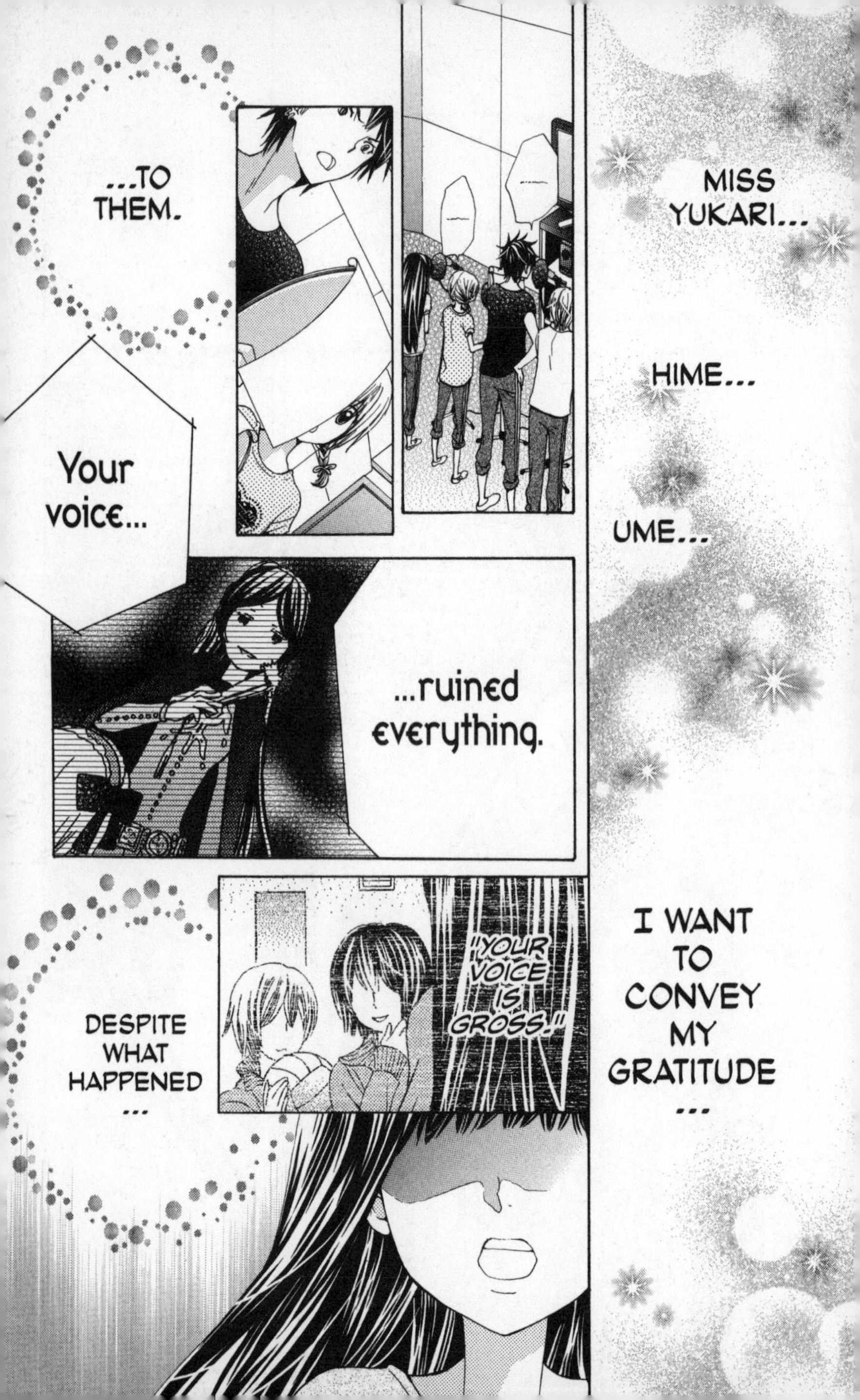

MISS YUKARI...
HIME...
UME...
I WANT TO CONVEY MY GRATITUDE...
...TO THEM.
Your voice...
...ruined everything.
"YOUR VOICE IS GROSS."
DESPITE WHAT HAPPENED...

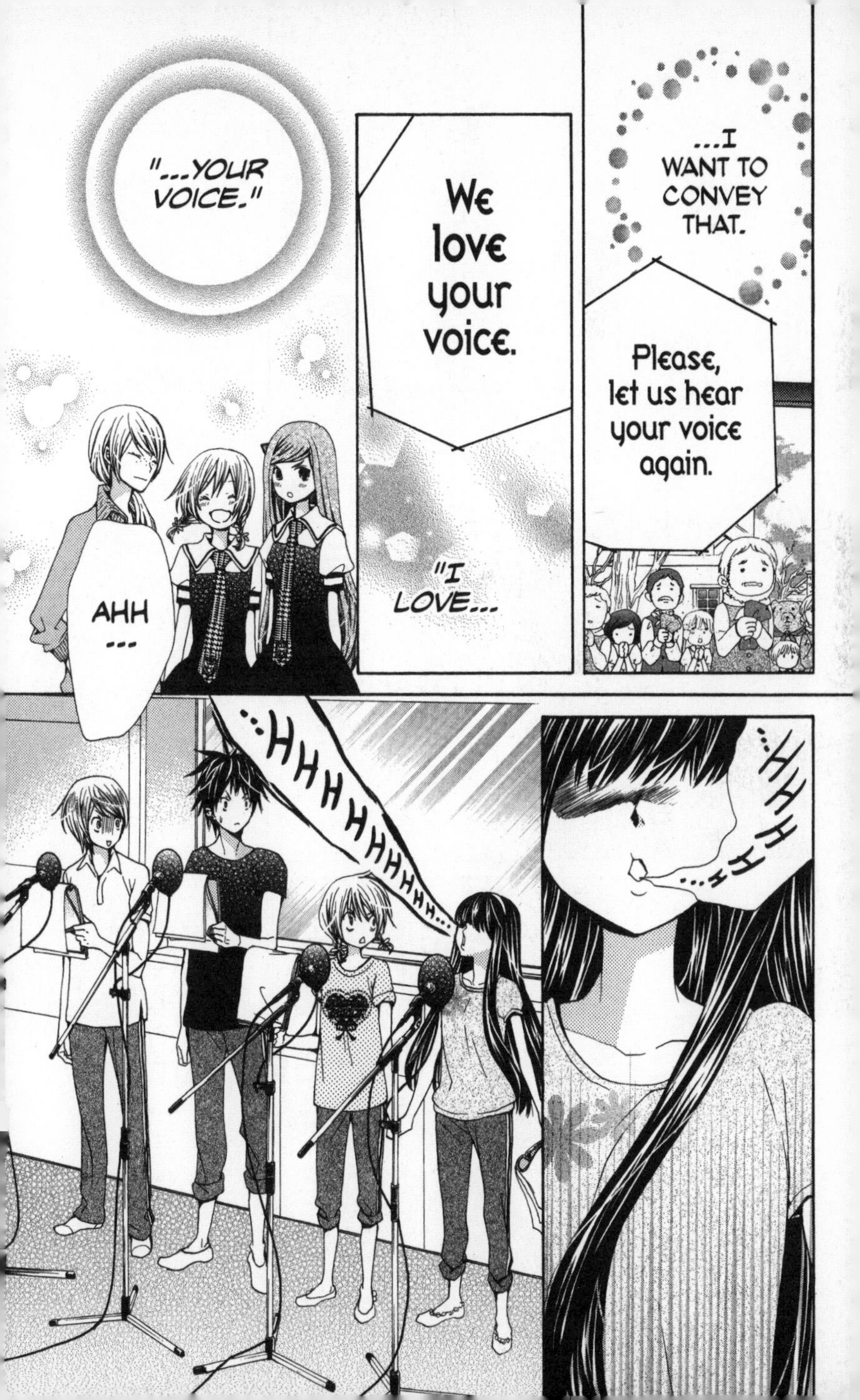
...I WANT TO CONVEY THAT.
Please, let us hear your voice again.
We love your voice.
"I LOVE...
"...YOUR VOICE."
AHH ---
...HHHHH...
...HHHHHHHHHHHH...

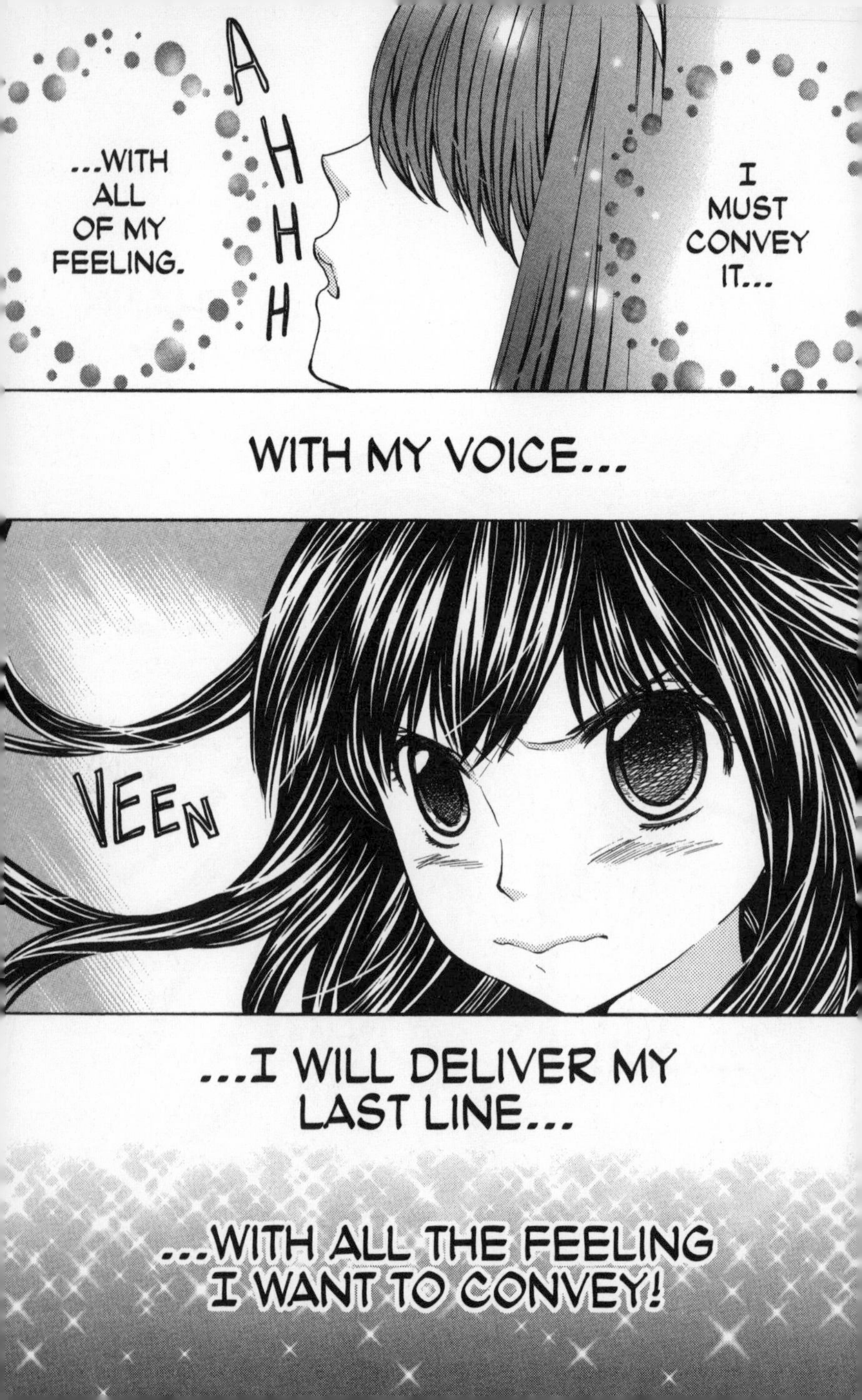
I MUST CONVEY IT...
AHHH
...WITH ALL OF MY FEELING.
WITH MY VOICE...
VEEN
...I WILL DELIVER MY LAST LINE...
...WITH ALL THE FEELING I WANT TO CONVEY!

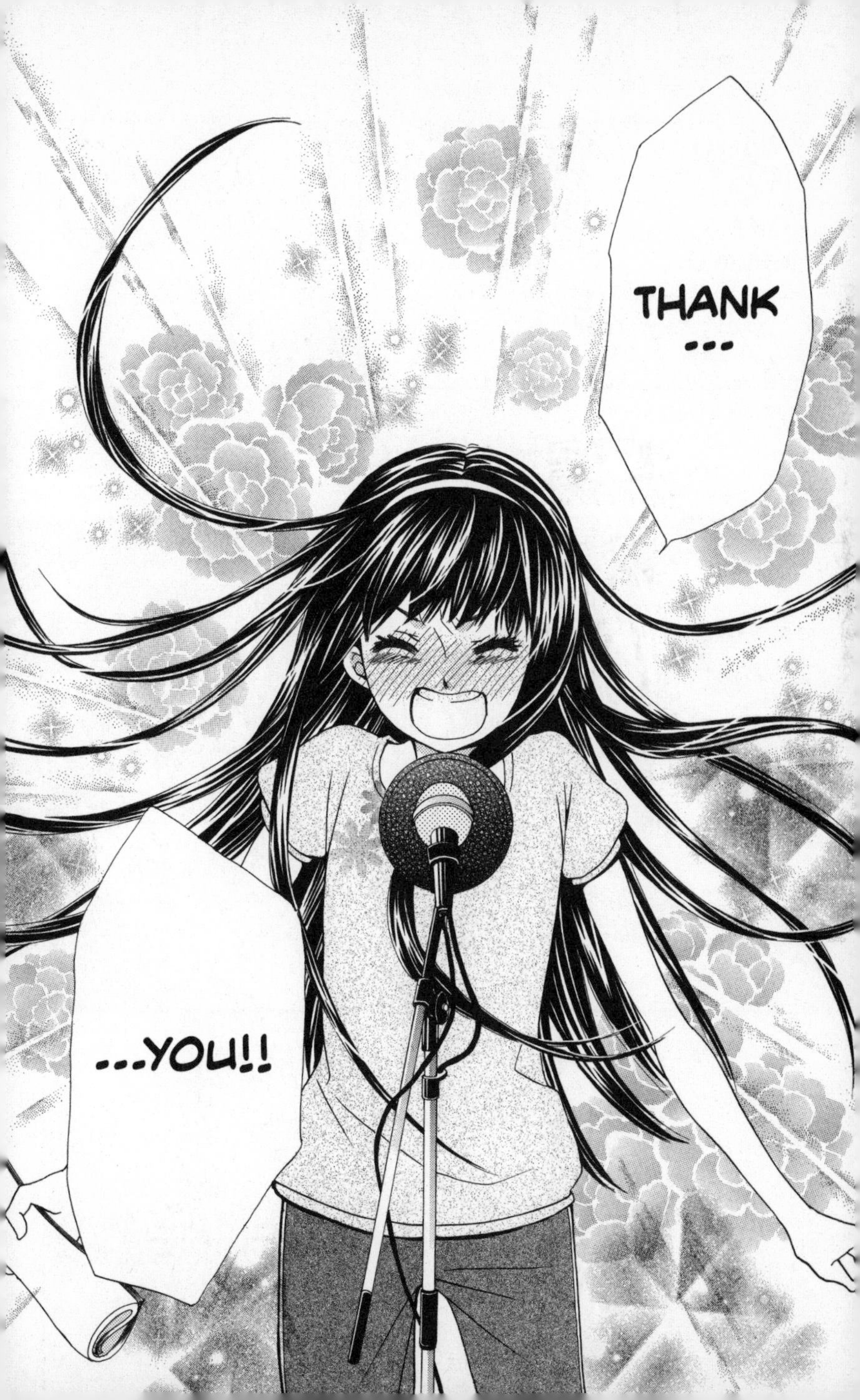
THANK
...
...YOU!!

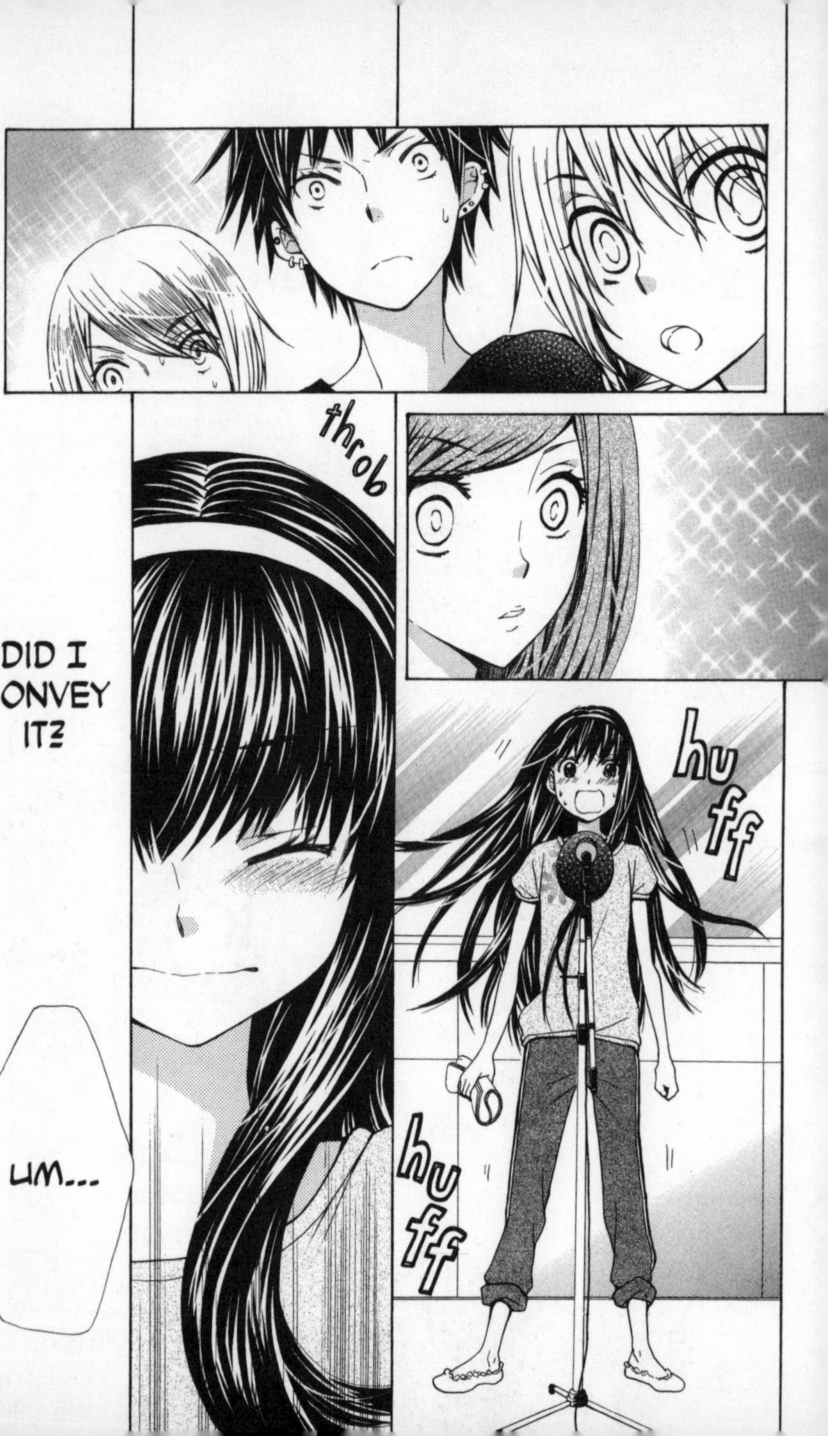
throb
huff
huff
DID I CONVEY IT?
UM...

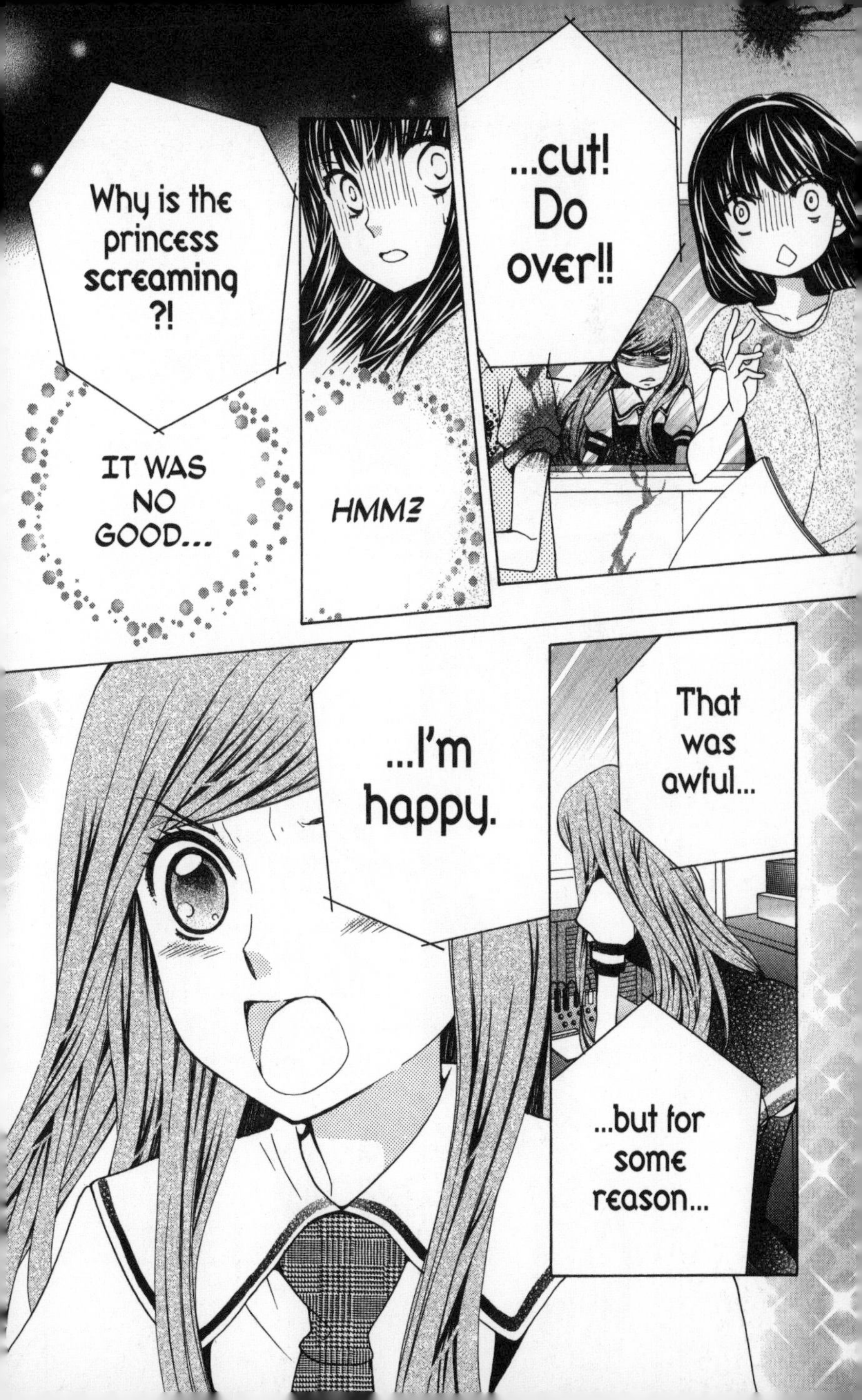

...cut! Do over!!
HMM?
Why is the princess screaming ?!
IT WAS NO GOOD...
That was awful...
...but for some reason...
...I'm happy.

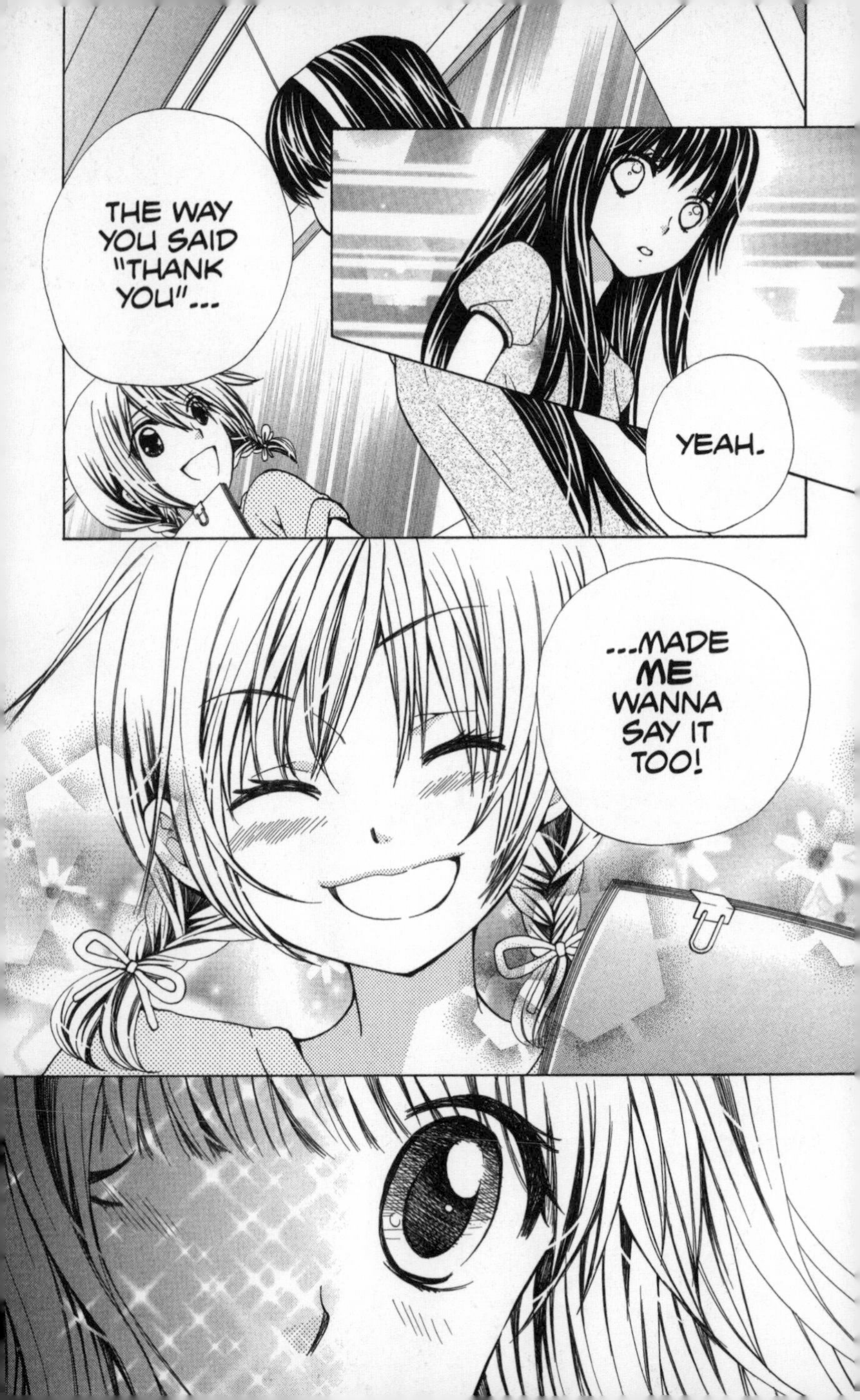
YEAH.
THE WAY YOU SAID "THANK YOU"...
...MADE ME WANNA SAY IT TOO!

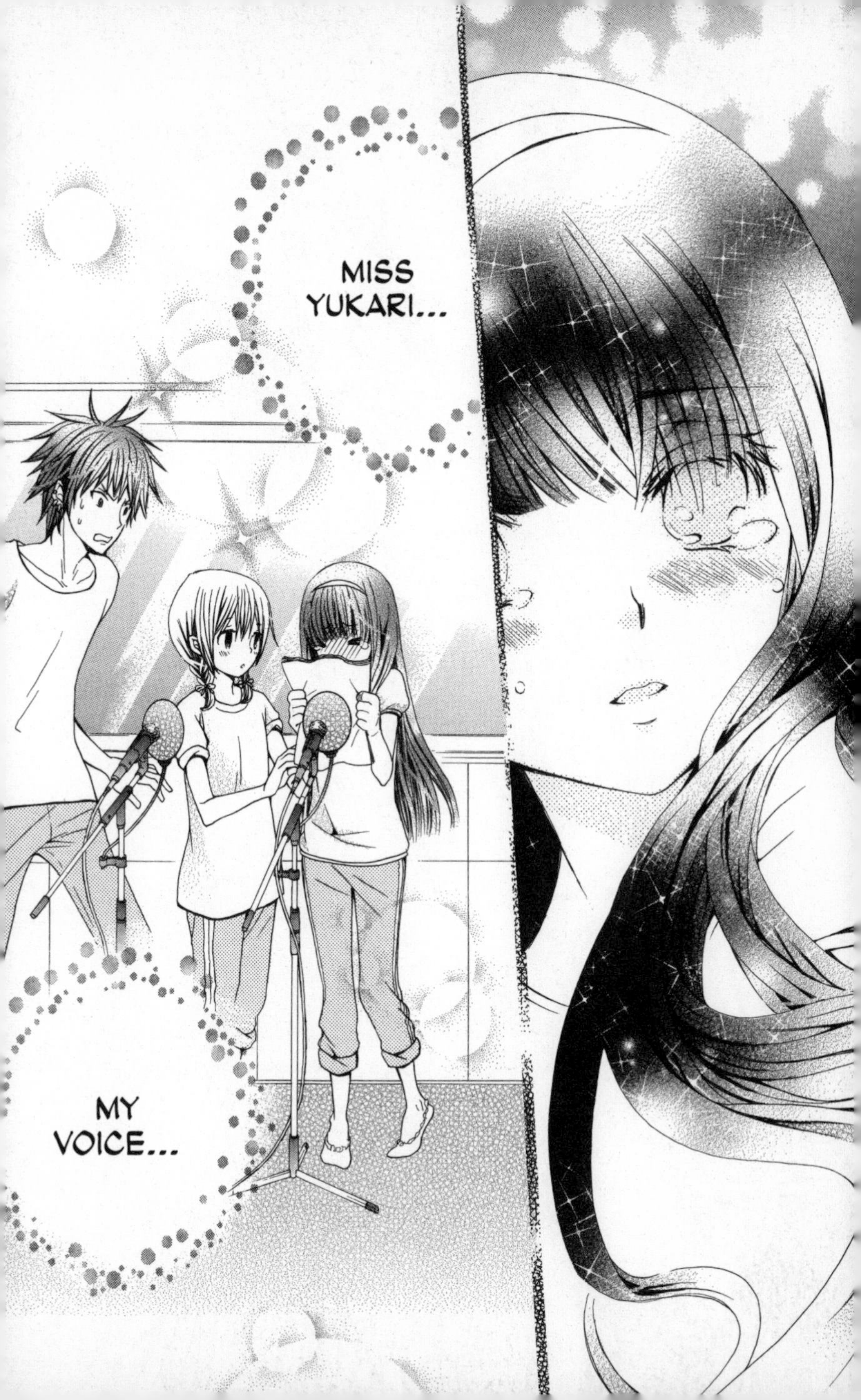
MISS YUKARI...
MY VOICE...

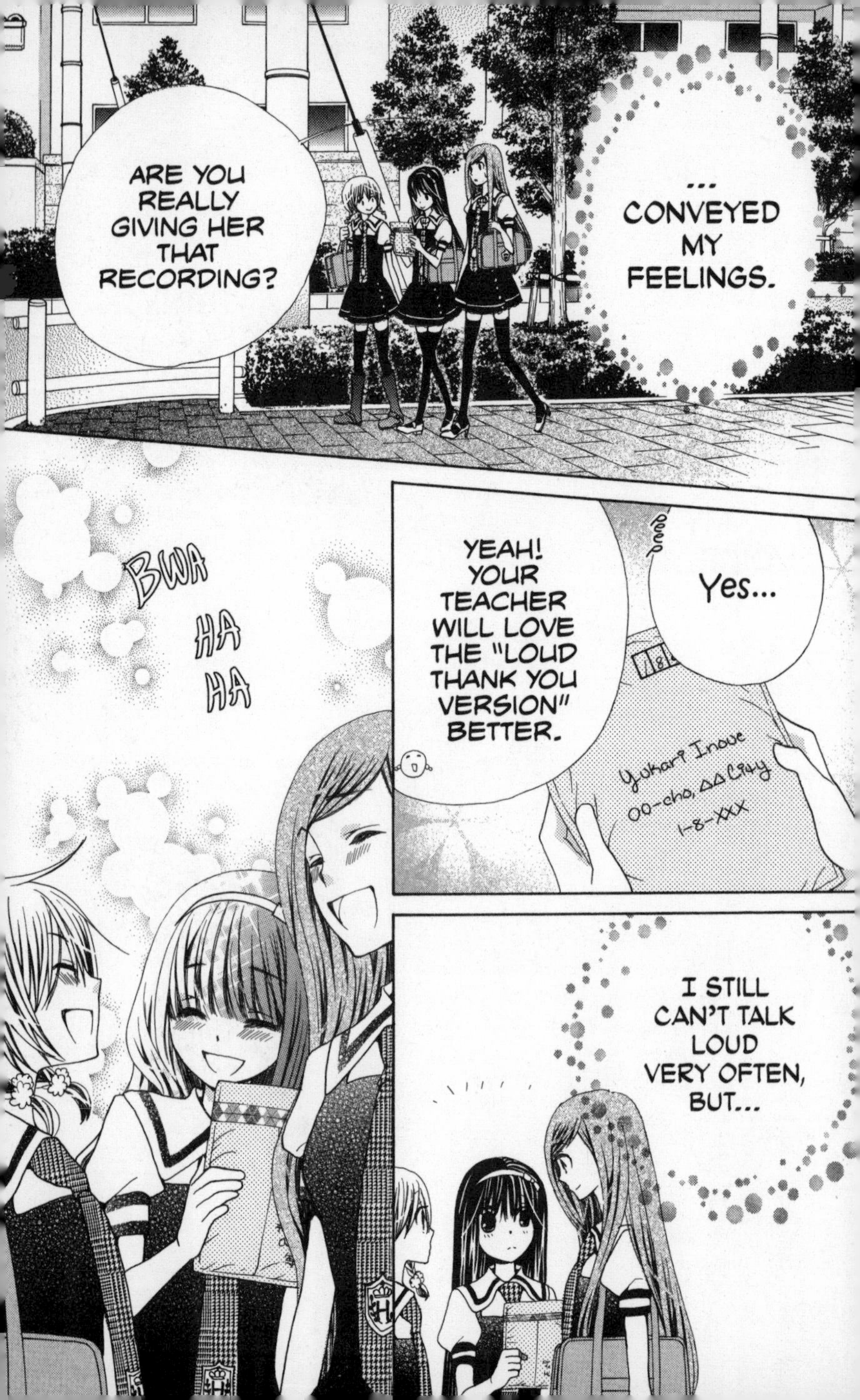
...CONVEYED MY FEELINGS.
ARE YOU REALLY GIVING HER THAT RECORDING?
Yes...
YEAH! YOUR TEACHER WILL LOVE THE "LOUD THANK YOU VERSION" BETTER.
Yukari Inoue
OO-cho, ΔΔ City
1-8-XXX
I STILL CAN'T TALK LOUD VERY OFTEN, BUT...
BWA HA HA

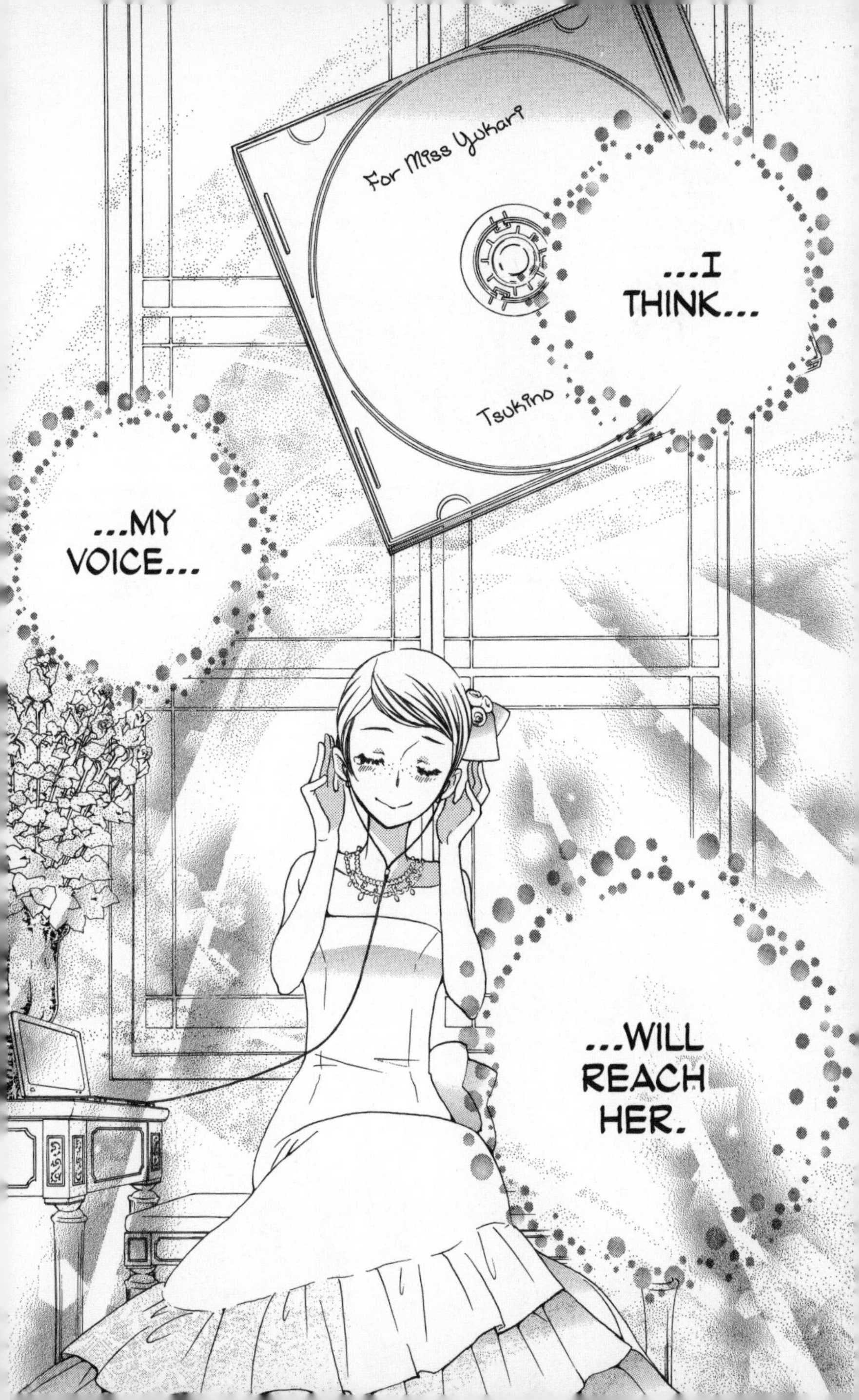
For Miss Yukari
Tsukino
...I THINK...
...MY VOICE...
...WILL REACH HER.

Chapter 42

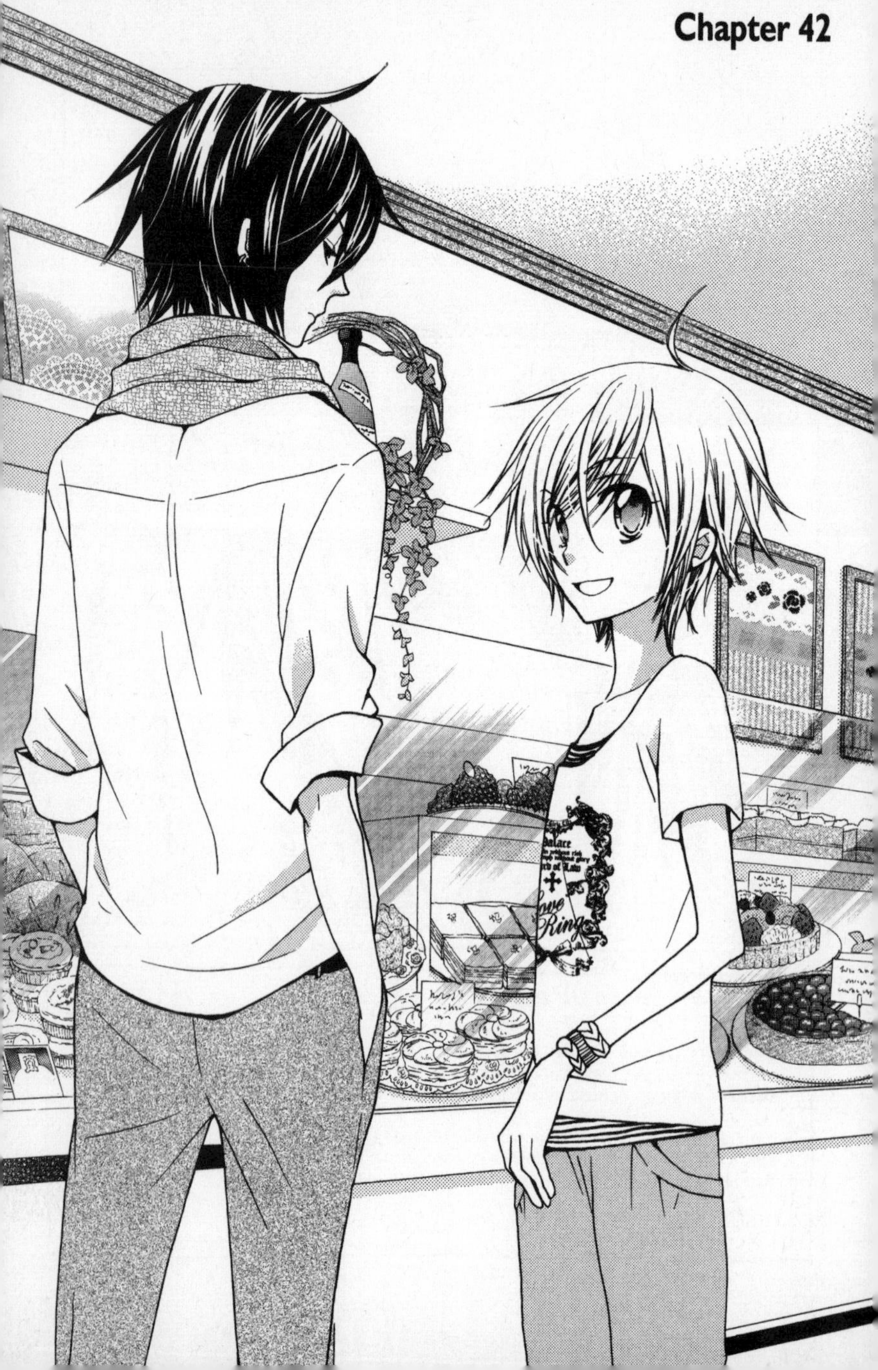
Ring

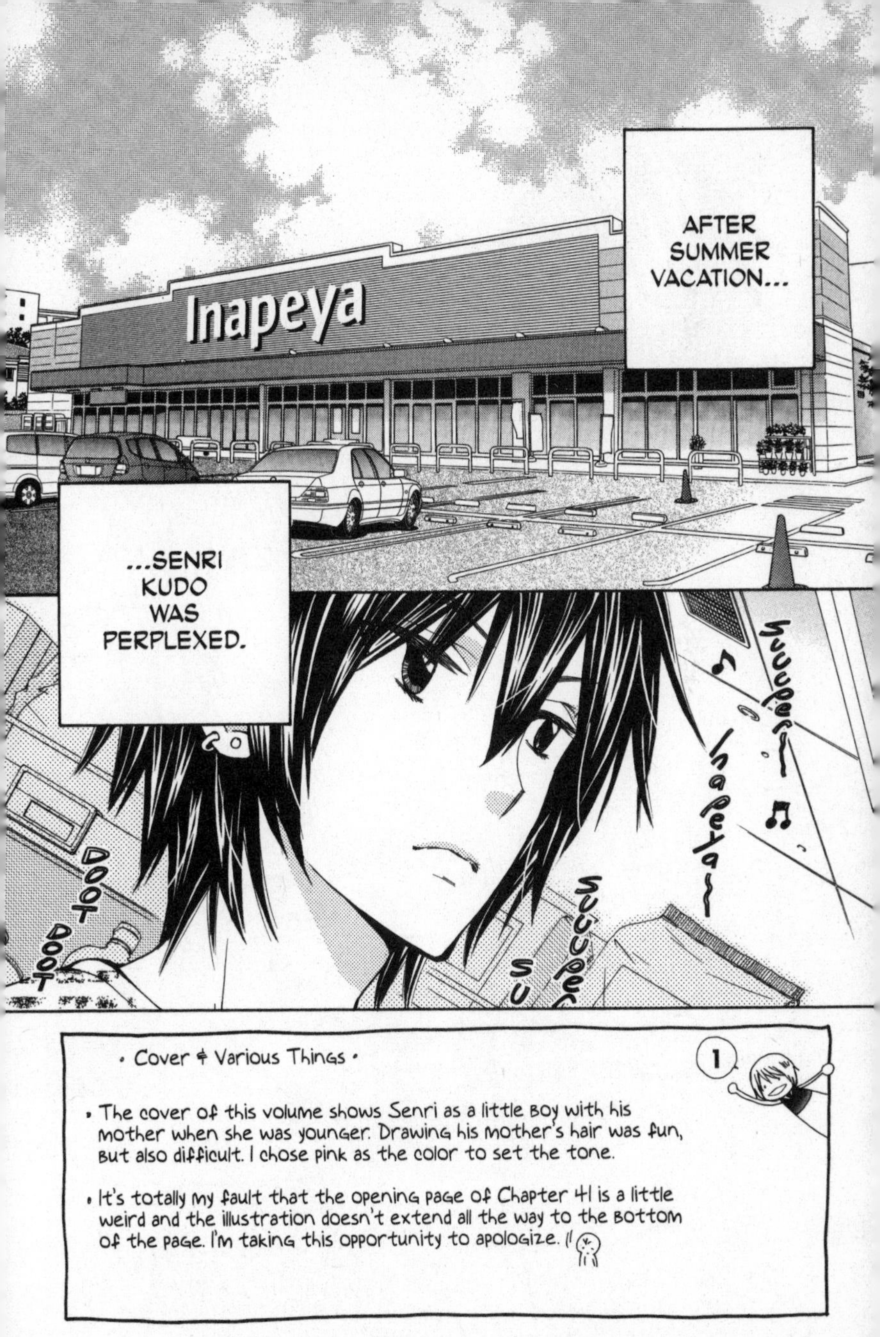
Inapeya
AFTER SUMMER VACATION...
...SENRI KUDO WAS PERPLEXED.
Suuuper~ Inapeya~
SUUUPER SU
DOOT DOOT

• Cover & Various Things •

1

• The cover of this volume shows Senri as a little boy with his mother when she was younger. Drawing his mother's hair was fun, but also difficult. I chose pink as the color to set the tone.

• It's totally my fault that the opening page of Chapter 41 is a little weird and the illustration doesn't extend all the way to the bottom of the page. I'm taking this opportunity to apologize.

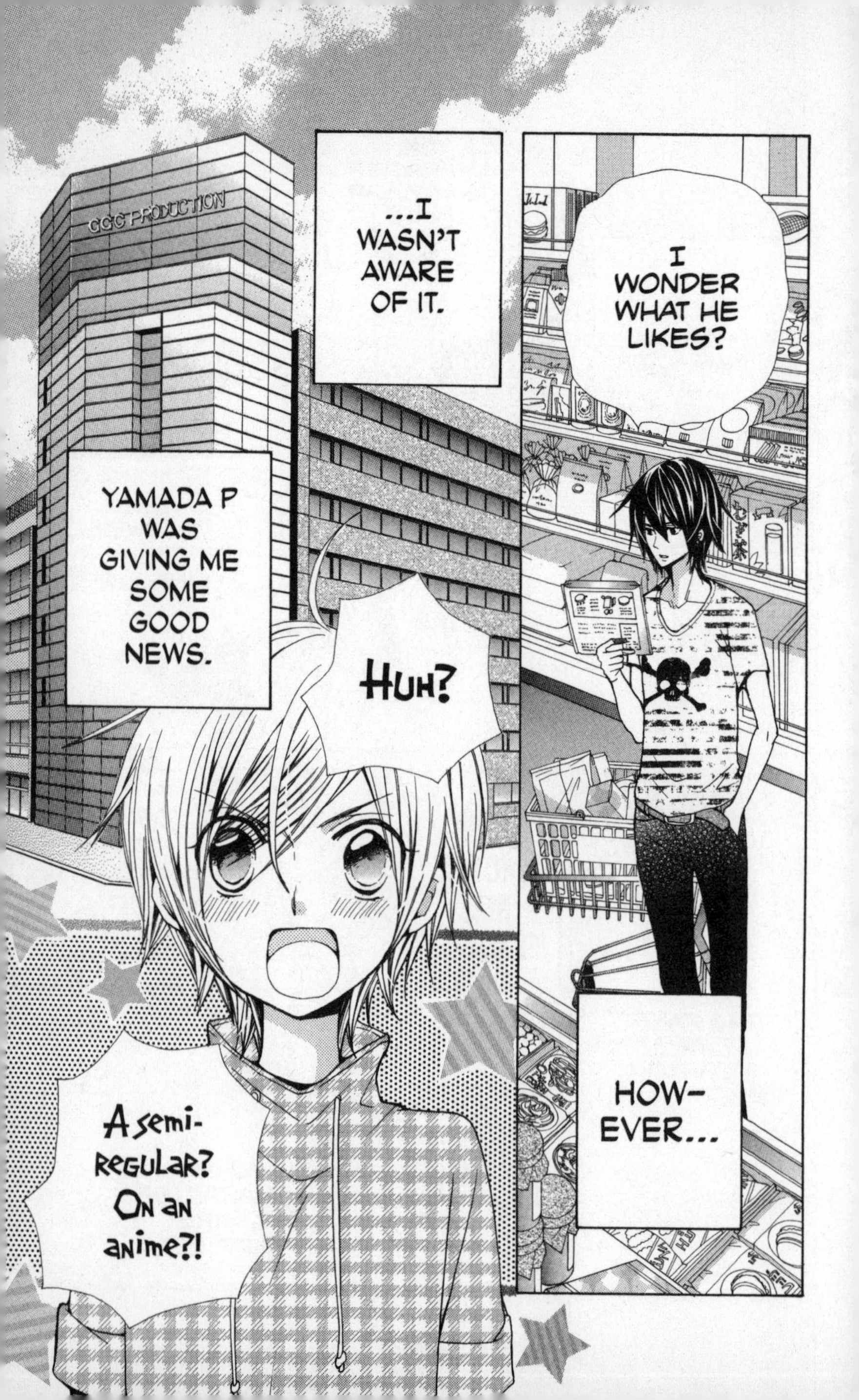
I WONDER WHAT HE LIKES?
HOW-EVER...
...I WASN'T AWARE OF IT.
YAMADA P WAS GIVING ME SOME GOOD NEWS.
HUH?
A semi-regular? On an anime?!

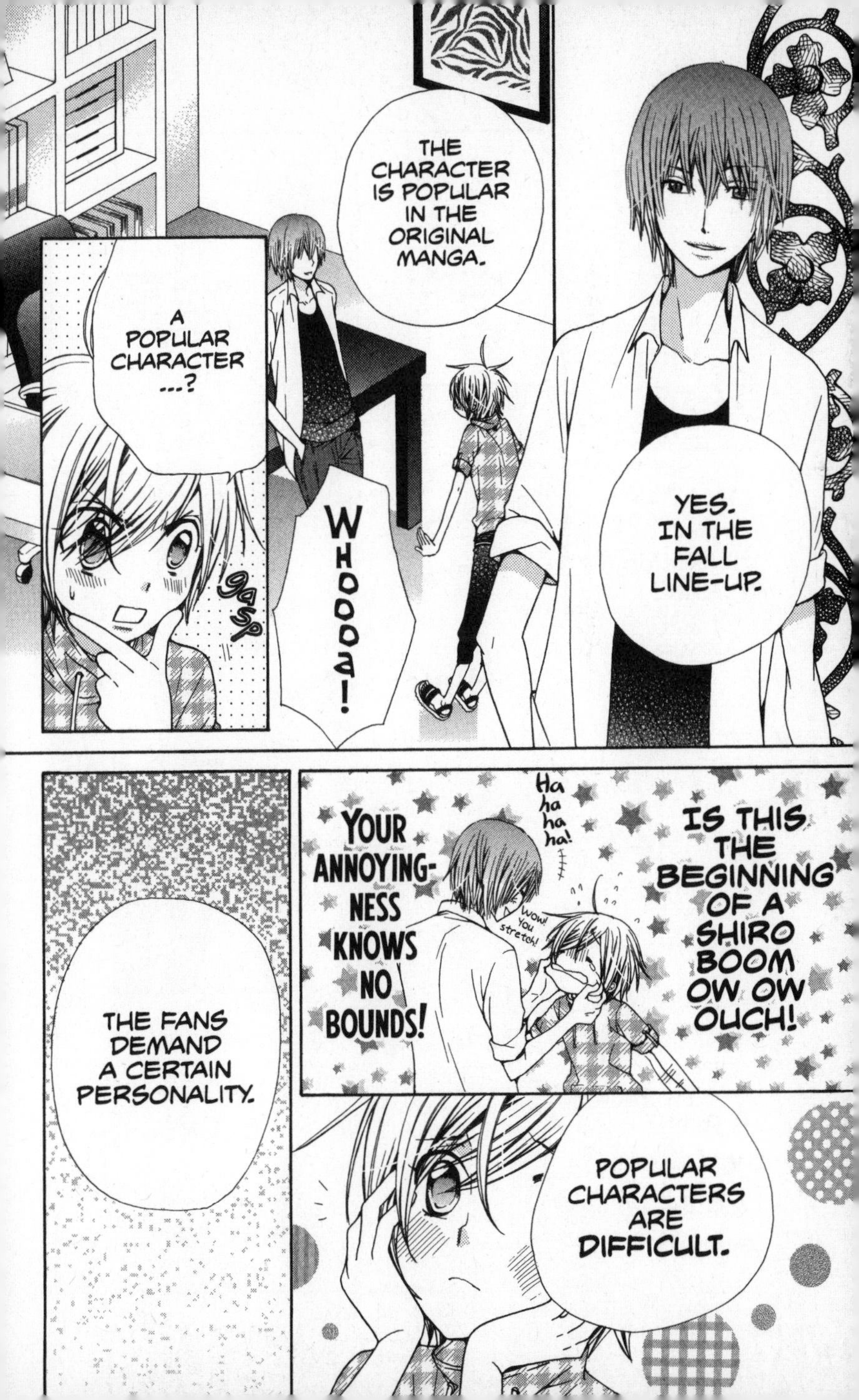
THE CHARACTER IS POPULAR IN THE ORIGINAL MANGA.
A POPULAR CHARACTER ...?
gasp
YES. IN THE FALL LINE-UP.
WHOOOa!
IS THIS THE BEGINNING OF A SHIRO BOOM OW OW OUCH!
Ha ha ha ha!
Wow! You stretch!
YOUR ANNOYING-NESS KNOWS NO BOUNDS!
POPULAR CHARACTERS ARE DIFFICULT.
THE FANS DEMAND A CERTAIN PERSONALITY.

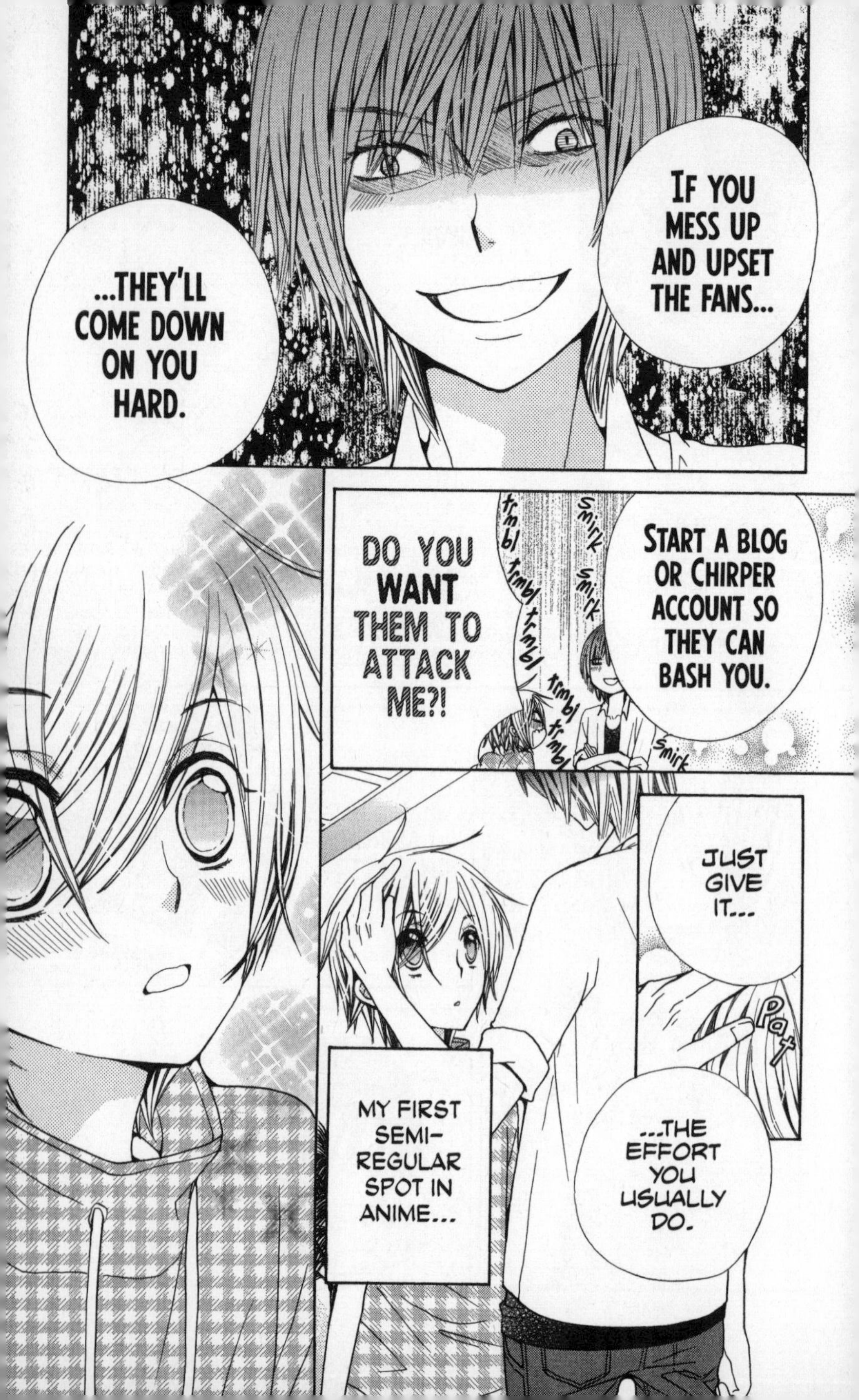
IF YOU MESS UP AND UPSET THE FANS...
...THEY'LL COME DOWN ON YOU HARD.
START A BLOG OR CHIRPER ACCOUNT SO THEY CAN BASH YOU.
smirk smirk
smirk
DO YOU WANT THEM TO ATTACK ME?!
trmbl trmbl trmbl trmbl
trmbl trmbl
JUST GIVE IT...
Pat
...THE EFFORT YOU USUALLY DO.
MY FIRST SEMI-REGULAR SPOT IN ANIME...

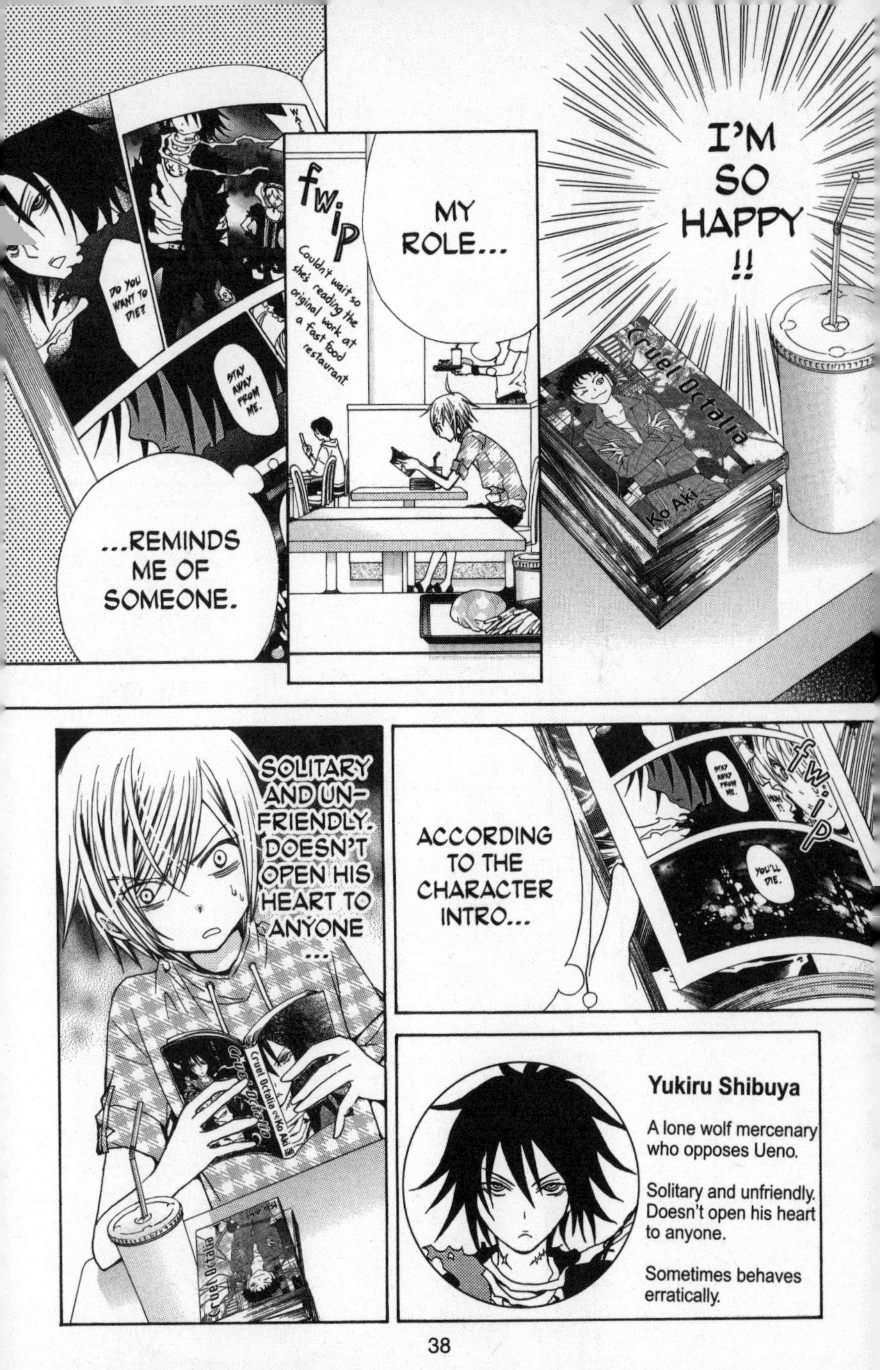
I'M SO HAPPY!!
Cruel Octalia
Ko Aki
fwip
MY ROLE...
Couldn't wait so she's reading the original work at a fast food restaurant.
DO YOU WANT TO DIE?
STAY AWAY FROM ME.
...REMINDS ME OF SOMEONE.
fwip
STAY AWAY FROM ME.
YOU'LL DIE.
ACCORDING TO THE CHARACTER INTRO...
Yukiru Shibuya
A lone wolf mercenary who opposes Ueno.
Solitary and unfriendly. Doesn't open his heart to anyone.
Sometimes behaves erratically.
SOLITARY AND UNFRIENDLY. DOESN'T OPEN HIS HEART TO ANYONE...
Cruel Octalia
Ko Aki
Cruel Octalia

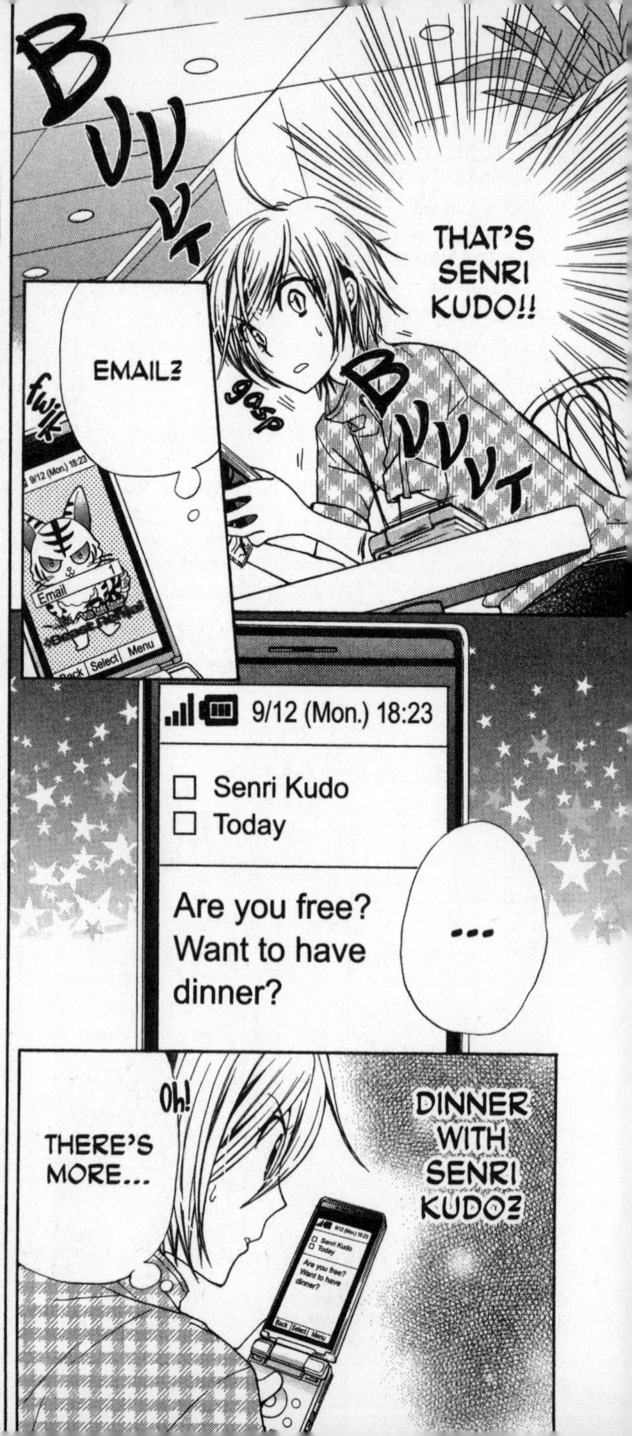
BUVVVT
THAT'S SENRI KUDO!!
gasp
BUVVVT
EMAIL?
fwip
9/12 (Mon.) 18:23
Senri Kudo
Today
Are you free? Want to have dinner?
...
DINNER WITH SENRI KUDO?
Oh!
THERE'S MORE...

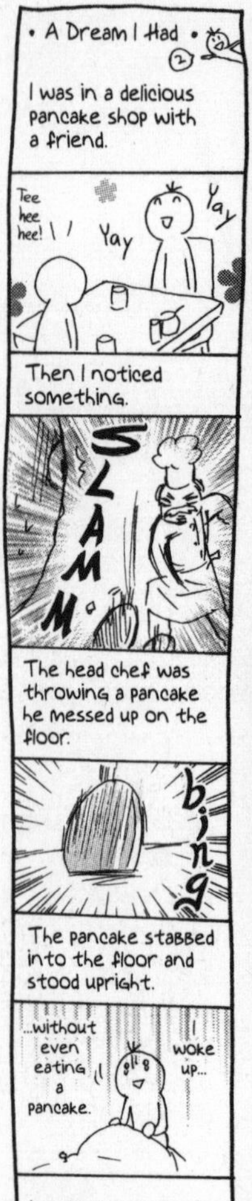
• A Dream I Had •
2
I was in a delicious pancake shop with a friend.
Tee hee hee!
Yay
Yay
Then I noticed something.
SLAMM
The head chef was throwing a pancake he messed up on the floor.
bing
The pancake stabbed into the floor and stood upright.
I woke up...
...without even eating a pancake.
I made toast, but I burned it. It was the last piece of bread though, so I ate it. Was my dream foretelling this?
What a pointless story!

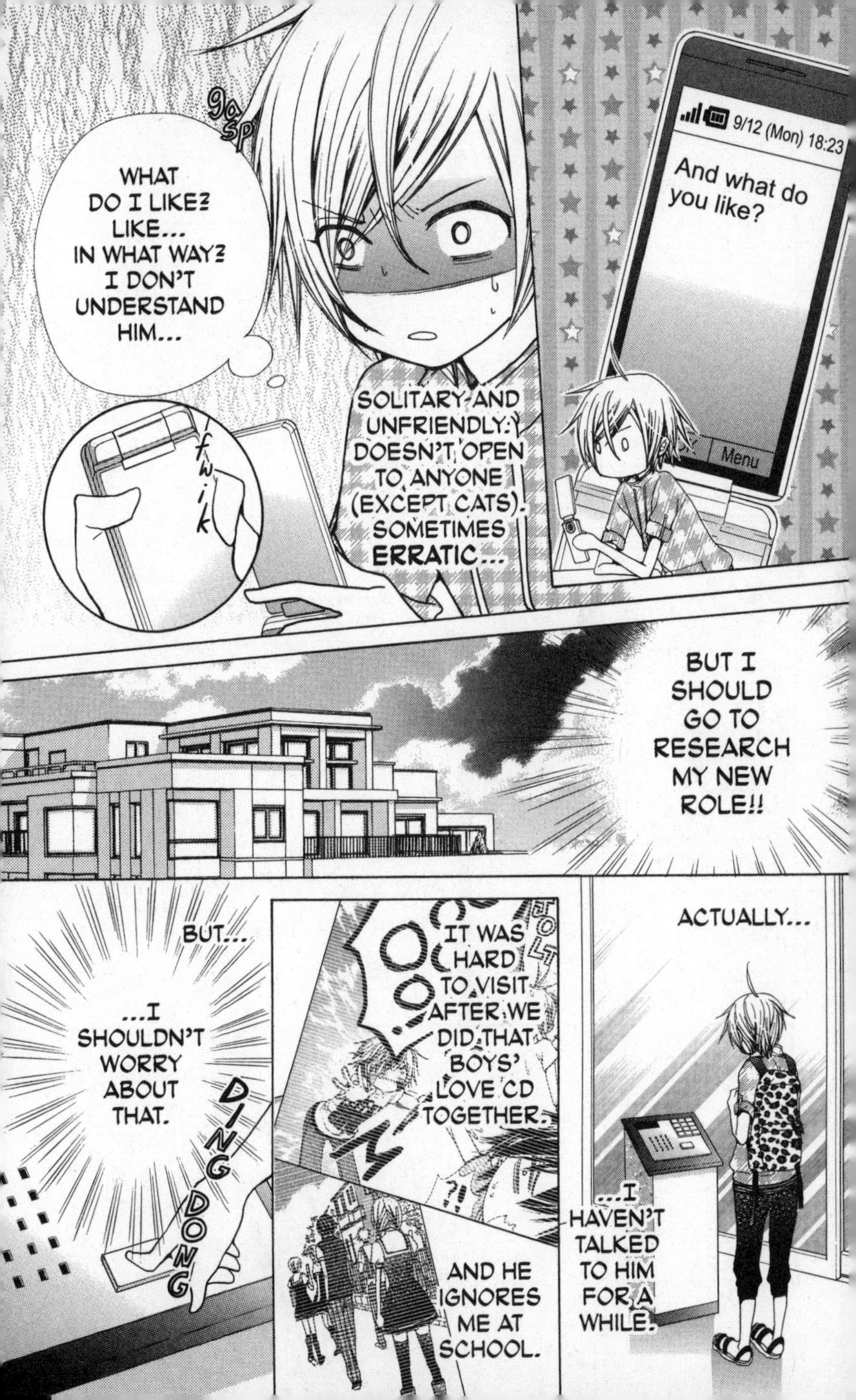

9/12 (Mon) 18:23
And what do you like?
Menu
gasp
WHAT DO I LIKE? LIKE... IN WHAT WAY? I DON'T UNDERSTAND HIM...
SOLITARY AND UNFRIENDLY. DOESN'T OPEN TO ANYONE (EXCEPT CATS). SOMETIMES ERRATIC...
fwik
BUT I SHOULD GO TO RESEARCH MY NEW ROLE!!
ACTUALLY...
...I HAVEN'T TALKED TO HIM FOR A WHILE.
IT WAS HARD TO VISIT AFTER WE DID THAT BOYS' LOVE CD TOGETHER.
?!
AND HE IGNORES ME AT SCHOOL.
BUT...
...I SHOULDN'T WORRY ABOUT THAT.
DING DONG

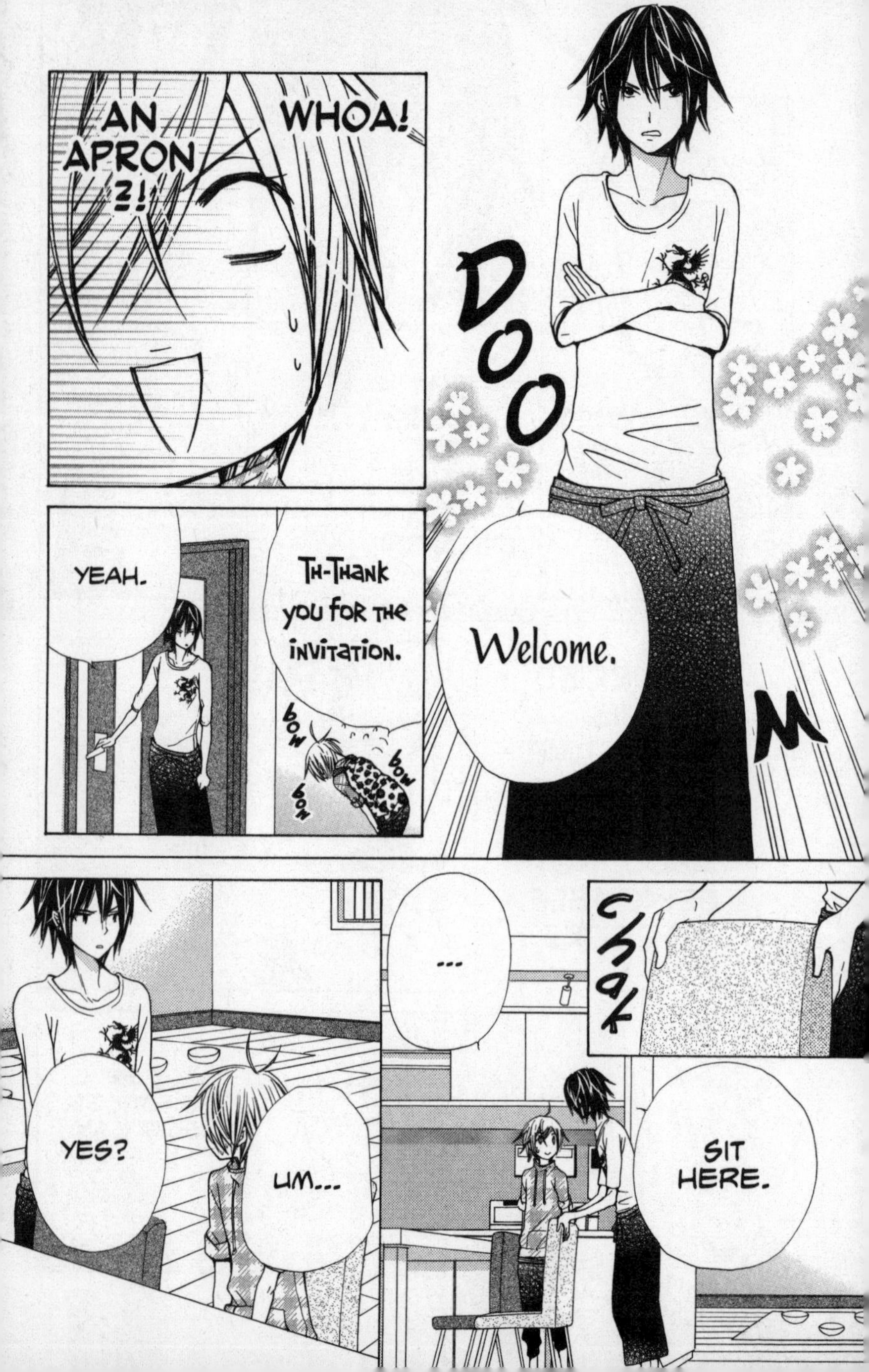
DOOOM
Welcome.
WHOA!
AN APRON?!
Th-Thank you for the invitation.
bow
bow
bow
YEAH.
chak
SIT HERE.
...
UM...
YES?

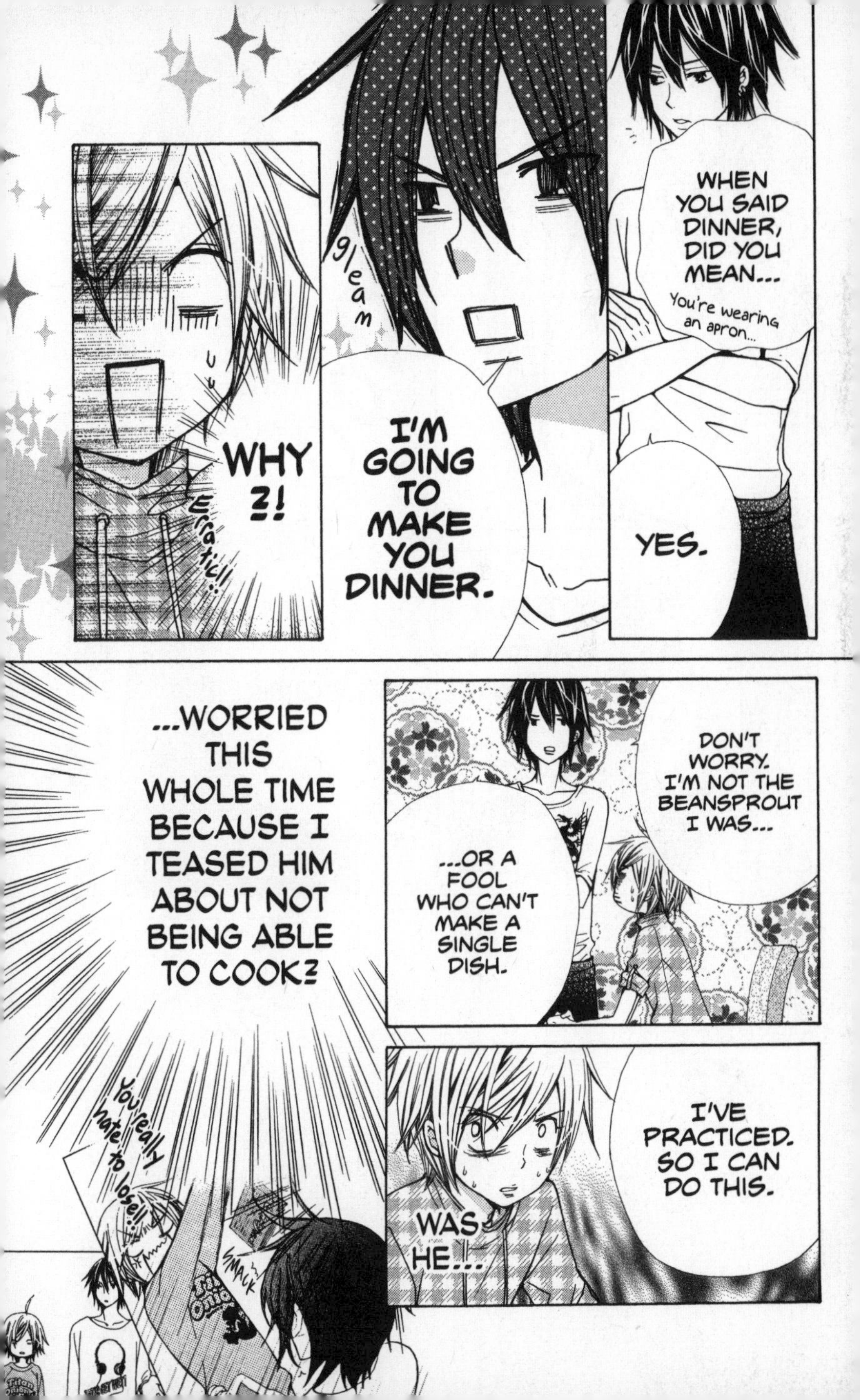
WHEN YOU SAID DINNER, DID YOU MEAN...
You're wearing an apron...
YES.
gleam
I'M GOING TO MAKE YOU DINNER.
WHY?!
Erratic!!
DON'T WORRY. I'M NOT THE BEANSPROUT I WAS...
...OR A FOOL WHO CAN'T MAKE A SINGLE DISH.
I'VE PRACTICED. SO I CAN DO THIS.
WAS HE...
...WORRIED THIS WHOLE TIME BECAUSE I TEASED HIM ABOUT NOT BEING ABLE TO COOK?
You really hate to lose!!
SMACK

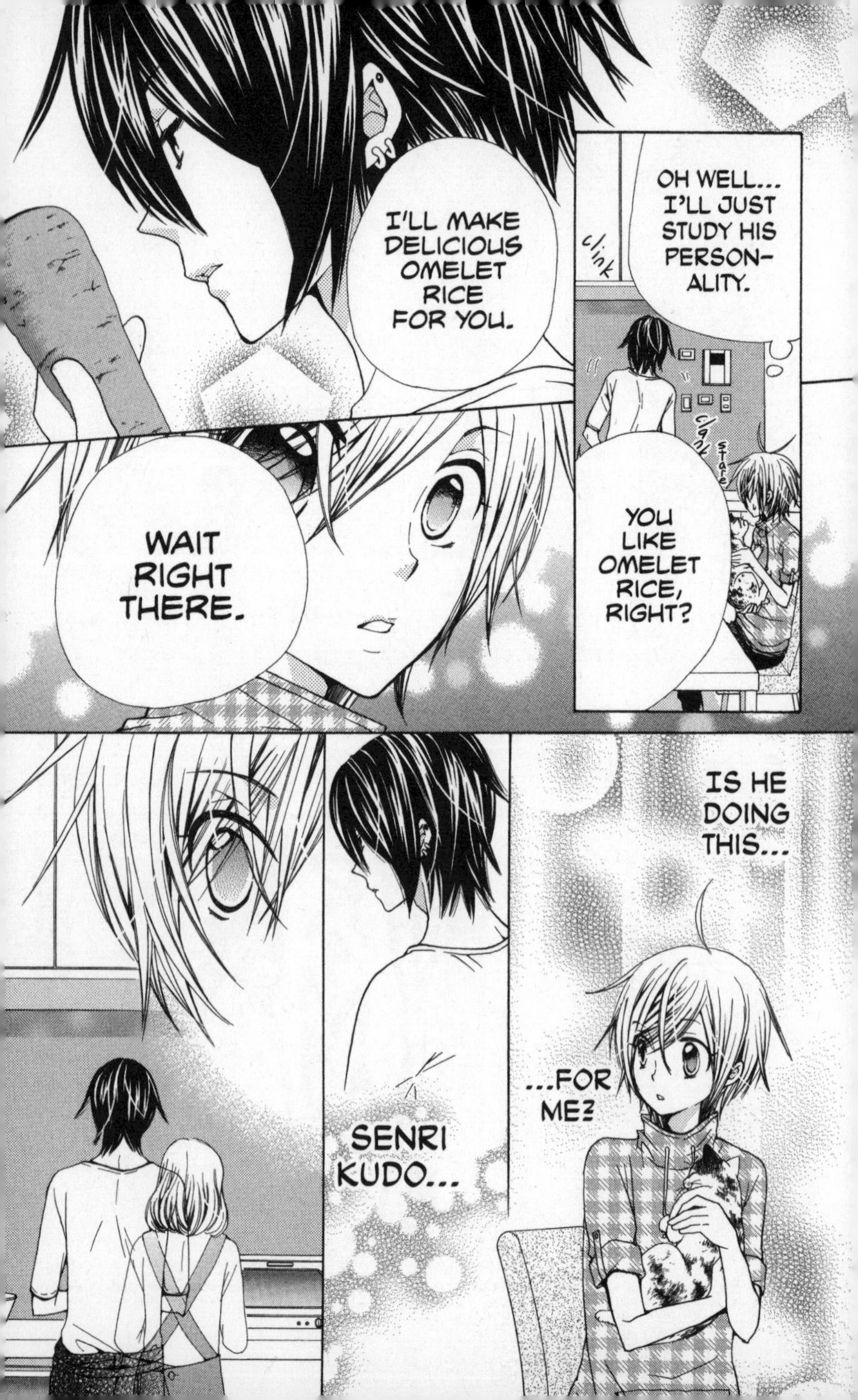
OH WELL... I'LL JUST STUDY HIS PERSON-ALITY.
clink
clank
stare
YOU LIKE OMELET RICE, RIGHT?
I'LL MAKE DELICIOUS OMELET RICE FOR YOU.
WAIT RIGHT THERE.
IS HE DOING THIS...
...FOR ME?
SENRI KUDO...

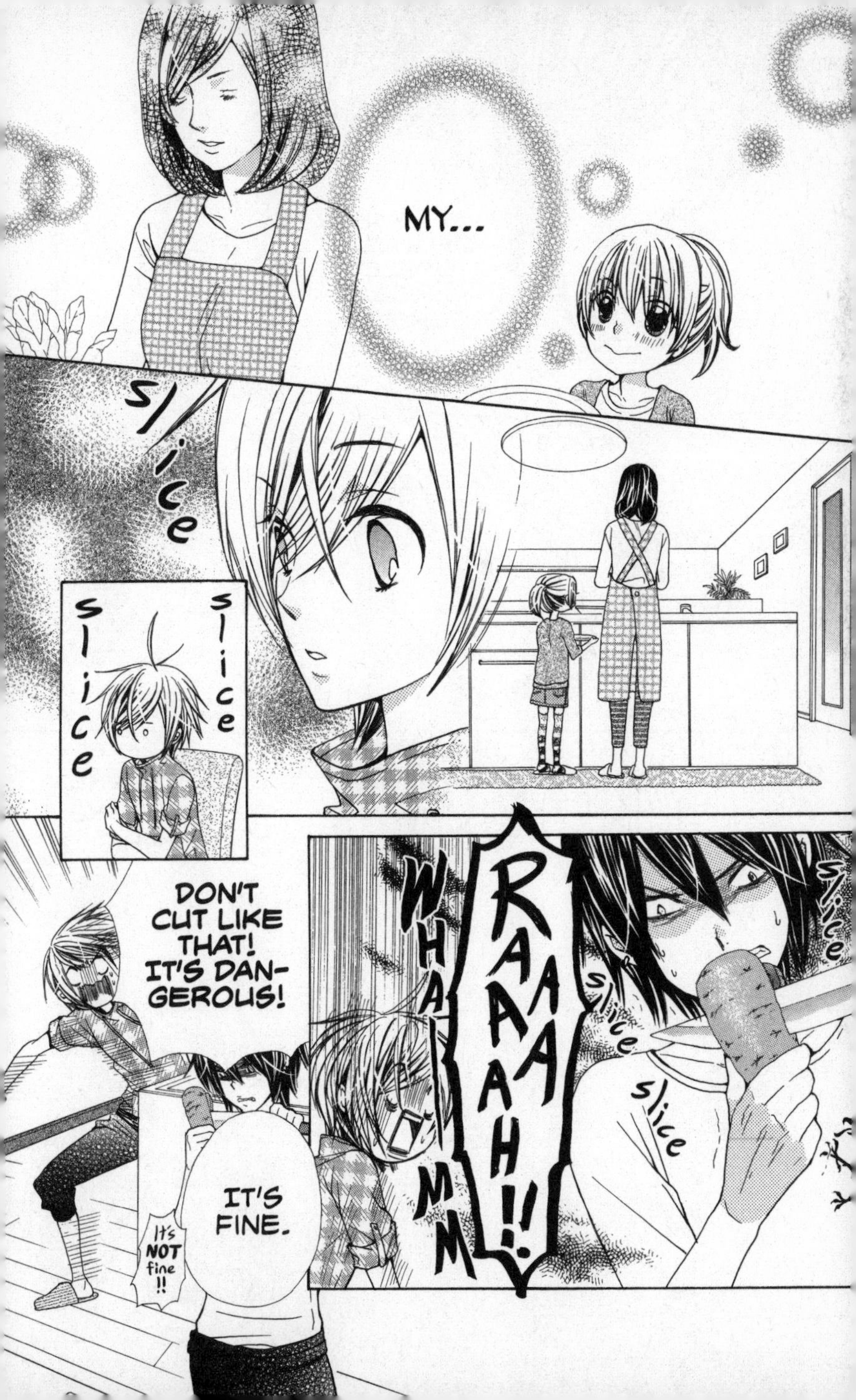
MY...
slice
slice slice
slice
RAAAAH!!
WHAM
slice
slice
DON'T CUT LIKE THAT! IT'S DAN-GEROUS!
IT'S FINE.
It's NOT fine!!

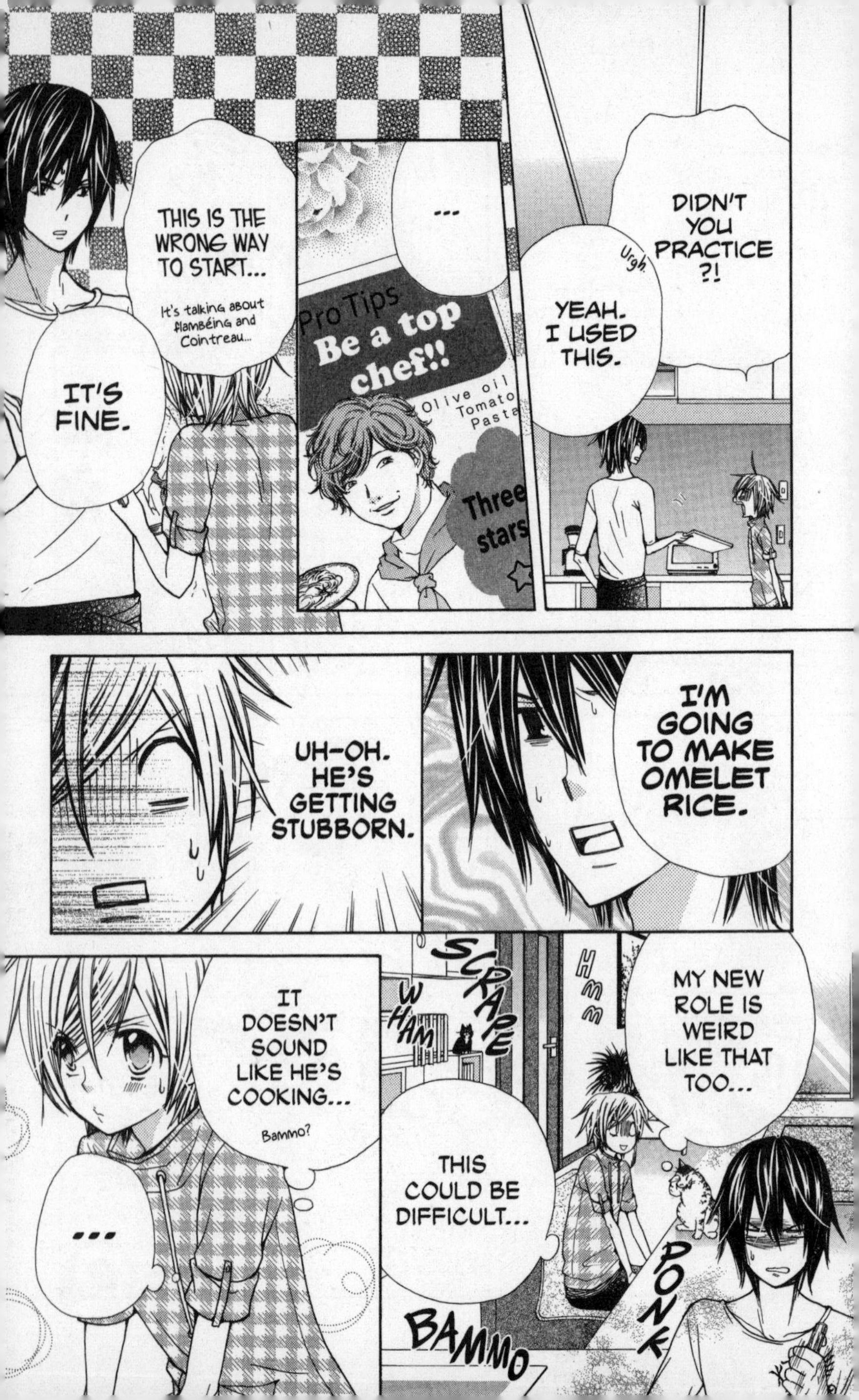
DIDN'T YOU PRACTICE ?!
Urgh.
YEAH. I USED THIS.
...
Pro Tips
Be a top chef!!
Olive oil
Tomato
Pasta
Three stars
THIS IS THE WRONG WAY TO START...
It's talking about flambéing and Cointreau...
IT'S FINE.
I'M GOING TO MAKE OMELET RICE.
UH-OH. HE'S GETTING STUBBORN.
Hmm
MY NEW ROLE IS WEIRD LIKE THAT TOO...
SCRAPE
WHAM
THIS COULD BE DIFFICULT...
PONK
BAMMO
IT DOESN'T SOUND LIKE HE'S COOKING...
Bammo?
...

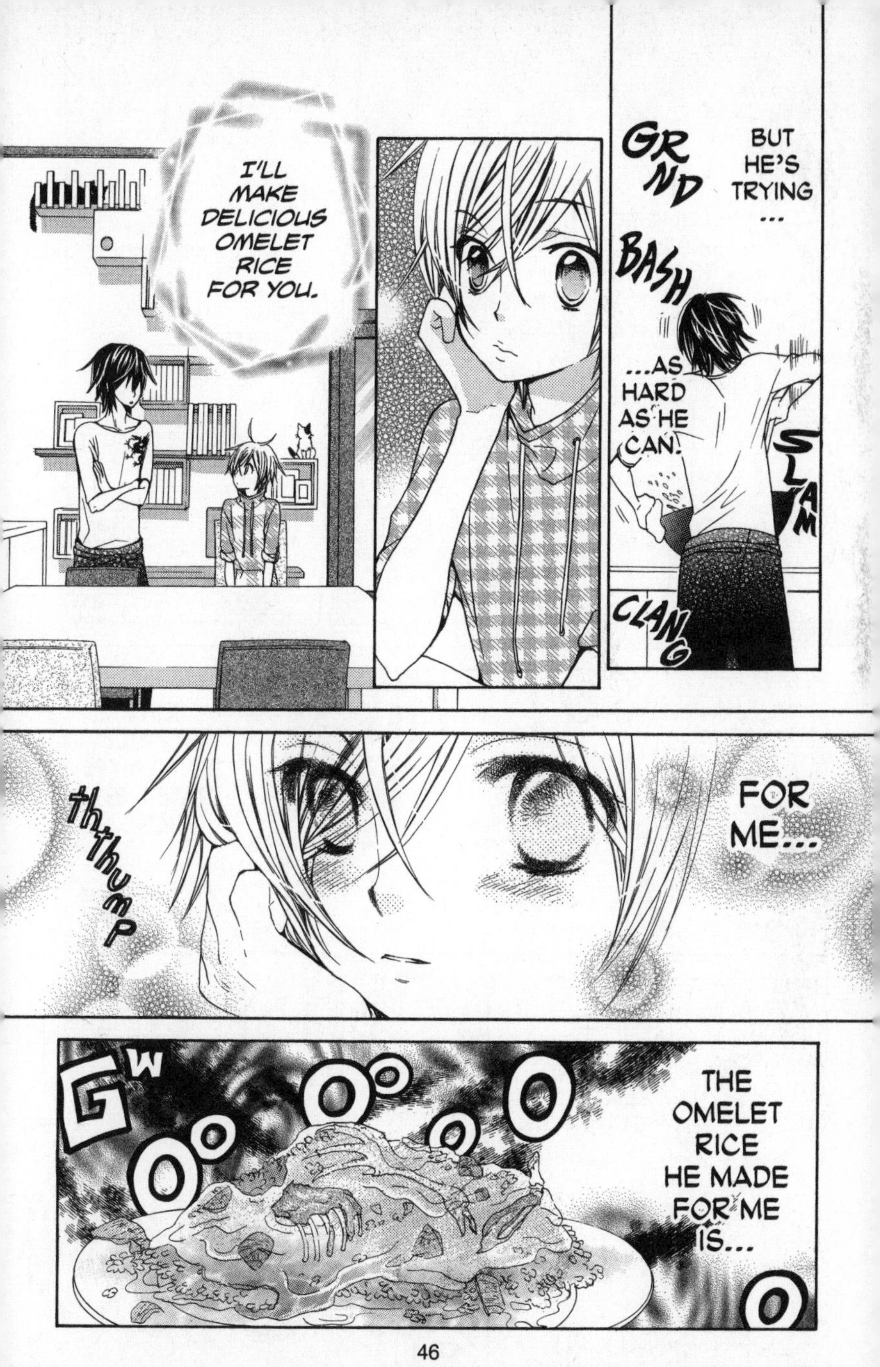
BUT HE'S TRYING ...
GRND
BASH
...AS HARD AS HE CAN.
SLAM
CLANG
I'LL MAKE DELICIOUS OMELET RICE FOR YOU.
FOR ME...
th-thump
THE OMELET RICE HE MADE FOR ME IS...
GWOOOOOOO

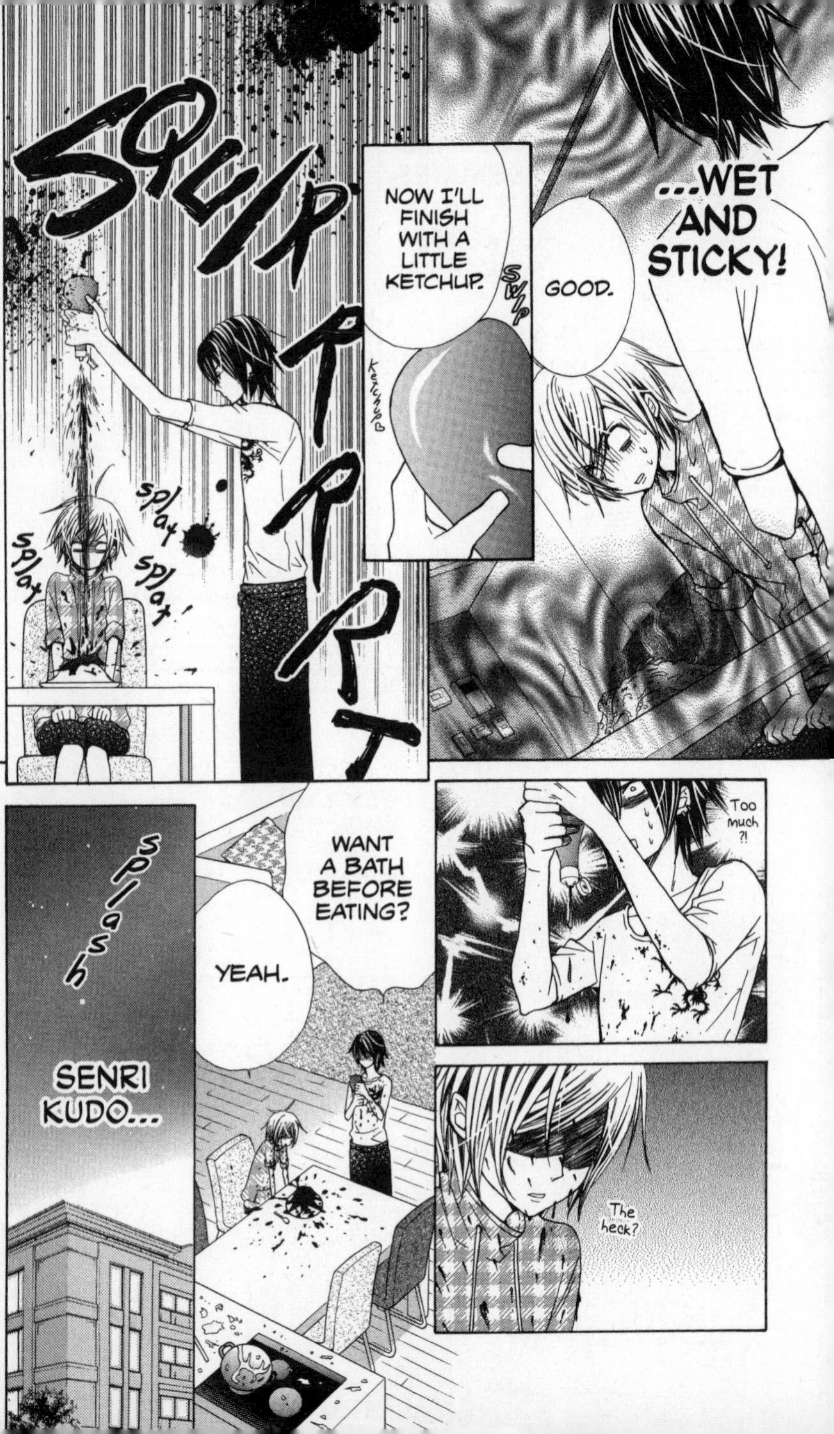
...WET AND STICKY!
GOOD.
swip
NOW I'LL FINISH WITH A LITTLE KETCHUP.
ketchup
splat
splat
splat
Too much?!
The heck?
WANT A BATH BEFORE EATING?
YEAH.
splash
SENRI KUDO...

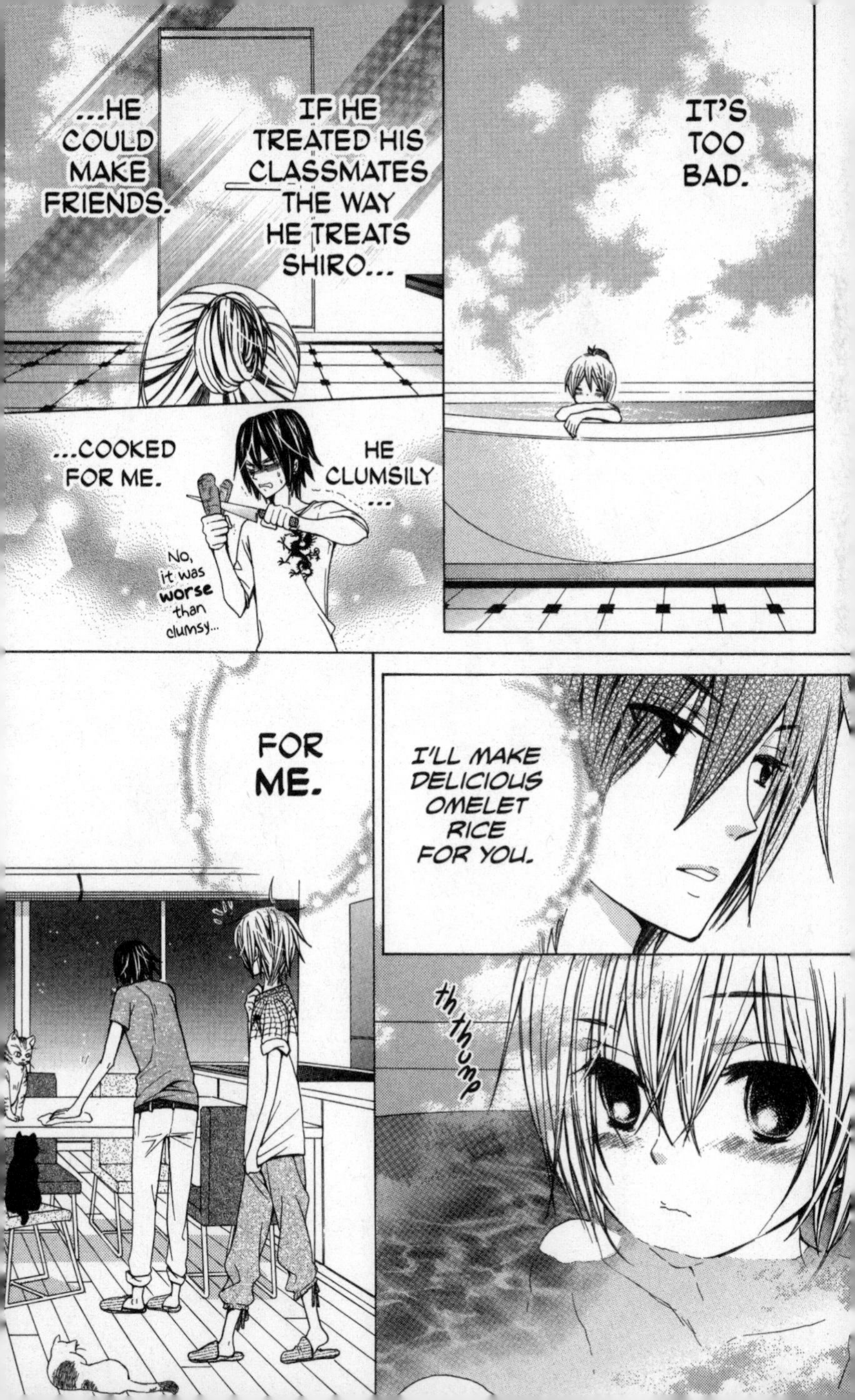
IT'S TOO BAD.
IF HE TREATED HIS CLASSMATES THE WAY HE TREATS SHIRO...
...HE COULD MAKE FRIENDS.
HE CLUMSILY...
...COOKED FOR ME.
No, it was worse than clumsy...
I'LL MAKE DELICIOUS OMELET RICE FOR YOU.
th thump
FOR ME.

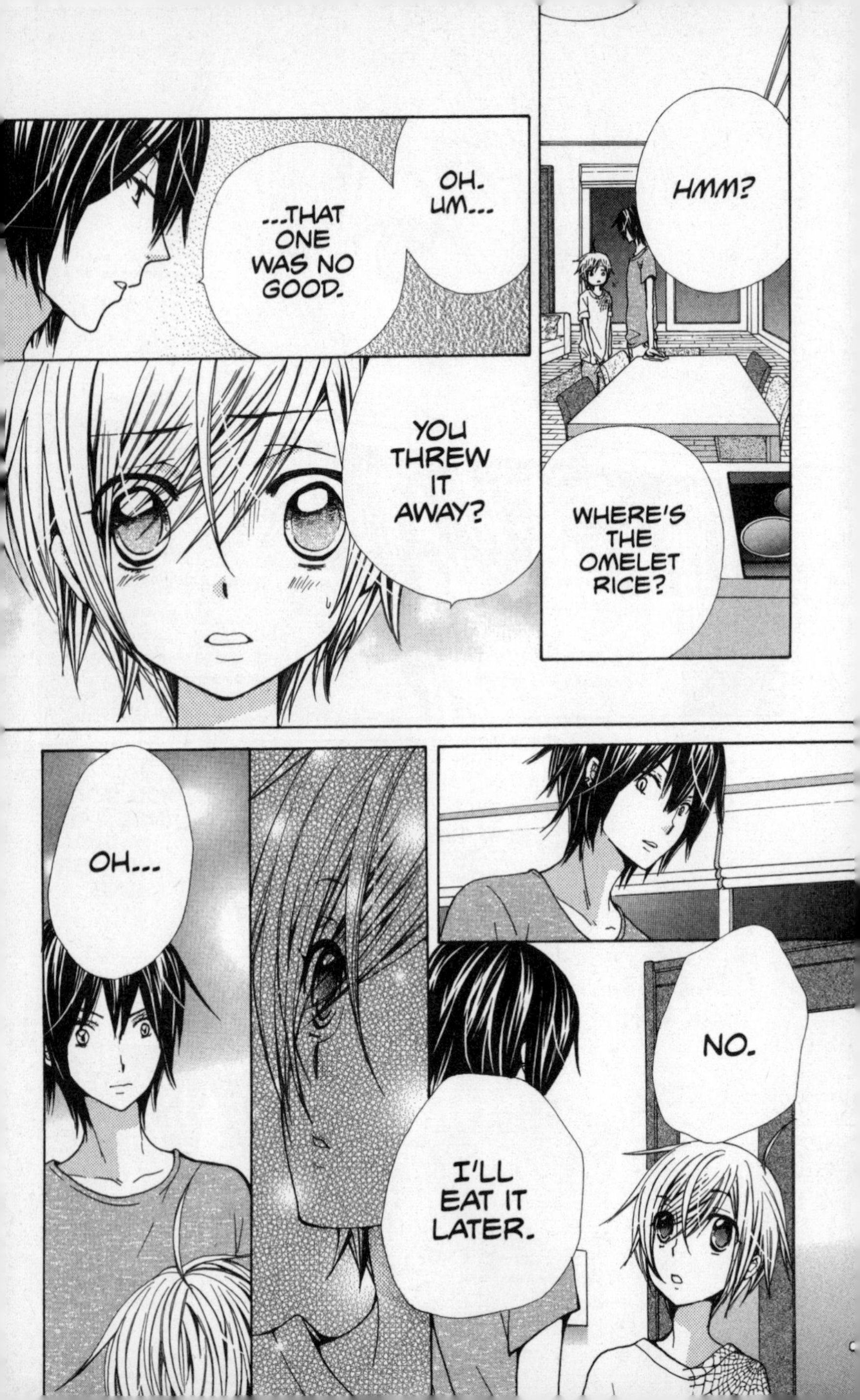
HMM?
WHERE'S THE OMELET RICE?
OH. UM...
...THAT ONE WAS NO GOOD.
YOU THREW IT AWAY?
NO.
I'LL EAT IT LATER.
OH...

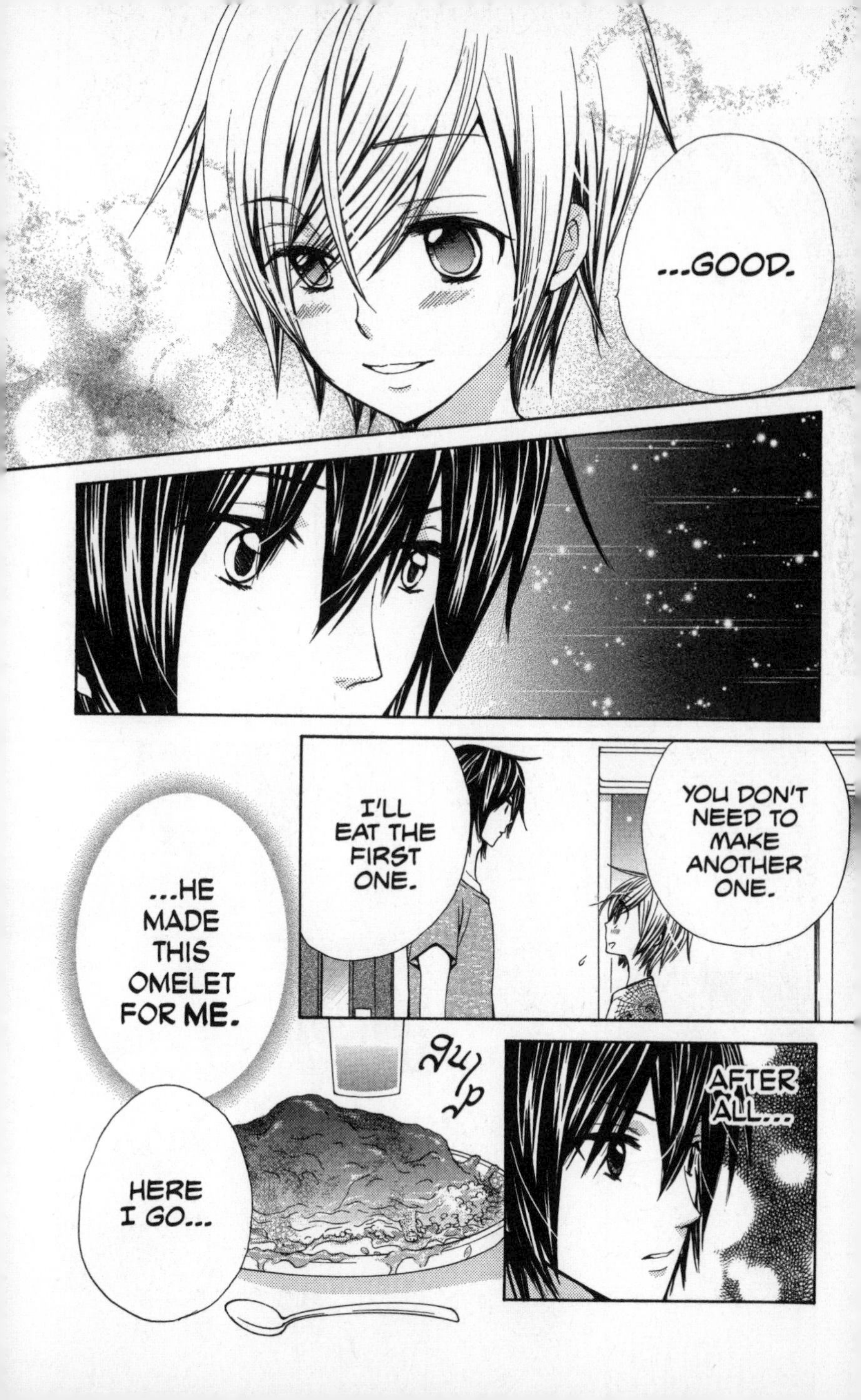
...GOOD.
YOU DON'T NEED TO MAKE ANOTHER ONE.
I'LL EAT THE FIRST ONE.
...HE MADE THIS OMELET FOR ME.
AFTER ALL...
gulp
HERE I GO...

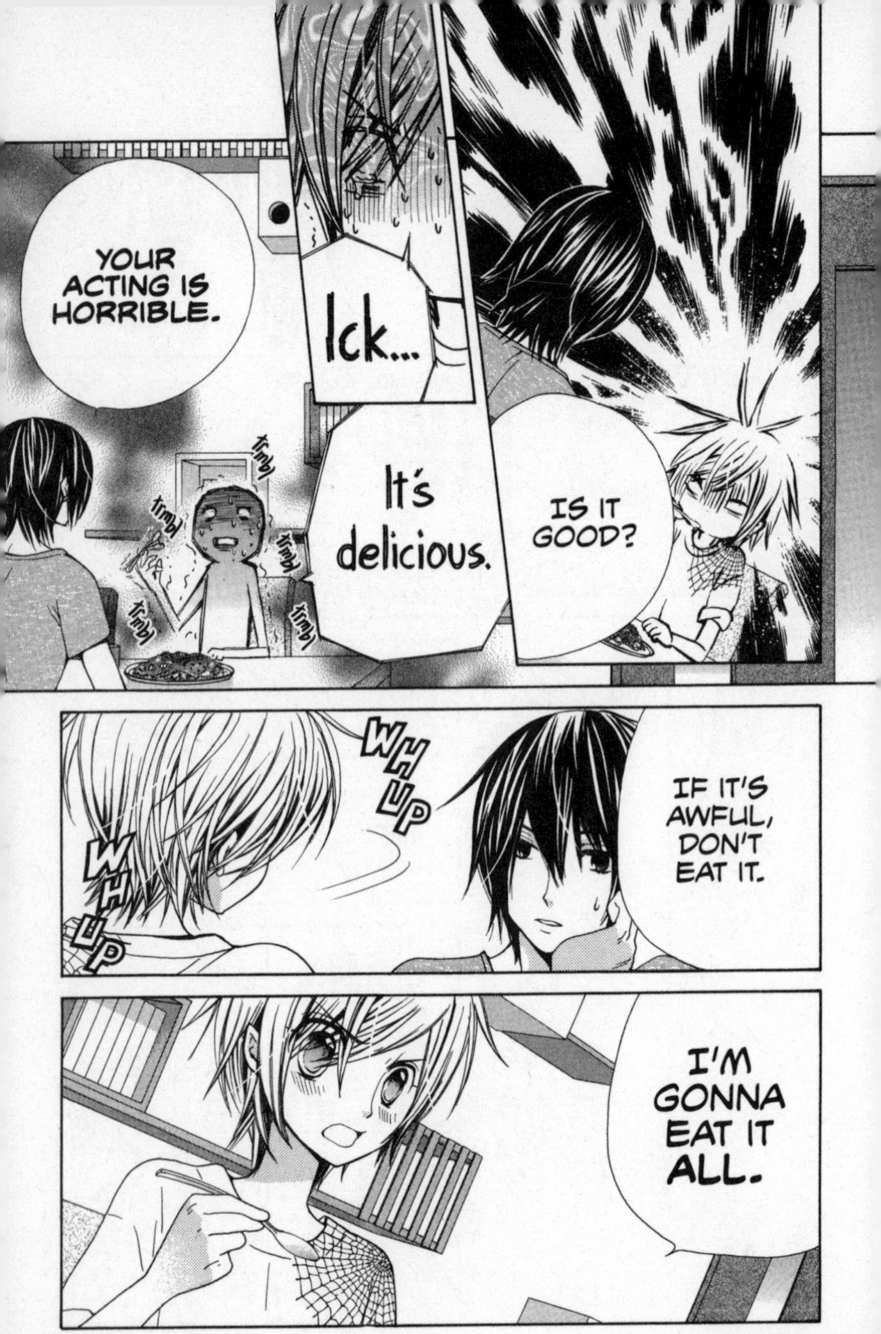
IS IT GOOD?
It's delicious.
Ick...
trmbl
trmbl
trmbl
trmbl
trmbl
YOUR ACTING IS HORRIBLE.
IF IT'S AWFUL, DON'T EAT IT.
WHUP
WHUP
I'M GONNA EAT IT ALL.

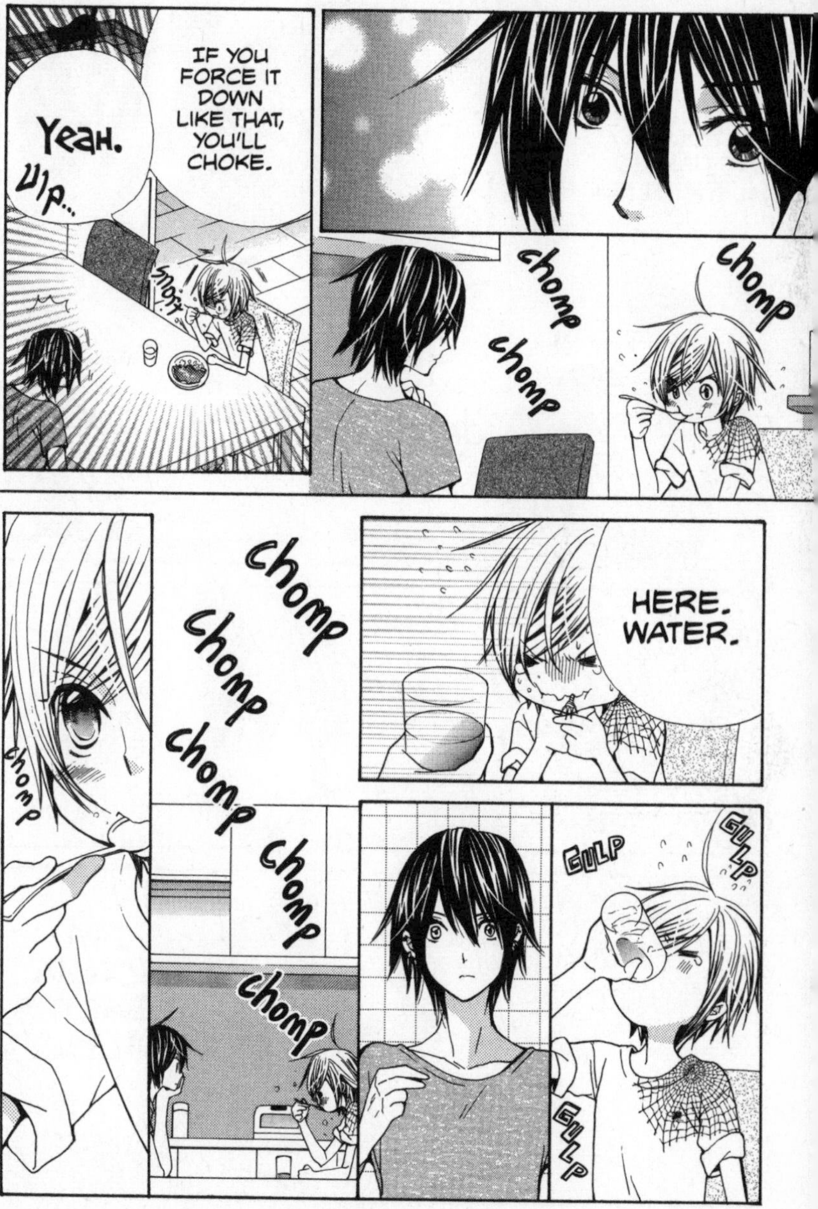
chomp
chomp
chomp
IF YOU FORCE IT DOWN LIKE THAT, YOU'LL CHOKE.
Yeah.
Ulp...
snort
HERE. WATER.
GULP
GULP
GULP
chomp
chomp
chomp
chomp
chomp
chomp

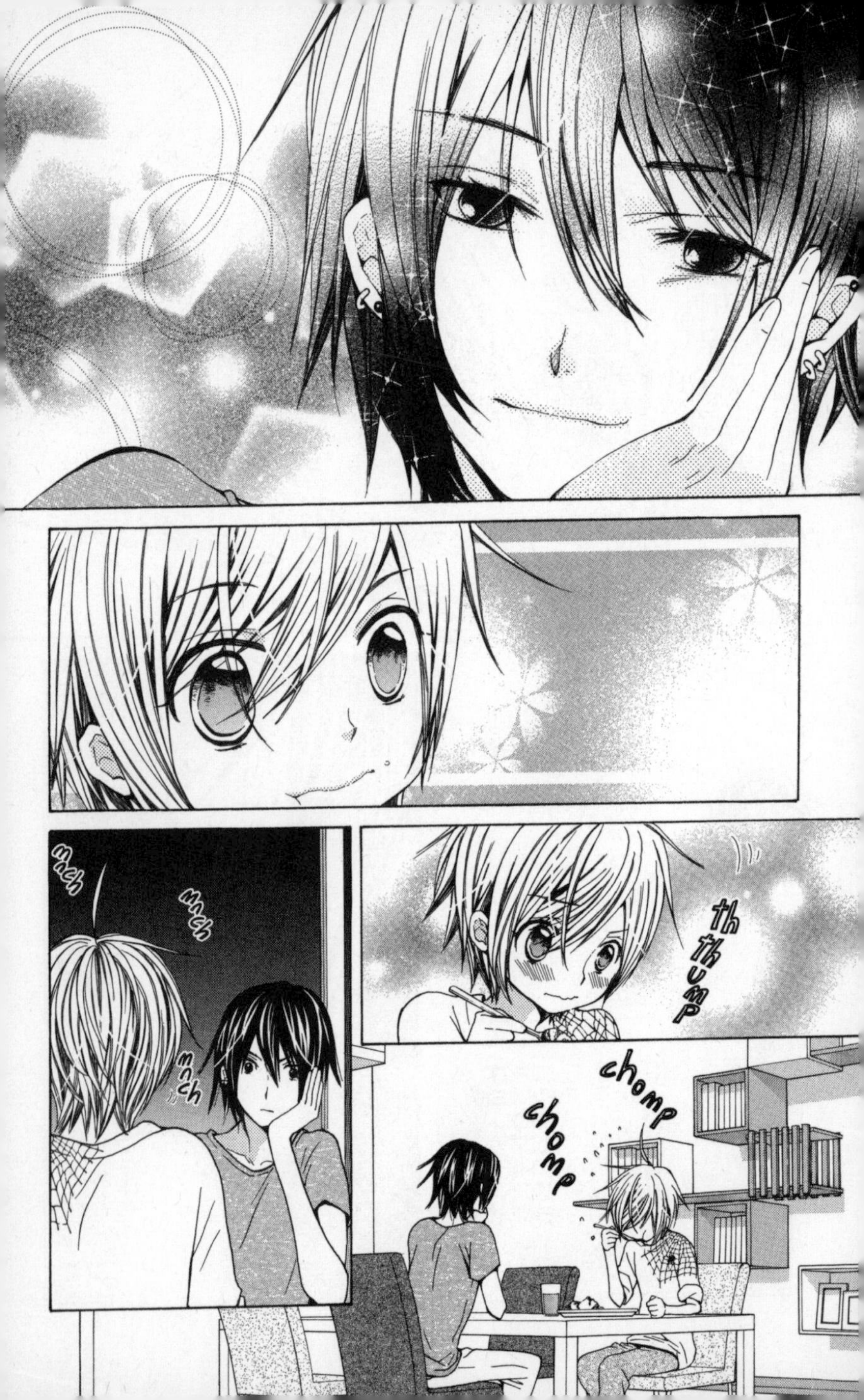
th thump
mnch
mnch
mnch
chomp
chomp

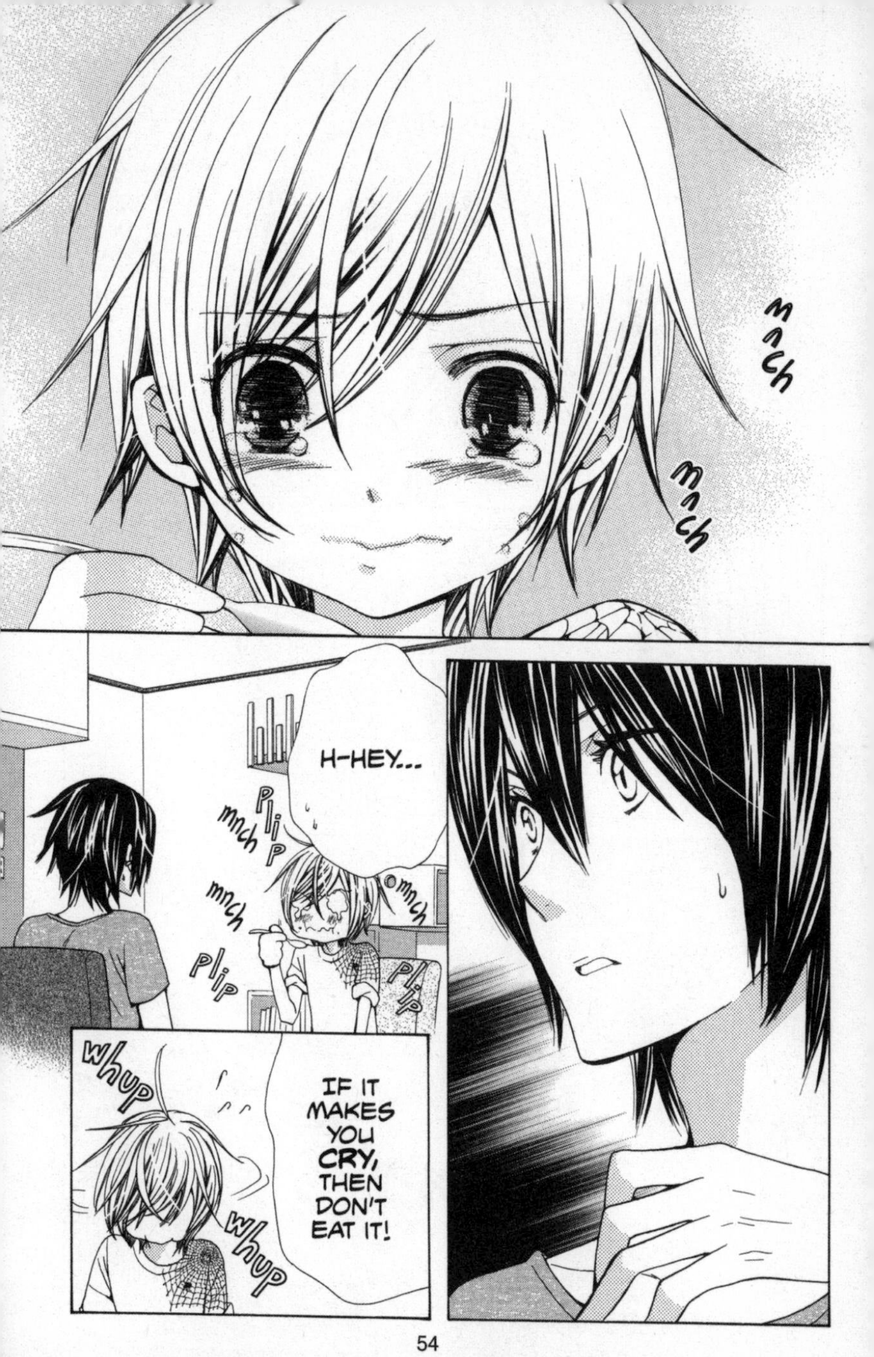
mnch
mnch
H-HEY...
plip
mnch
mnch
mnch
plip
plip
IF IT MAKES YOU CRY, THEN DON'T EAT IT!
whup
whup

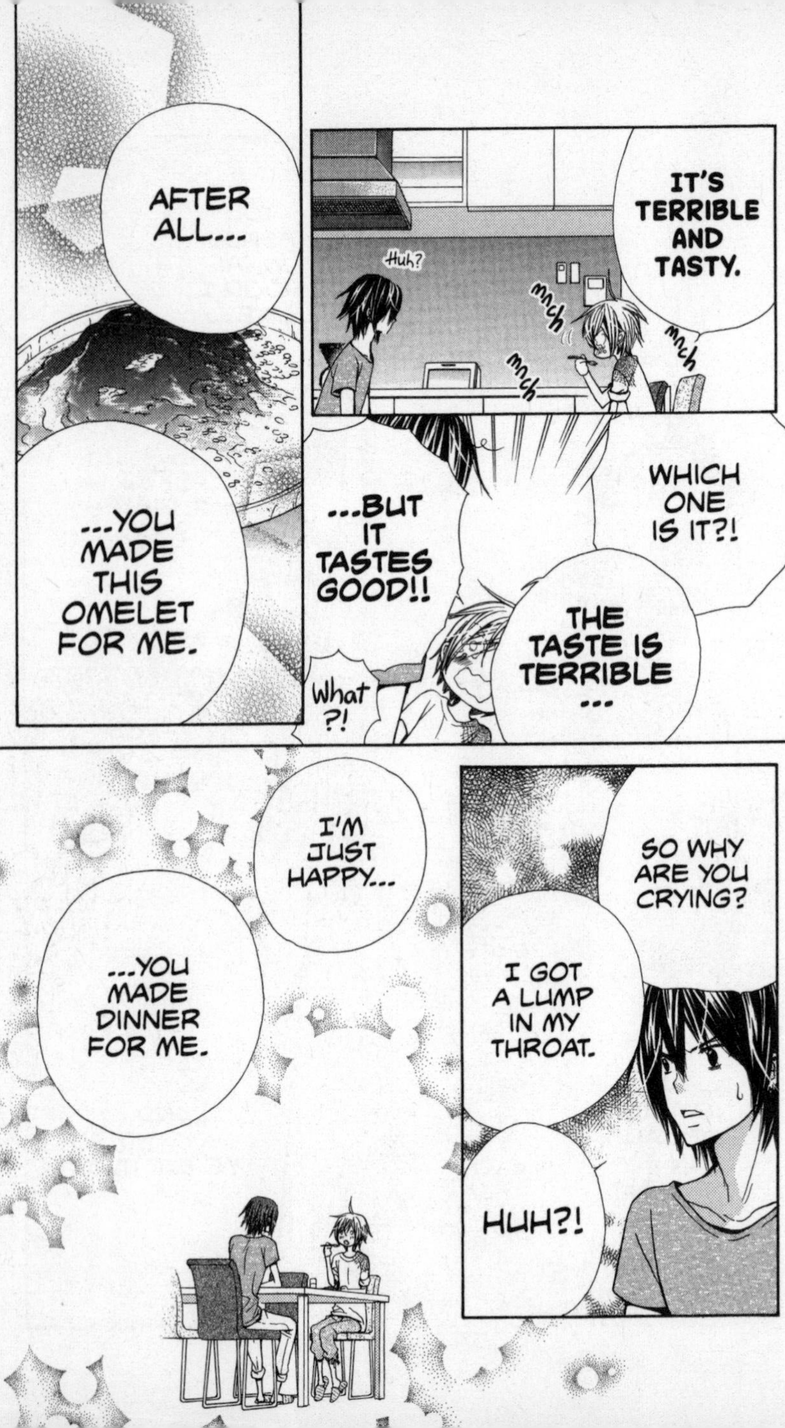
IT'S TERRIBLE AND TASTY.
Huh?
mnch
mnch
mnch
WHICH ONE IS IT?!
THE TASTE IS TERRIBLE...
...BUT IT TASTES GOOD!!
What?!
AFTER ALL...
...YOU MADE THIS OMELET FOR ME.
SO WHY ARE YOU CRYING?
I GOT A LUMP IN MY THROAT.
HUH?!
I'M JUST HAPPY...
...YOU MADE DINNER FOR ME.

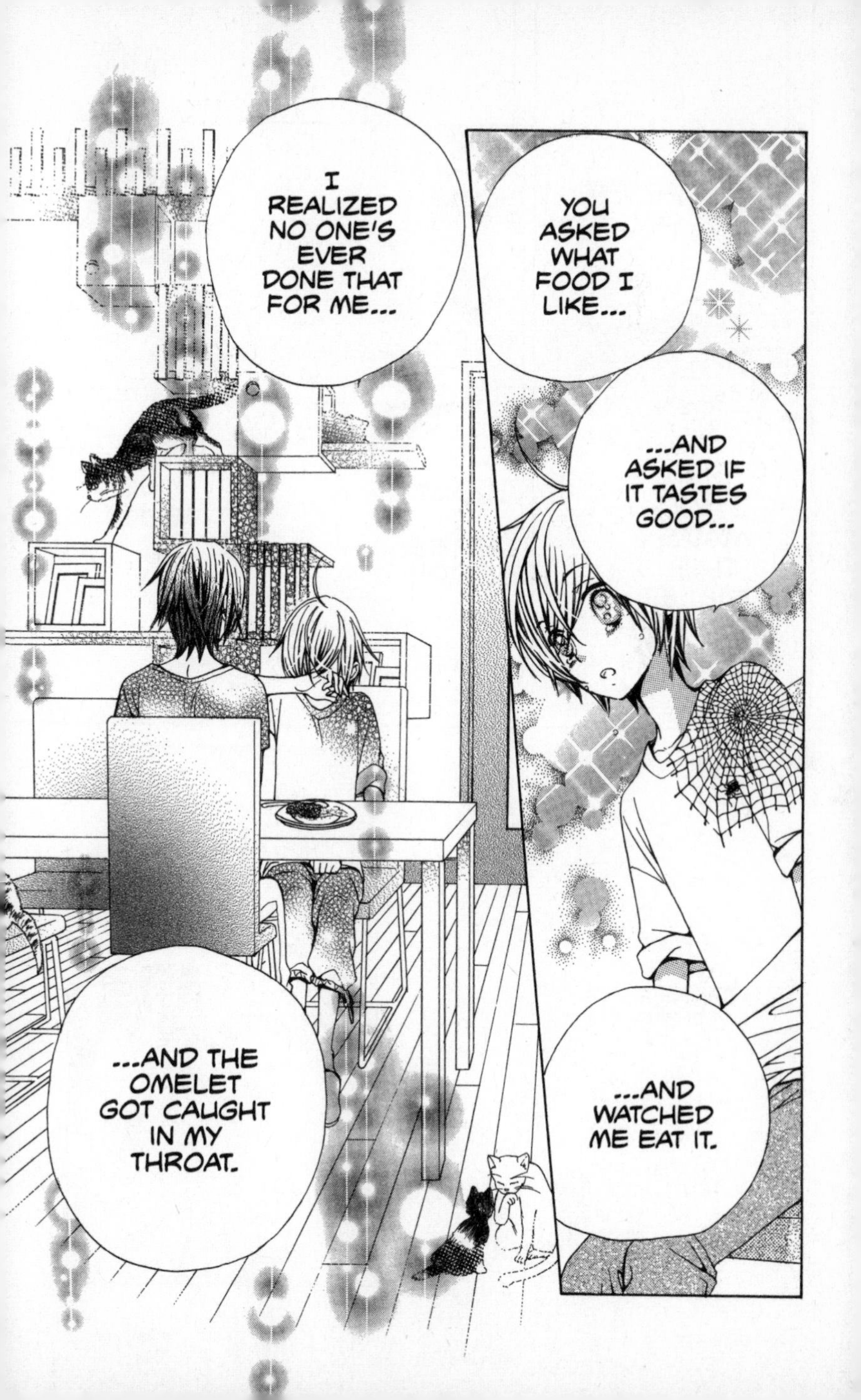
YOU ASKED WHAT FOOD I LIKE...
...AND ASKED IF IT TASTES GOOD...
...AND WATCHED ME EAT IT.
I REALIZED NO ONE'S EVER DONE THAT FOR ME...
...AND THE OMELET GOT CAUGHT IN MY THROAT.

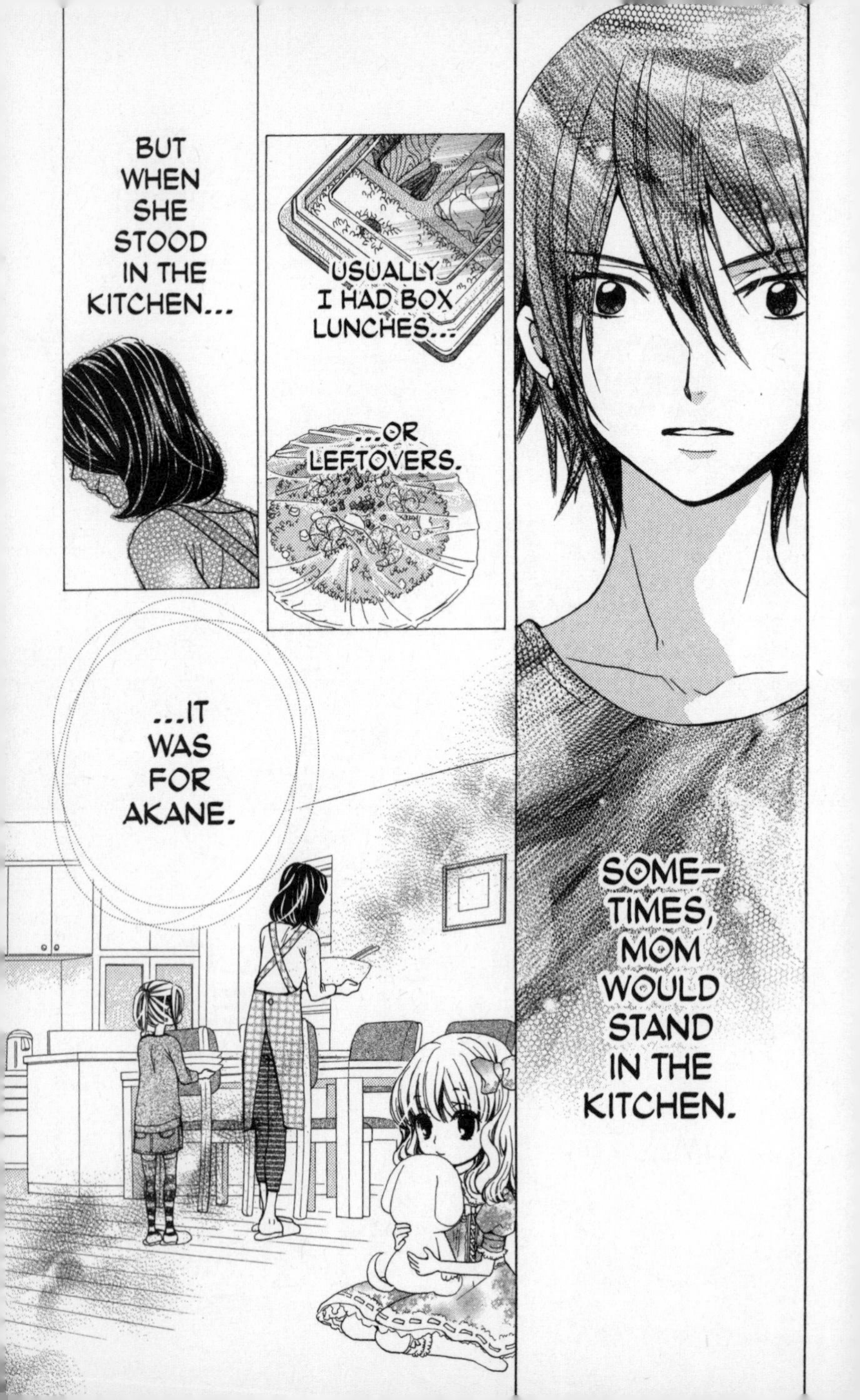
SOME-TIMES, MOM WOULD STAND IN THE KITCHEN.
USUALLY I HAD BOX LUNCHES...
...OR LEFTOVERS.
BUT WHEN SHE STOOD IN THE KITCHEN...
...IT WAS FOR AKANE.

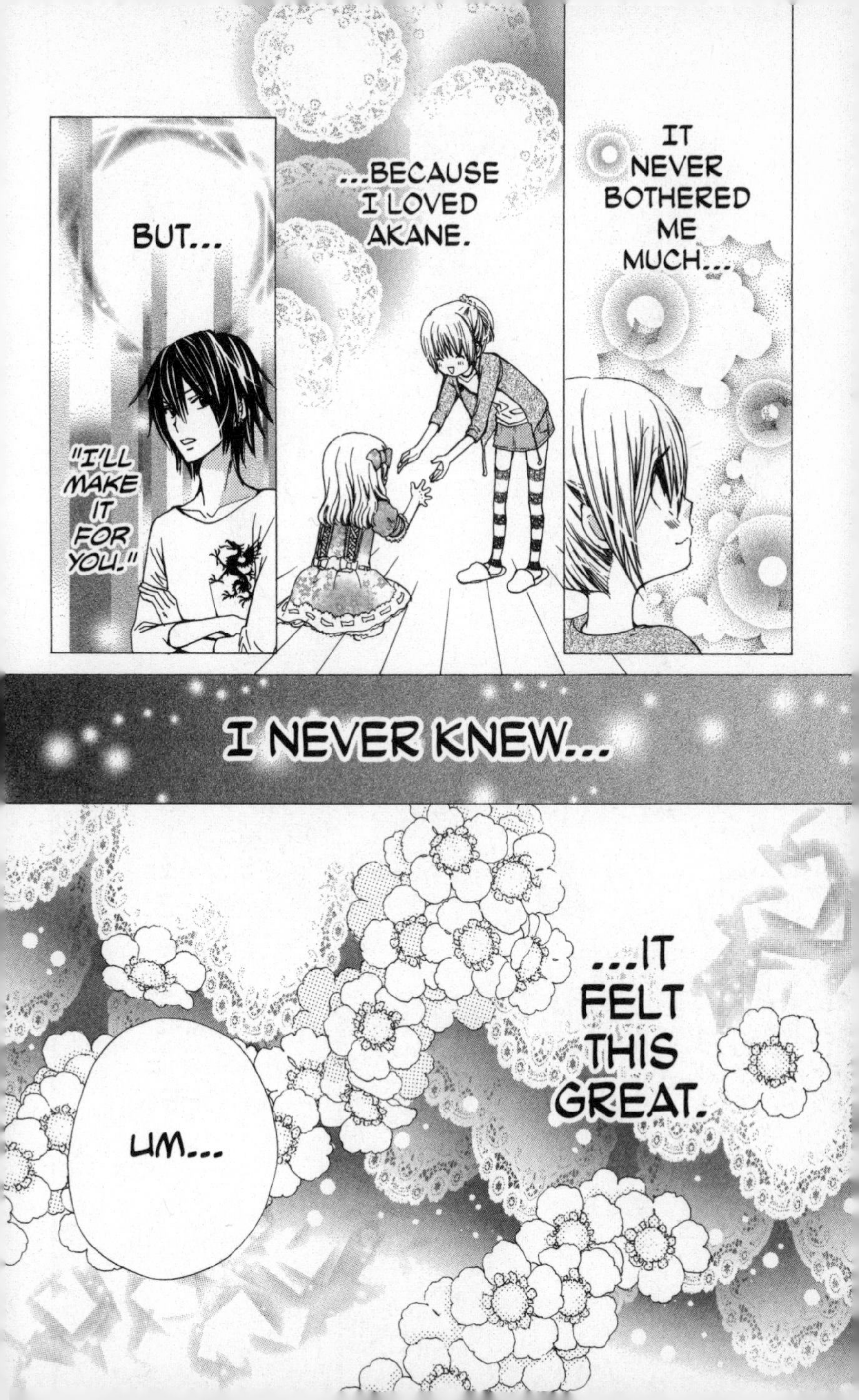
IT NEVER BOTHERED ME MUCH...
...BECAUSE I LOVED AKANE.
BUT...
"I'LL MAKE IT FOR YOU."
I NEVER KNEW...
...IT FELT THIS GREAT.
UM...

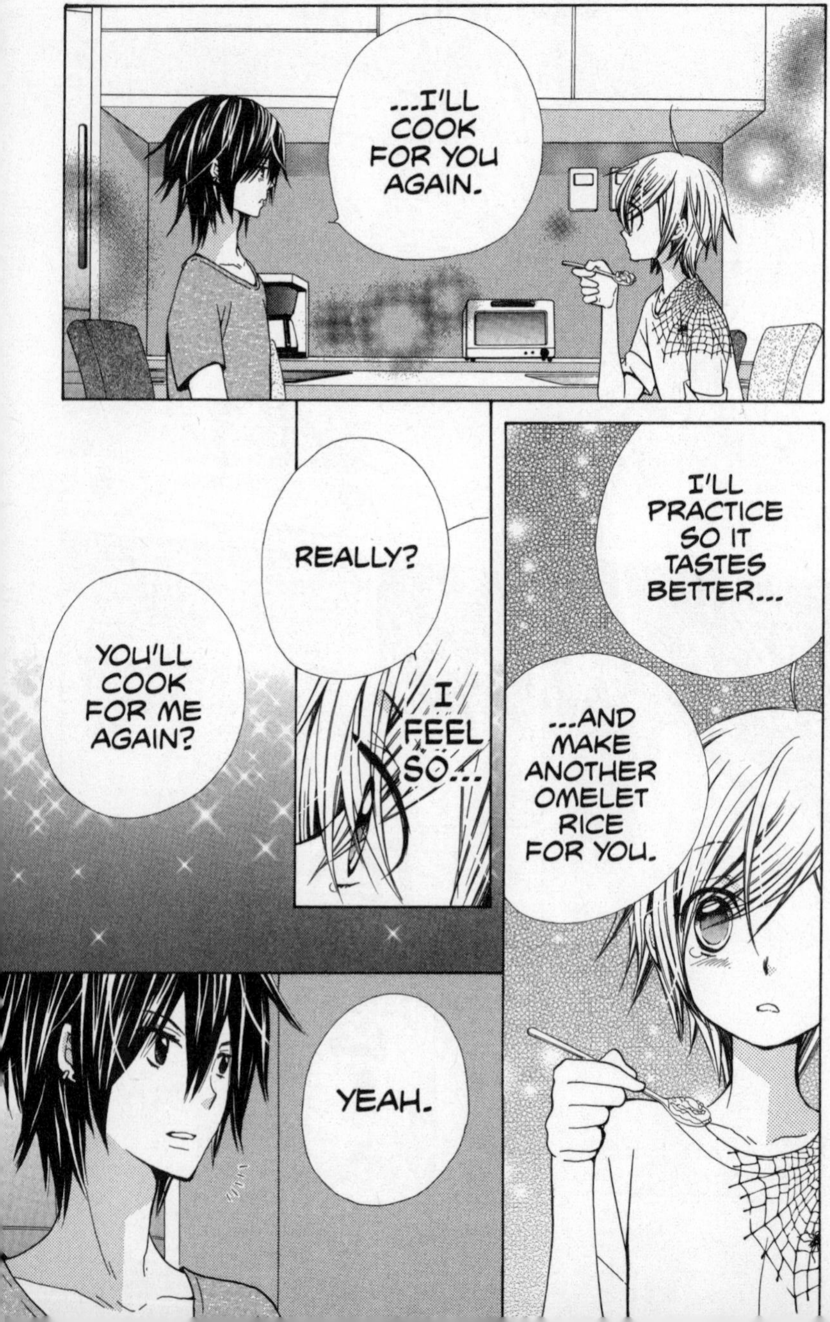
...I'LL COOK FOR YOU AGAIN.
I'LL PRACTICE SO IT TASTES BETTER...
...AND MAKE ANOTHER OMELET RICE FOR YOU.
REALLY?
I FEEL SO...
YOU'LL COOK FOR ME AGAIN?
YEAH.

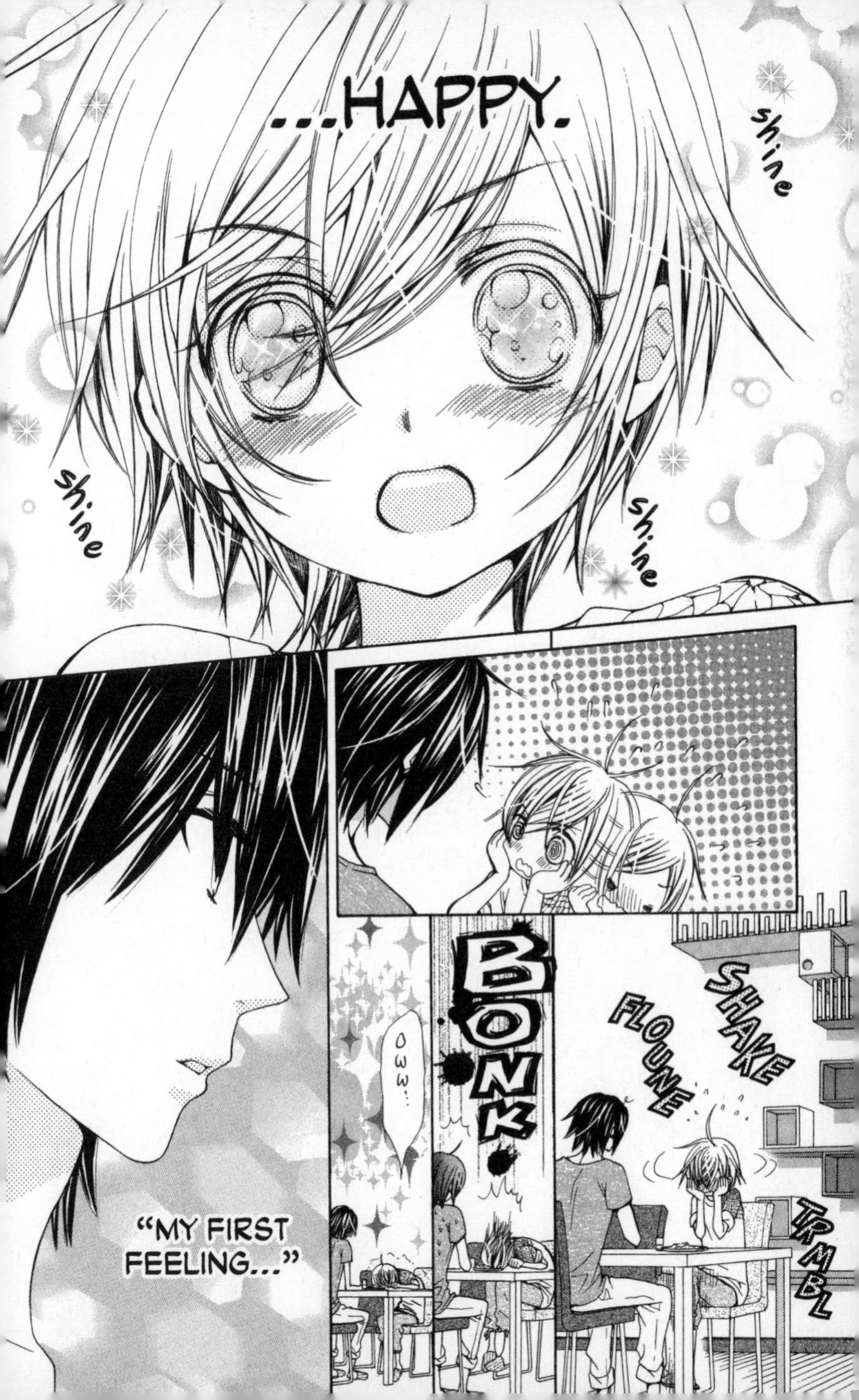

shine
...HAPPY.
shine
shine
SHAKE
TRMBL
FLOUNE
BONK
Oww...
"MY FIRST FEELING..."

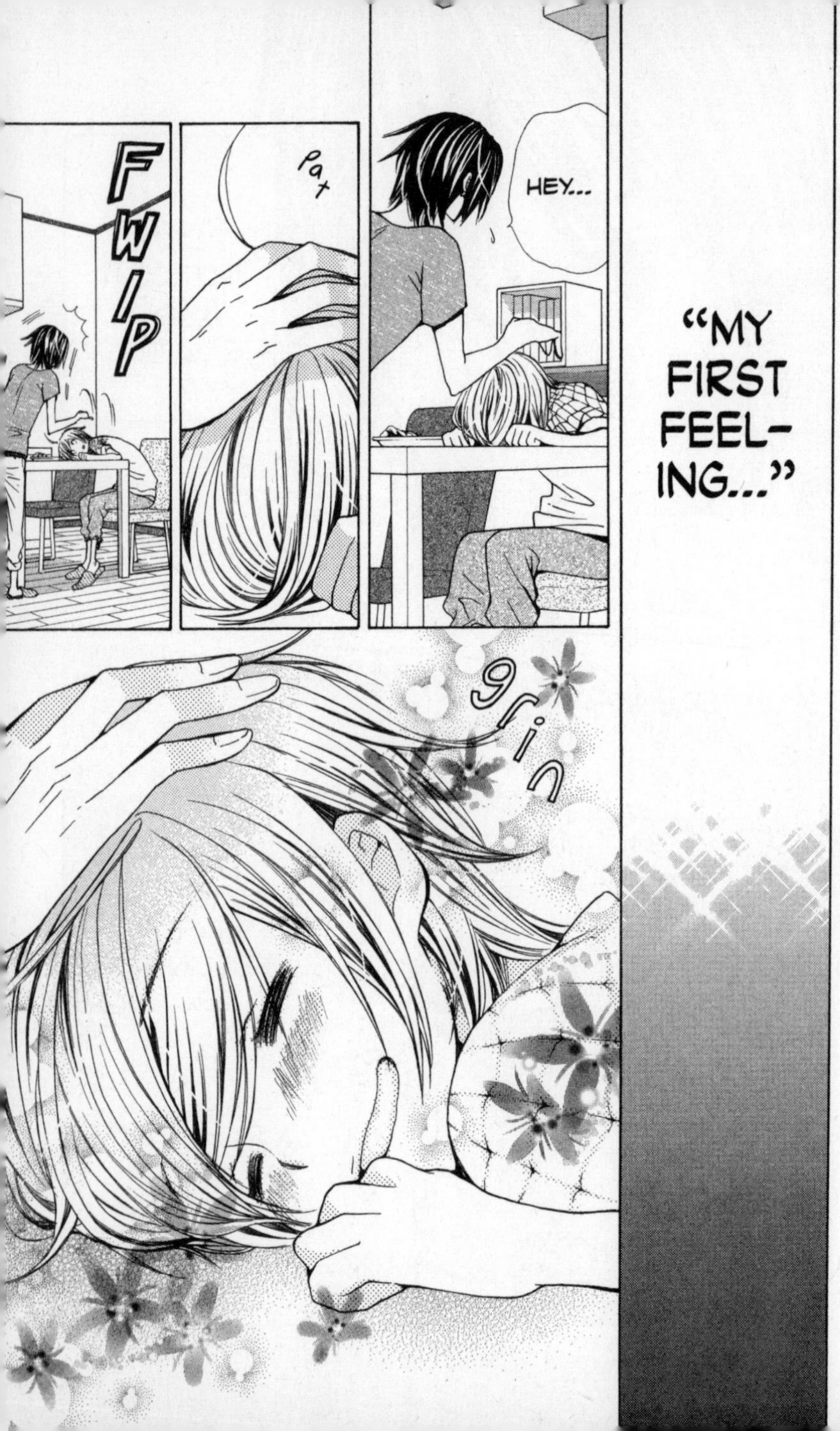
"MY FIRST FEELING..."
HEY...
pat
FWIP
grin

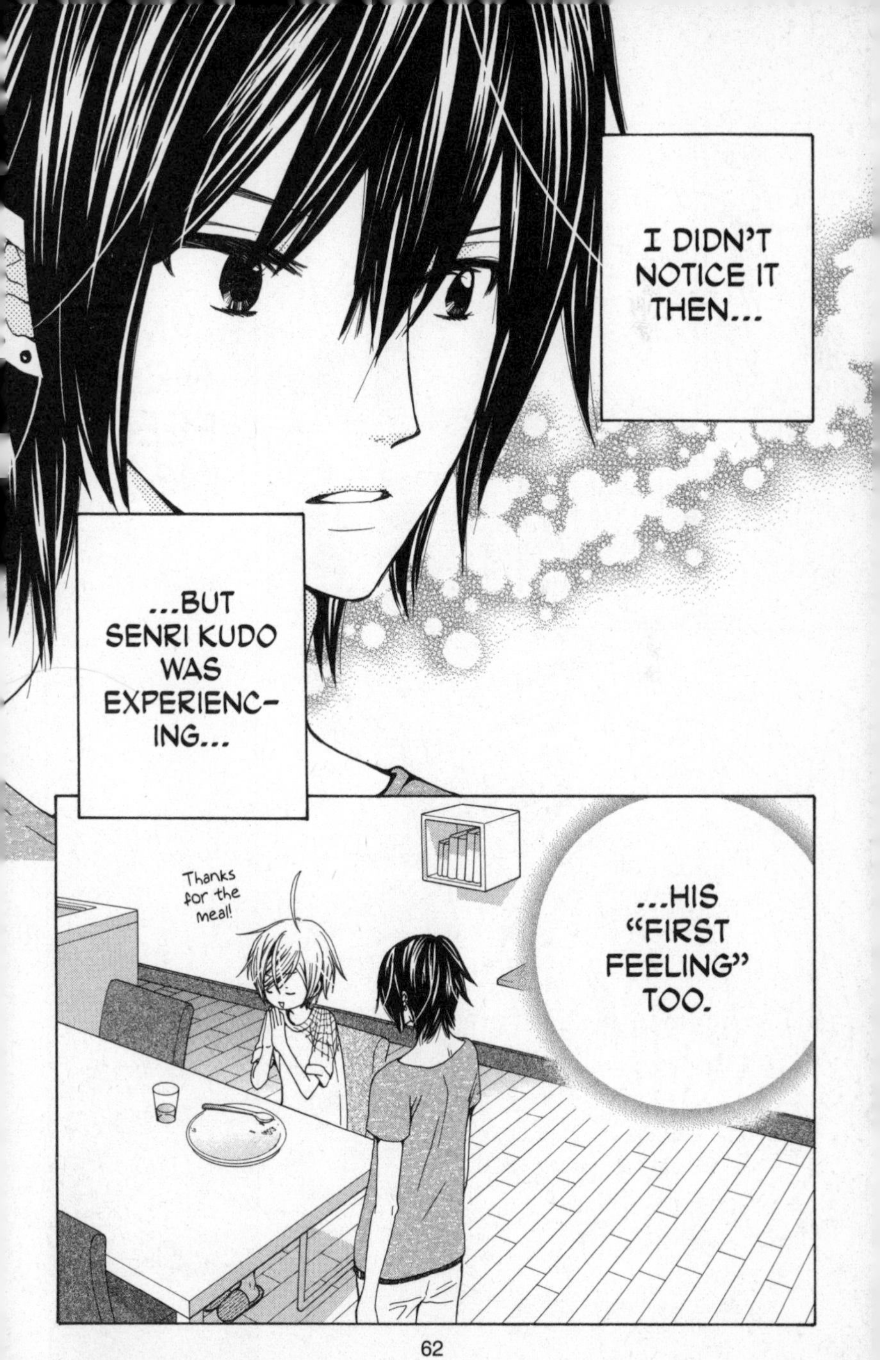
I DIDN'T NOTICE IT THEN...
...BUT SENRI KUDO WAS EXPERIENC-ING...
...HIS "FIRST FEELING" TOO.
Thanks for the meal!

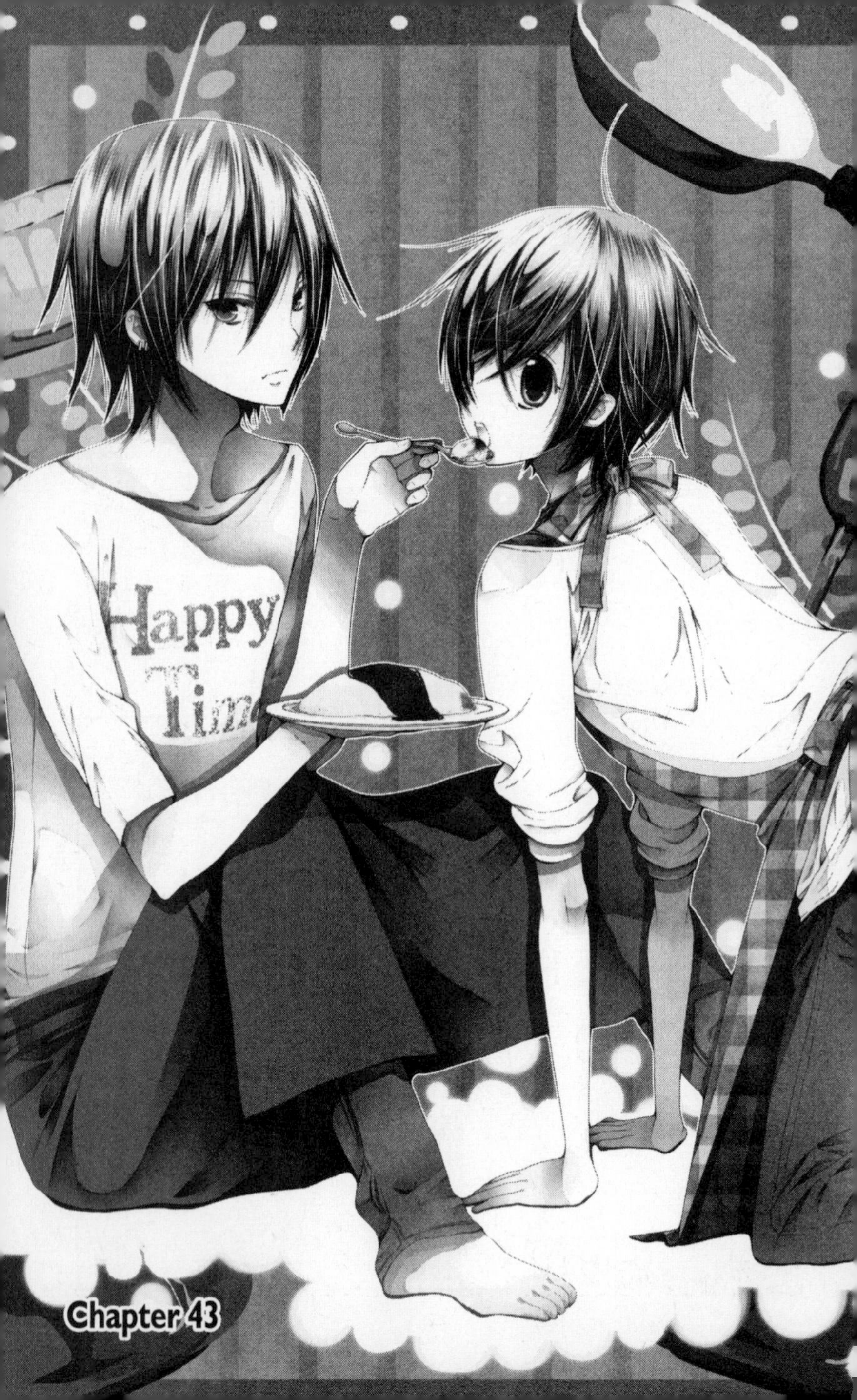
Happy
Chapter 43

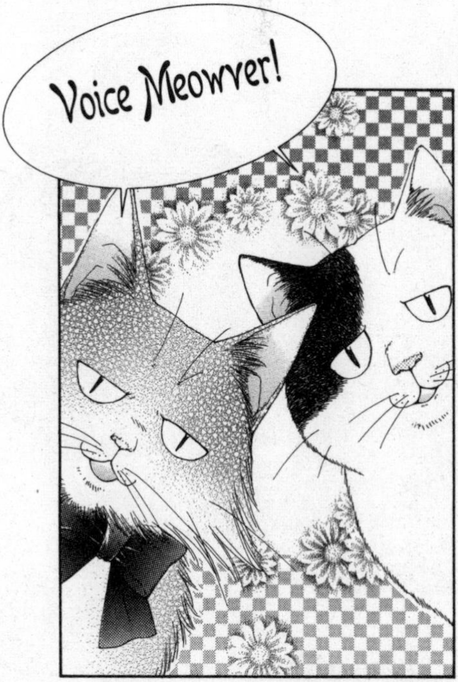
Voice Meowver!

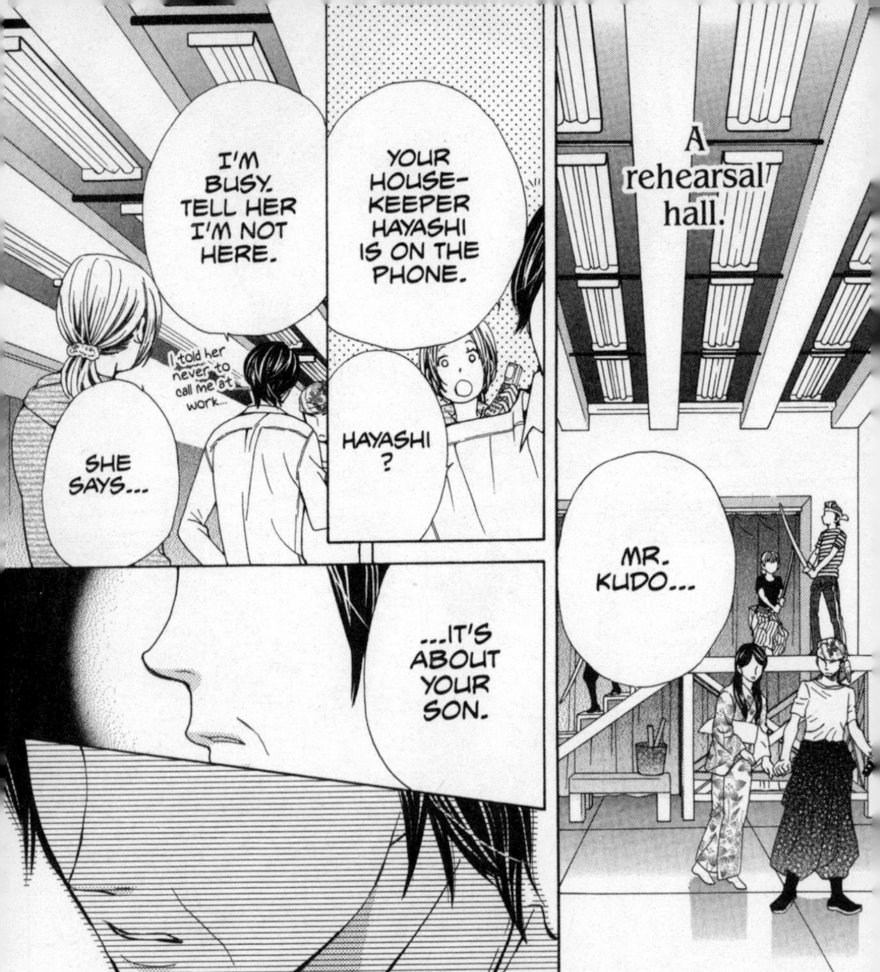
A rehearsal hall.
MR. KUDO...
YOUR HOUSE-KEEPER HAYASHI IS ON THE PHONE.
HAYASHI?
I'M BUSY. TELL HER I'M NOT HERE.
I told her never to call me at work...
SHE SAYS...
...IT'S ABOUT YOUR SON.

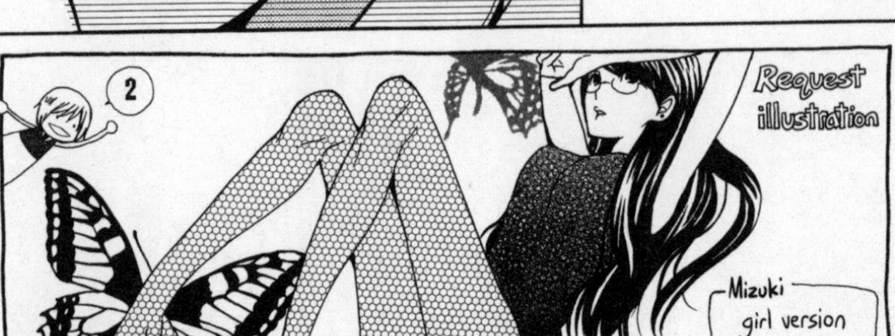
Request illustration
2
Mizuki girl version

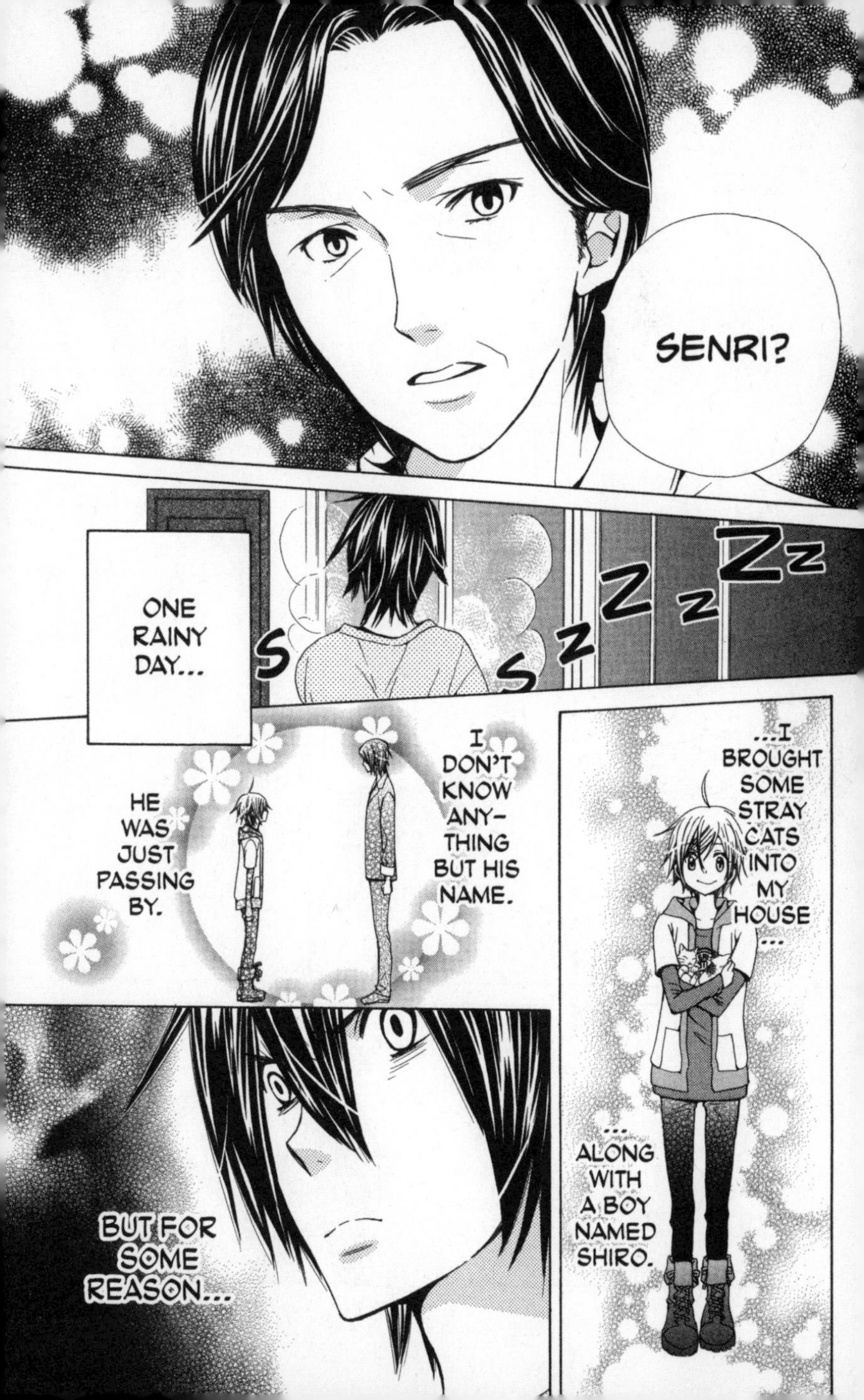
SENRI?
ONE RAINY DAY...
S
SZ
Z z
Zz
...I BROUGHT SOME STRAY CATS INTO MY HOUSE...
...ALONG WITH A BOY NAMED SHIRO.
I DON'T KNOW ANY-THING BUT HIS NAME.
HE WAS JUST PASSING BY.
BUT FOR SOME REASON...

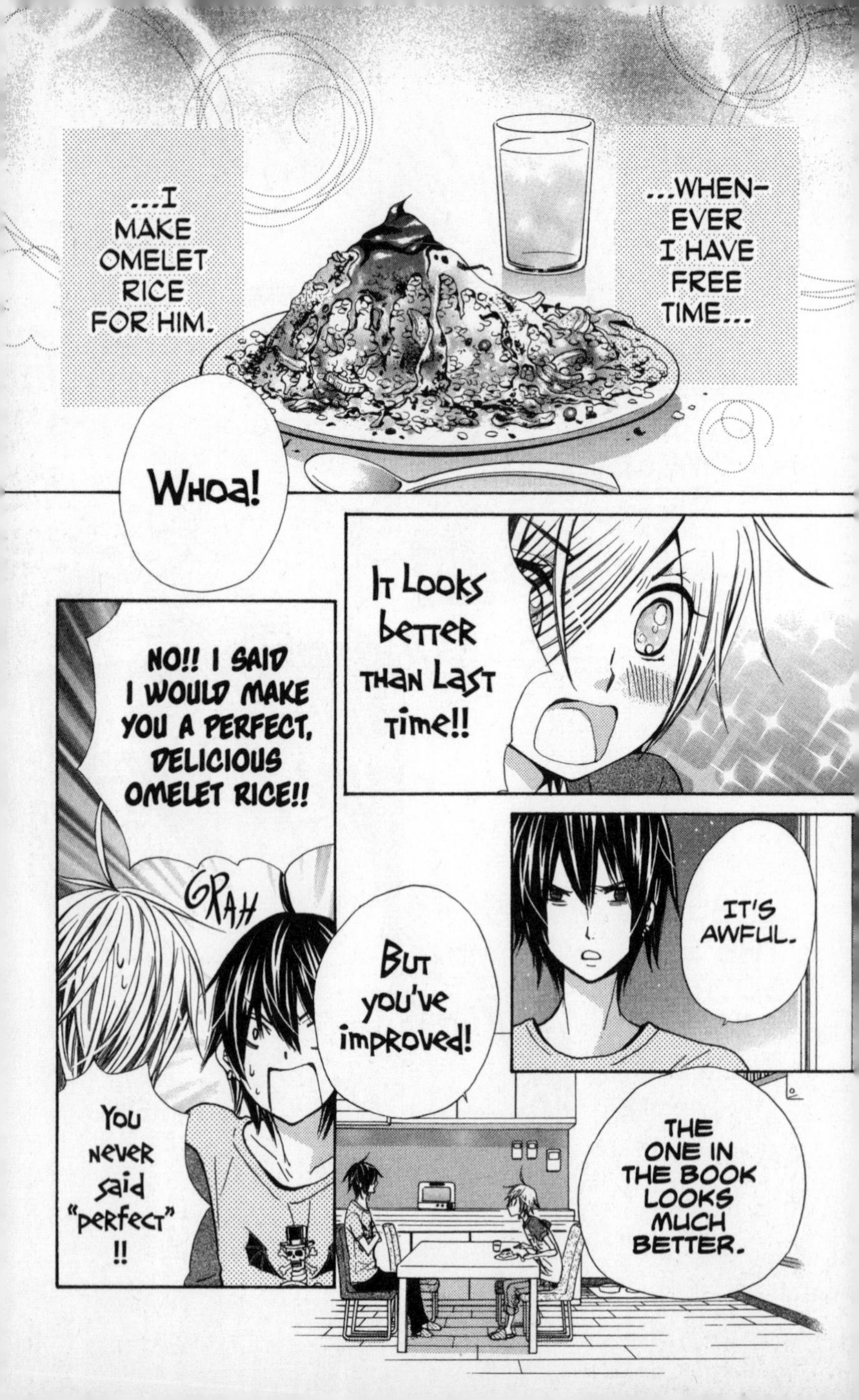
...WHEN-EVER I HAVE FREE TIME...
...I MAKE OMELET RICE FOR HIM.
Whoa!
It Looks better than Last time!!
IT'S AWFUL.
THE ONE IN THE BOOK LOOKS MUCH BETTER.
But you've improved!
NO!! I SAID I WOULD MAKE YOU A PERFECT, DELICIOUS OMELET RICE!!
GRAH
You never said "perfect" !!

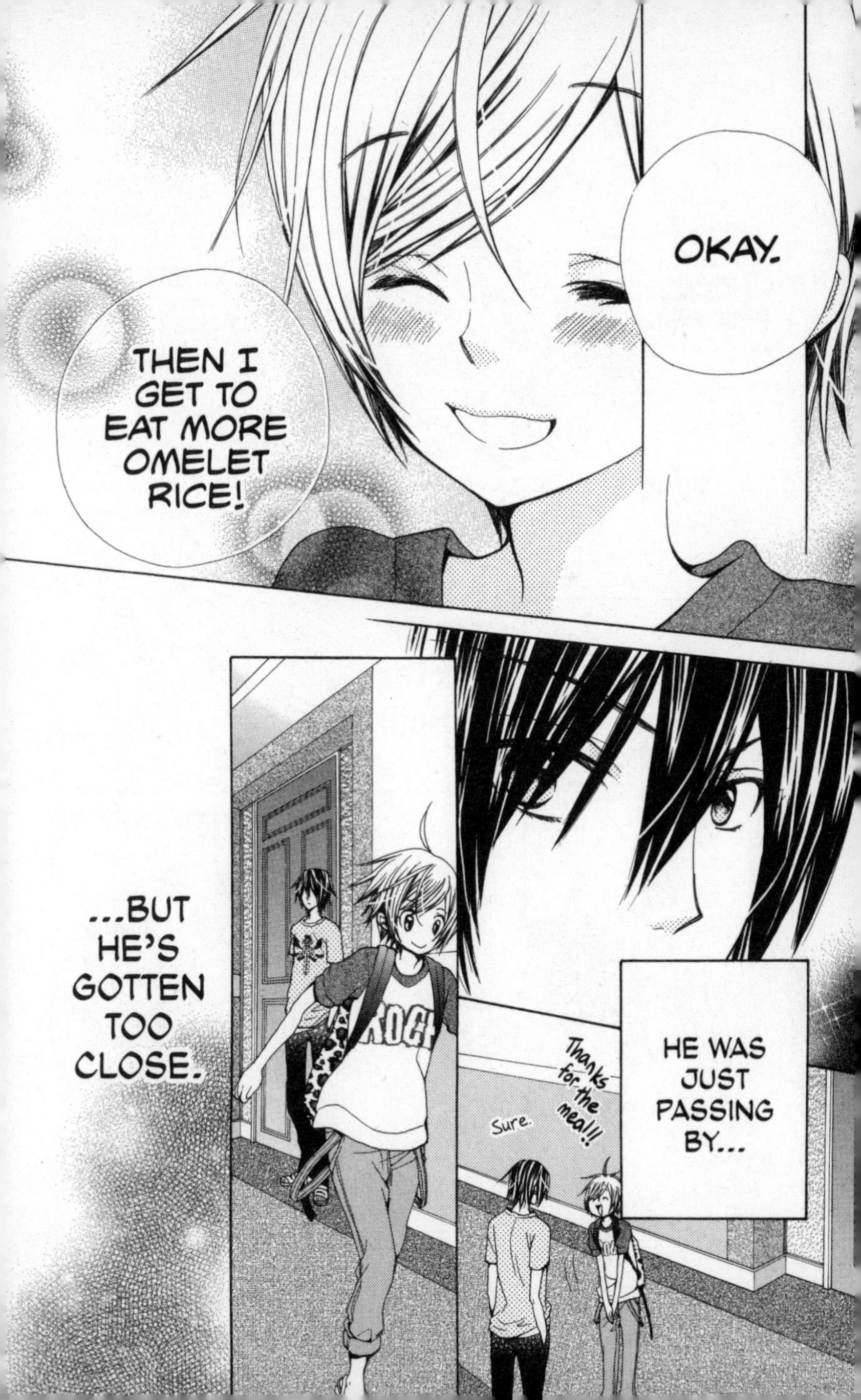
OKAY.
THEN I GET TO EAT MORE OMELET RICE!
HE WAS JUST PASSING BY...
Thanks for the meal!!
Sure.
...BUT HE'S GOTTEN TOO CLOSE.

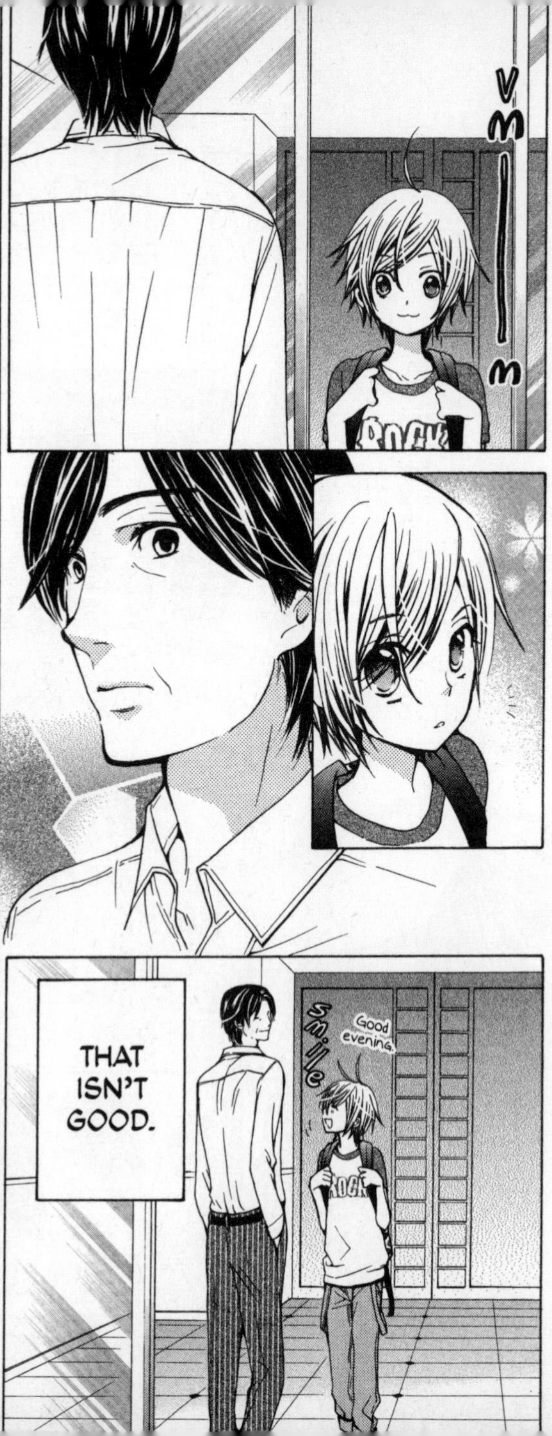
Vm——m
Good evening.
smile
THAT ISN'T GOOD.

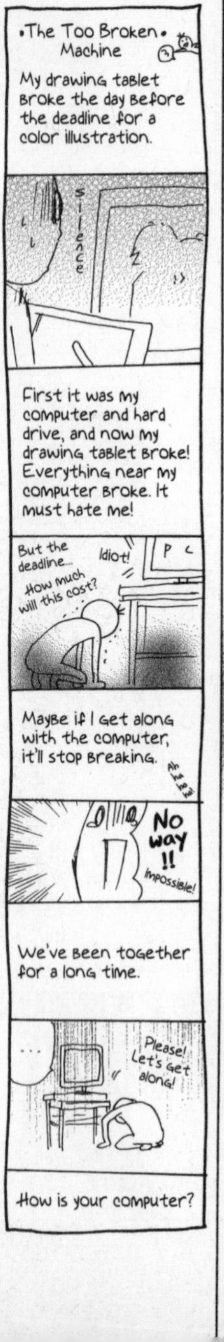
•The Too Broken• Machine
My drawing tablet broke the day before the deadline for a color illustration.
silence
First it was my computer and hard drive, and now my drawing tablet broke! Everything near my computer broke. It must hate me!
But the deadline...
Idiot!
How much will this cost?
Maybe if I get along with the computer, it'll stop breaking.
No way!!
Impossible!
We've been together for a long time.
...
Please! Let's get along!
How is your computer?

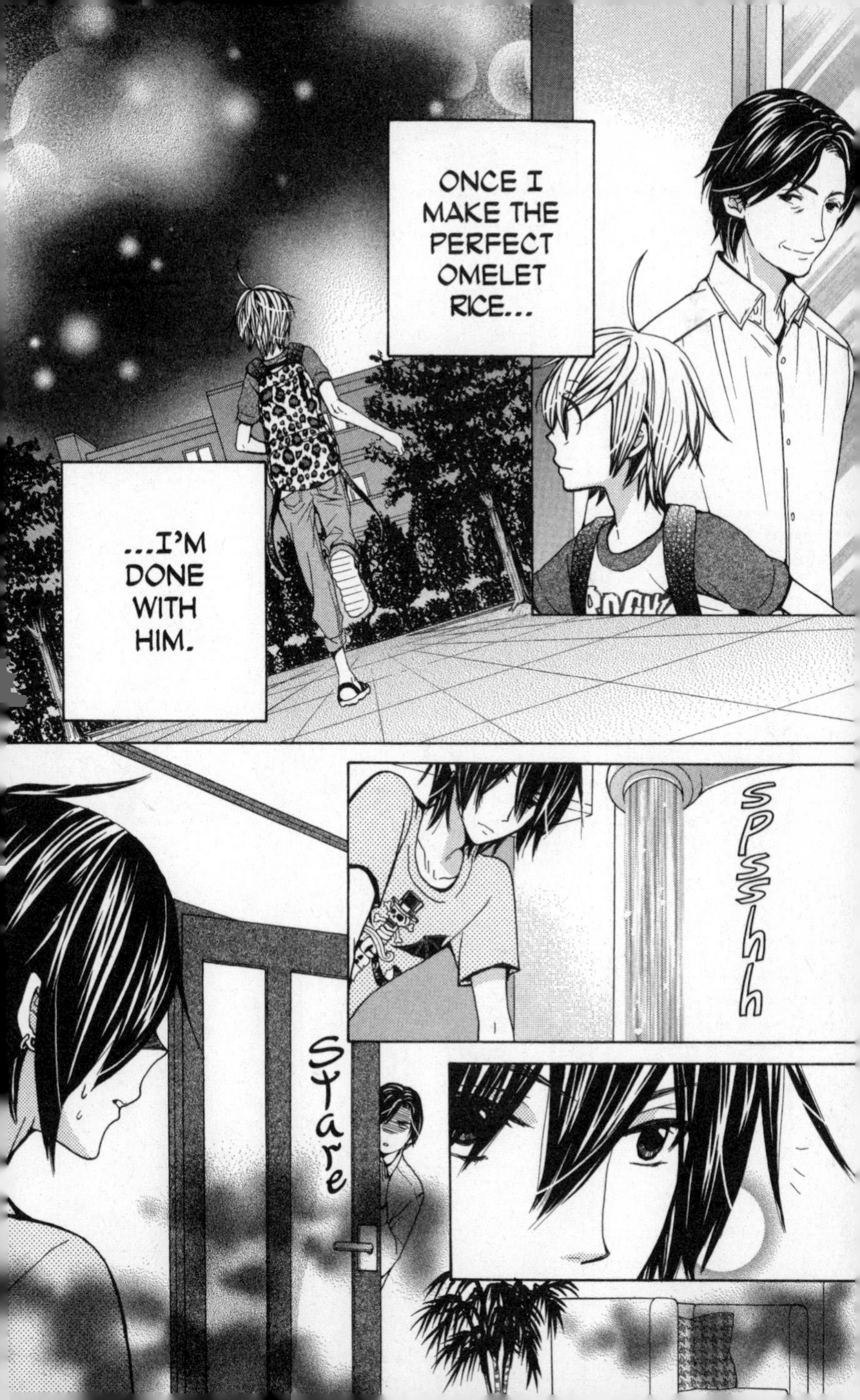
ONCE I MAKE THE PERFECT OMELET RICE...
...I'M DONE WITH HIM.
SPSSHH
STARE

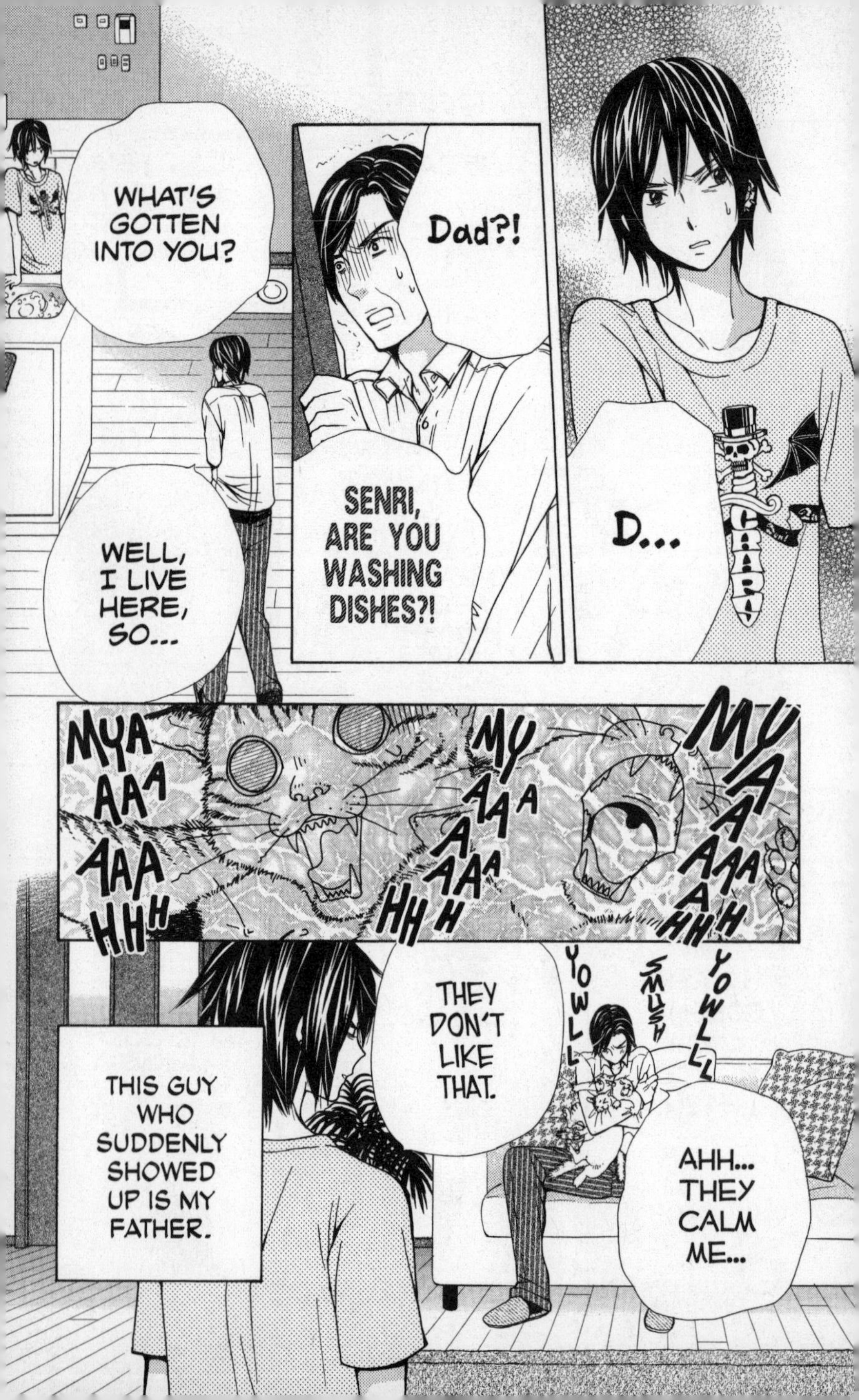
D...
Dad?!
SENRI, ARE YOU WASHING DISHES?!
WHAT'S GOTTEN INTO YOU?
WELL, I LIVE HERE, SO...
MYAAAAAAAHH
MYAAAAAAAAHH
MYAAAAAAHHH
YOWLLL
SMUSH
YOWLLL
AHH... THEY CALM ME...
THEY DON'T LIKE THAT.
THIS GUY WHO SUDDENLY SHOWED UP IS MY FATHER.

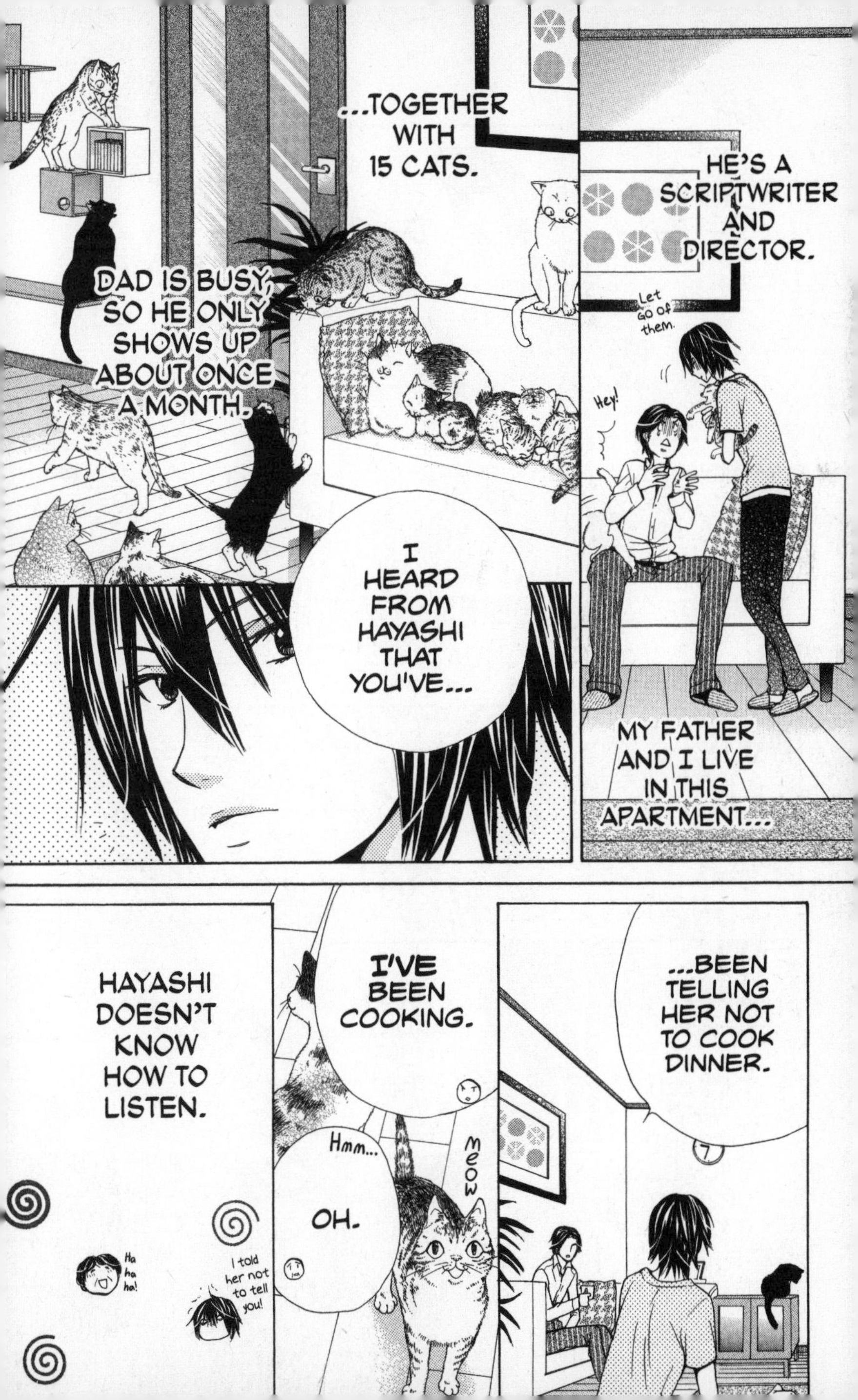
HE'S A SCRIPTWRITER AND DIRECTOR.
Let go of them.
Hey!
MY FATHER AND I LIVE IN THIS APARTMENT...
...TOGETHER WITH 15 CATS.
DAD IS BUSY, SO HE ONLY SHOWS UP ABOUT ONCE A MONTH.
I HEARD FROM HAYASHI THAT YOU'VE...
...BEEN TELLING HER NOT TO COOK DINNER.
I'VE BEEN COOKING.
MEOW
Hmm...
OH.
HAYASHI DOESN'T KNOW HOW TO LISTEN.
I told her not to tell you!
Ha ha ha!

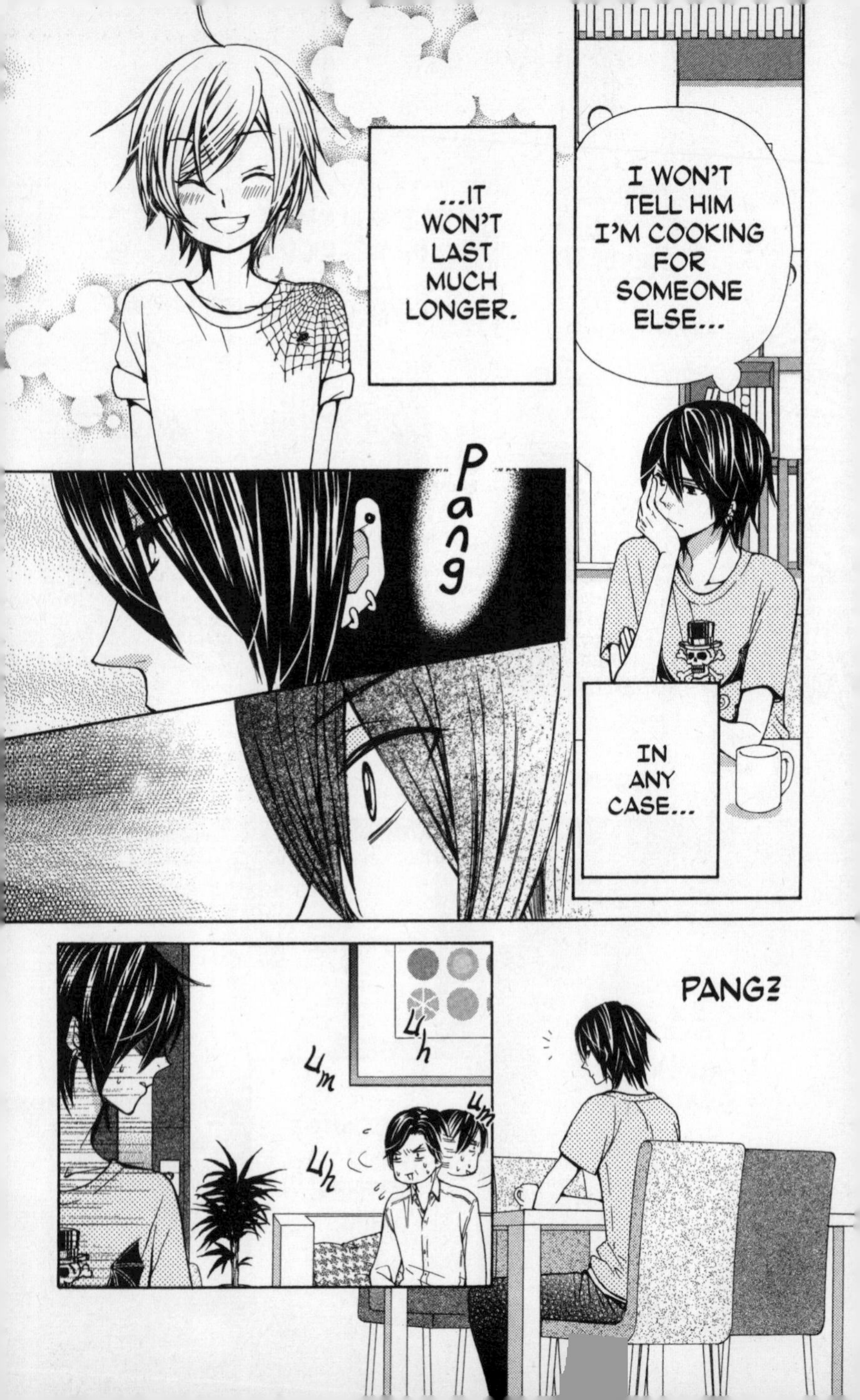
I WON'T TELL HIM I'M COOKING FOR SOMEONE ELSE...
IN ANY CASE...
...IT WON'T LAST MUCH LONGER.
Pang
PANG?
Uh
Um
Um
Uh

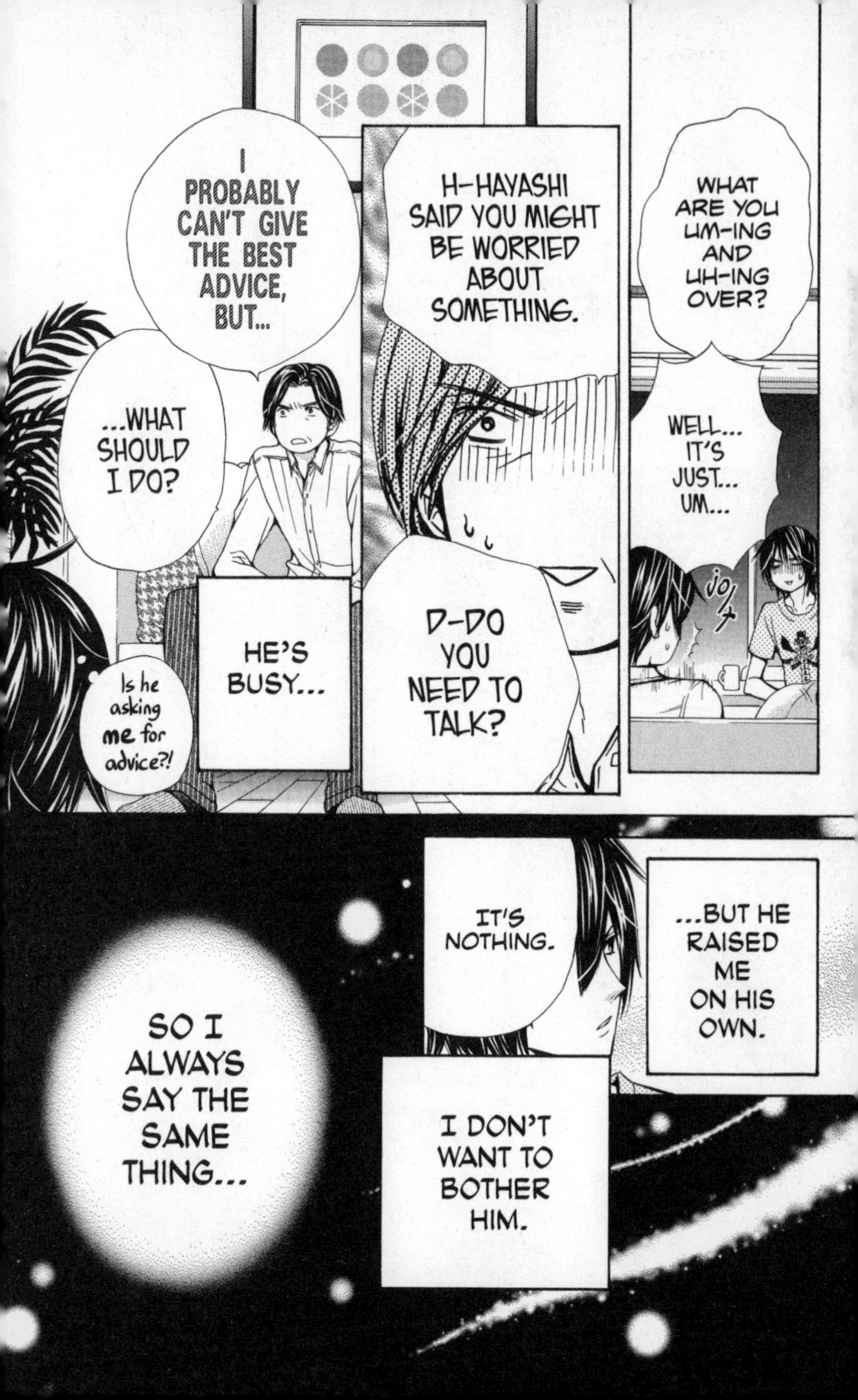
WHAT ARE YOU UM-ING AND UH-ING OVER?
WELL... IT'S JUST... UM...
H-HAYASHI SAID YOU MIGHT BE WORRIED ABOUT SOMETHING.
D-DO YOU NEED TO TALK?
I PROBABLY CAN'T GIVE THE BEST ADVICE, BUT...
...WHAT SHOULD I DO?
HE'S BUSY...
Is he asking me for advice?!
...BUT HE RAISED ME ON HIS OWN.
IT'S NOTHING.
I DON'T WANT TO BOTHER HIM.
SO I ALWAYS SAY THE SAME THING...

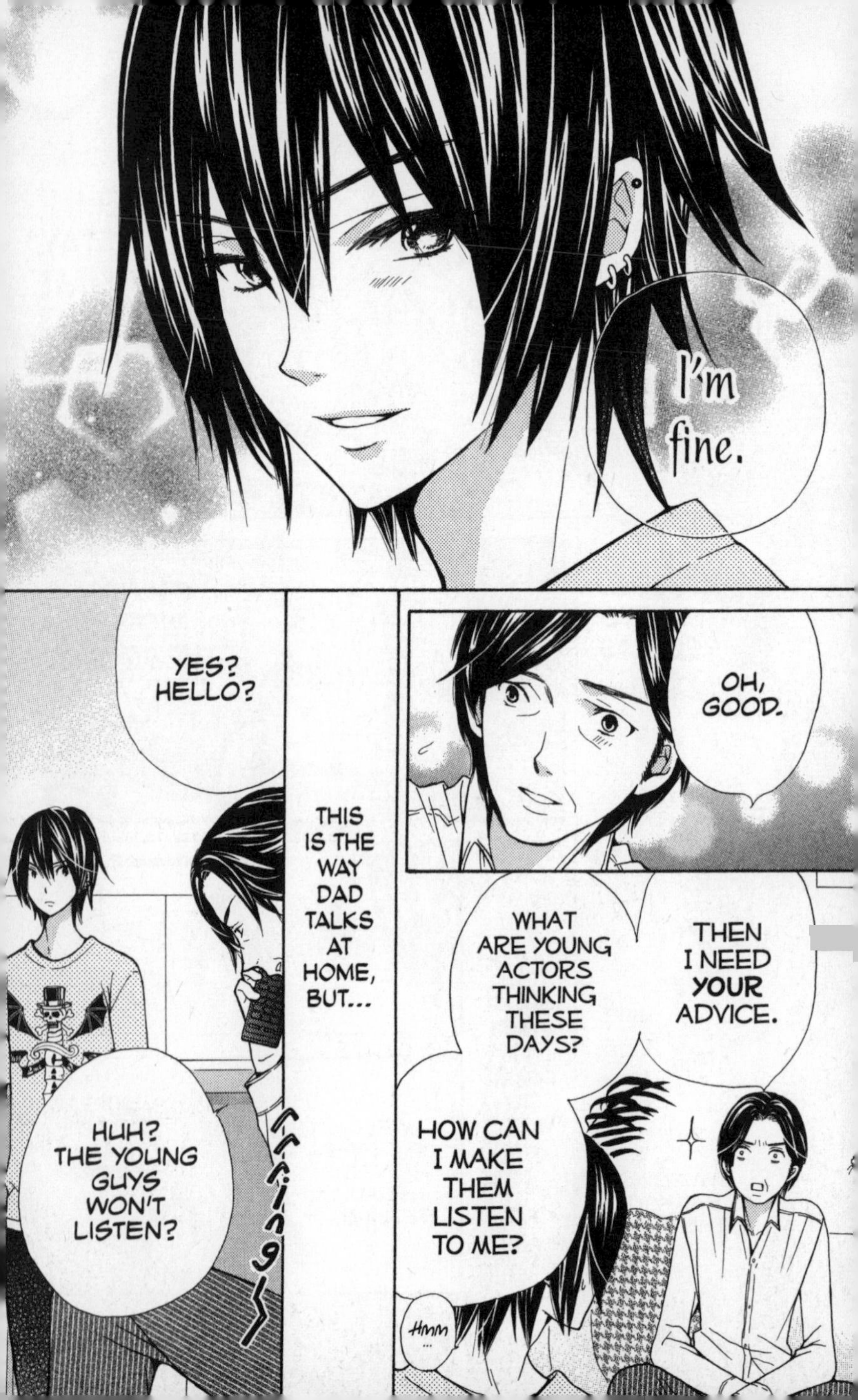
I'm fine.
OH, GOOD.
THEN I NEED YOUR ADVICE.
WHAT ARE YOUNG ACTORS THINKING THESE DAYS?
HOW CAN I MAKE THEM LISTEN TO ME?
Hmm...
THIS IS THE WAY DAD TALKS AT HOME, BUT...
YES? HELLO?
rrring~
HUH? THE YOUNG GUYS WON'T LISTEN?

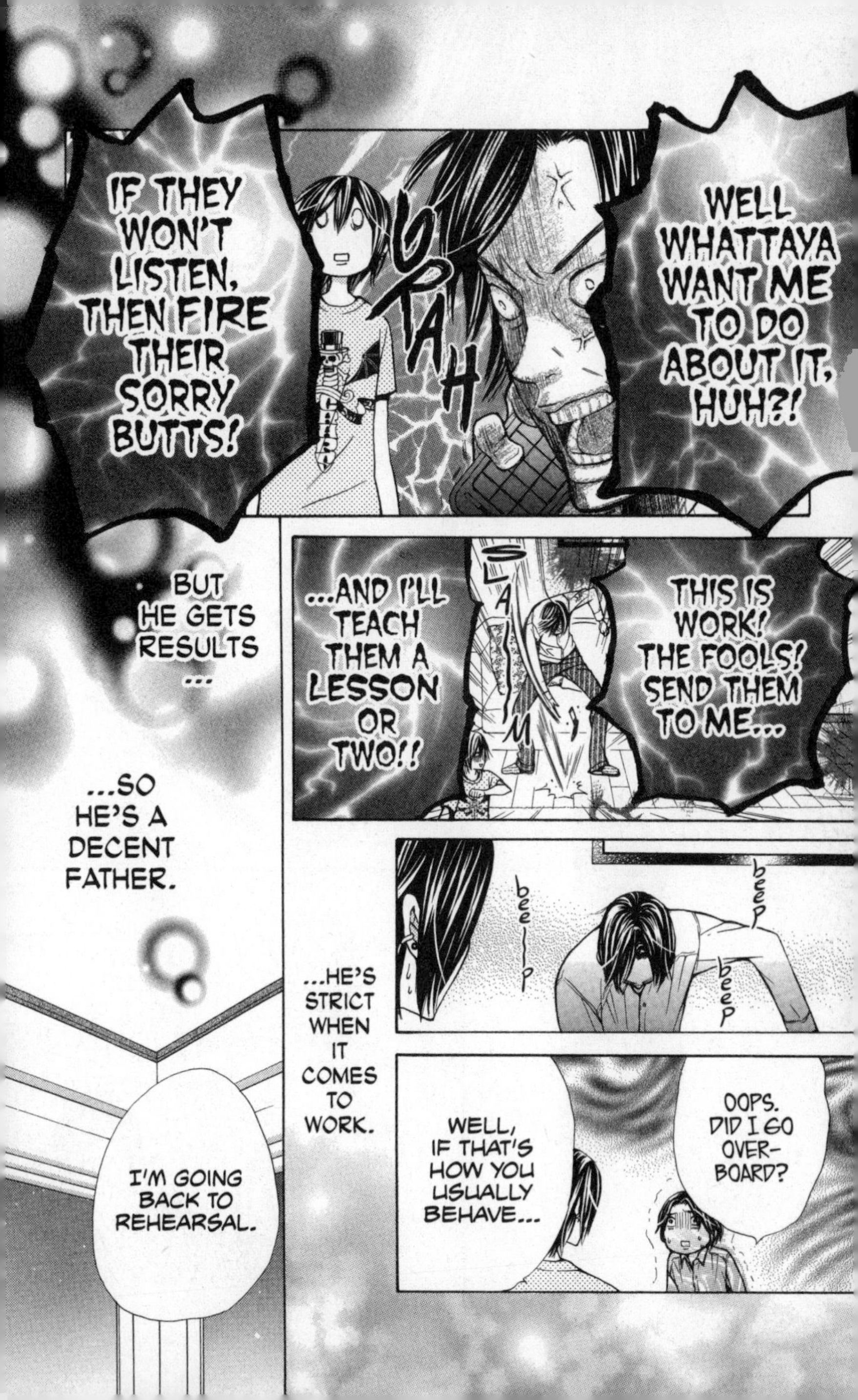
WELL WHATTAYA WANT ME TO DO ABOUT IT, HUH?!
IF THEY WON'T LISTEN, THEN FIRE THEIR SORRY BUTTS!
THIS IS WORK! THE FOOLS! SEND THEM TO ME...
SLAM
...AND I'LL TEACH THEM A LESSON OR TWO!!
beep
beep
bee-p
...HE'S STRICT WHEN IT COMES TO WORK.
OOPS. DID I GO OVER-BOARD?
WELL, IF THAT'S HOW YOU USUALLY BEHAVE...
BUT HE GETS RESULTS...
...SO HE'S A DECENT FATHER.
I'M GOING BACK TO REHEARSAL.

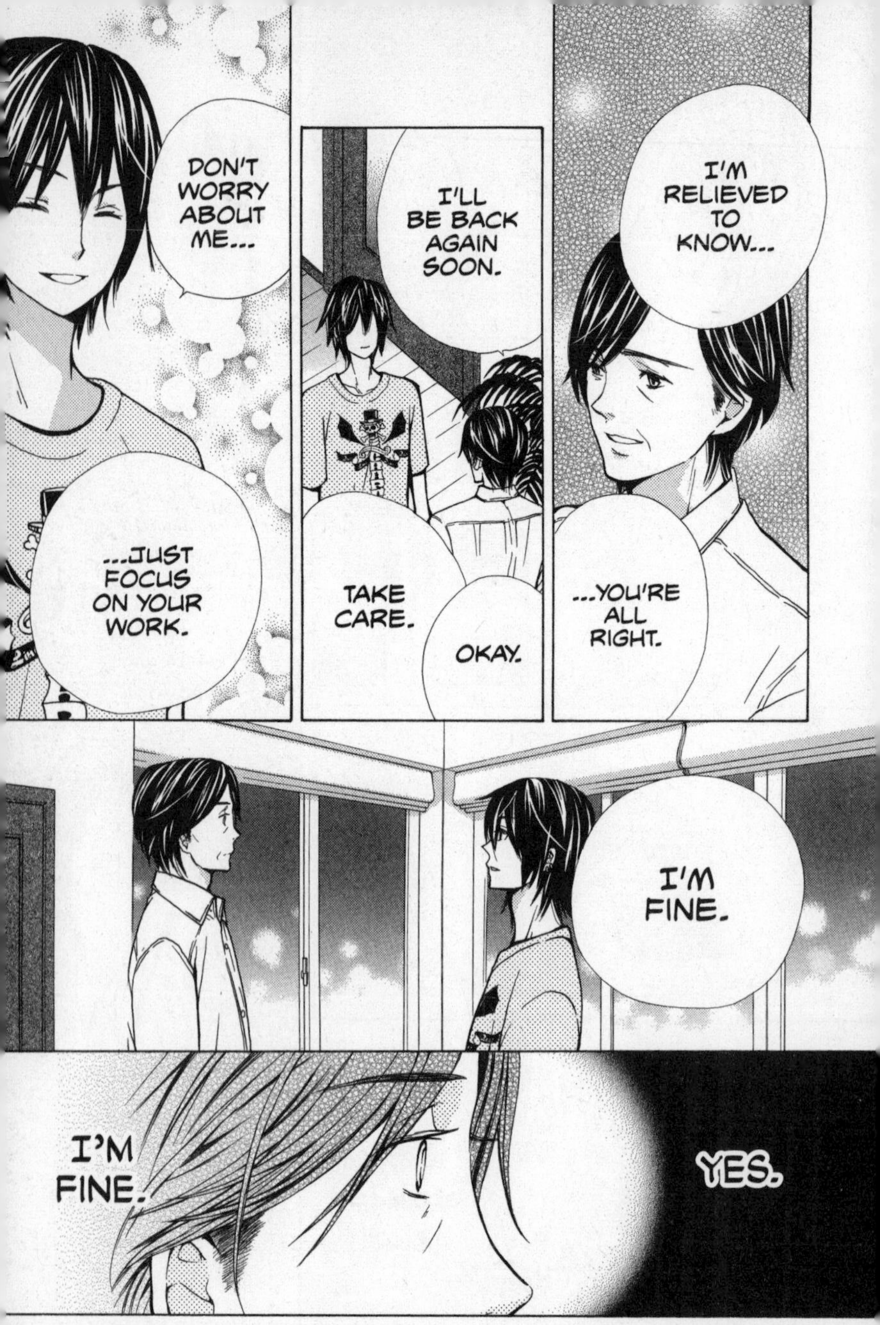
I'M RELIEVED TO KNOW...
...YOU'RE ALL RIGHT.
I'LL BE BACK AGAIN SOON.
OKAY.
TAKE CARE.
DON'T WORRY ABOUT ME...
...JUST FOCUS ON YOUR WORK.
I'M FINE.
YES.
I'M FINE.

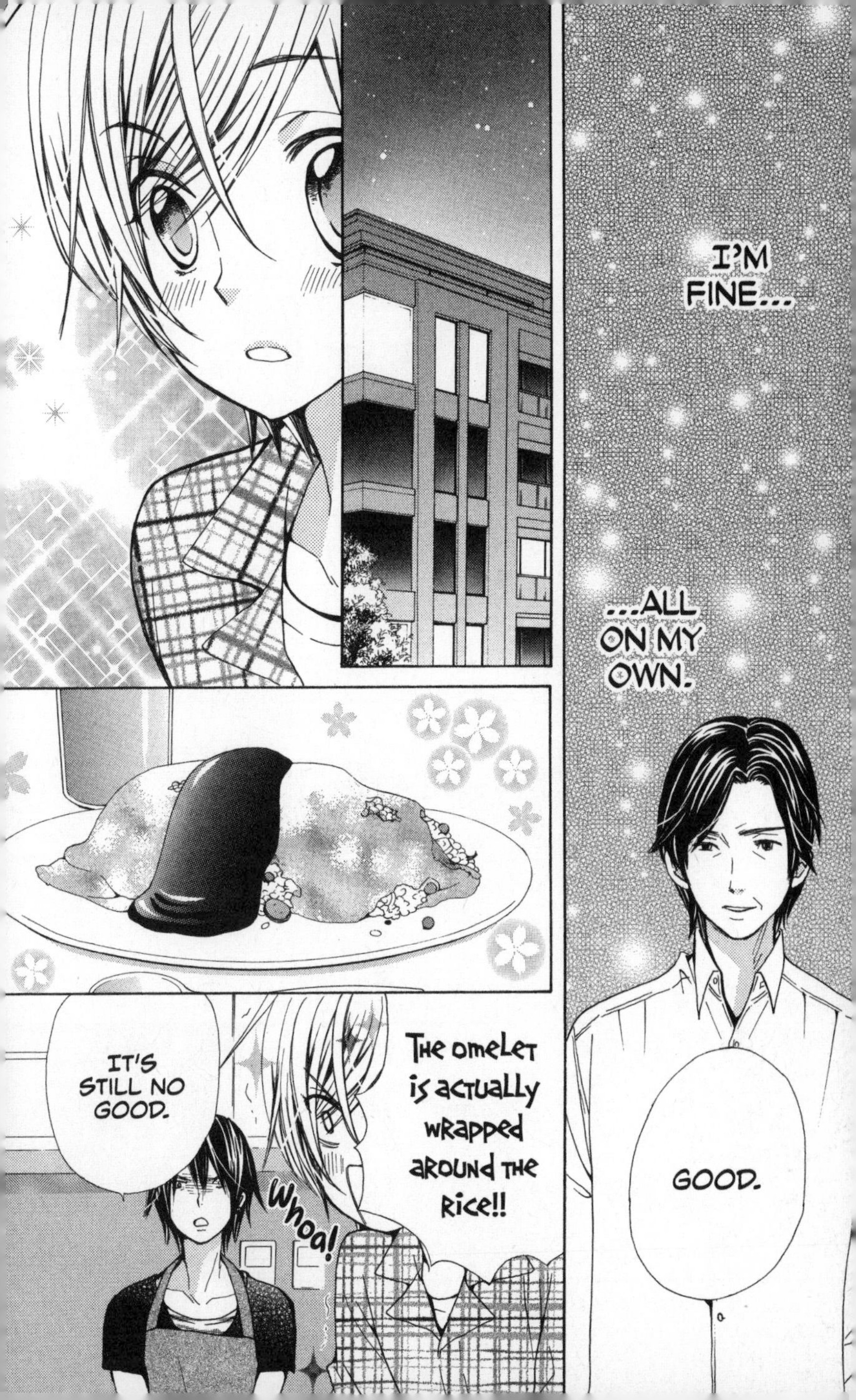
I'M FINE...
...ALL ON MY OWN.
GOOD.
The omelet is actually wrapped around the rice!!
IT'S STILL NO GOOD.
Whoa!

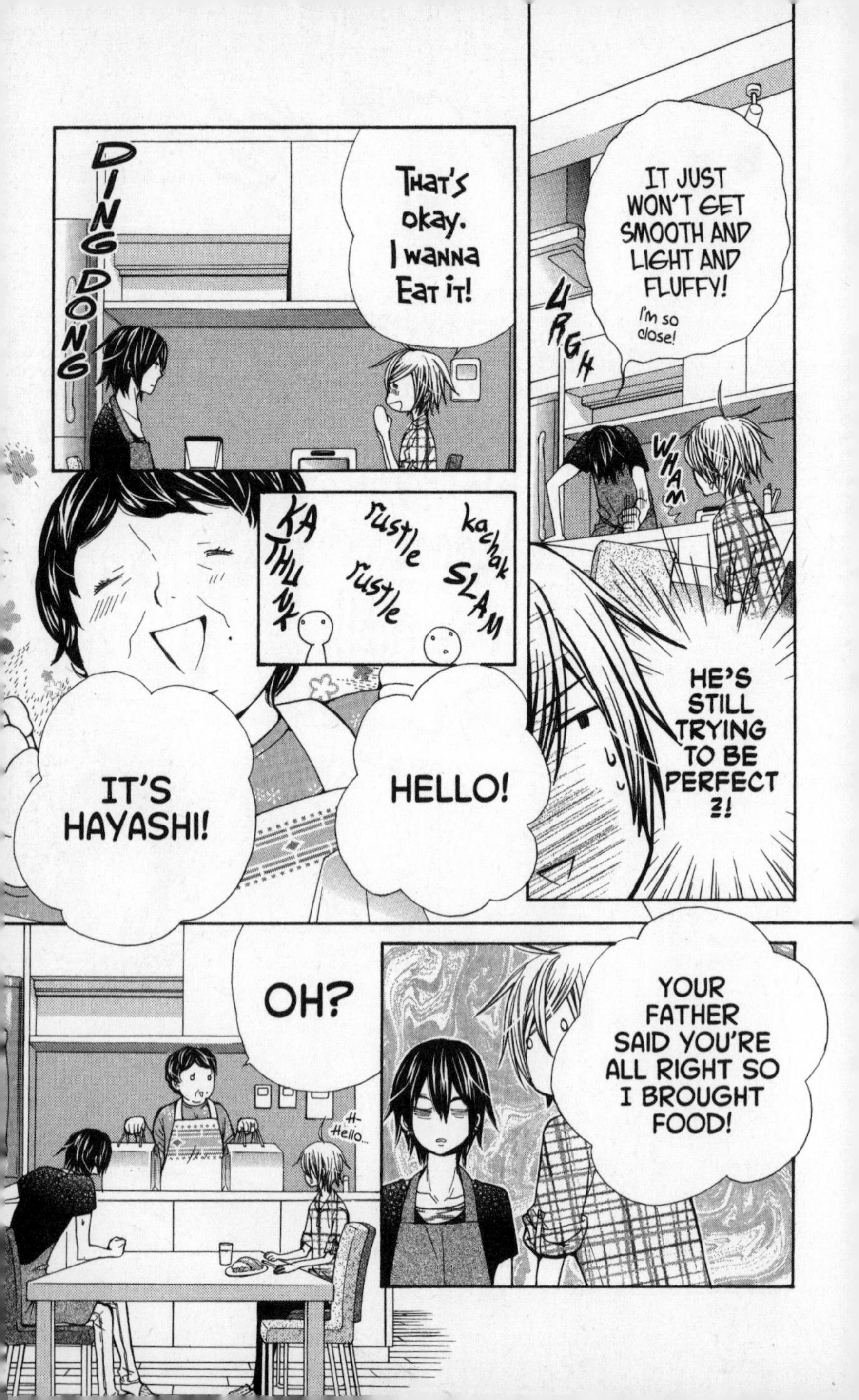
IT JUST WON'T GET SMOOTH AND LIGHT AND FLUFFY!
I'm so close!
URGH
WHAM
HE'S STILL TRYING TO BE PERFECT?!
That's okay. I wanna Eat it!
DING DONG
KATHUNK
rustle
kachak
rustle
SLAM
HELLO!
IT'S HAYASHI!
YOUR FATHER SAID YOU'RE ALL RIGHT SO I BROUGHT FOOD!
OH?
H- Hello...

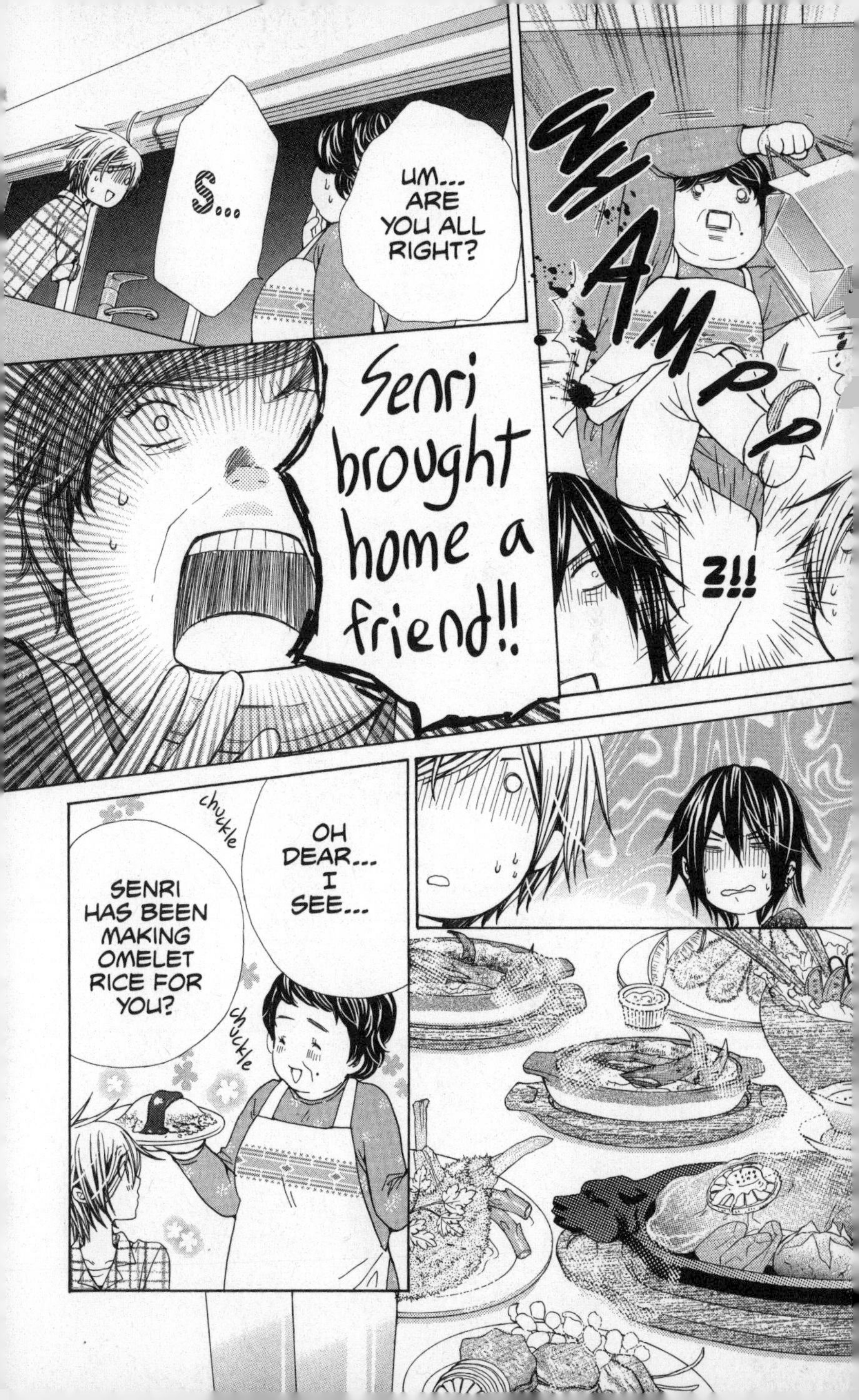
WHAMPP
UM... ARE YOU ALL RIGHT?
S...
?!!
Senri brought home a friend!!
OH DEAR... I SEE...
chuckle
SENRI HAS BEEN MAKING OMELET RICE FOR YOU?
chuckle

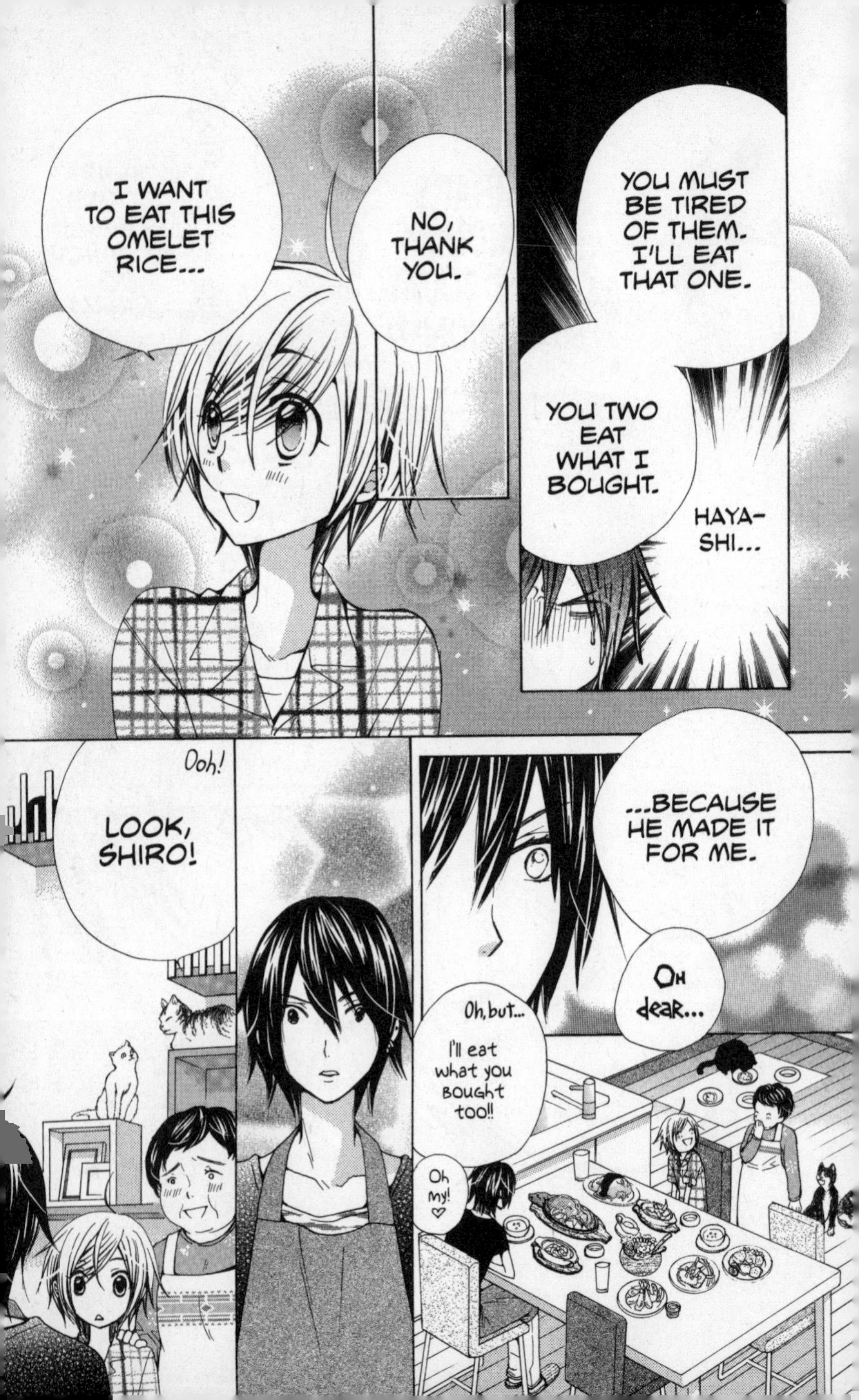
YOU MUST BE TIRED OF THEM. I'LL EAT THAT ONE.
YOU TWO EAT WHAT I BOUGHT.
HAYA-SHI...
NO, THANK YOU.
I WANT TO EAT THIS OMELET RICE...
...BECAUSE HE MADE IT FOR ME.
OH dear...
Oh, but...
I'll eat what you bought too!!
Oh my! ♥
Ooh!
LOOK, SHIRO!

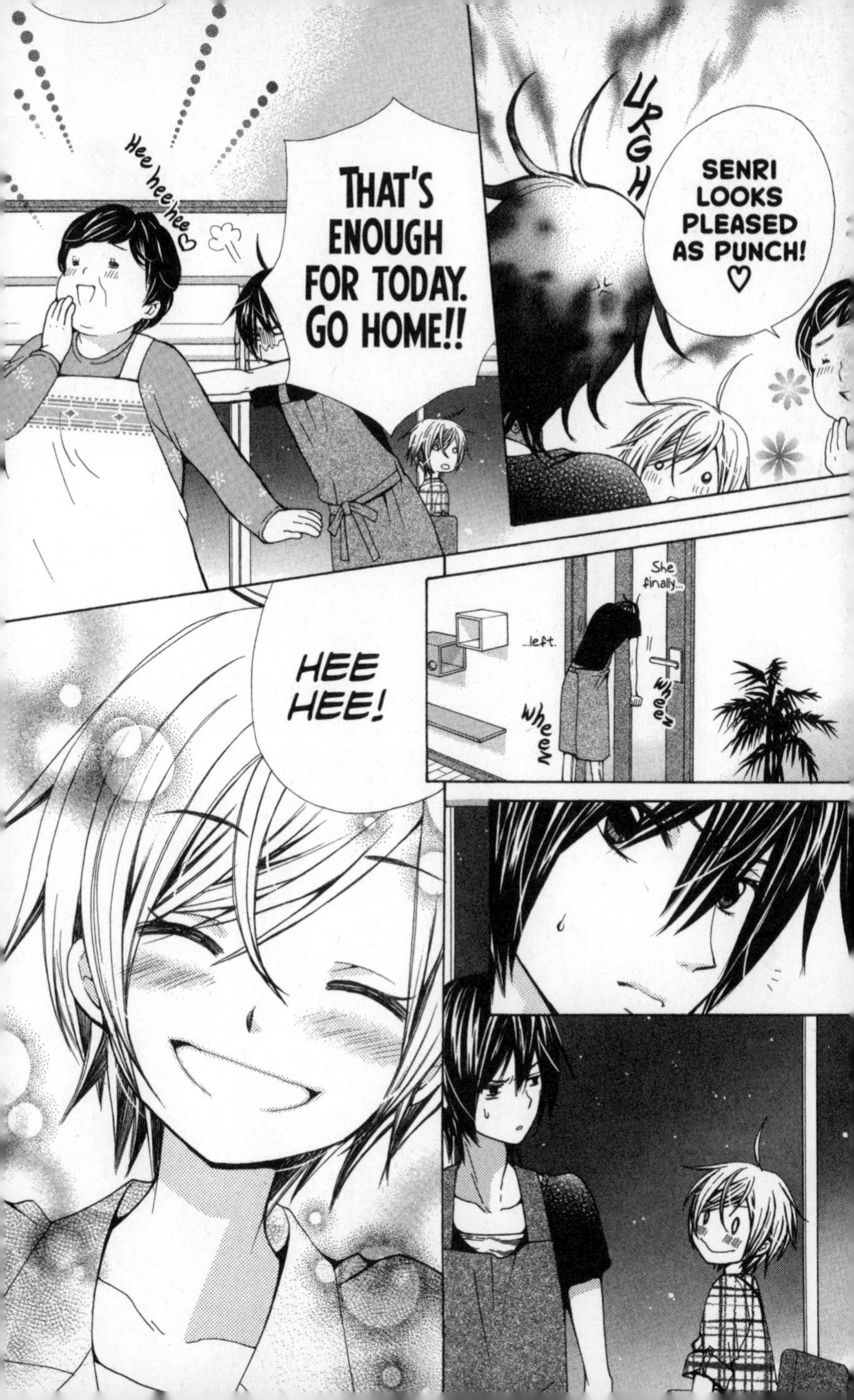
URGH
SENRI LOOKS PLEASED AS PUNCH! ♡
THAT'S ENOUGH FOR TODAY. GO HOME!!
Hee hee hee ♡
She finally...
...left.
wheez
wheez
HEE HEE!

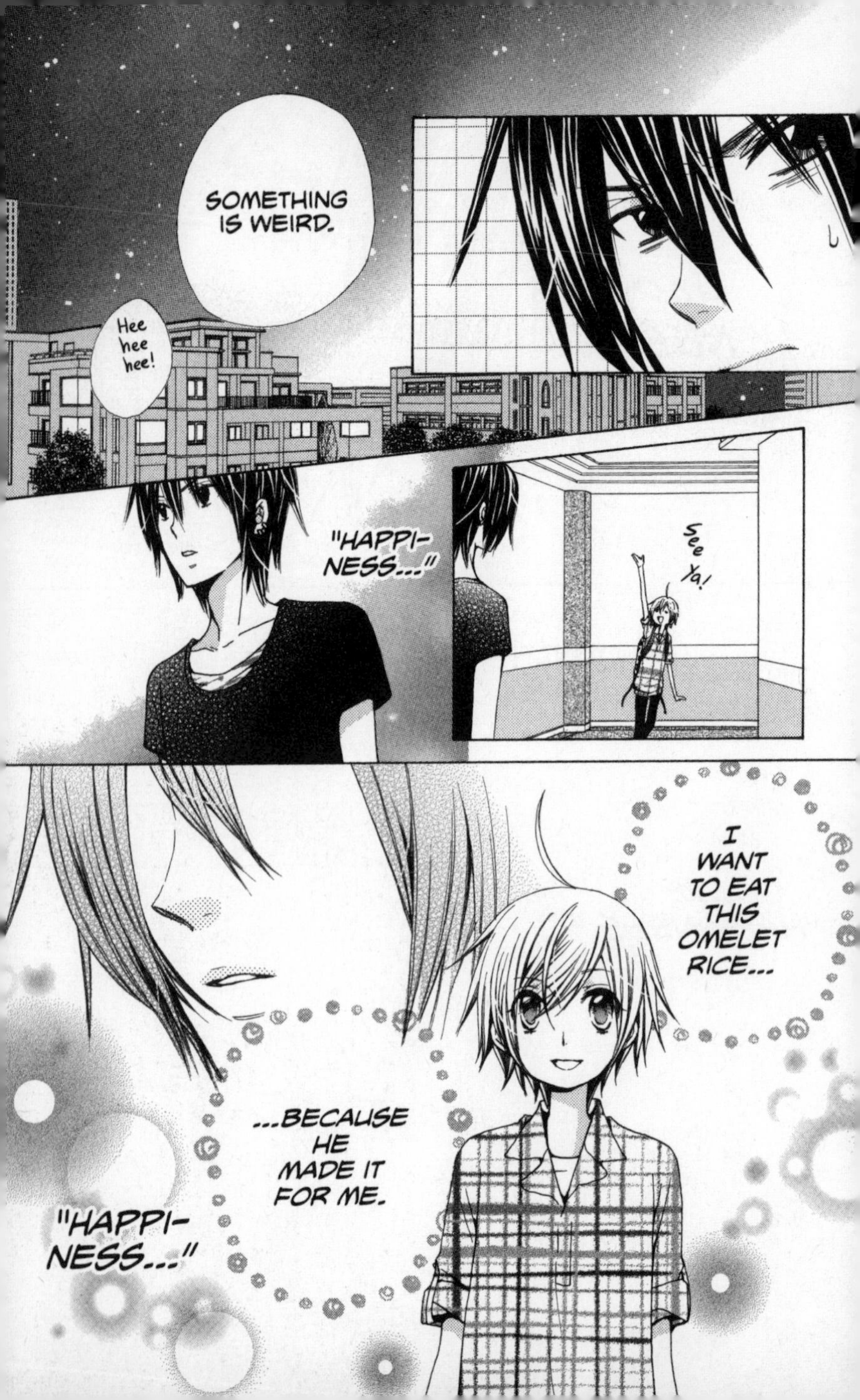
SOMETHING IS WEIRD.
Hee hee hee!
See ya!
"HAPPI-NESS..."
I WANT TO EAT THIS OMELET RICE...
...BECAUSE HE MADE IT FOR ME.
"HAPPI-NESS..."

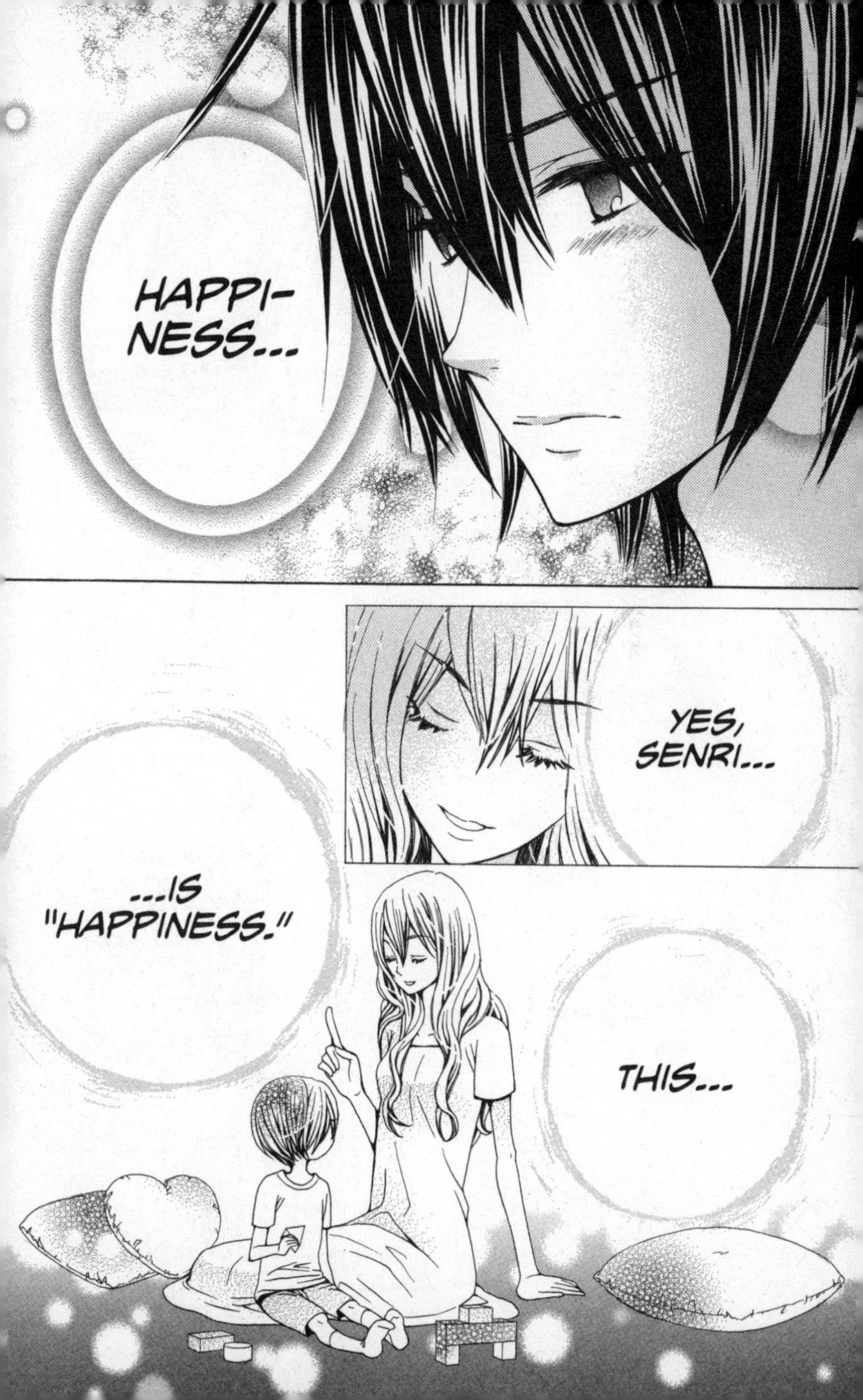
HAPPI-
NESS...
YES,
SENRI...
THIS...
...IS
"HAPPINESS."

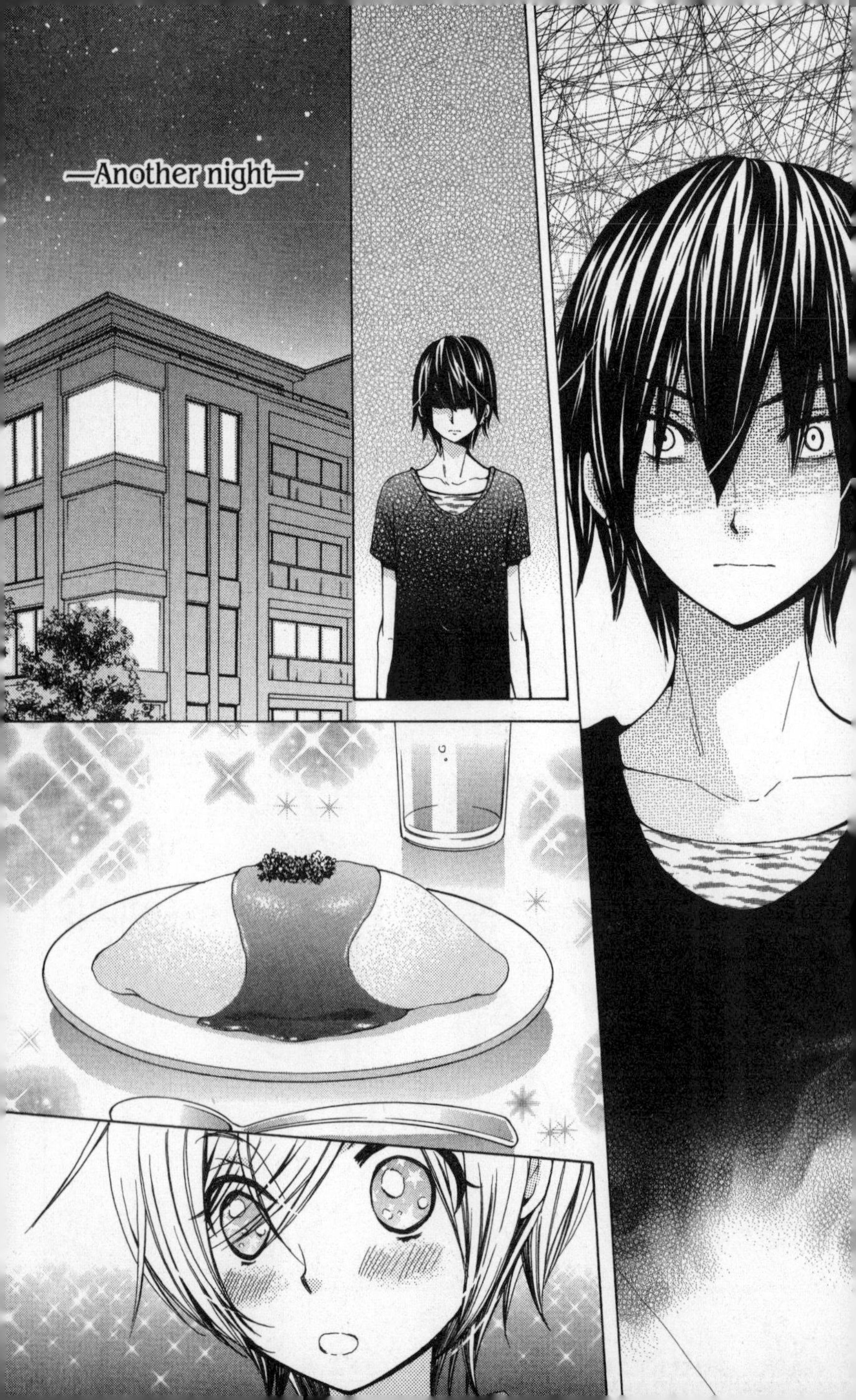
—Another night—

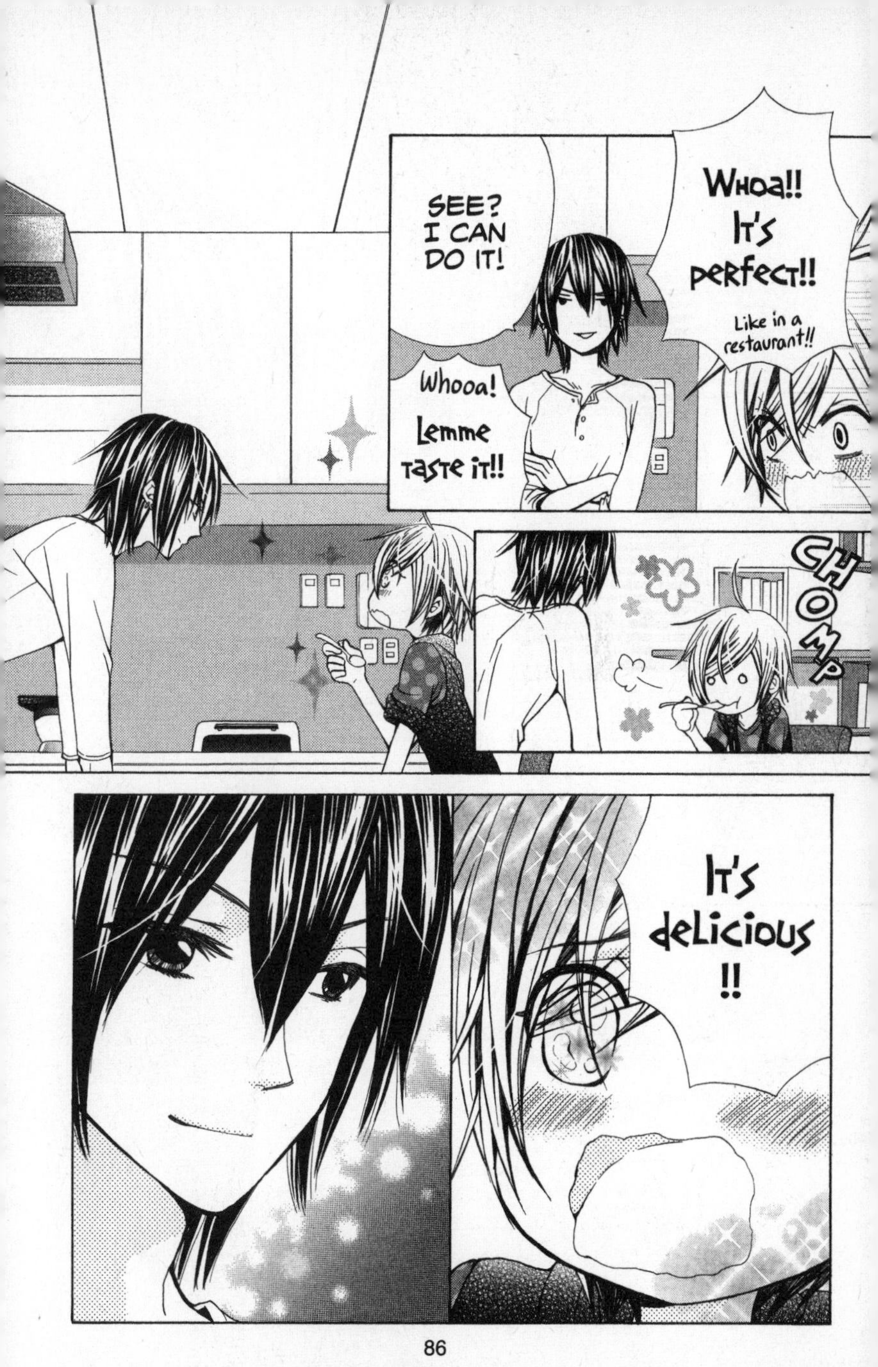
Whoa!! It's perfect!!
Like in a restaurant!!
SEE? I CAN DO IT!
Whooa! Lemme taste it!!
CHOMP
It's delicious !!

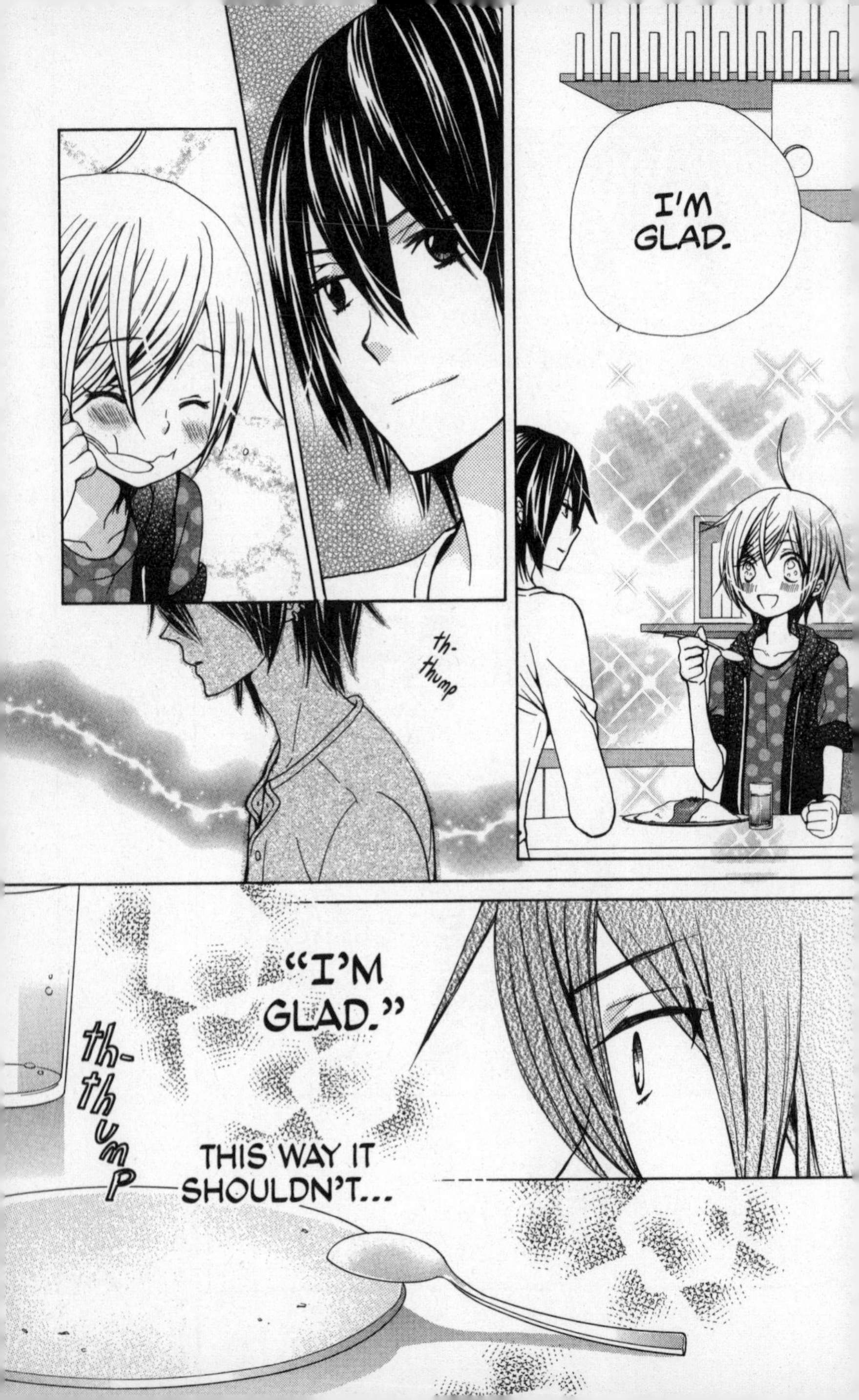
I'M GLAD.
th-thump
"I'M GLAD."
th-thump
THIS WAY IT SHOULDN'T...

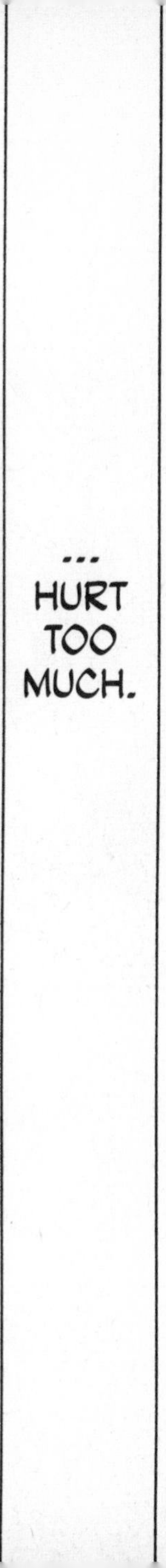
...
HURT
TOO
MUCH.

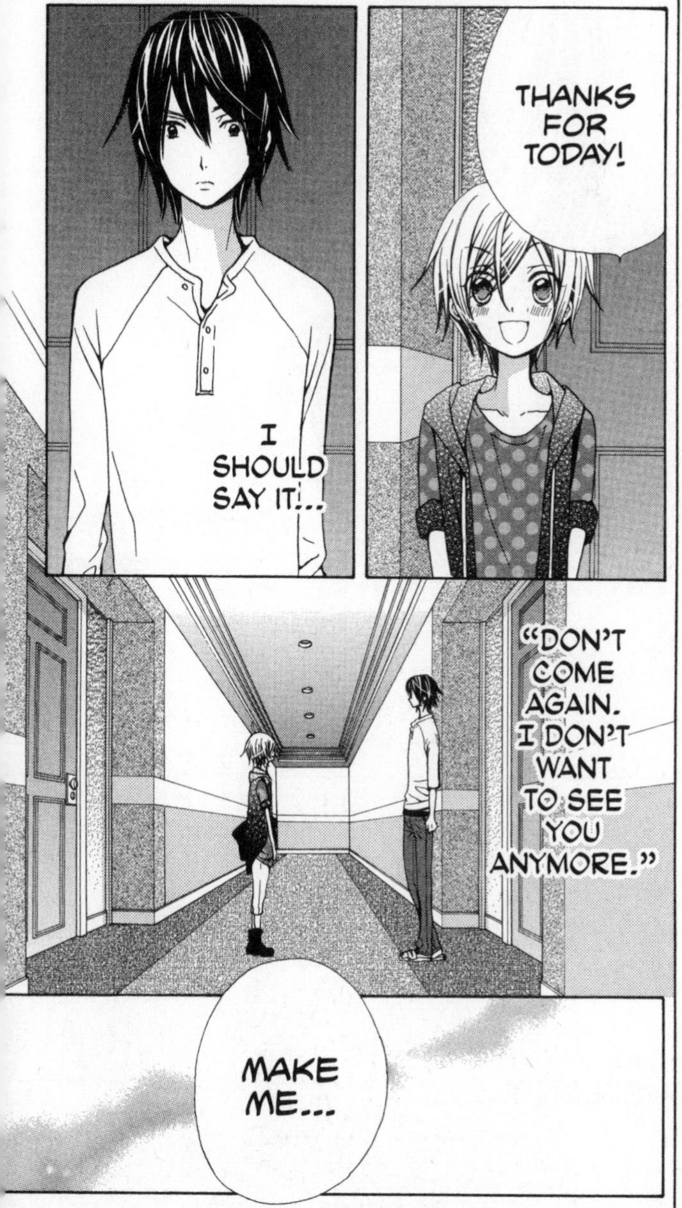
THANKS FOR TODAY!
I SHOULD SAY IT...
"DON'T COME AGAIN. I DON'T WANT TO SEE YOU ANYMORE."
MAKE ME...

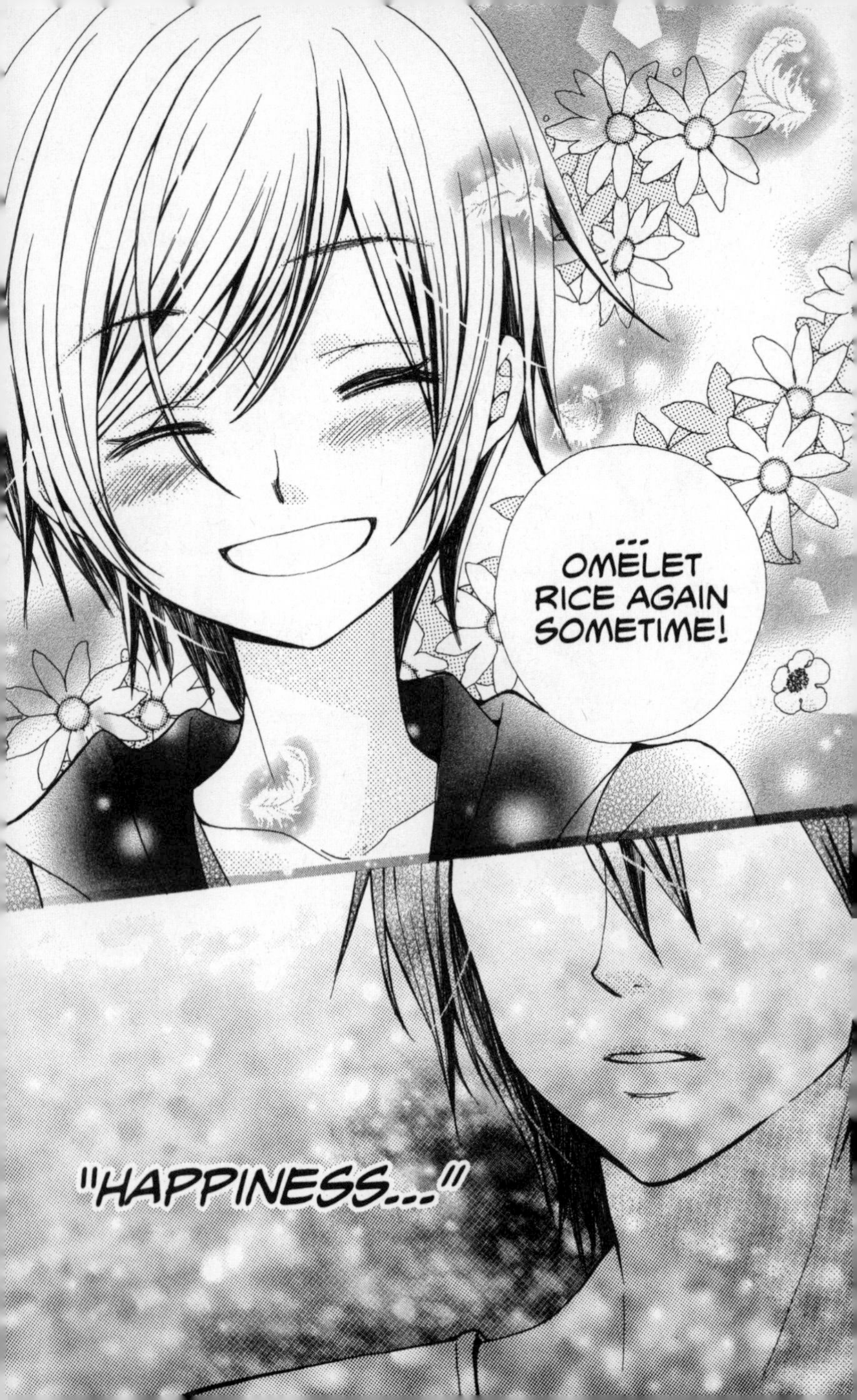
...
OMELET RICE AGAIN SOMETIME!
"HAPPINESS..."

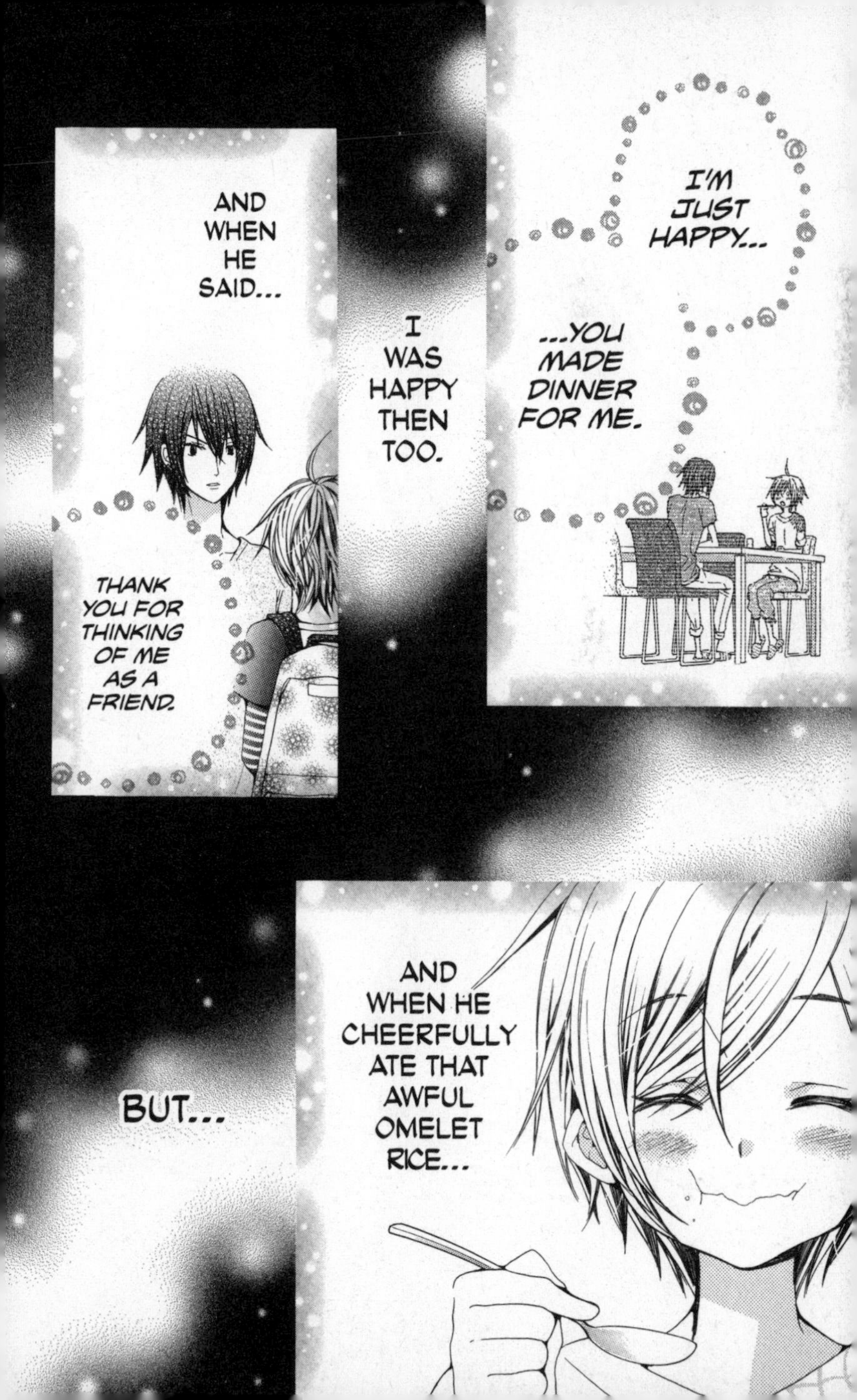
I'M JUST HAPPY...
...YOU MADE DINNER FOR ME.
I WAS HAPPY THEN TOO.
AND WHEN HE SAID...
THANK YOU FOR THINKING OF ME AS A FRIEND.
AND WHEN HE CHEERFULLY ATE THAT AWFUL OMELET RICE...
BUT...

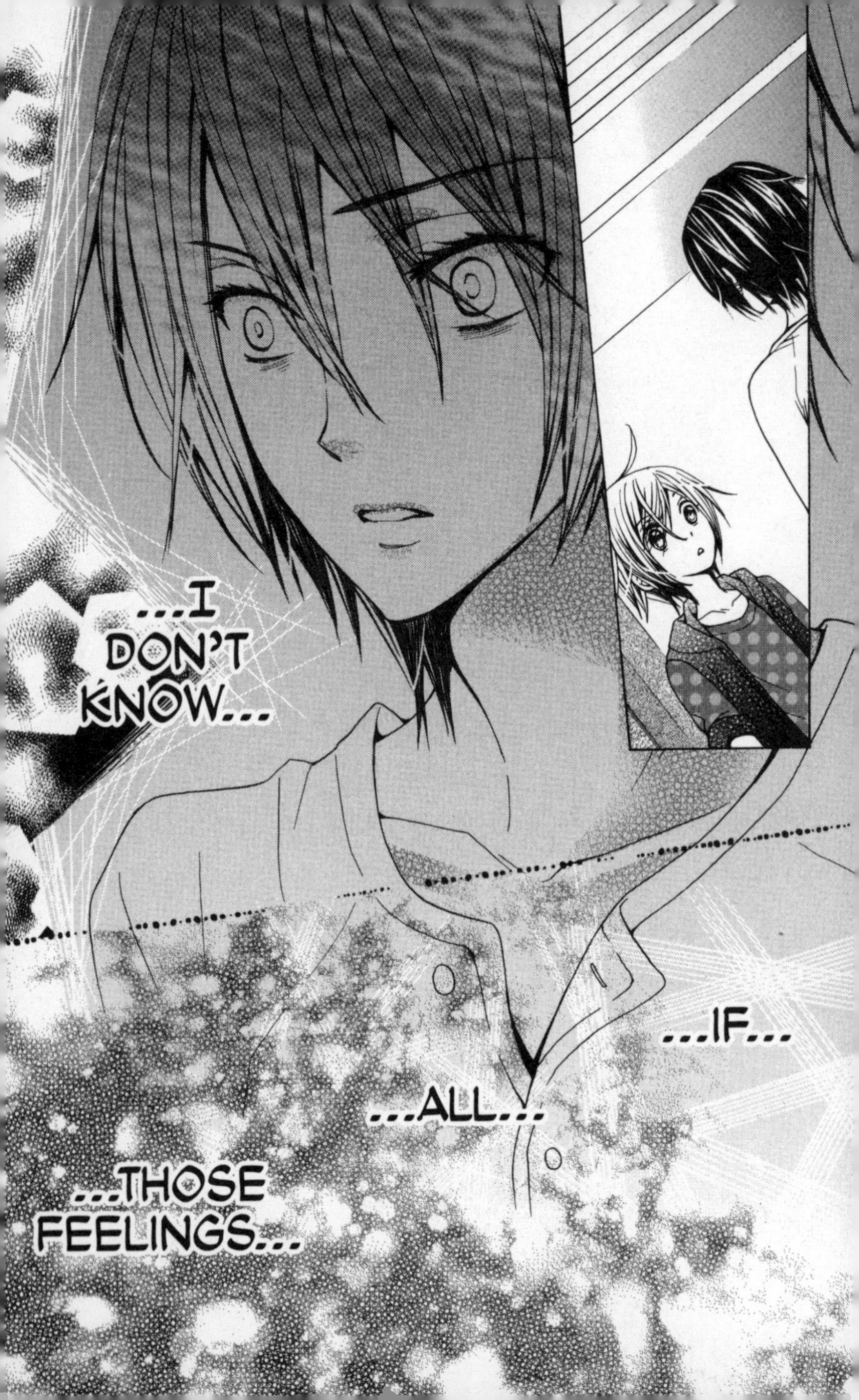
...I DON'T KNOW...
...IF...
...ALL...
...THOSE FEELINGS...

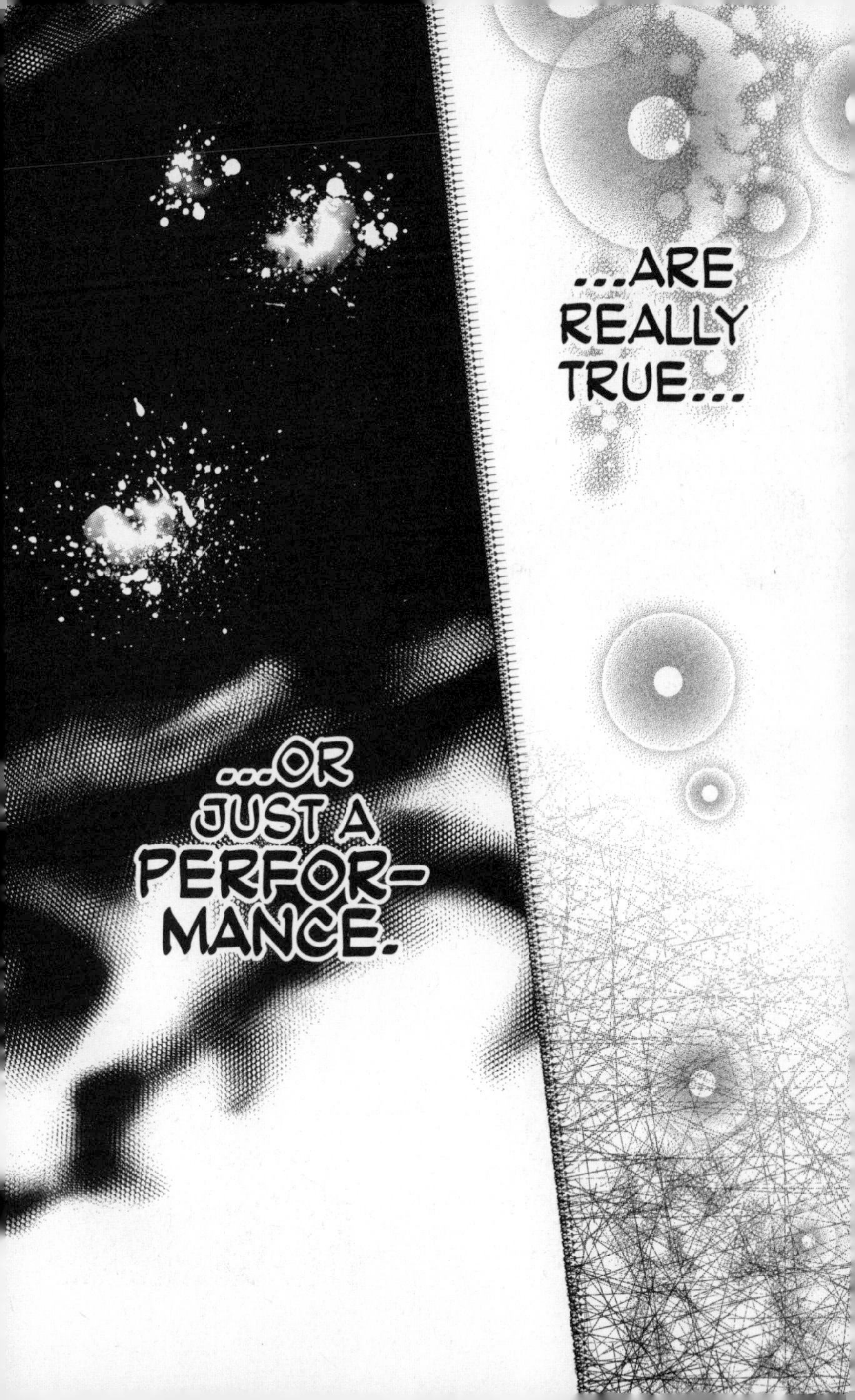
...ARE REALLY TRUE...
...OR JUST A PERFOR-MANCE.

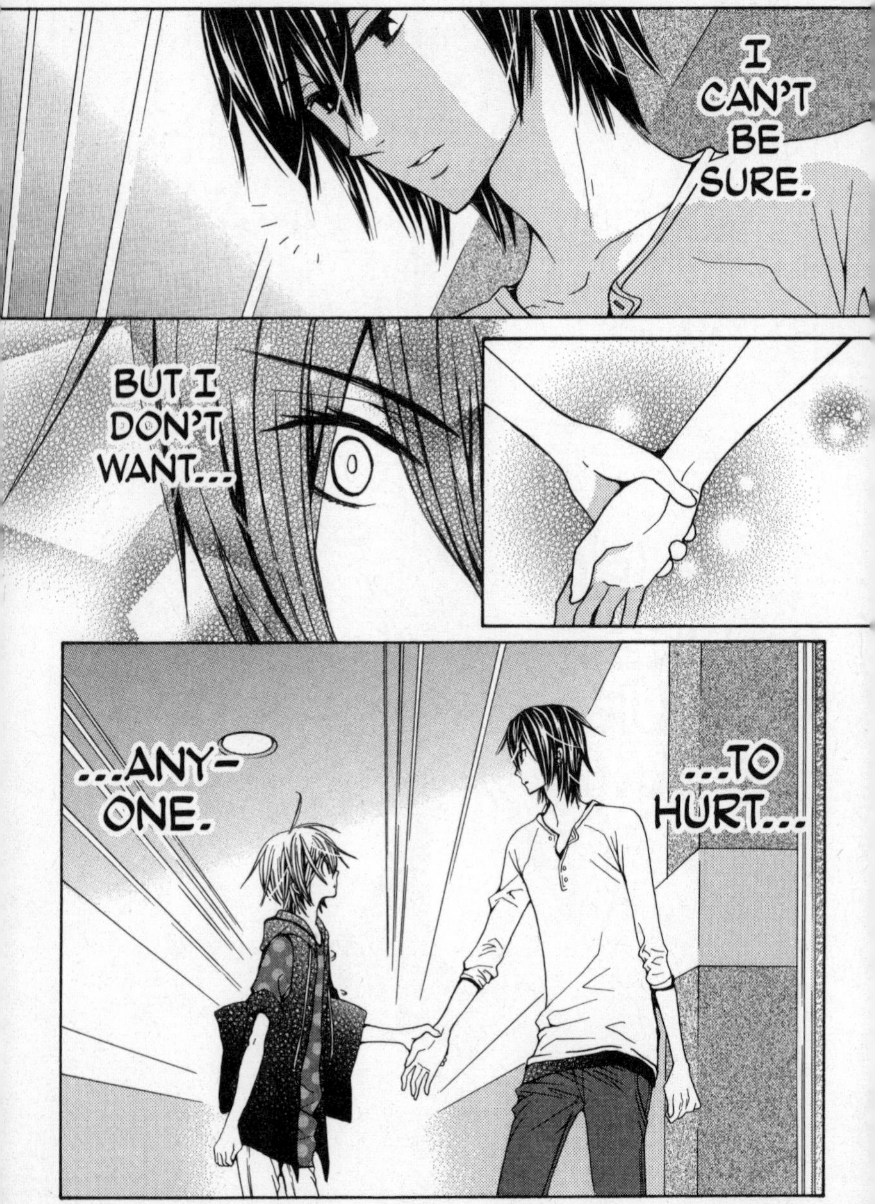
I CAN'T BE SURE.
BUT I DON'T WANT...
...TO HURT...
...ANY-ONE.

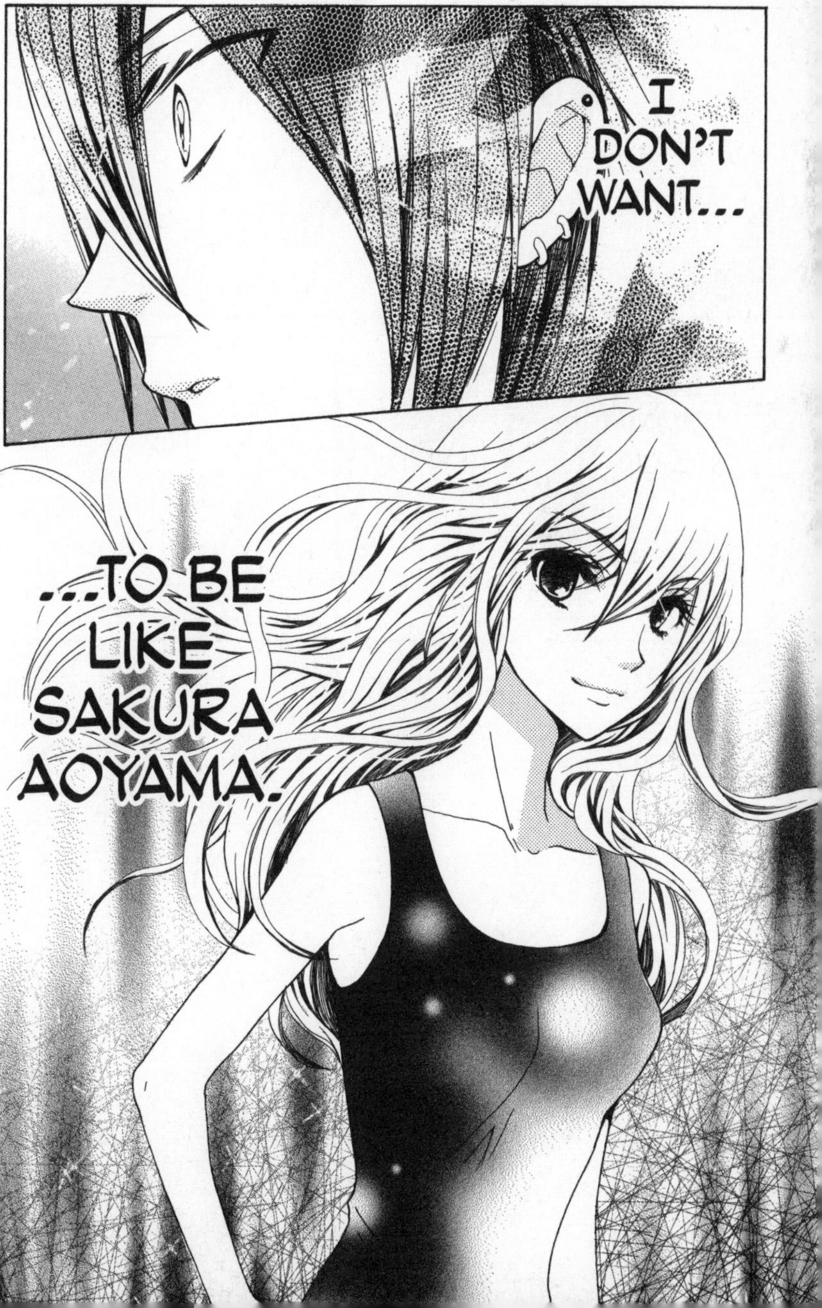
I DON'T WANT...
...TO BE LIKE SAKURA AOYAMA.

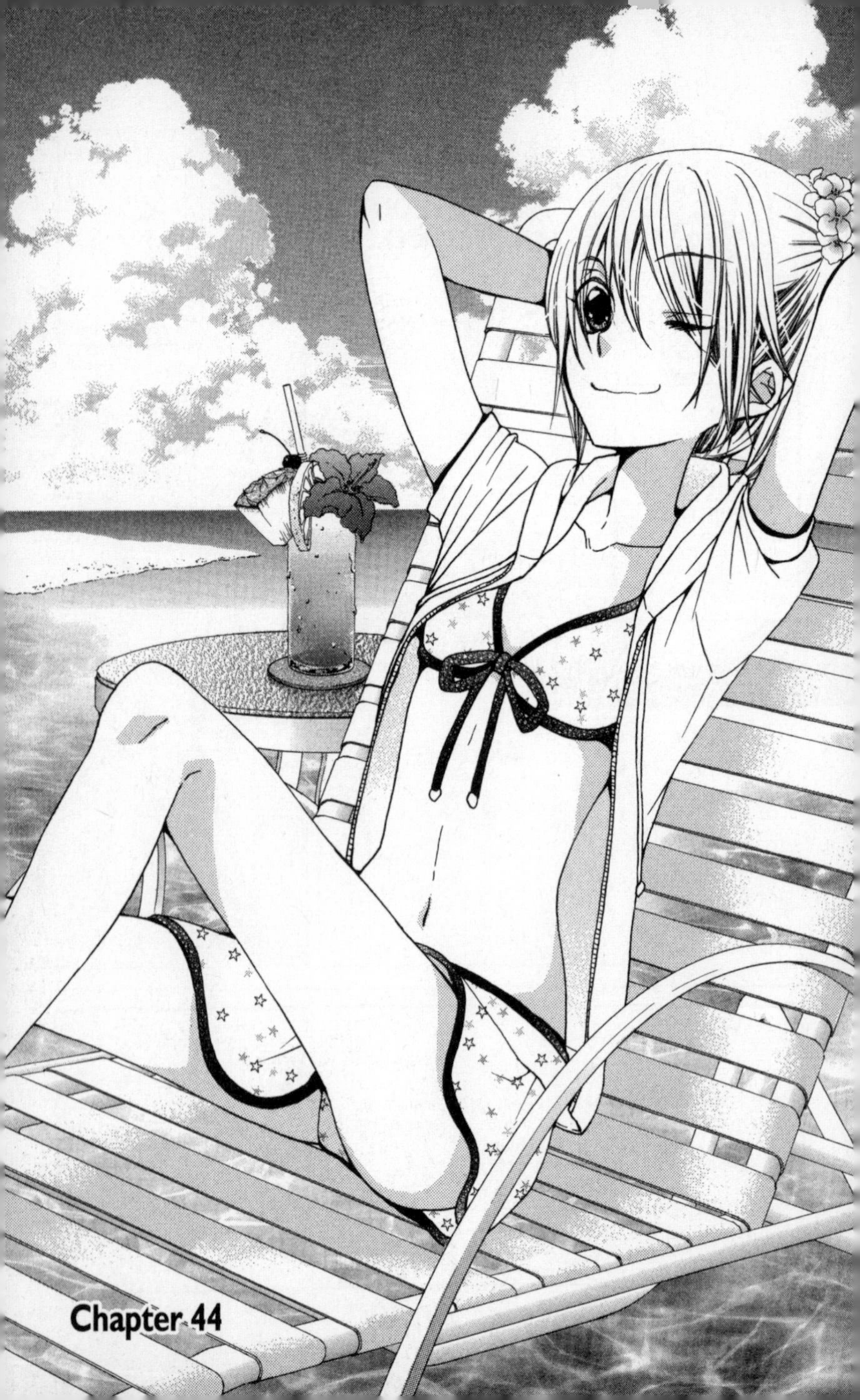

Chapter 44

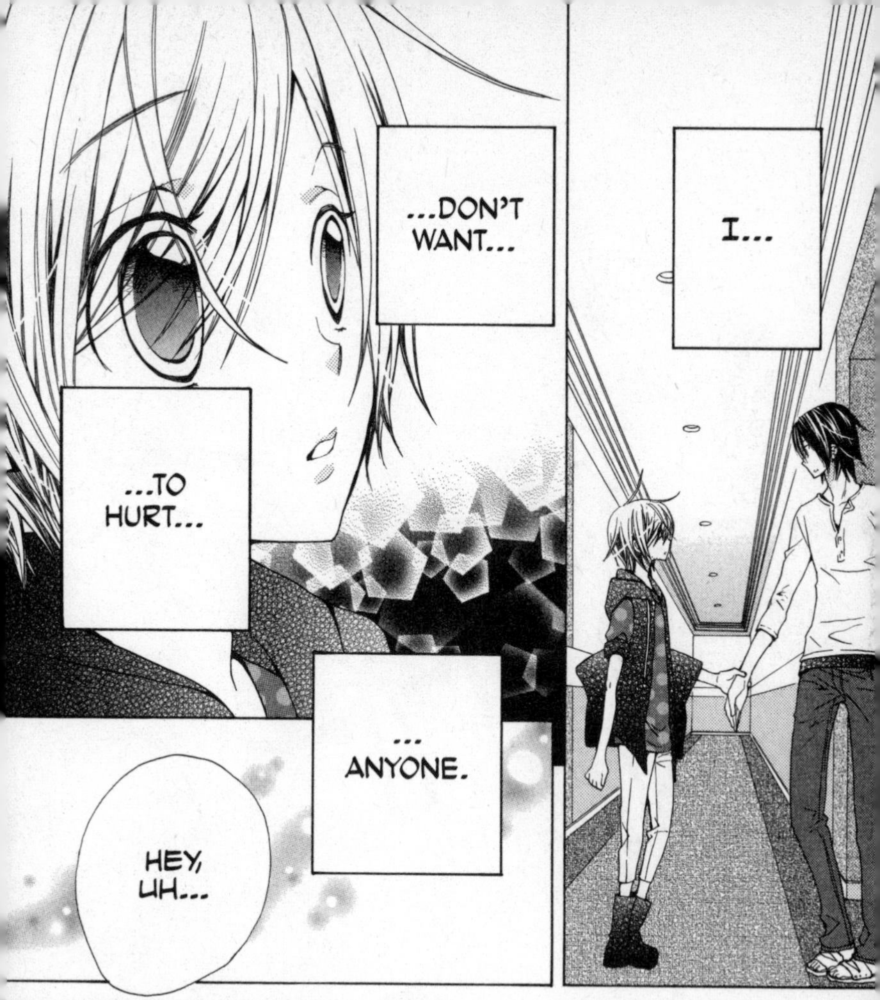
I...
...DON'T WANT...
...TO HURT...
... ANYONE.
HEY, UH...

• Who's Coming to Dinner? •

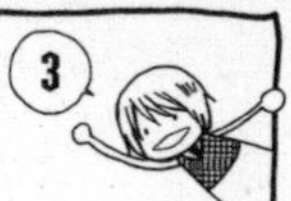
3

In the manga, Mizuki often shows up at Shiro's for dinner, but he usually lets Shiro know beforehand. I enjoy drawing those scenes.

Or maybe I just enjoy drawing eating scenes...

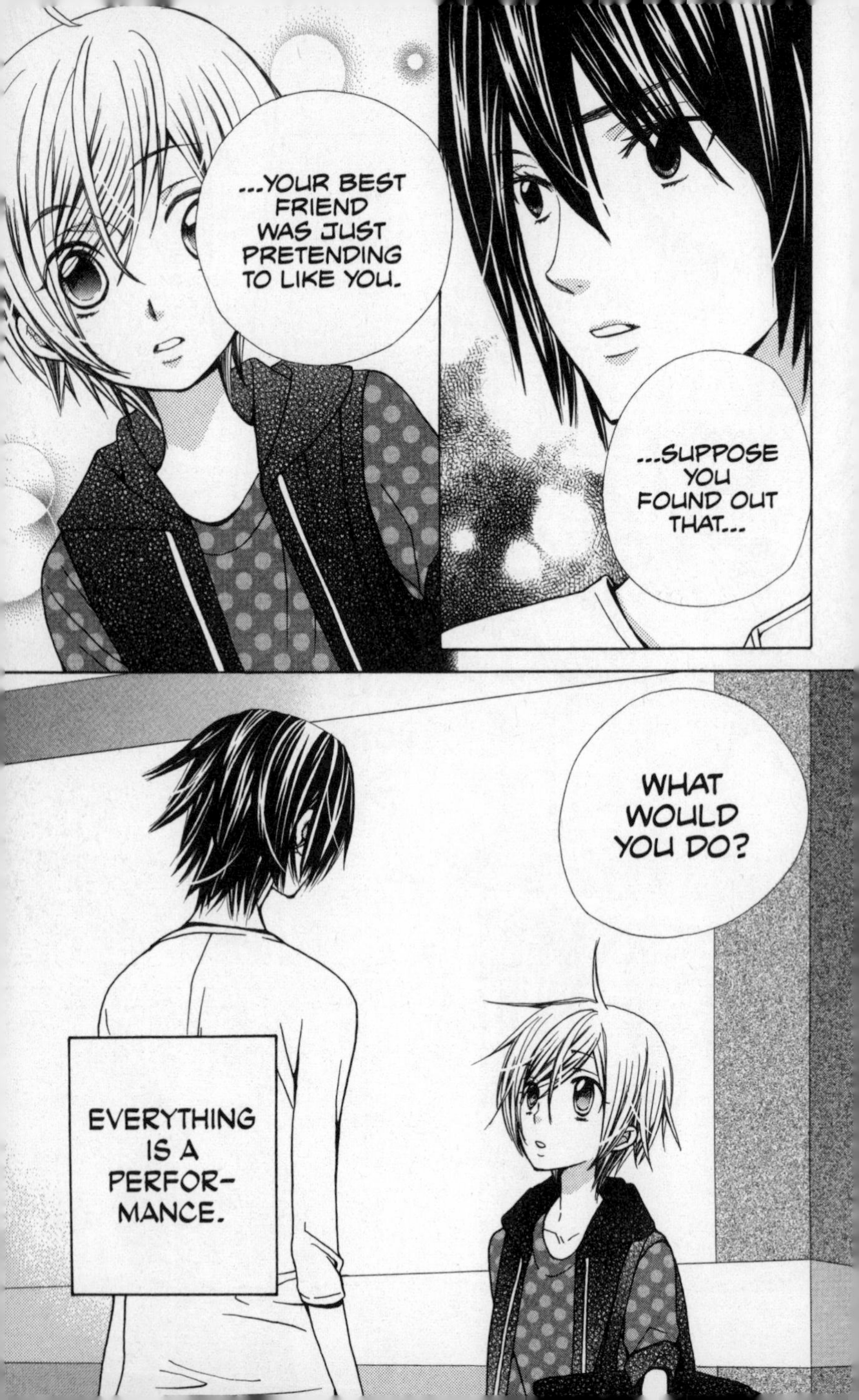
...SUPPOSE YOU FOUND OUT THAT...
...YOUR BEST FRIEND WAS JUST PRETENDING TO LIKE YOU.
WHAT WOULD YOU DO?
EVERYTHING IS A PERFOR-MANCE.

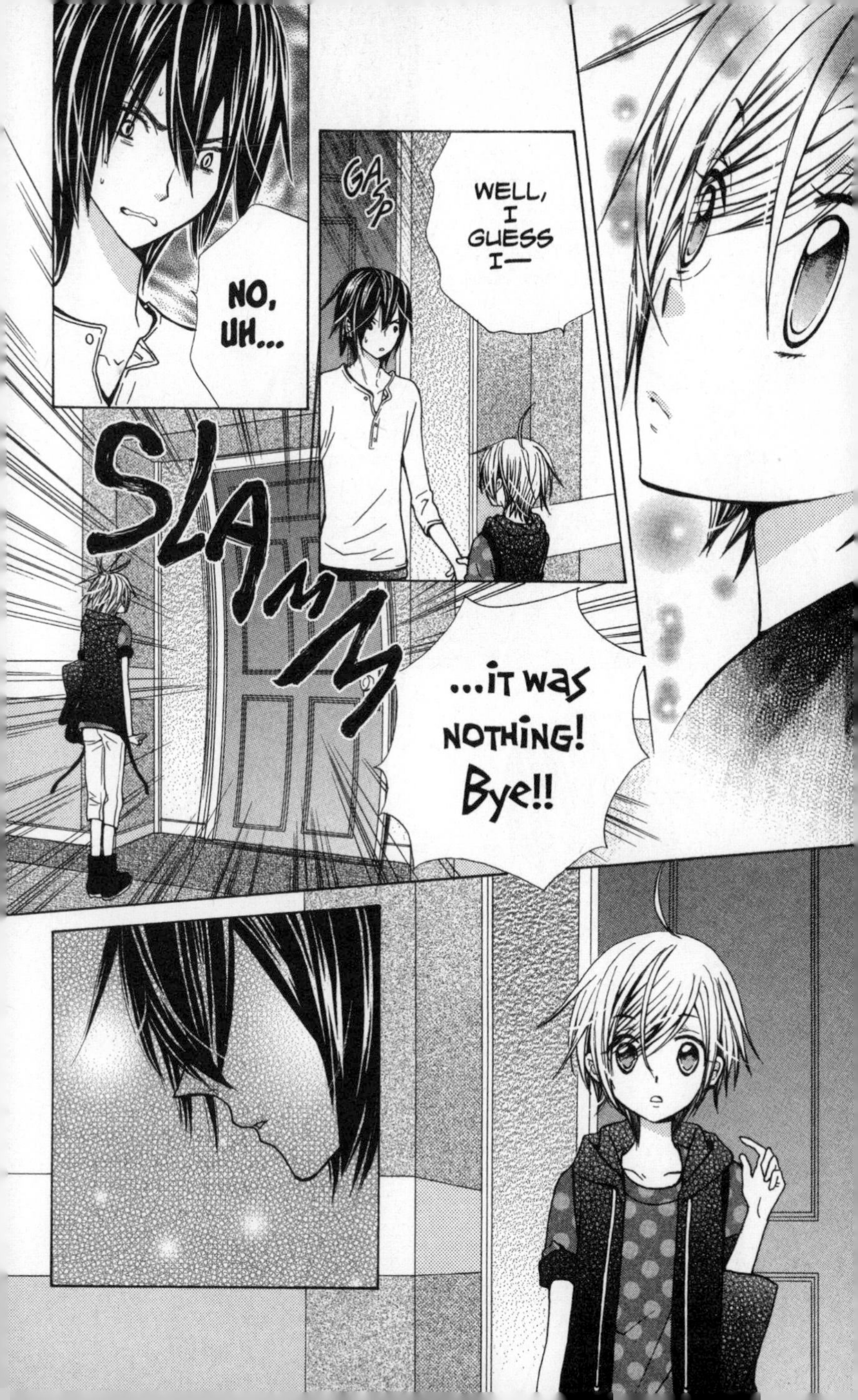
GASP
WELL, I GUESS I—
NO, UH...
...it was NOTHING! Bye!!
SLAMM

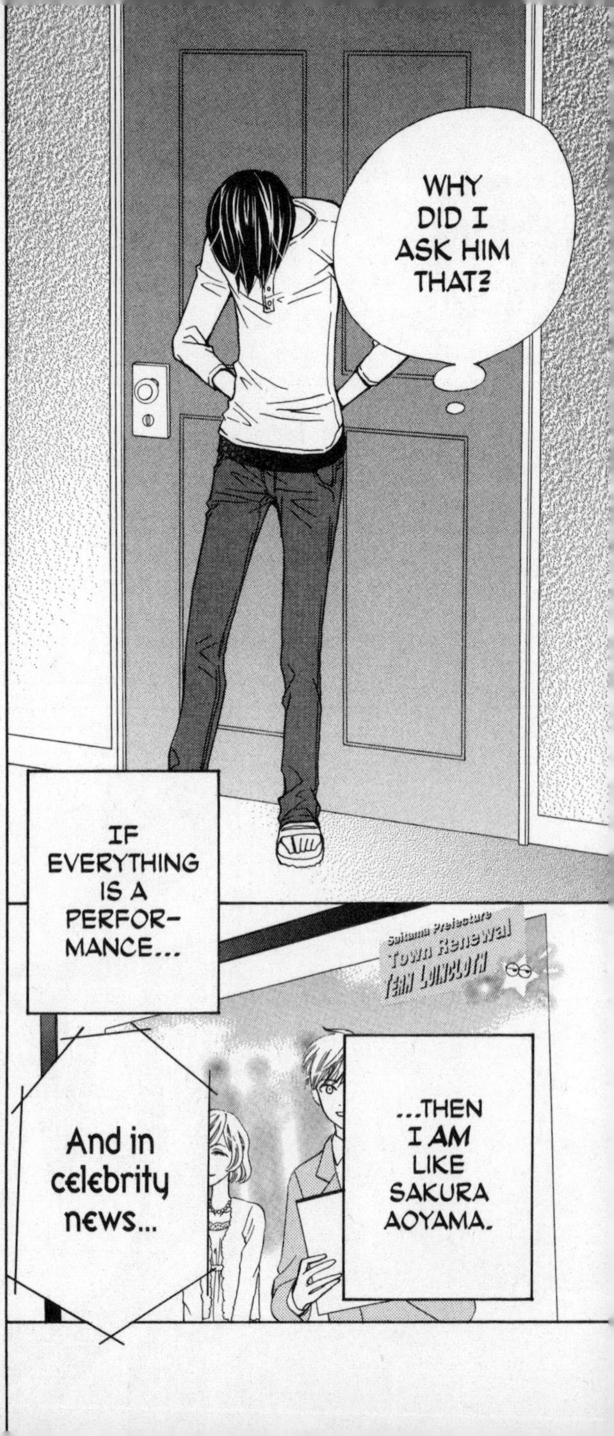
WHY DID I ASK HIM THAT?
IF EVERYTHING IS A PERFORMANCE...
...THEN I AM LIKE SAKURA AOYAMA.
Saitama Prefecture Town Renewal
And in celebrity news...

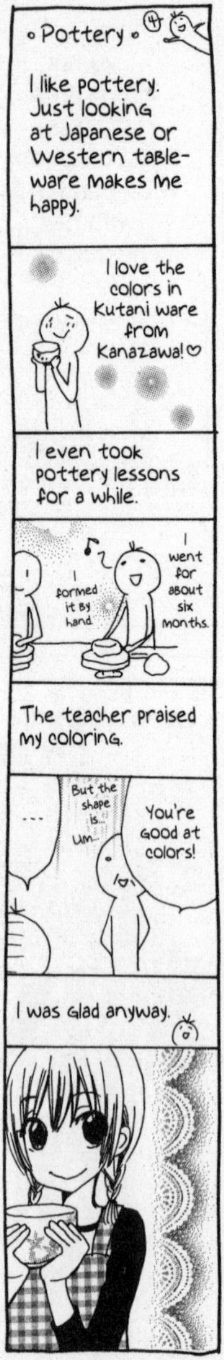
Pottery ④
I like pottery. Just looking at Japanese or Western tableware makes me happy.
I love the colors in Kutani ware from Kanazawa!♡
I even took pottery lessons for a while.
I formed it by hand.
I went for about six months.
The teacher praised my coloring.
You're good at colors!
But the shape is... Um...
...
I was glad anyway.

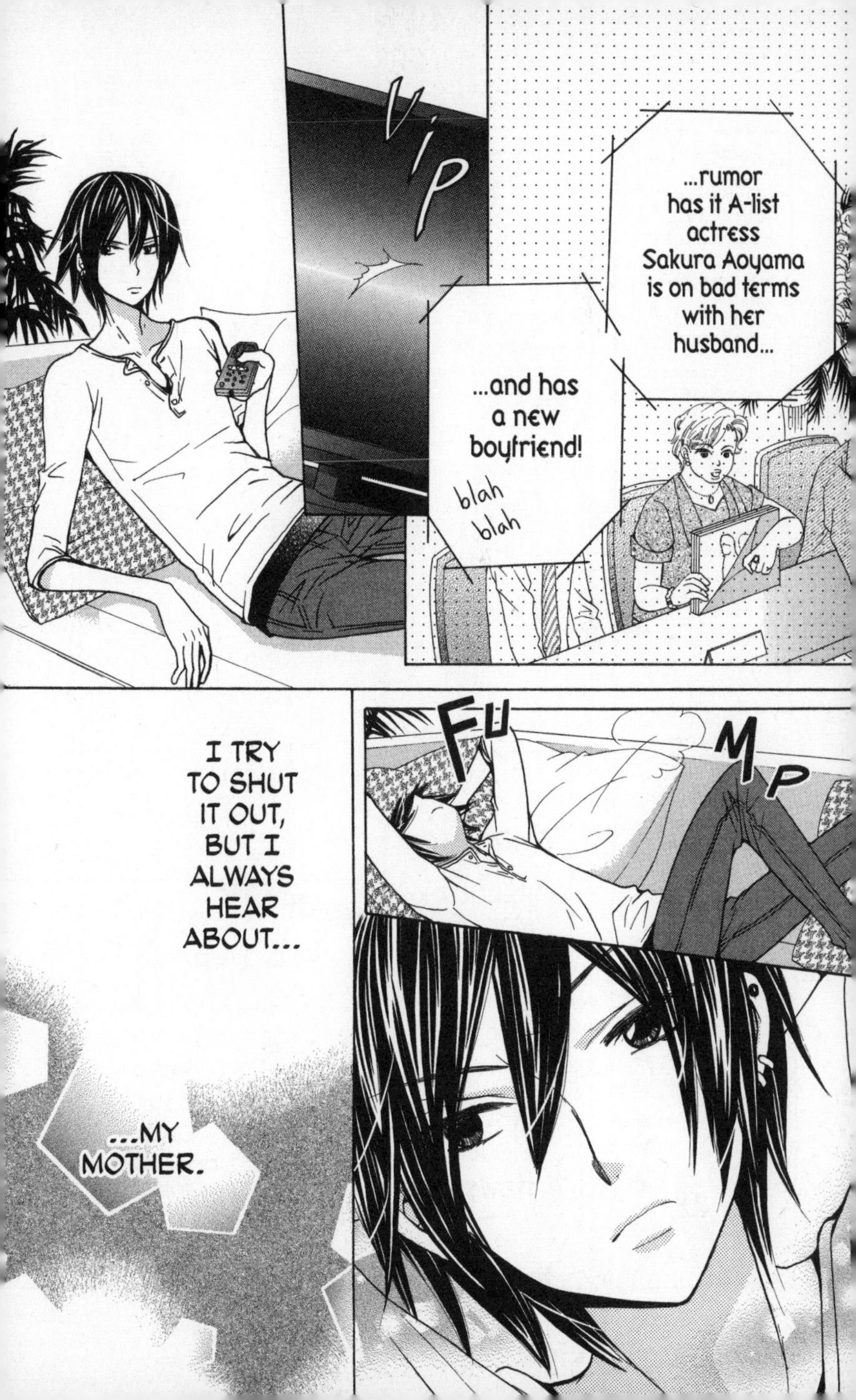
...rumor has it A-list actress Sakura Aoyama is on bad terms with her husband...
...and has a new boyfriend!
blah blah
VIP
FUMP
I TRY TO SHUT IT OUT, BUT I ALWAYS HEAR ABOUT...
...MY MOTHER.

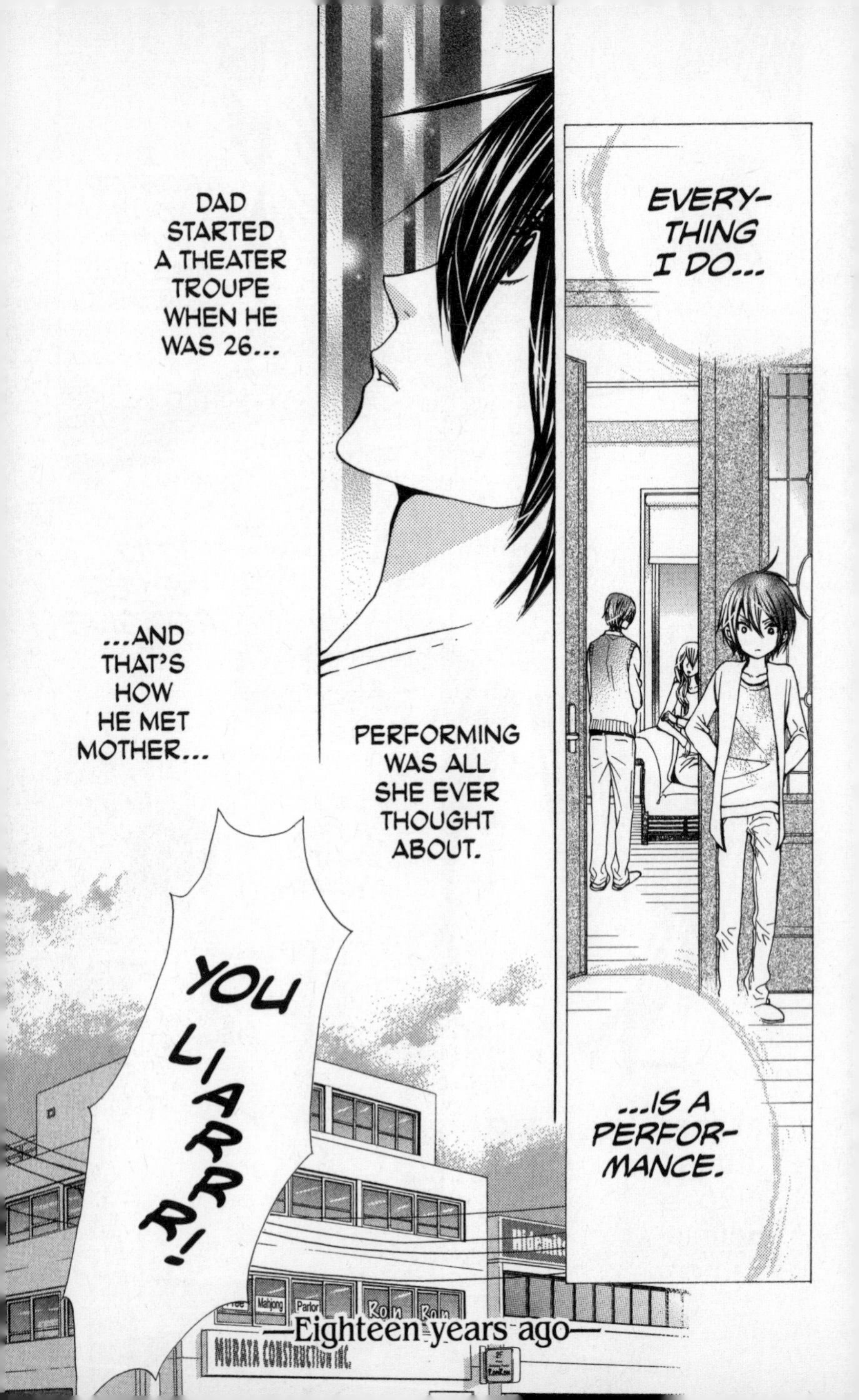
EVERY-THING I DO...
...IS A PERFORMANCE.
PERFORMING WAS ALL SHE EVER THOUGHT ABOUT.
DAD STARTED A THEATER TROUPE WHEN HE WAS 26...
...AND THAT'S HOW HE MET MOTHER...
YOU LIARRR!
Mahjong Parlor
Ron Ron
MURATA CONSTRUCTION INC.
—Eighteen years ago—

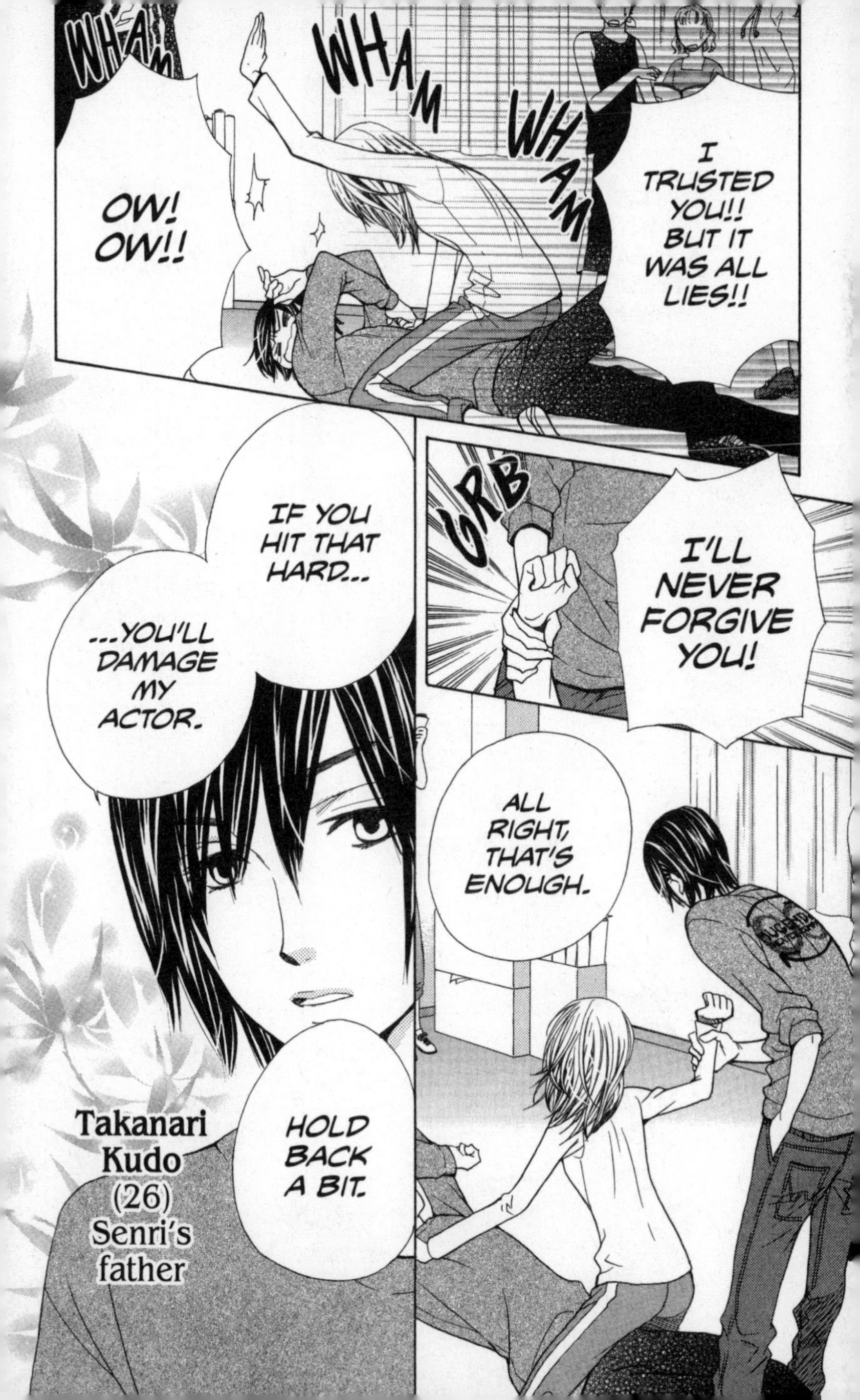
I TRUSTED YOU!! BUT IT WAS ALL LIES!!
WHAM
WHAM
WHAM
OW! OW!!
GRB
I'LL NEVER FORGIVE YOU!
ALL RIGHT, THAT'S ENOUGH.
IF YOU HIT THAT HARD...
...YOU'LL DAMAGE MY ACTOR.
HOLD BACK A BIT.
Takanari Kudo (26) Senri's father

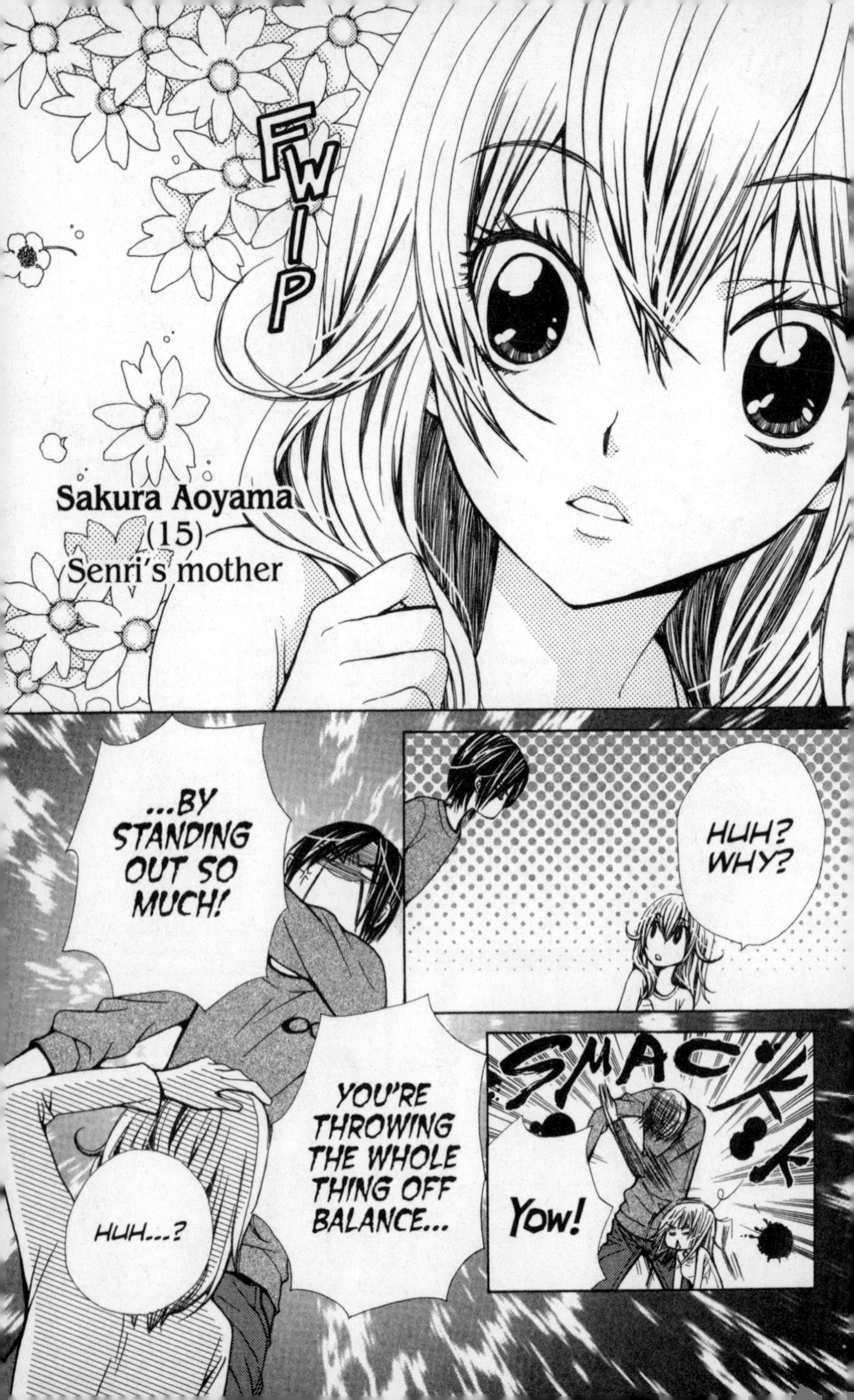
FWIP
Sakura Aoyama
(15)
Senri's mother
HUH? WHY?
SMACK
YOW!
...BY STANDING OUT SO MUCH!
YOU'RE THROWING THE WHOLE THING OFF BALANCE...
HUH...?

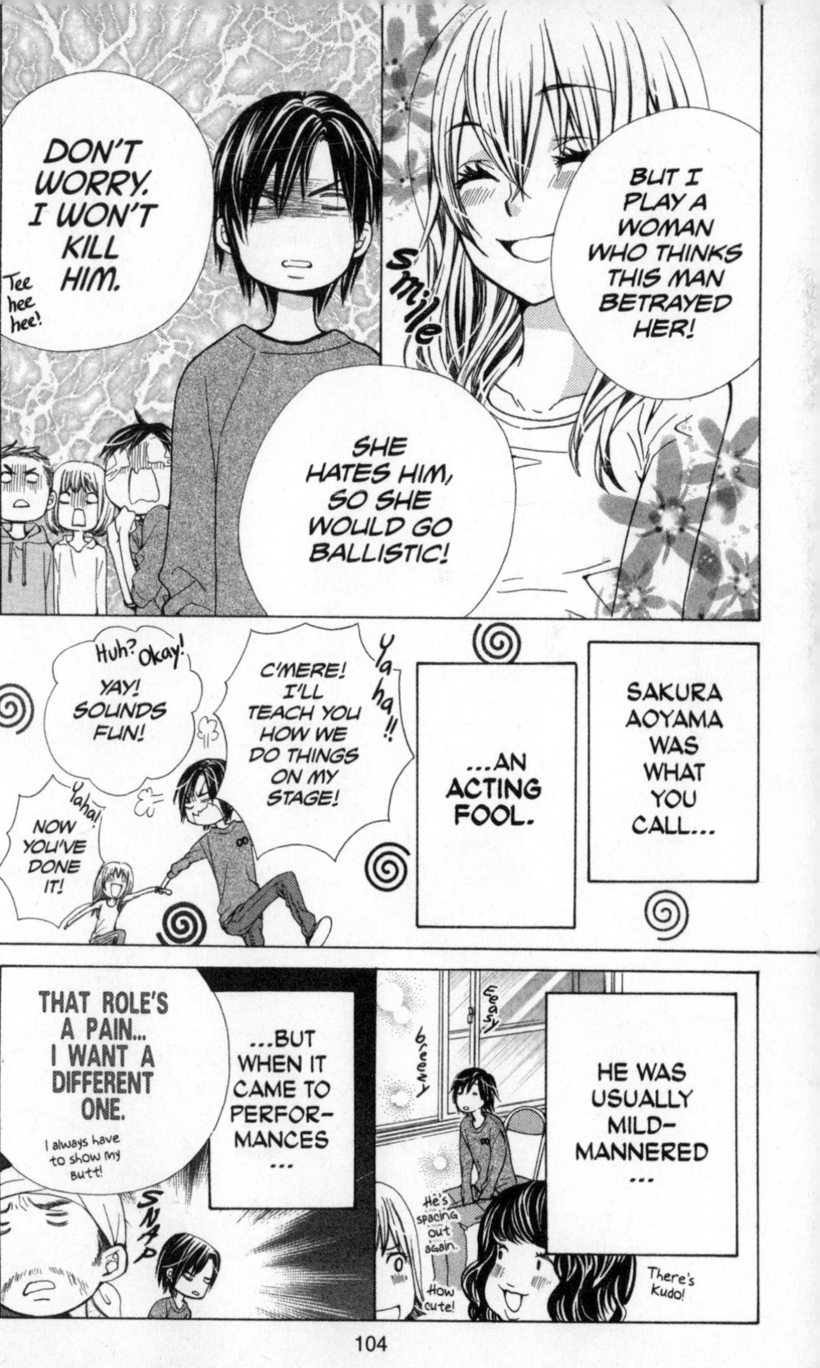
smile
BUT I PLAY A WOMAN WHO THINKS THIS MAN BETRAYED HER!
SHE HATES HIM, SO SHE WOULD GO BALLISTIC!
DON'T WORRY. I WON'T KILL HIM.
Tee hee hee!
SAKURA AOYAMA WAS WHAT YOU CALL...
...AN ACTING FOOL.
Yaha!!
C'MERE! I'LL TEACH YOU HOW WE DO THINGS ON MY STAGE!
Huh? Okay!
YAY! SOUNDS FUN!
Yaha!
NOW YOU'VE DONE IT!
HE WAS USUALLY MILD-MANNERED ...
Easy
breezy
There's Kudo!
He's spacing out again.
How cute!
...BUT WHEN IT CAME TO PERFORMANCES ...
THAT ROLE'S A PAIN... I WANT A DIFFERENT ONE.
I always have to show my butt!
SNAP

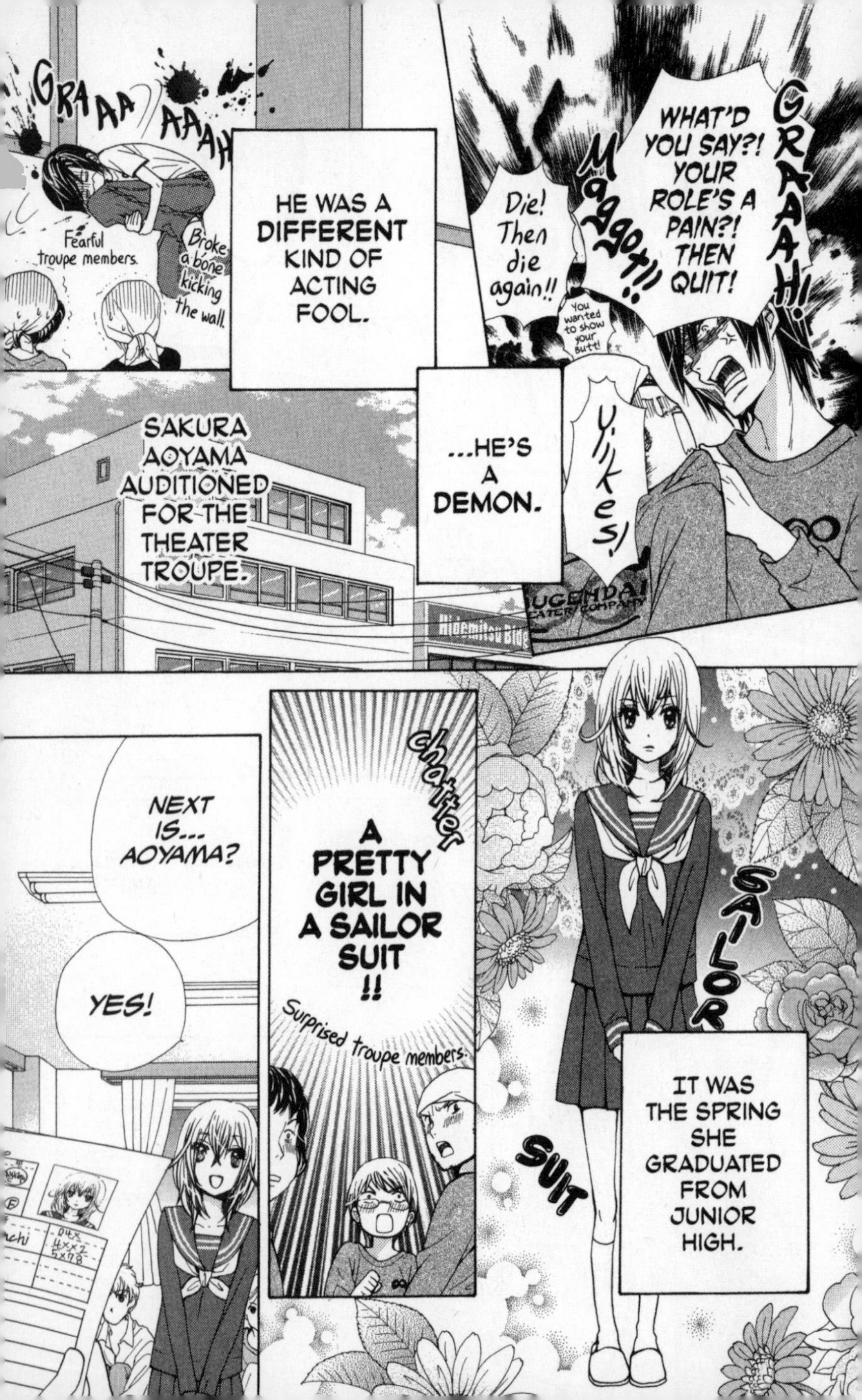
GRAAAH!
WHAT'D YOU SAY?! YOUR ROLE'S A PAIN?! THEN QUIT!
Maggot!!
Die! Then die again!!
You wanted to show your butt!
HE WAS A DIFFERENT KIND OF ACTING FOOL.
GRAAAAAAAAH
Broke a bone kicking the wall.
Fearful troupe members.
Yiiikes!
...HE'S A DEMON.
UGENDAI THEATER COMPANY
SAKURA AOYAMA AUDITIONED FOR THE THEATER TROUPE.
Hidemitsu Bldg
SAILOR SUIT
IT WAS THE SPRING SHE GRADUATED FROM JUNIOR HIGH.
chatter
A PRETTY GIRL IN A SAILOR SUIT !!
Surprised troupe members.
NEXT IS... AOYAMA?
YES!

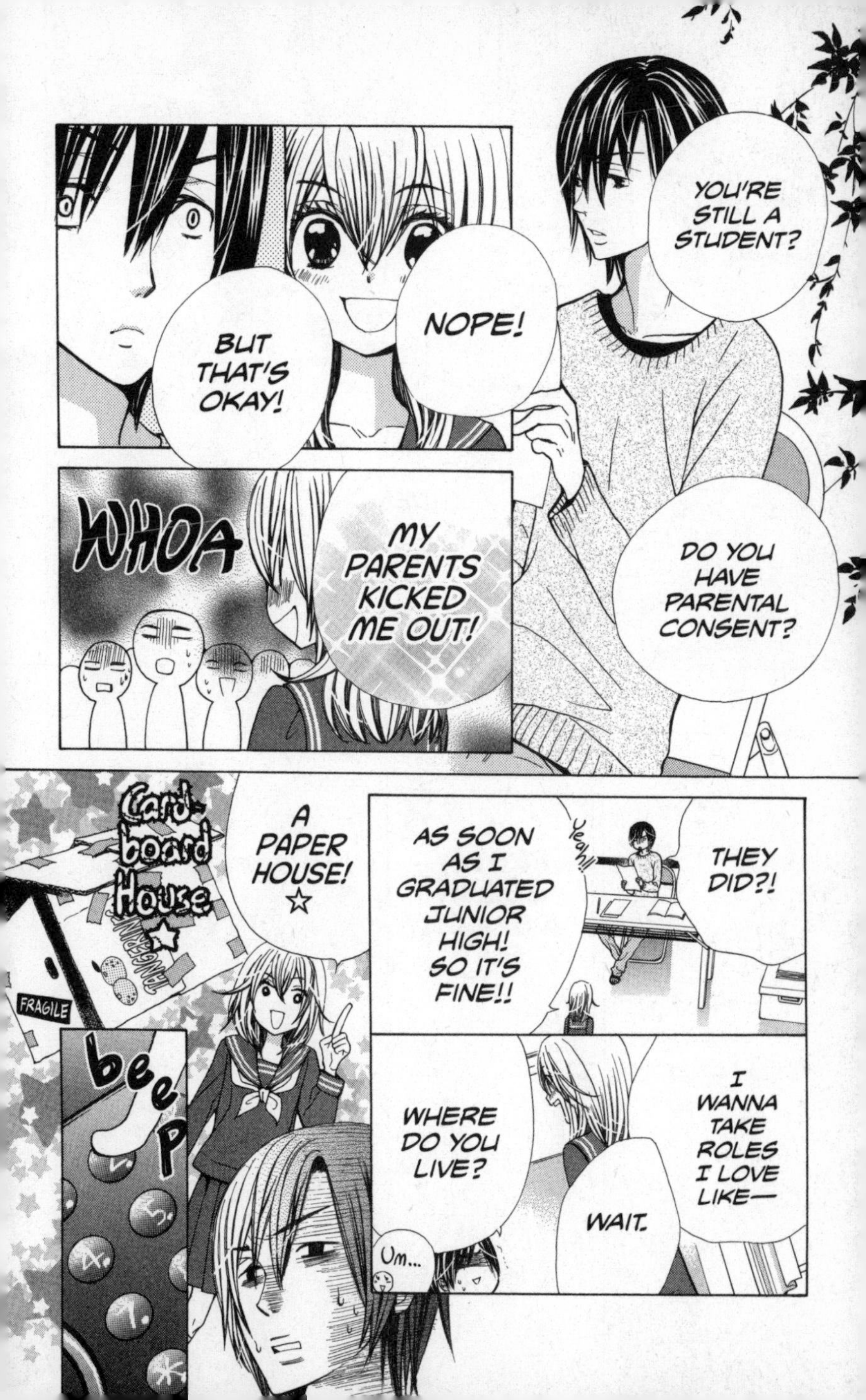
YOU'RE STILL A STUDENT?
DO YOU HAVE PARENTAL CONSENT?
NOPE!
BUT THAT'S OKAY!
MY PARENTS KICKED ME OUT!
WHOA
THEY DID?!
Yeah!!
AS SOON AS I GRADUATED JUNIOR HIGH! SO IT'S FINE!!
I WANNA TAKE ROLES I LOVE LIKE—
WAIT.
WHERE DO YOU LIVE?
Um...
A PAPER HOUSE! ☆
Card-board House ☆
TANGERINES
FRAGILE
beep

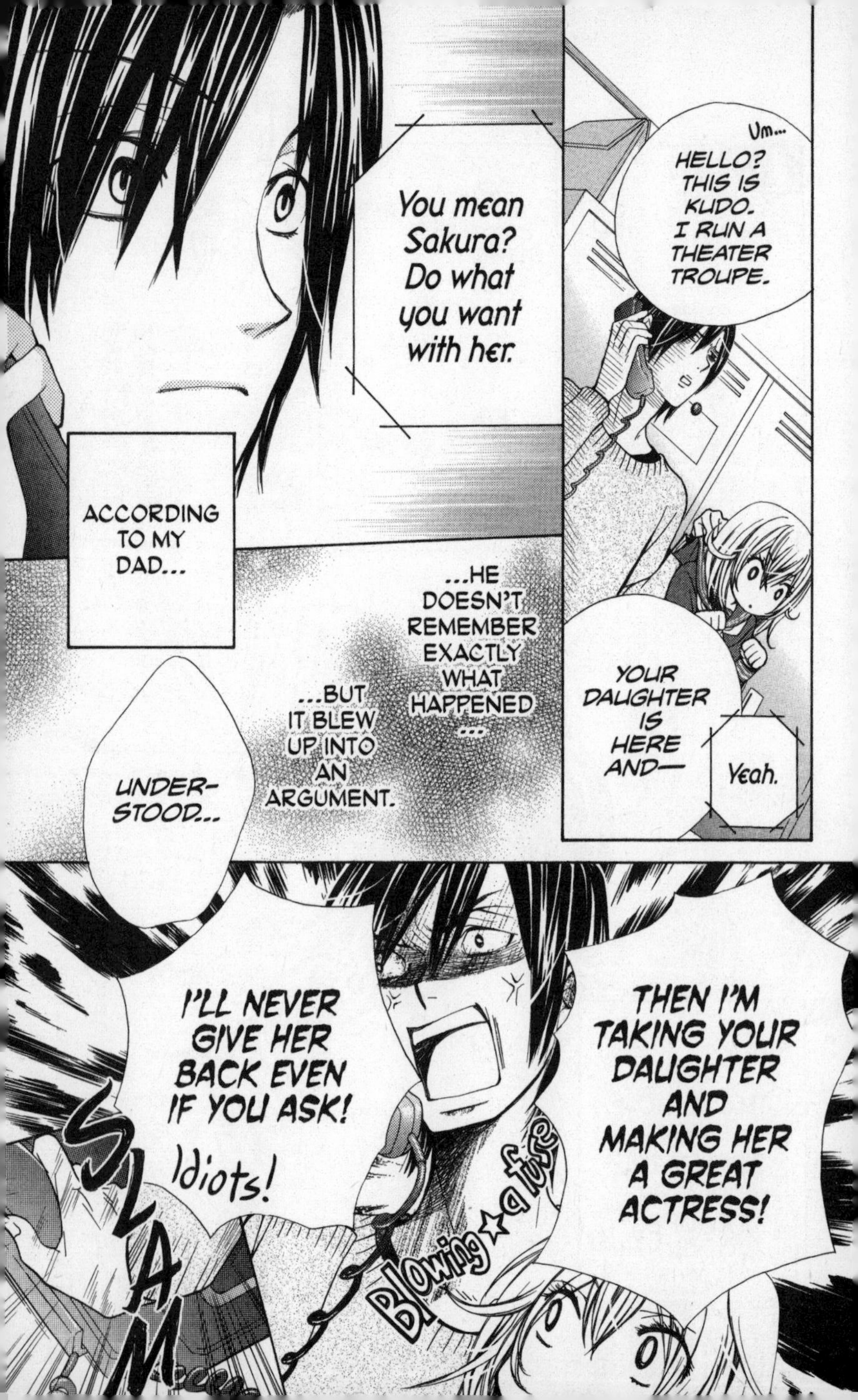
Um...
HELLO? THIS IS KUDO. I RUN A THEATER TROUPE.
YOUR DAUGHTER IS HERE AND—
Yeah.
You mean Sakura? Do what you want with her.
ACCORDING TO MY DAD...
...HE DOESN'T REMEMBER EXACTLY WHAT HAPPENED...
...BUT IT BLEW UP INTO AN ARGUMENT.
UNDER-STOOD...
THEN I'M TAKING YOUR DAUGHTER AND MAKING HER A GREAT ACTRESS!
I'LL NEVER GIVE HER BACK EVEN IF YOU ASK!
Idiots!
Blowing☆a fuse
SLAM

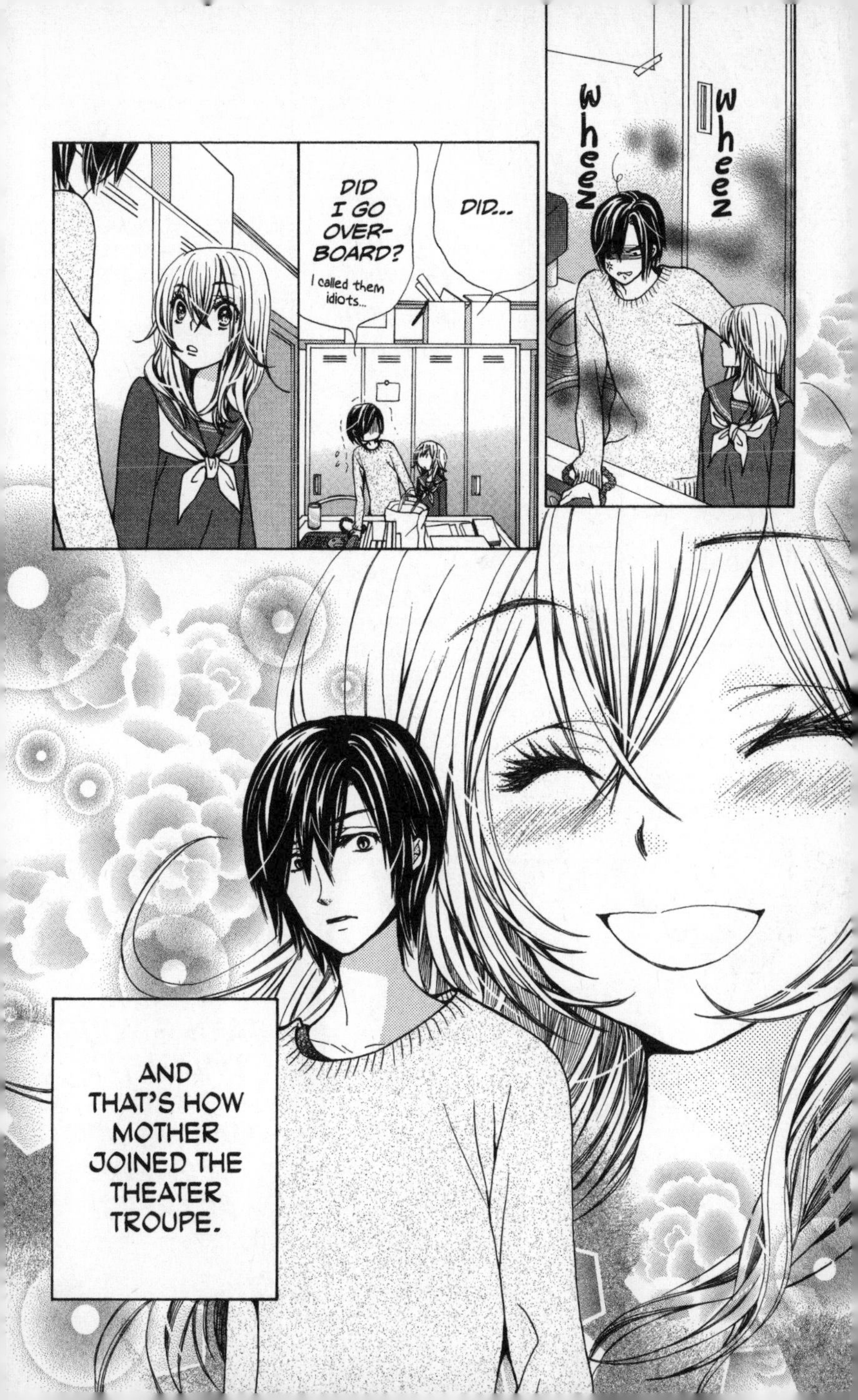
wheez
wheez
DID...
DID I GO OVER-BOARD?
I called them idiots...
AND THAT'S HOW MOTHER JOINED THE THEATER TROUPE.

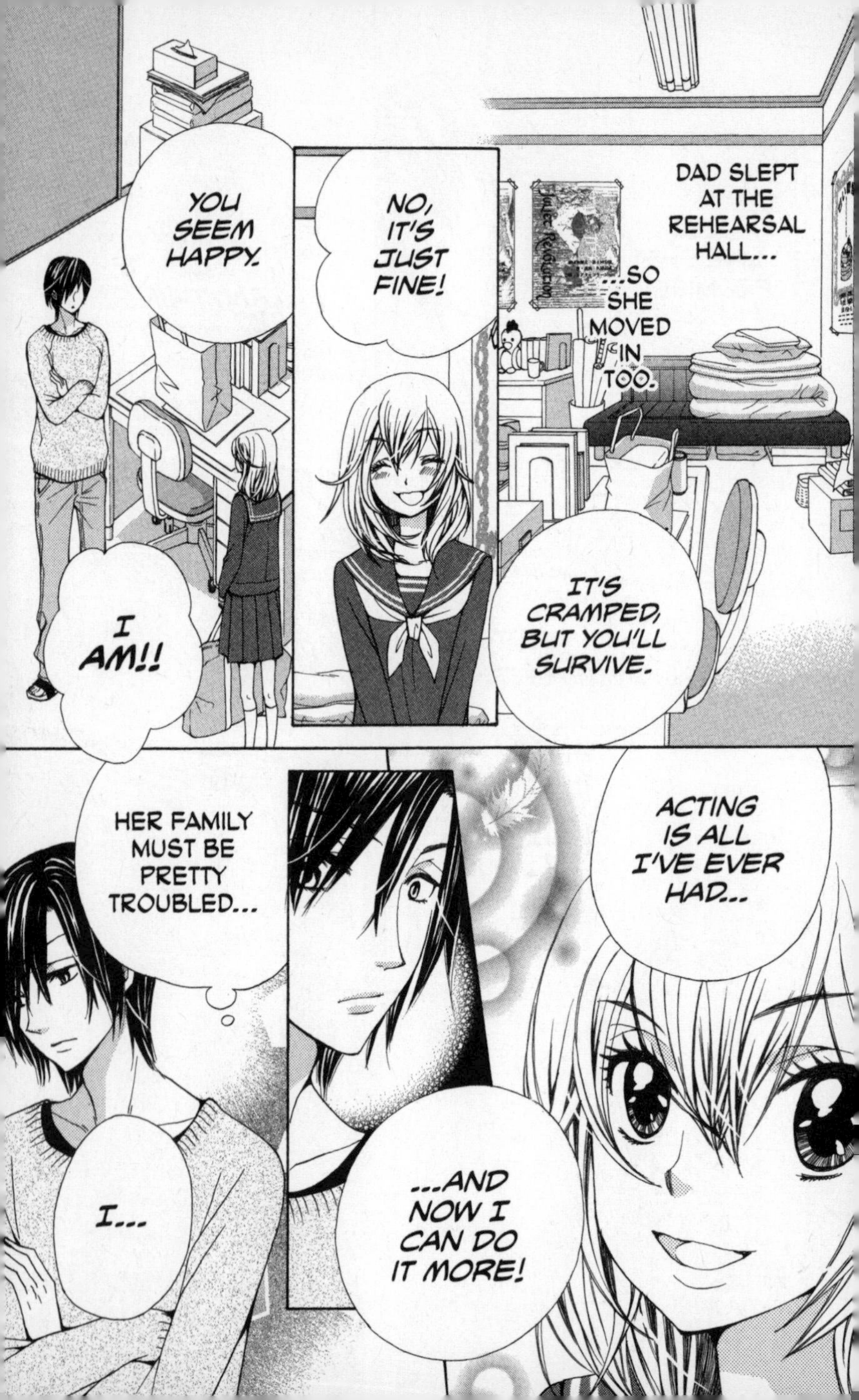
DAD SLEPT AT THE REHEARSAL HALL...
...SO SHE MOVED IN TOO.
IT'S CRAMPED, BUT YOU'LL SURVIVE.
NO, IT'S JUST FINE!
YOU SEEM HAPPY.
I AM!!
ACTING IS ALL I'VE EVER HAD...
...AND NOW I CAN DO IT MORE!
HER FAMILY MUST BE PRETTY TROUBLED...
I...

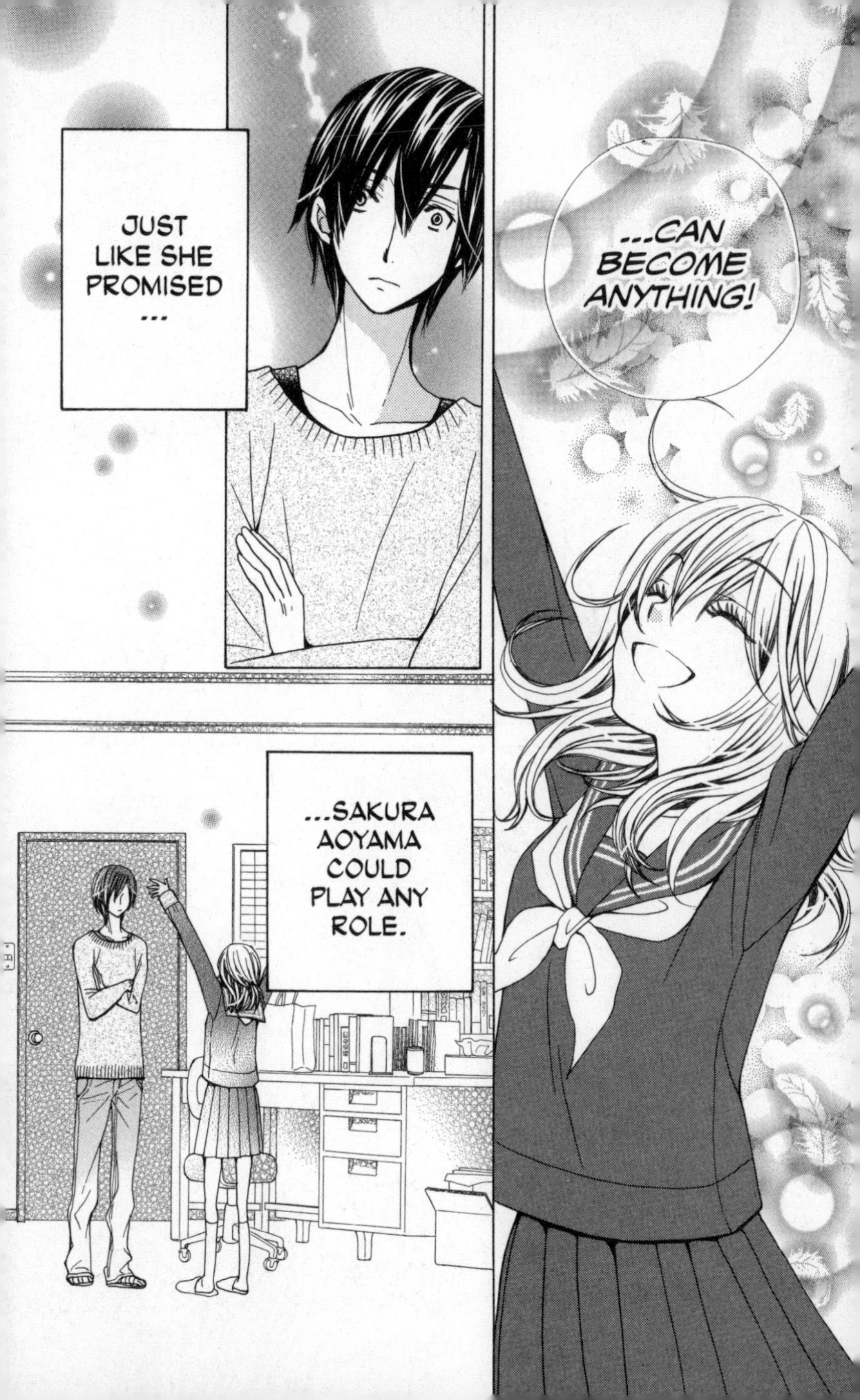
...CAN BECOME ANYTHING!
JUST LIKE SHE PROMISED ...
...SAKURA AOYAMA COULD PLAY ANY ROLE.

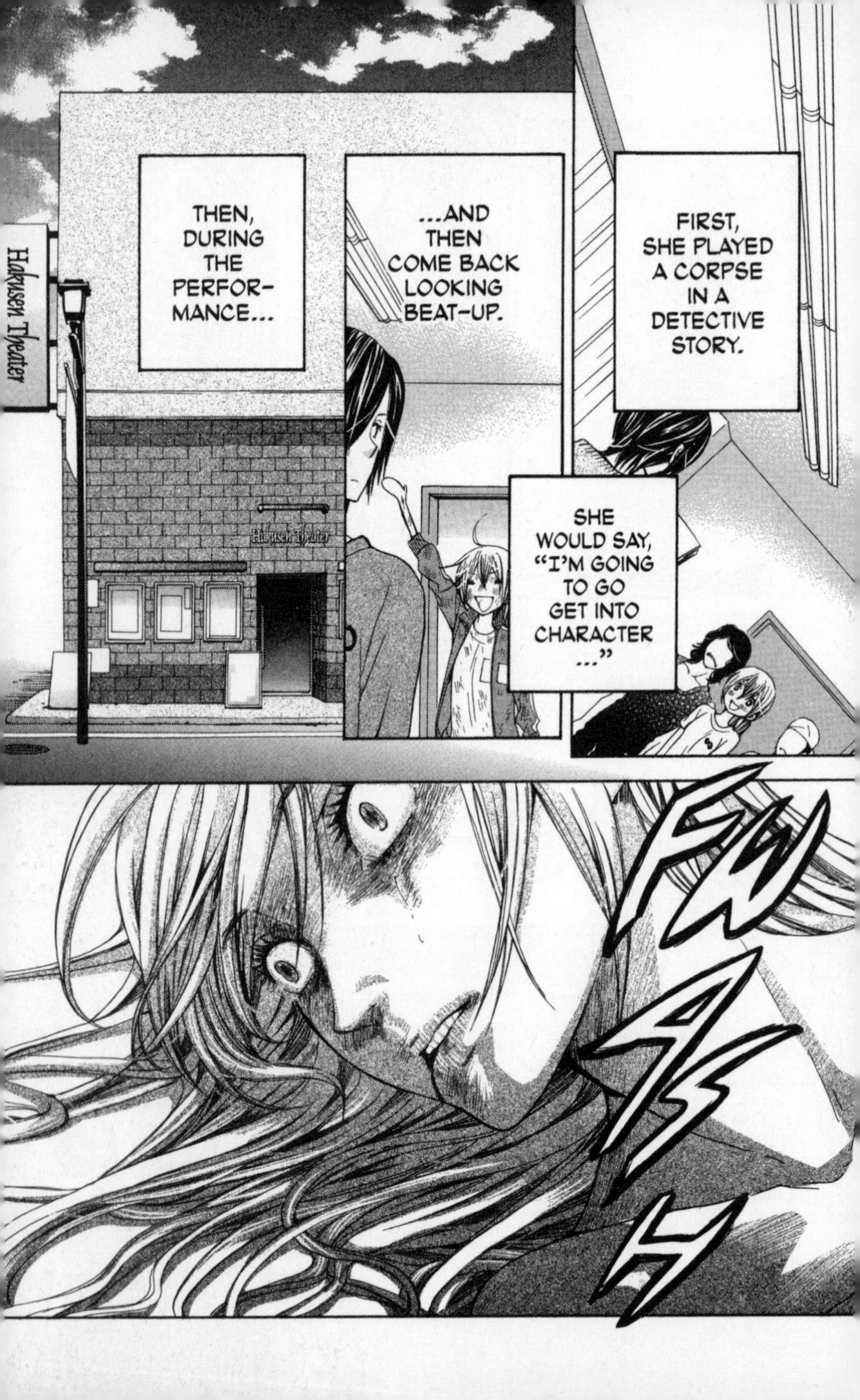

FIRST, SHE PLAYED A CORPSE IN A DETECTIVE STORY.
SHE WOULD SAY, "I'M GOING TO GO GET INTO CHARACTER..."
...AND THEN COME BACK LOOKING BEAT-UP.
THEN, DURING THE PERFORMANCE...
Hakusen Theater
Hakusen Theater
FWASH

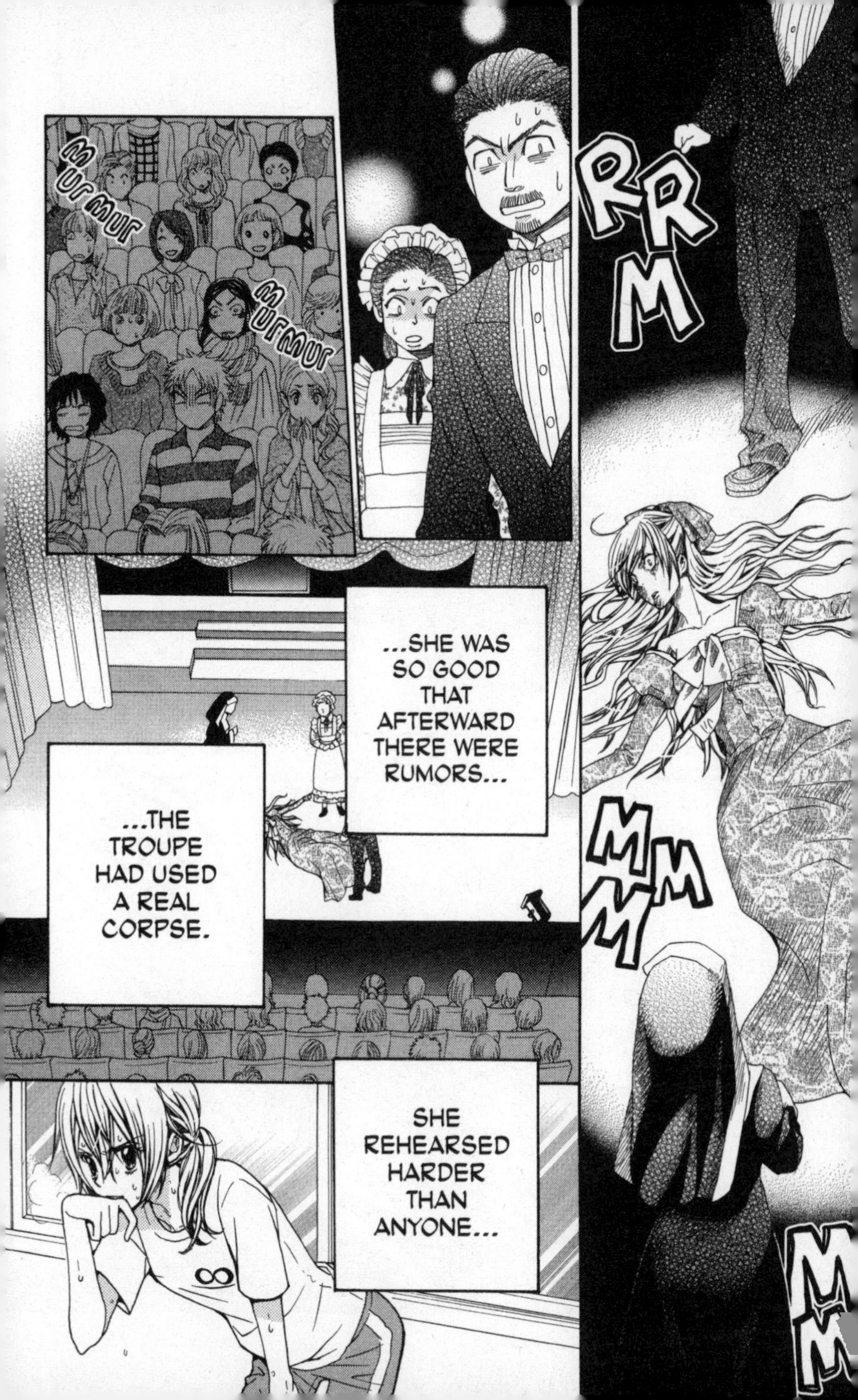
RRM
MMMM
MMM
MURMUR
MURMUR
...SHE WAS SO GOOD THAT AFTERWARD THERE WERE RUMORS...
...THE TROUPE HAD USED A REAL CORPSE.
SHE REHEARSED HARDER THAN ANYONE...

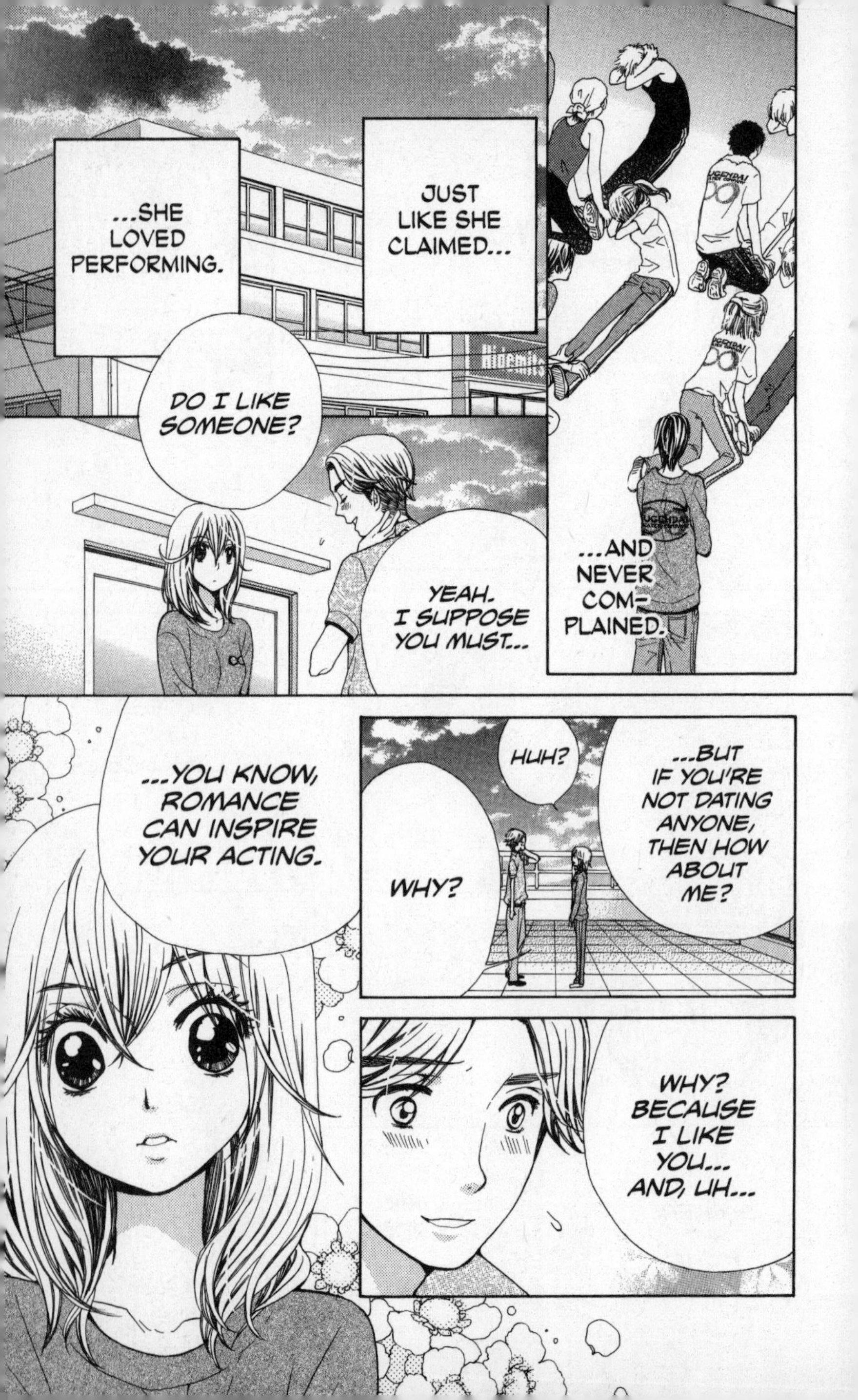
JUST LIKE SHE CLAIMED...
...SHE LOVED PERFORMING.
...AND NEVER COM-PLAINED.
DO I LIKE SOMEONE?
YEAH. I SUPPOSE YOU MUST...
...BUT IF YOU'RE NOT DATING ANYONE, THEN HOW ABOUT ME?
HUH?
WHY?
WHY? BECAUSE I LIKE YOU... AND, UH...
...YOU KNOW, ROMANCE CAN INSPIRE YOUR ACTING.

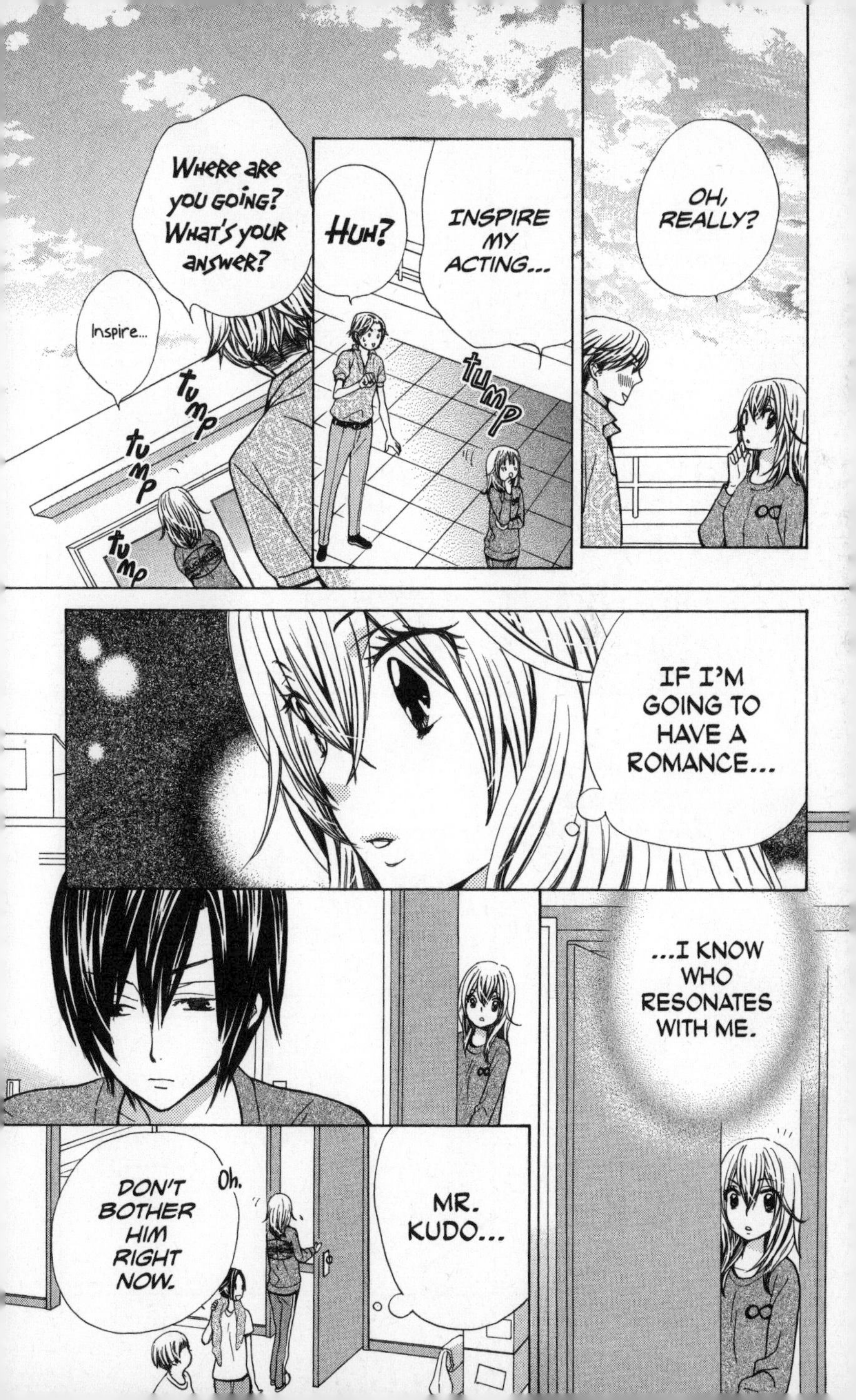
OH, REALLY?
INSPIRE MY ACTING...
HUH?
tump
Where are you going? What's your answer?
Inspire...
tump
tump
tump
tump
IF I'M GOING TO HAVE A ROMANCE...
...I KNOW WHO RESONATES WITH ME.
MR. KUDO...
Oh.
DON'T BOTHER HIM RIGHT NOW.

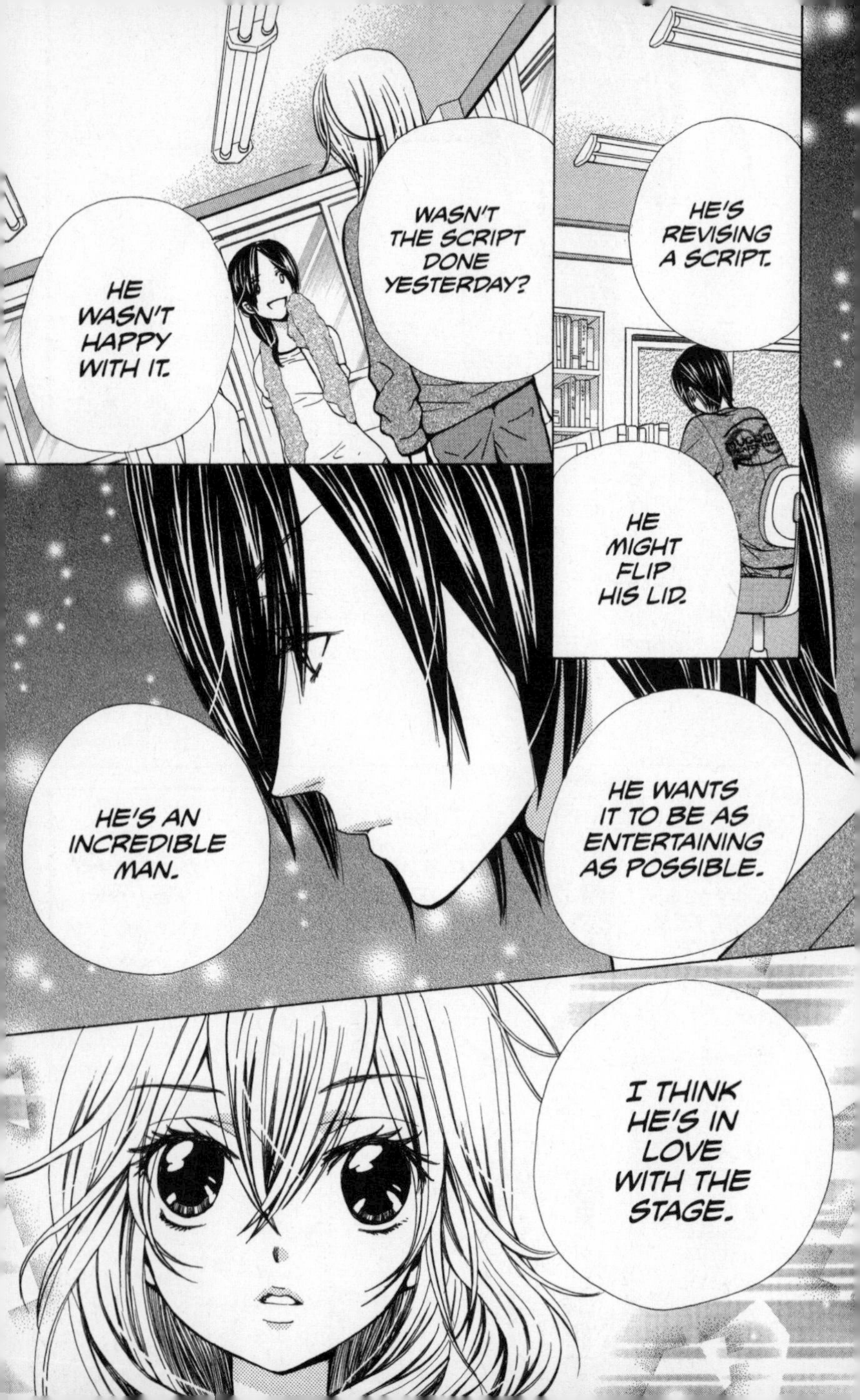
HE'S REVISING A SCRIPT.
HE MIGHT FLIP HIS LID.
WASN'T THE SCRIPT DONE YESTERDAY?
HE WASN'T HAPPY WITH IT.
HE WANTS IT TO BE AS ENTERTAINING AS POSSIBLE.
HE'S AN INCREDIBLE MAN.
I THINK HE'S IN LOVE WITH THE STAGE.

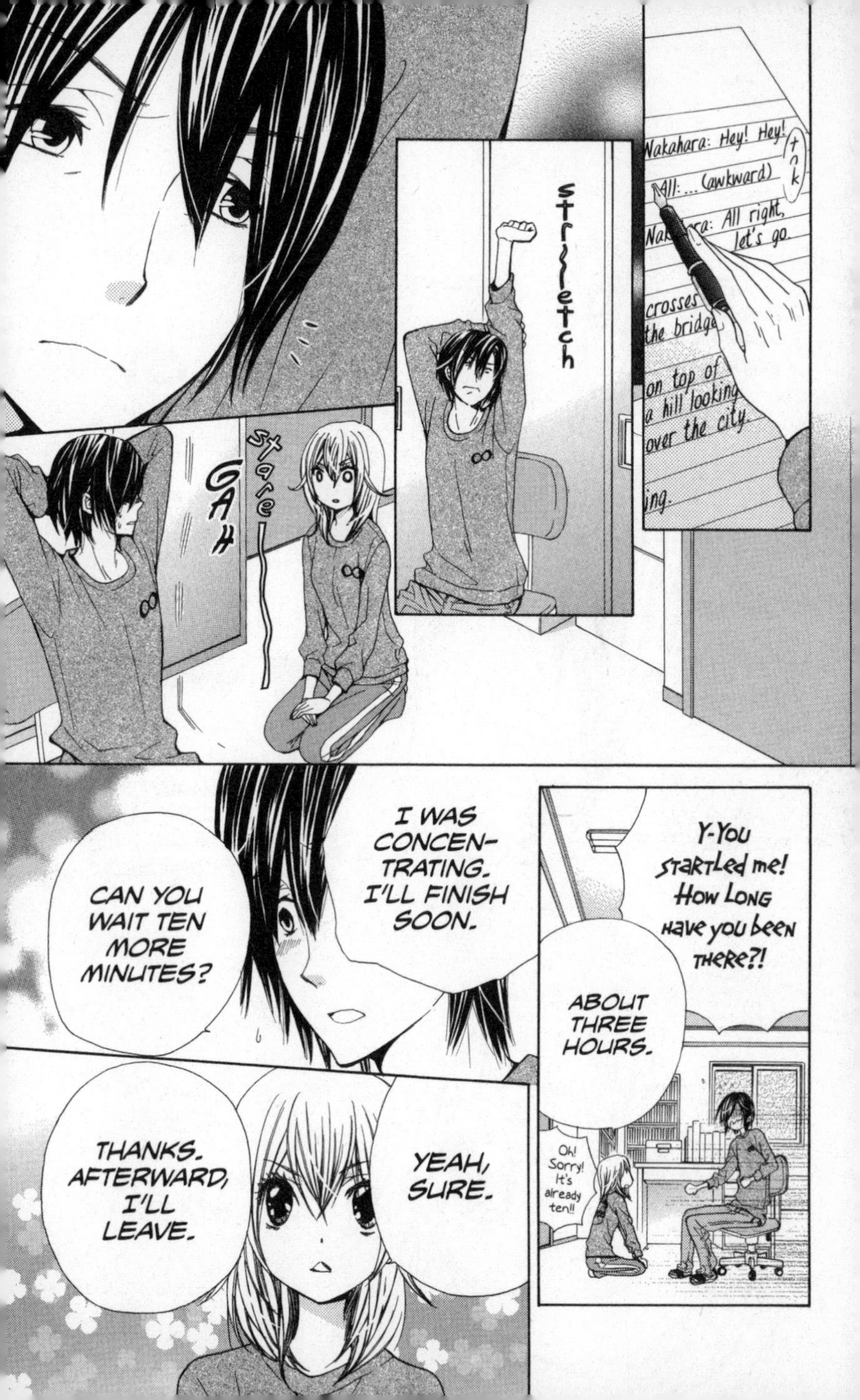
Nakahara: Hey! Hey!
tnk
All: ... (awkward)
ra: All right, let's go.
crosses the bridge
on top of a hill looking over the city.
ing.
stretch
stare
GAH
Y-You startled me! How long have you been there?!
About three hours.
Oh! Sorry! It's already ten!!
I was concentrating. I'll finish soon.
Can you wait ten more minutes?
Yeah, sure.
Thanks. Afterward, I'll leave.

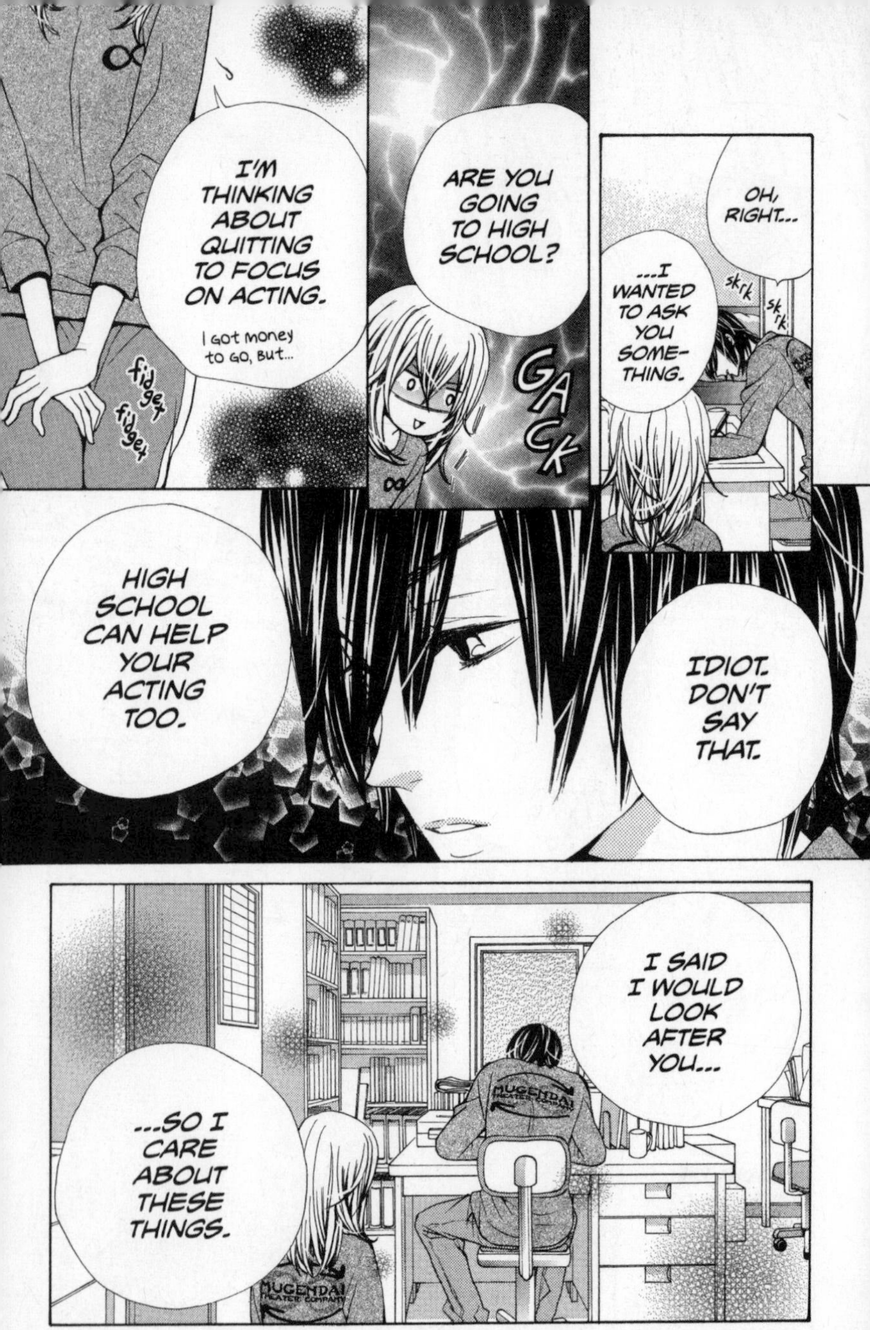
OH, RIGHT...
...I WANTED TO ASK YOU SOMETHING.
skrk
skrk
ARE YOU GOING TO HIGH SCHOOL?
GACK
I'M THINKING ABOUT QUITTING TO FOCUS ON ACTING.
I got money to go, but...
fidget
fidget
IDIOT. DON'T SAY THAT.
HIGH SCHOOL CAN HELP YOUR ACTING TOO.
I SAID I WOULD LOOK AFTER YOU...
...SO I CARE ABOUT THESE THINGS.

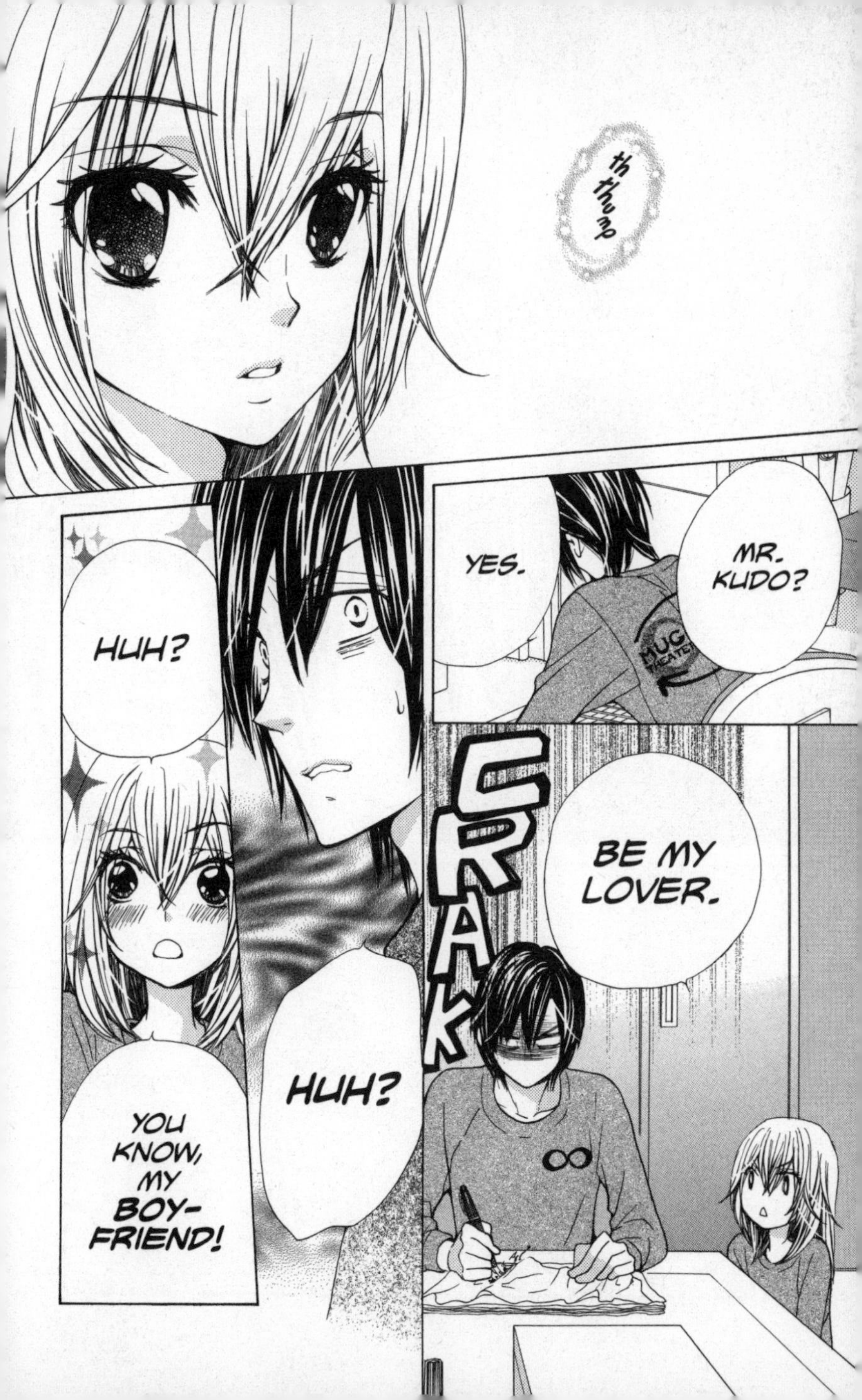
th thump
MR. KUDO?
YES.
CRAK
BE MY LOVER.
HUH?
HUH?
YOU KNOW, MY BOY-FRIEND!

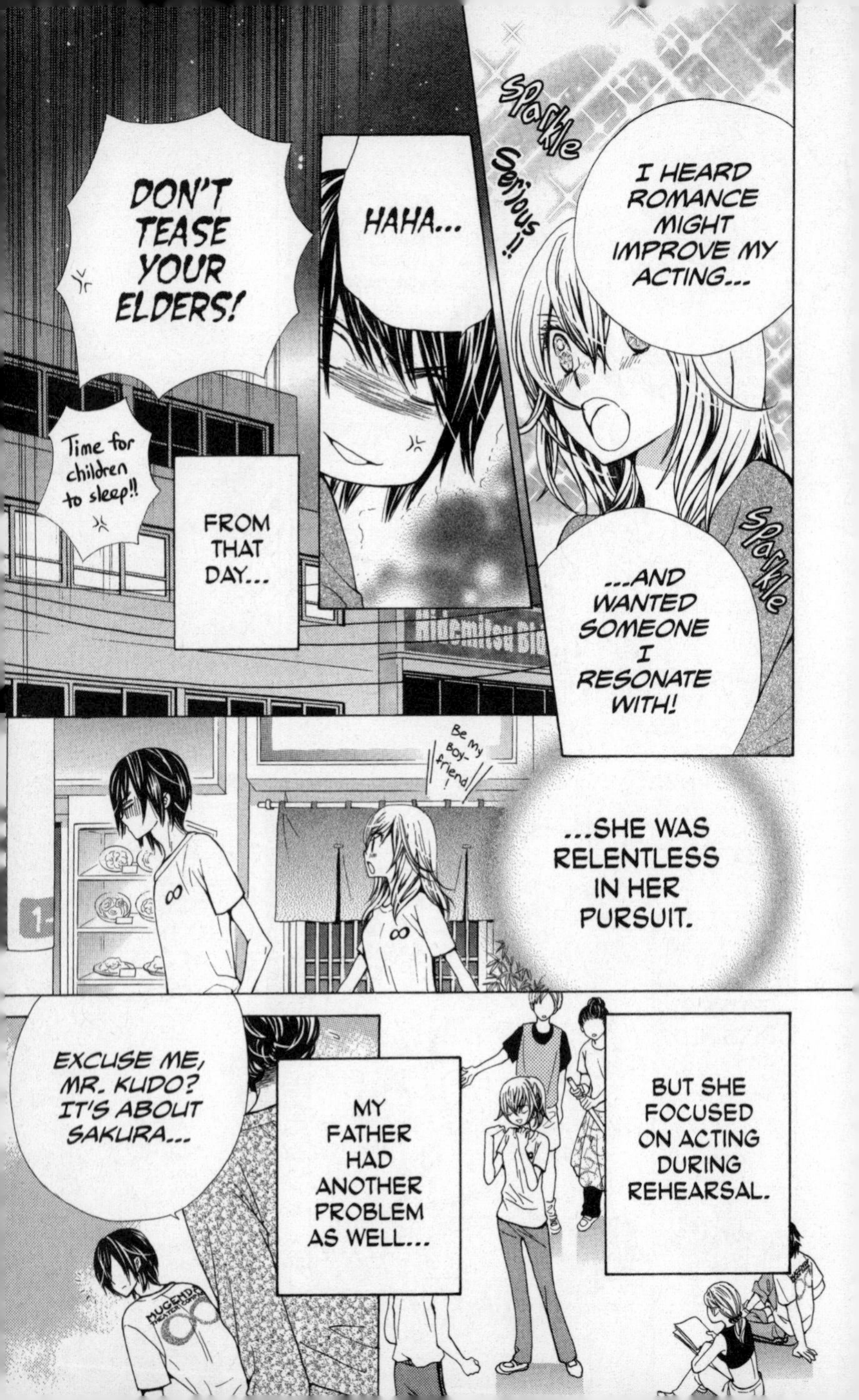
Sparkle
Serious!!
I HEARD ROMANCE MIGHT IMPROVE MY ACTING...
Sparkle
...AND WANTED SOMEONE I RESONATE WITH!
HAHA...
DON'T TEASE YOUR ELDERS!
Time for children to sleep!!
FROM THAT DAY...
...SHE WAS RELENTLESS IN HER PURSUIT.
Be my boyfriend!
BUT SHE FOCUSED ON ACTING DURING REHEARSAL.
MY FATHER HAD ANOTHER PROBLEM AS WELL...
EXCUSE ME, MR. KUDO? IT'S ABOUT SAKURA...
MUGENDO

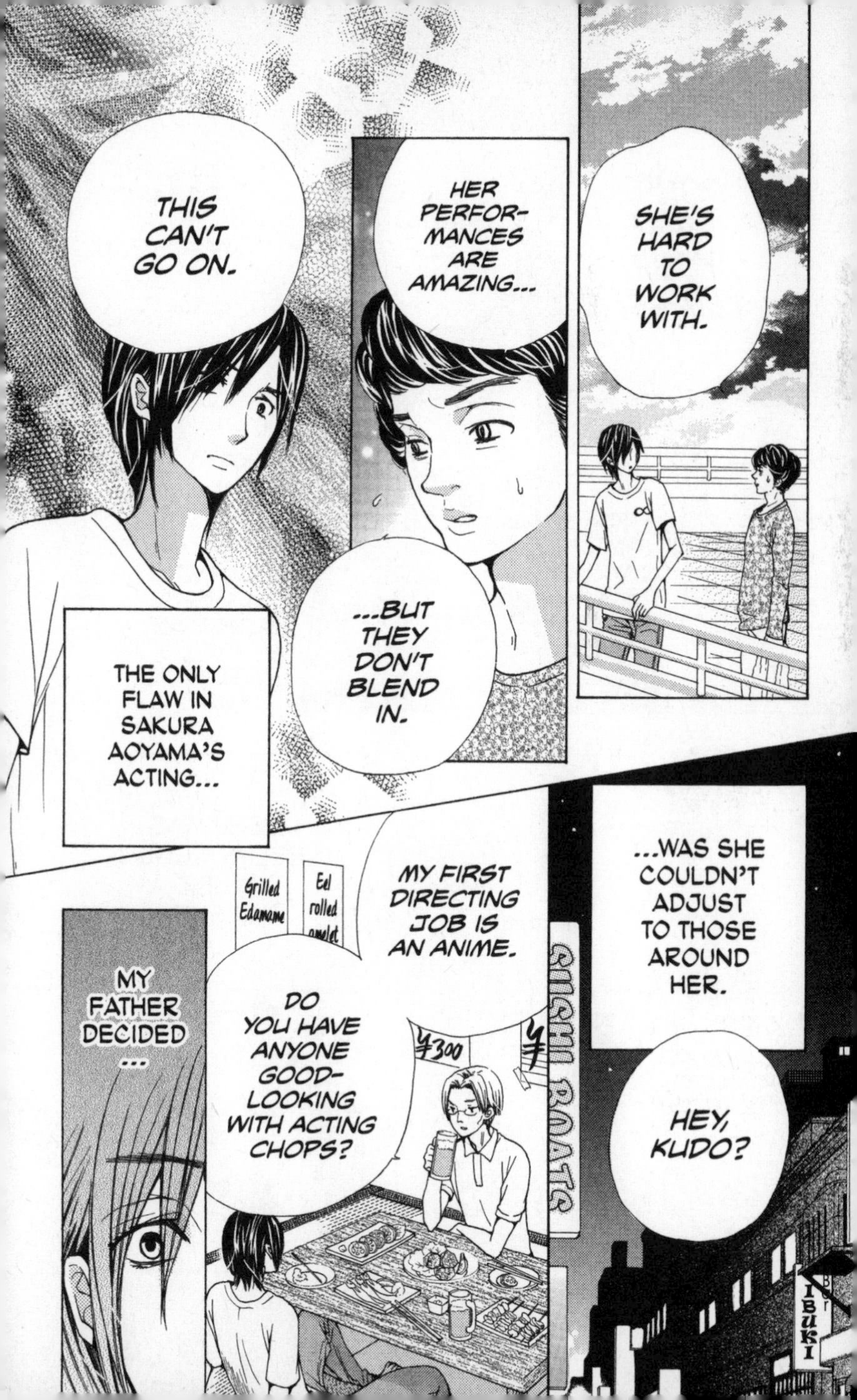
SHE'S HARD TO WORK WITH.
HER PERFOR-MANCES ARE AMAZING...
...BUT THEY DON'T BLEND IN.
THIS CAN'T GO ON.
THE ONLY FLAW IN SAKURA AOYAMA'S ACTING...
...WAS SHE COULDN'T ADJUST TO THOSE AROUND HER.
HEY, KUDO?
IBUKI
SUSHI BOATS
MY FIRST DIRECTING JOB IS AN ANIME.
DO YOU HAVE ANYONE GOOD-LOOKING WITH ACTING CHOPS?
¥300
Grilled Edamame
Eel rolled
MY FATHER DECIDED ...

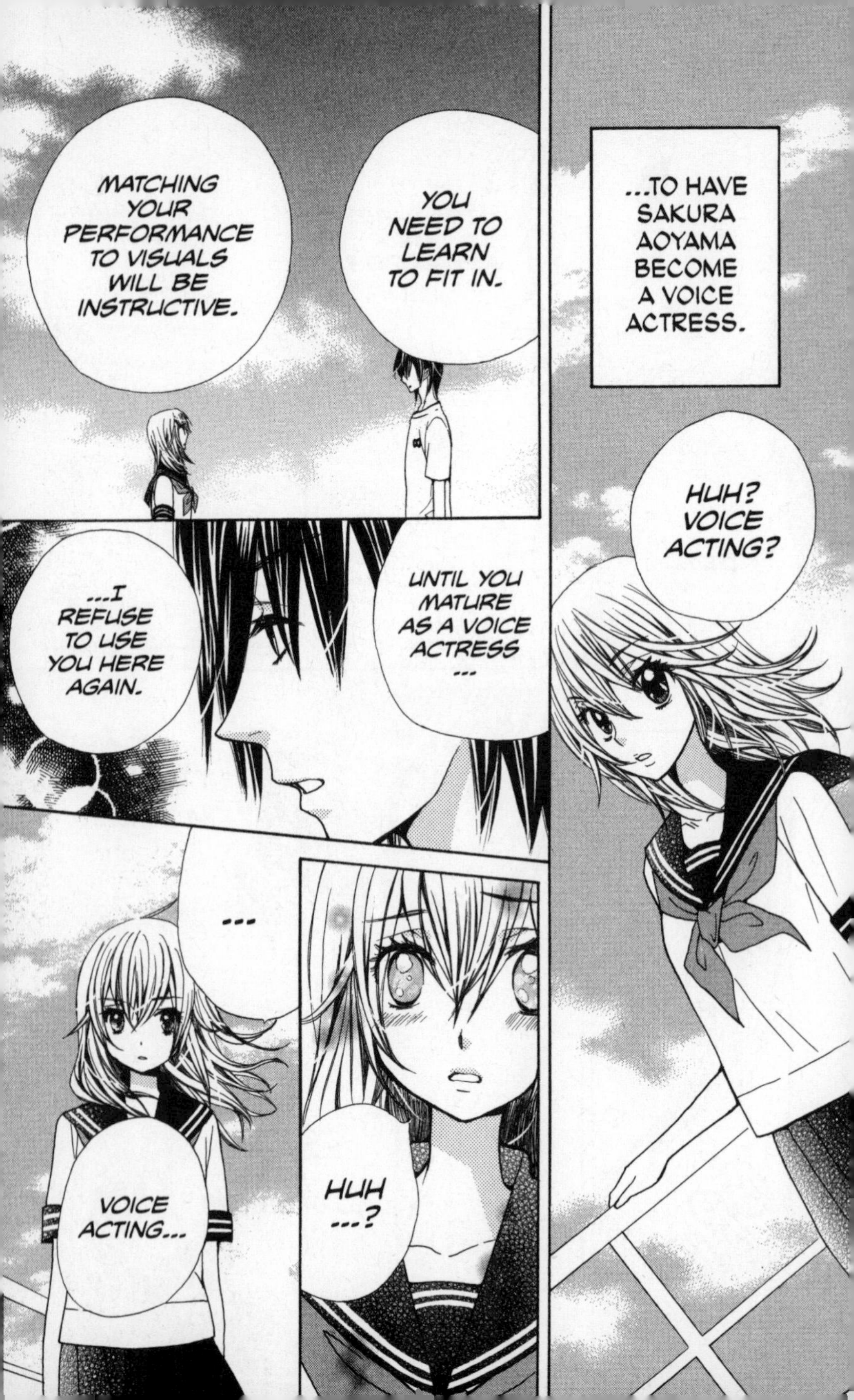
...TO HAVE SAKURA AOYAMA BECOME A VOICE ACTRESS.
HUH? VOICE ACTING?
YOU NEED TO LEARN TO FIT IN.
MATCHING YOUR PERFORMANCE TO VISUALS WILL BE INSTRUCTIVE.
UNTIL YOU MATURE AS A VOICE ACTRESS ...
...I REFUSE TO USE YOU HERE AGAIN.
HUH ...?
...
VOICE ACTING...

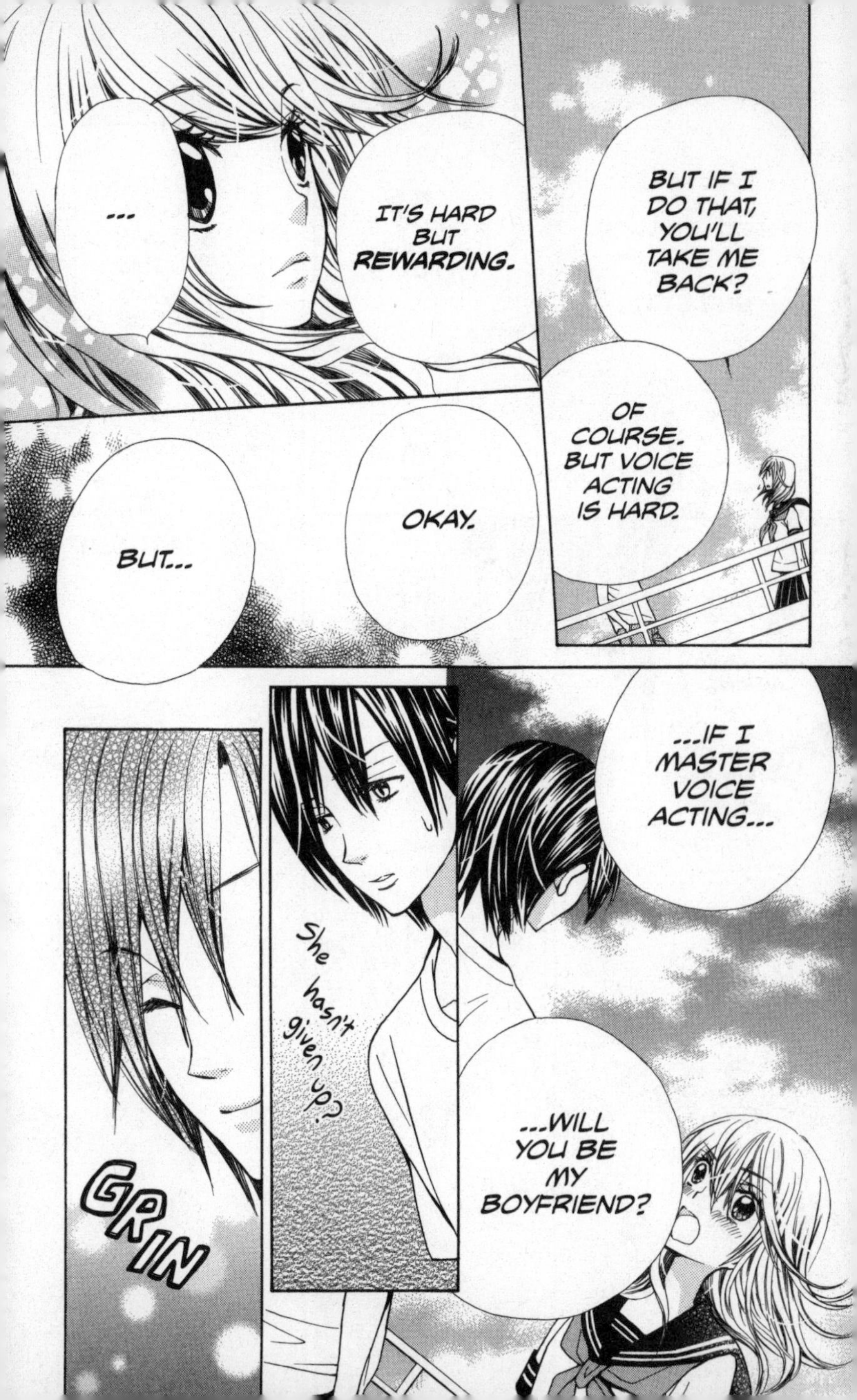
BUT IF I DO THAT, YOU'LL TAKE ME BACK?
OF COURSE. BUT VOICE ACTING IS HARD.
IT'S HARD BUT REWARDING.
...
OKAY.
BUT...
...IF I MASTER VOICE ACTING...
...WILL YOU BE MY BOYFRIEND?
She hasn't given up?
GRIN

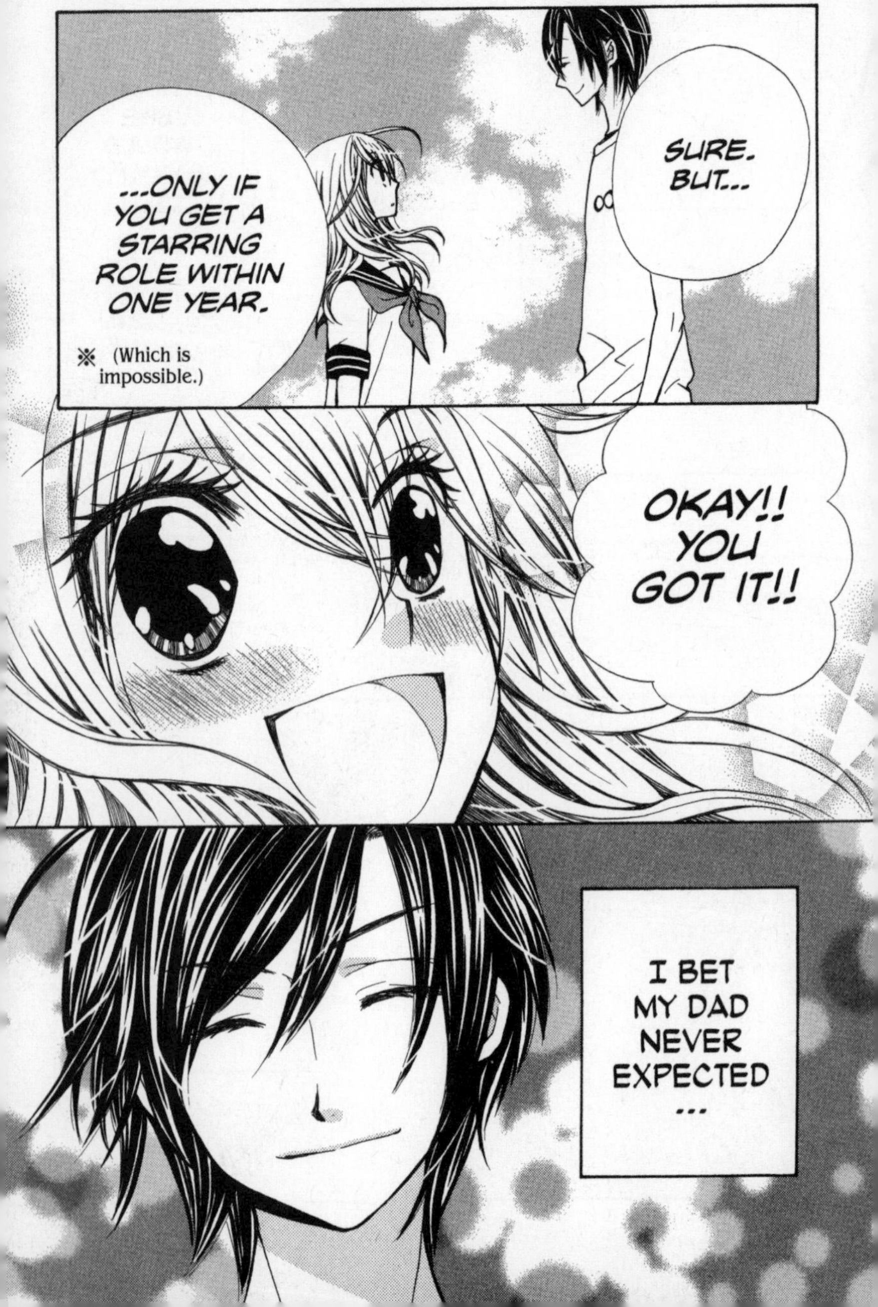
SURE. BUT...
...ONLY IF YOU GET A STARRING ROLE WITHIN ONE YEAR.
※ (Which is impossible.)
OKAY!! YOU GOT IT!!
I BET MY DAD NEVER EXPECTED ...

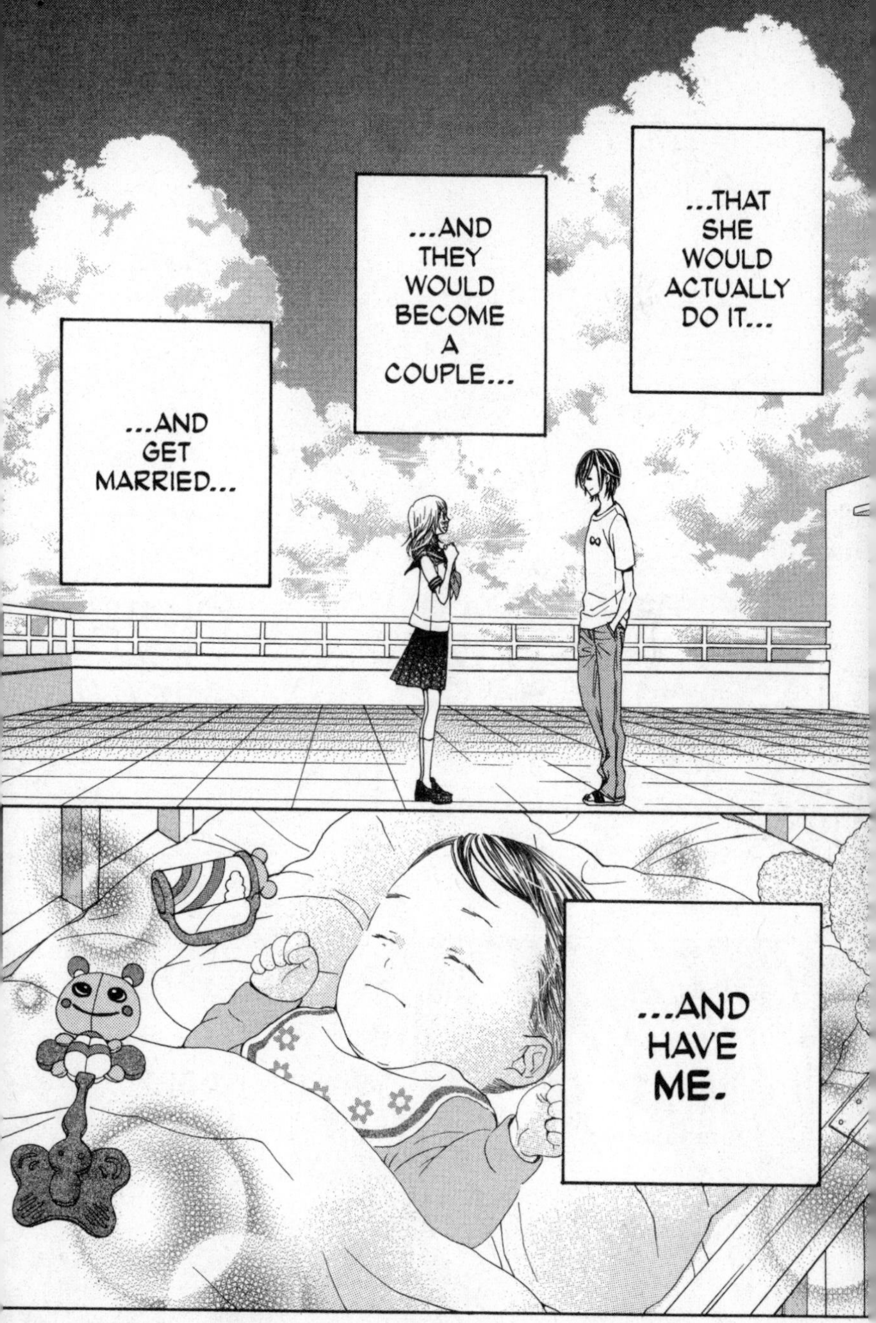
...THAT SHE WOULD ACTUALLY DO IT...
...AND THEY WOULD BECOME A COUPLE...
...AND GET MARRIED...
...AND HAVE **ME**.

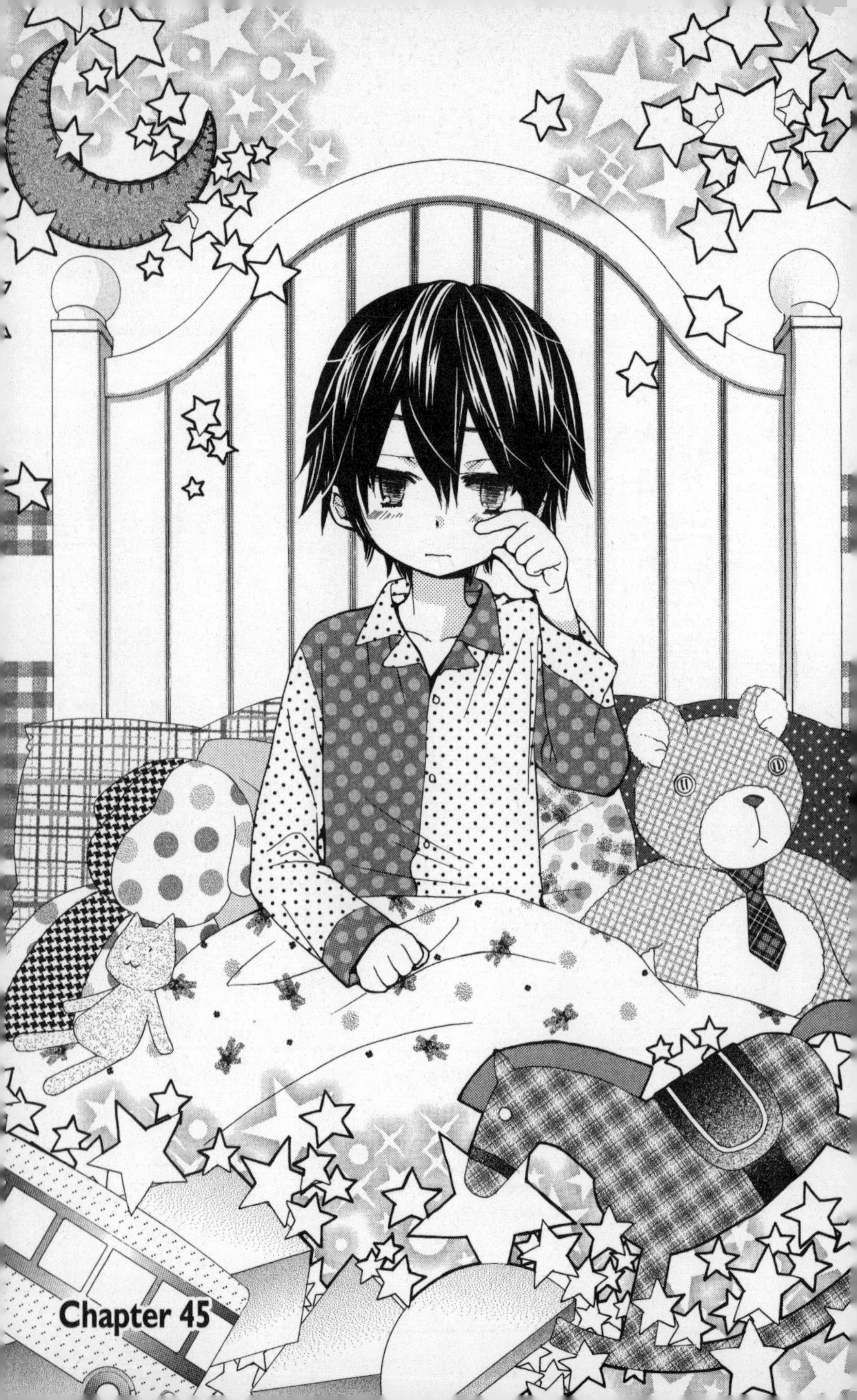
Chapter 45

chirp

WHEN I WAS LITTLE, MY FIRST THOUGHT IN THE MORNING...

...WAS "WHO IS MY MOTHER TODAY?"

chirp

chirp

④ • Things I Can't Help Buying •

I can't help buying material collections for digital graphics. They're like catalogs full of illustrations and patterns, and they're fun to look at. I guess I like looking at things like catalogs. It's fun, right? ♪
And now my bookshelves are out of control... Yep.

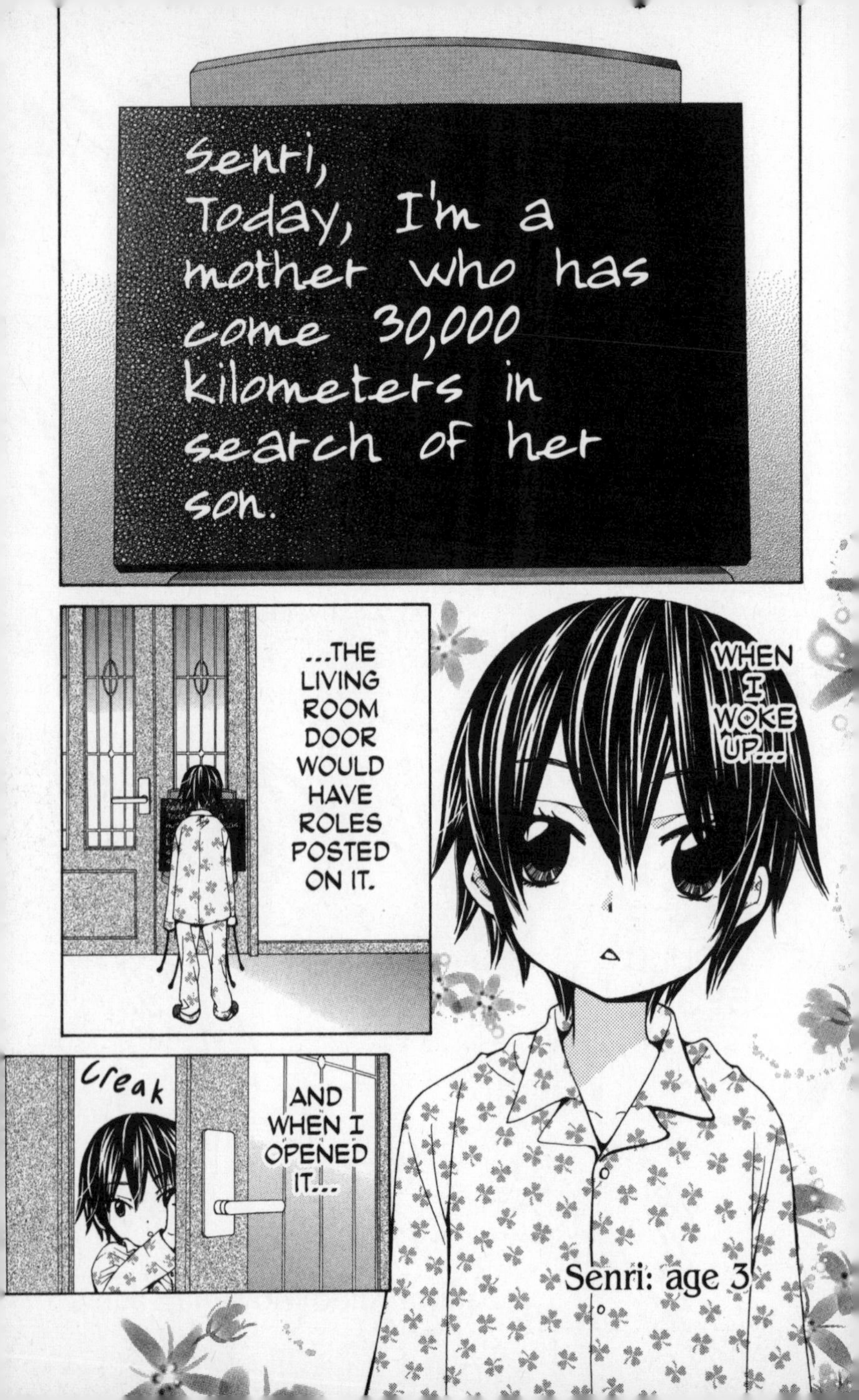
Senri,
Today, I'm a mother who has come 30,000 kilometers in search of her son.
WHEN I WOKE UP...
Senri: age 3
...THE LIVING ROOM DOOR WOULD HAVE ROLES POSTED ON IT.
AND WHEN I OPENED IT...
Creak

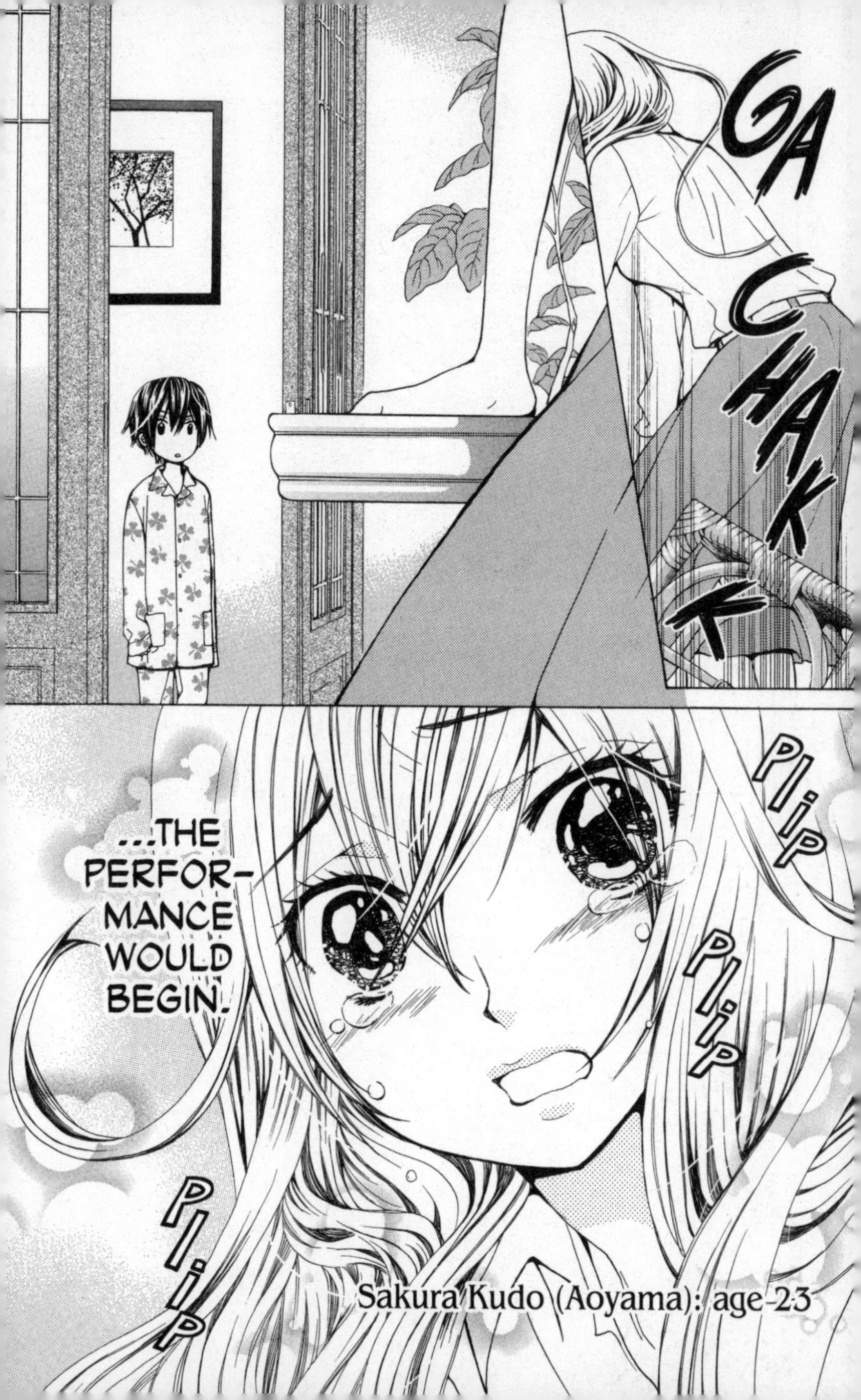
GACHAK
PLIP
...THE PERFORMANCE WOULD BEGIN...
PLIP
PLIP
Sakura Kudo (Aoyama): age 23

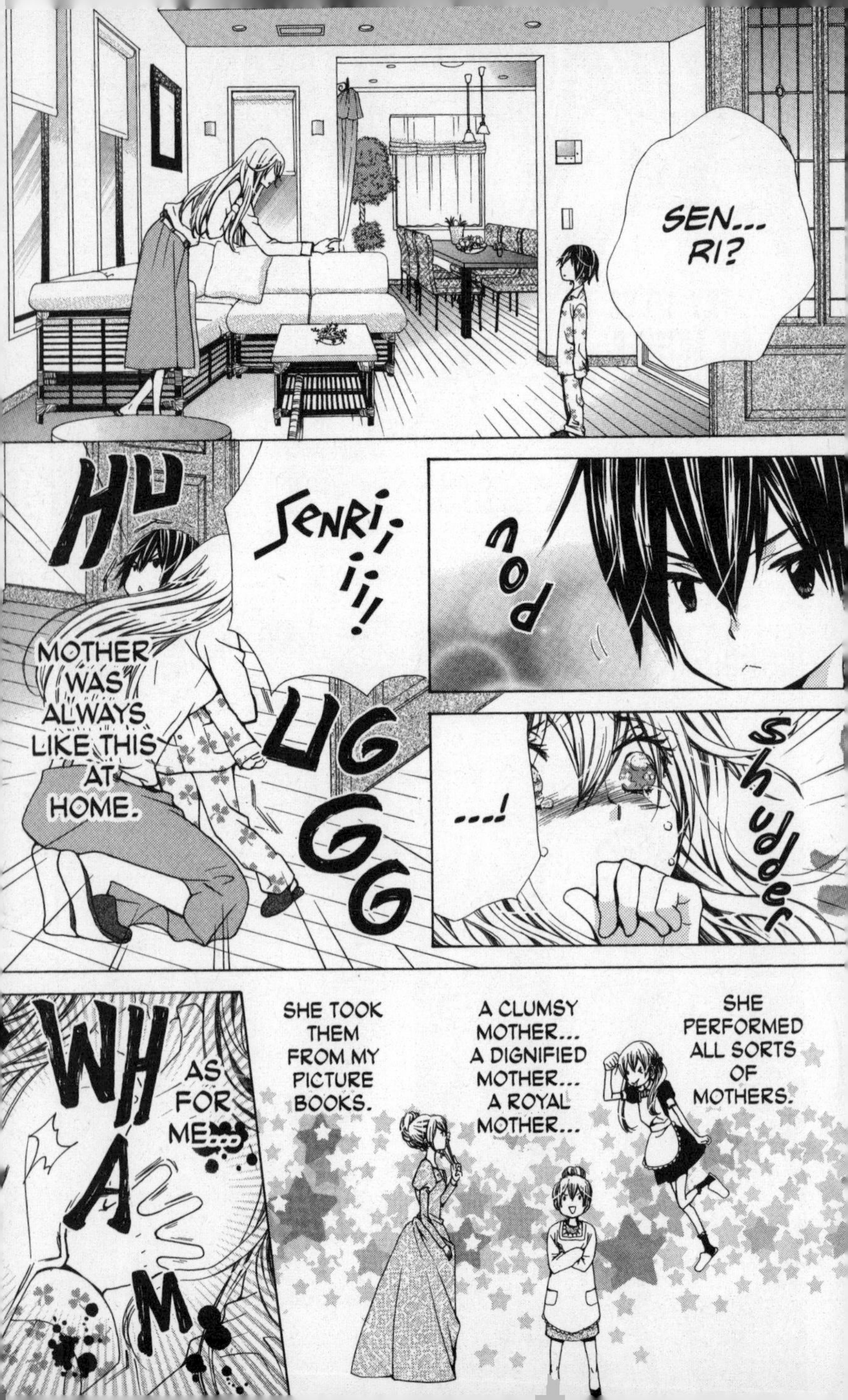
SEN... RI?
pou
...!
shudder
Senriiiii!
HUUGGG
MOTHER WAS ALWAYS LIKE THIS AT HOME.
SHE PERFORMED ALL SORTS OF MOTHERS.
A CLUMSY MOTHER... A DIGNIFIED MOTHER... A ROYAL MOTHER...
SHE TOOK THEM FROM MY PICTURE BOOKS.
AS FOR ME...
WHAM

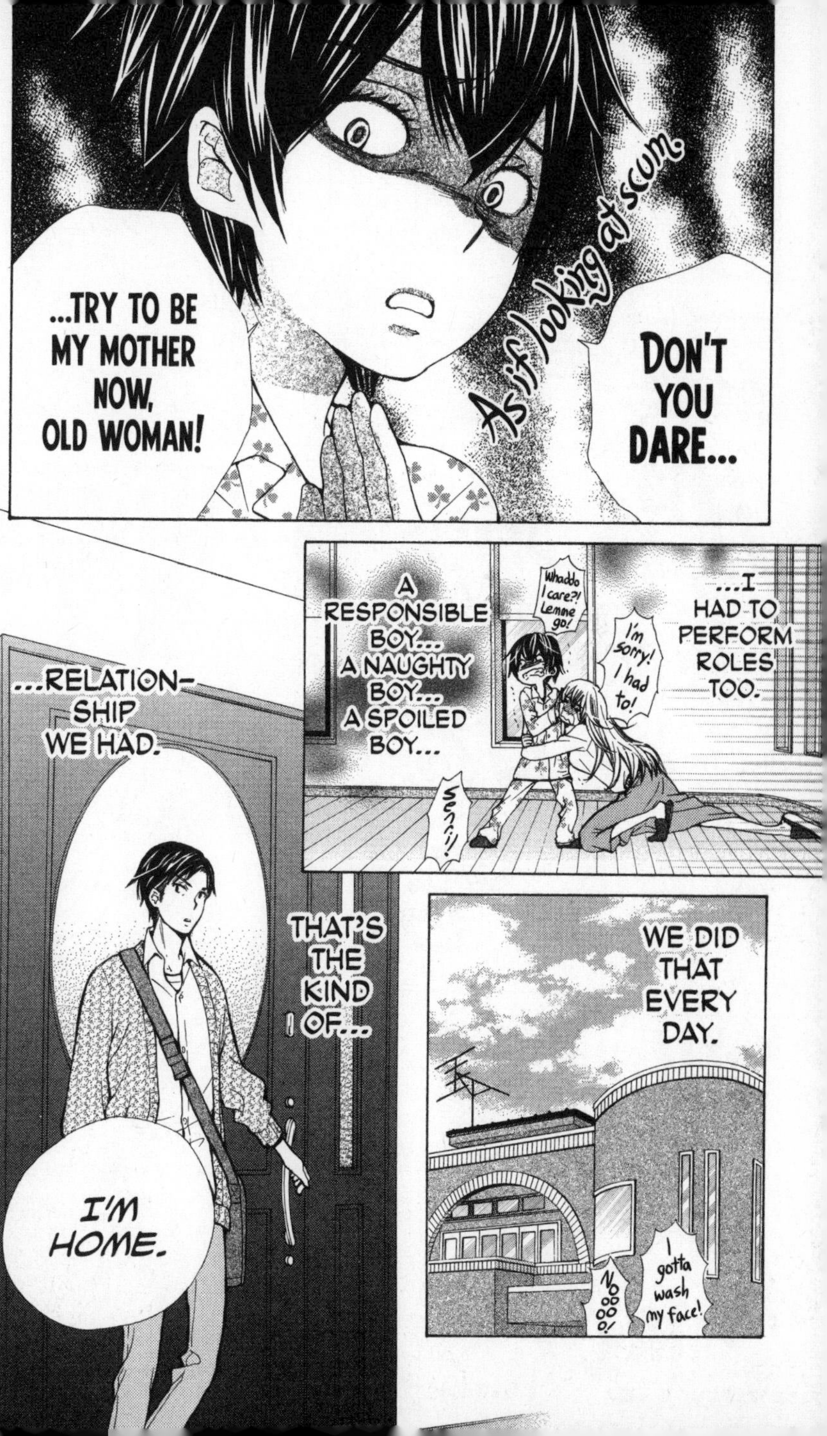
DON'T YOU DARE...
As if looking at scum.
...TRY TO BE MY MOTHER NOW, OLD WOMAN!
...I HAD TO PERFORM ROLES TOO.
I'm sorry! I had to!
Whaddo I care?! Lemme go!
A RESPONSIBLE BOY... A NAUGHTY BOY... A SPOILED BOY...
Senri!
WE DID THAT EVERY DAY.
I gotta wash my face!
Nooooo!
THAT'S THE KIND OF...
...RELATION-SHIP WE HAD.
I'M HOME.

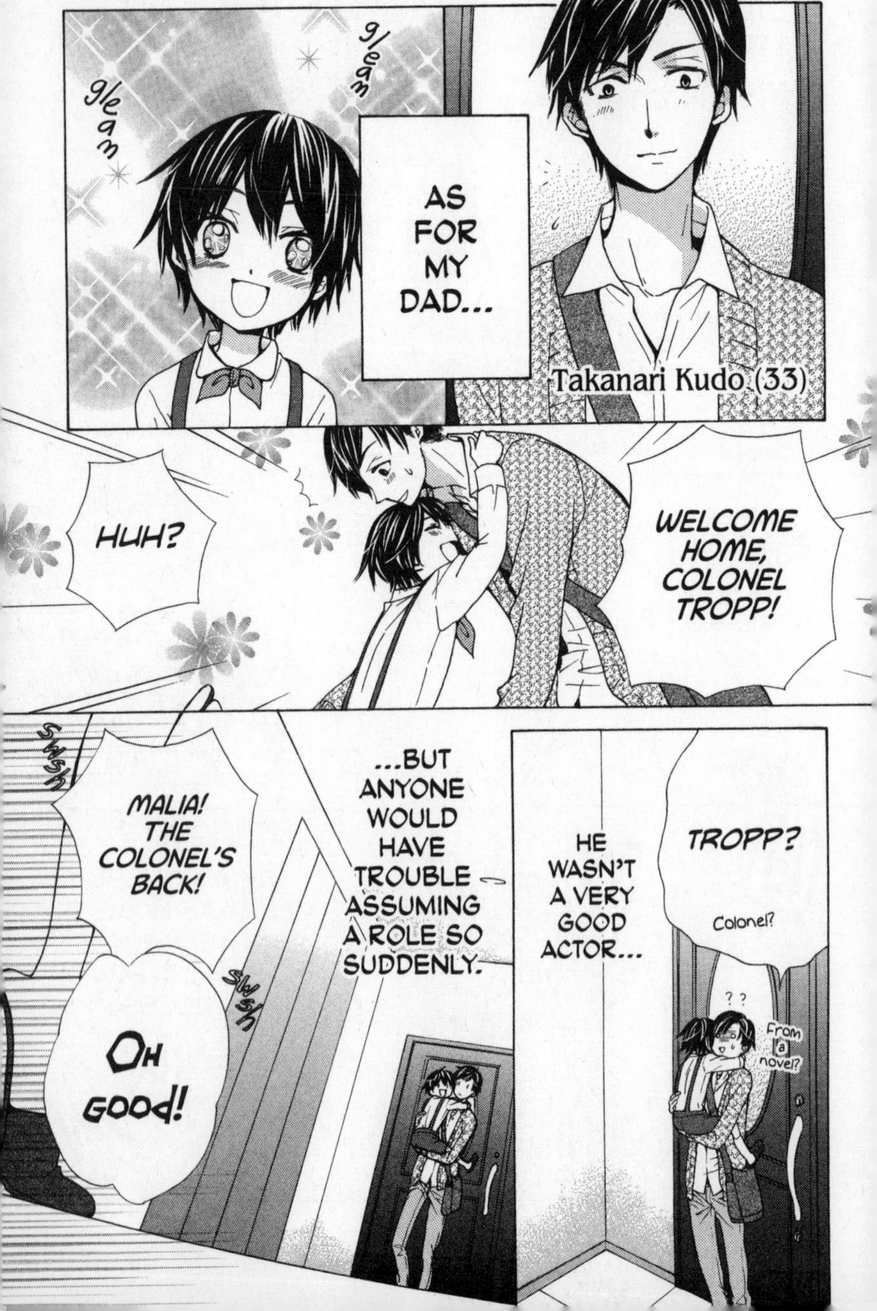
AS FOR MY DAD...
Takanari Kudo (33)
gleam
gleam
WELCOME HOME, COLONEL TROPP!
HUH?
TROPP?
Colonel?
? ?
From a novel?
HE WASN'T A VERY GOOD ACTOR...
...BUT ANYONE WOULD HAVE TROUBLE ASSUMING A ROLE SO SUDDENLY.
MALIA! THE COLONEL'S BACK!
SWSH
SWSH
OH GOOD!

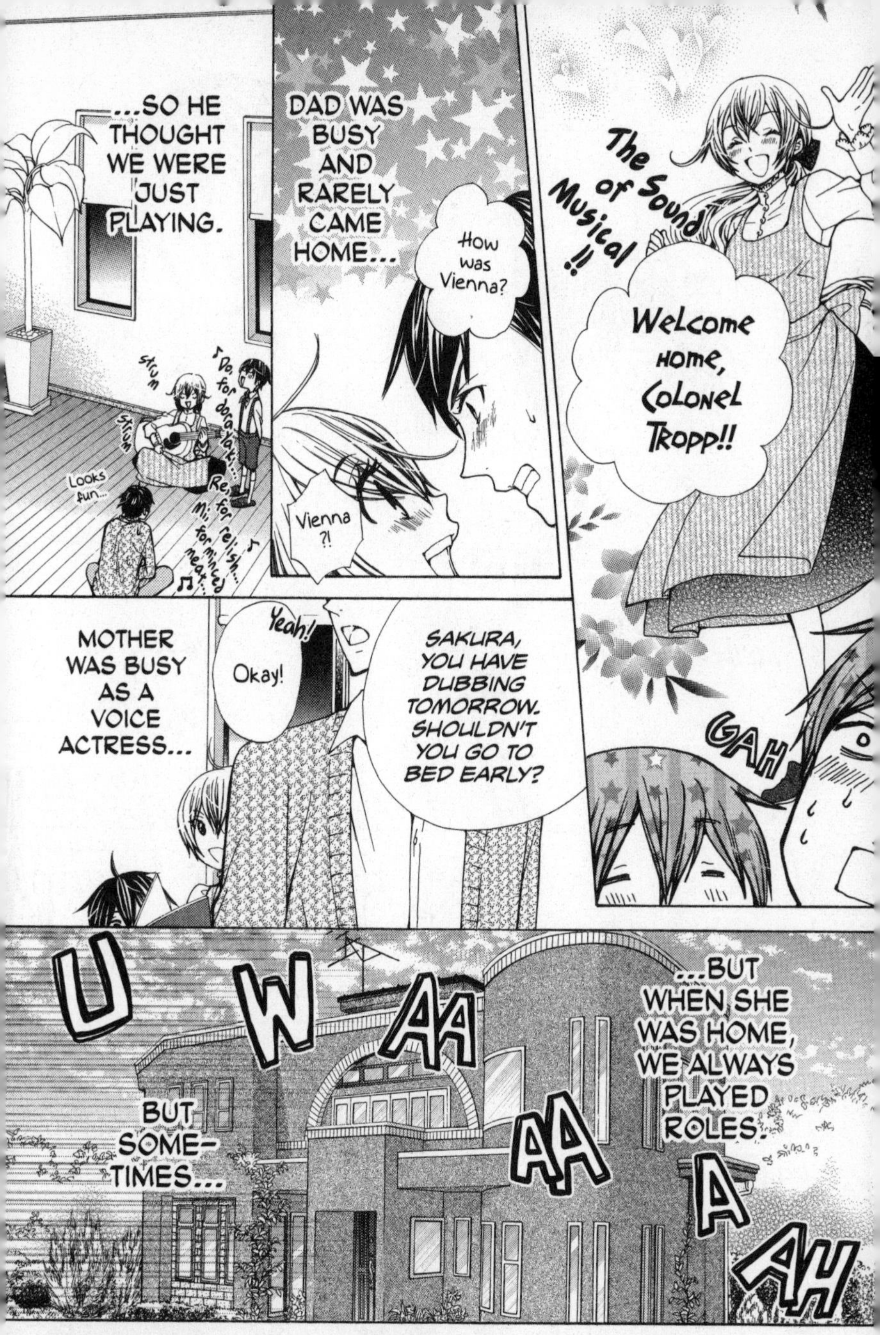
The Sound of Musical!!
Welcome home, Colonel Tropp!!
DAD WAS BUSY AND RARELY CAME HOME...
How was Vienna?
Vienna?!
...SO HE THOUGHT WE WERE JUST PLAYING.
strum
strum
♪Do, for dorayaki... Re, for relish... Mi, for minced meat...♪
Looks fun...
GAH
SAKURA, YOU HAVE DUBBING TOMORROW. SHOULDN'T YOU GO TO BED EARLY?
Yeah!
Okay!
MOTHER WAS BUSY AS A VOICE ACTRESS...
...BUT WHEN SHE WAS HOME, WE ALWAYS PLAYED ROLES.
UWAAAAAAH
BUT SOMETIMES...

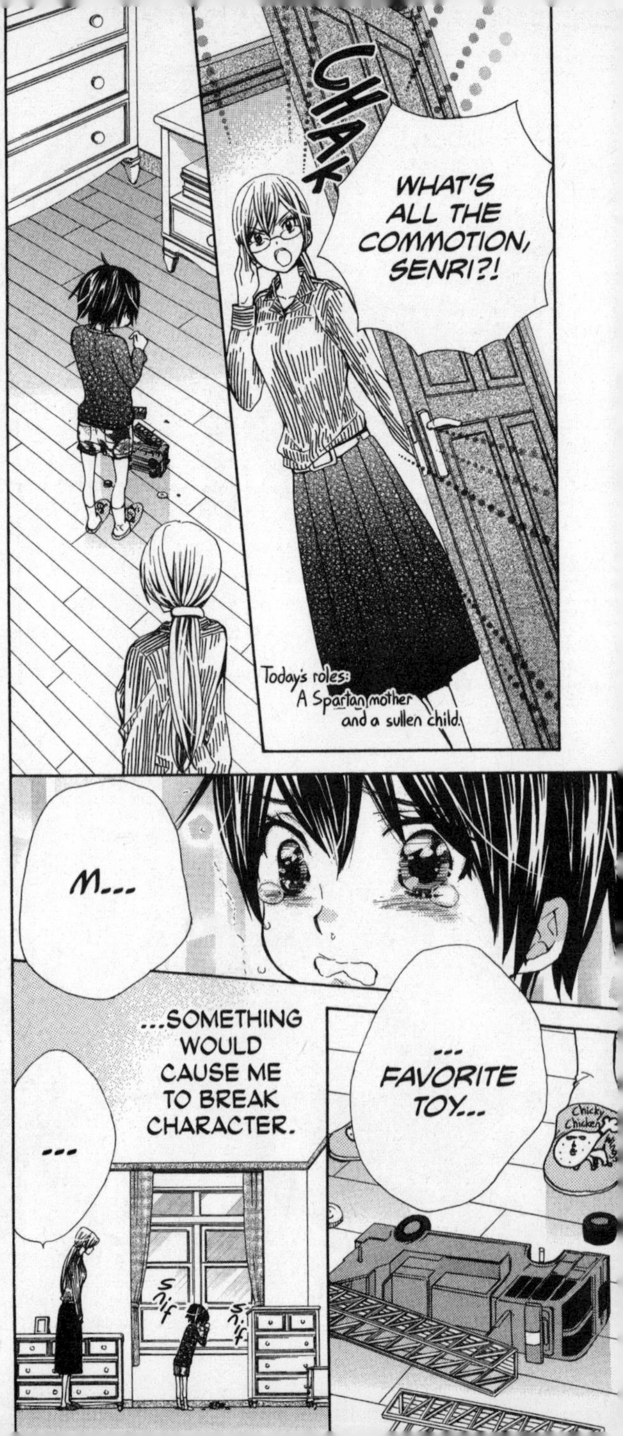
CHAK
WHAT'S ALL THE COMMOTION, SENRI?!
Today's roles: A Spartan mother and a sullen child.
M...
... FAVORITE TOY...
Chicky Chicken
...SOMETHING WOULD CAUSE ME TO BREAK CHARACTER.
...
snif
snif

Culture Festival ⑤

I went to the culture festival at a technical school where a friend lectures.

They had a "Paradise Road."

Kara-age Yakisoba

My friend lectures about manga, so I talked to the students.

They were all bright and perky. Their love for manga warmed my heart. I realized I should make sure never to lose my initial enthusiasm. Yep.

I have much to learn!

I also get letters from people trying to become voice actors and so forth. You all positively shine! I hope it goes well for everyone searching for their dream and facing various worries. I'll work hard, too. You encourage me!

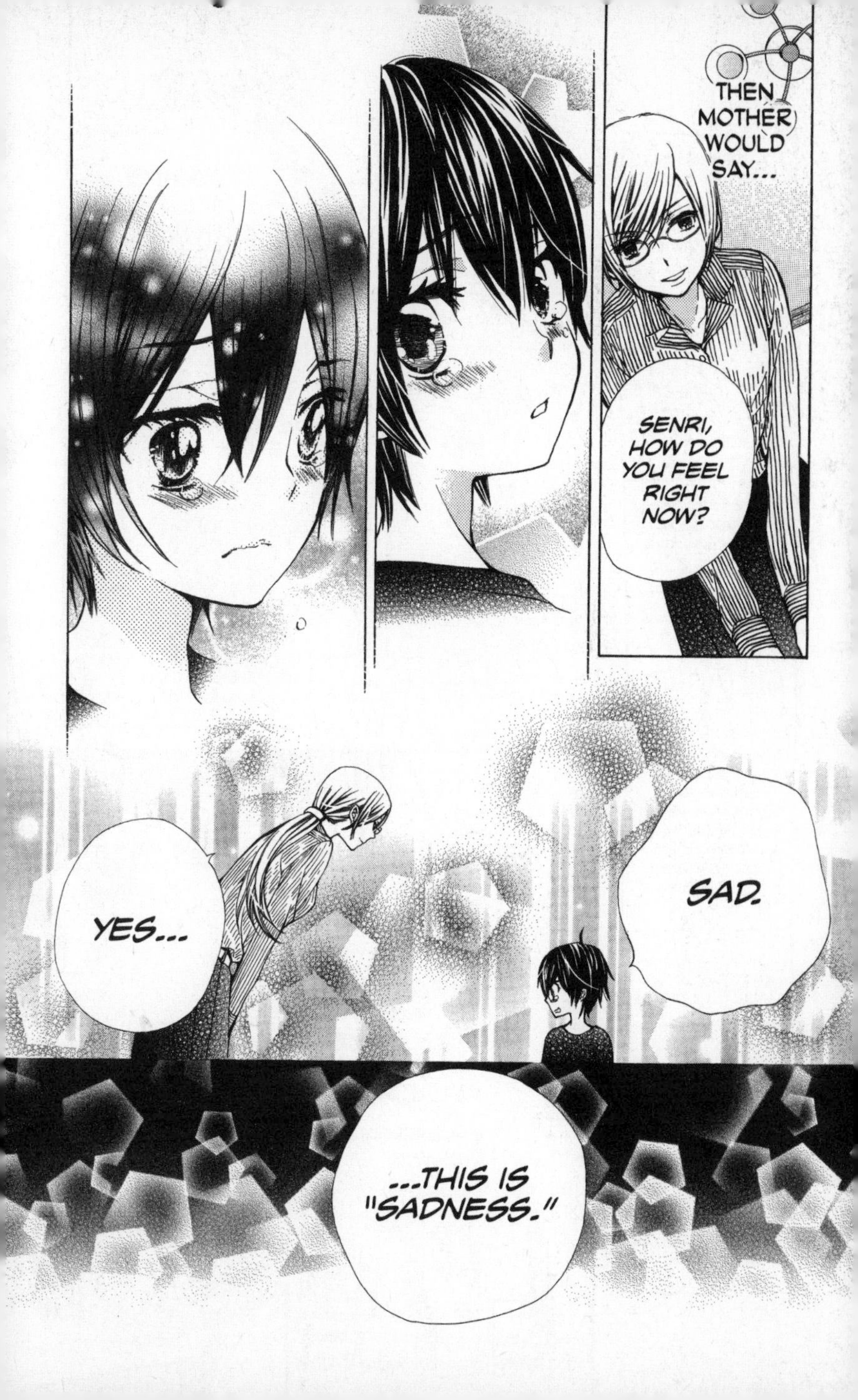
THEN MOTHER WOULD SAY...
SENRI, HOW DO YOU FEEL RIGHT NOW?
SAD.
YES...
...THIS IS "SADNESS."

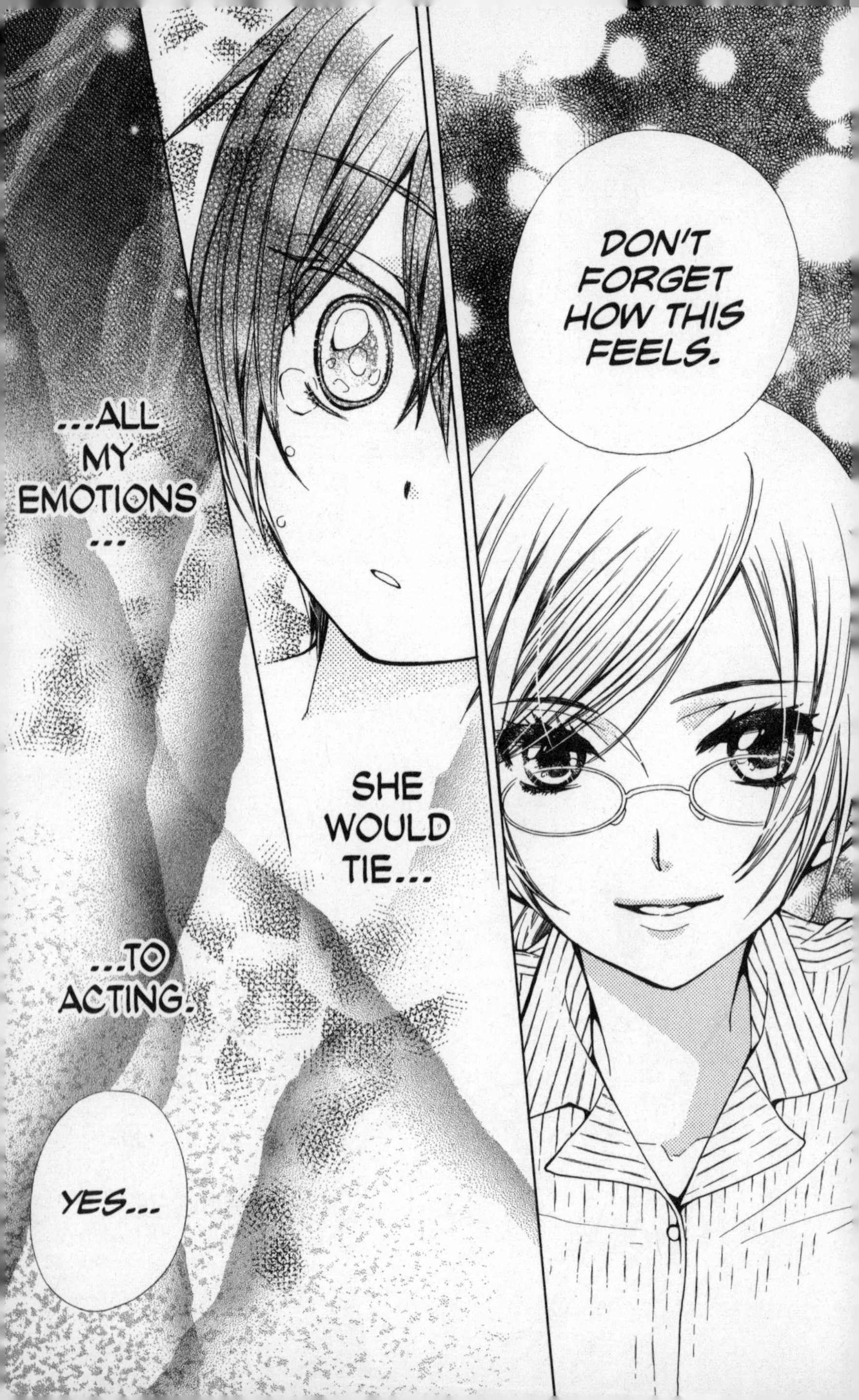
DON'T FORGET HOW THIS FEELS.
SHE WOULD TIE...
...ALL MY EMOTIONS ...
...TO ACTING.
YES...

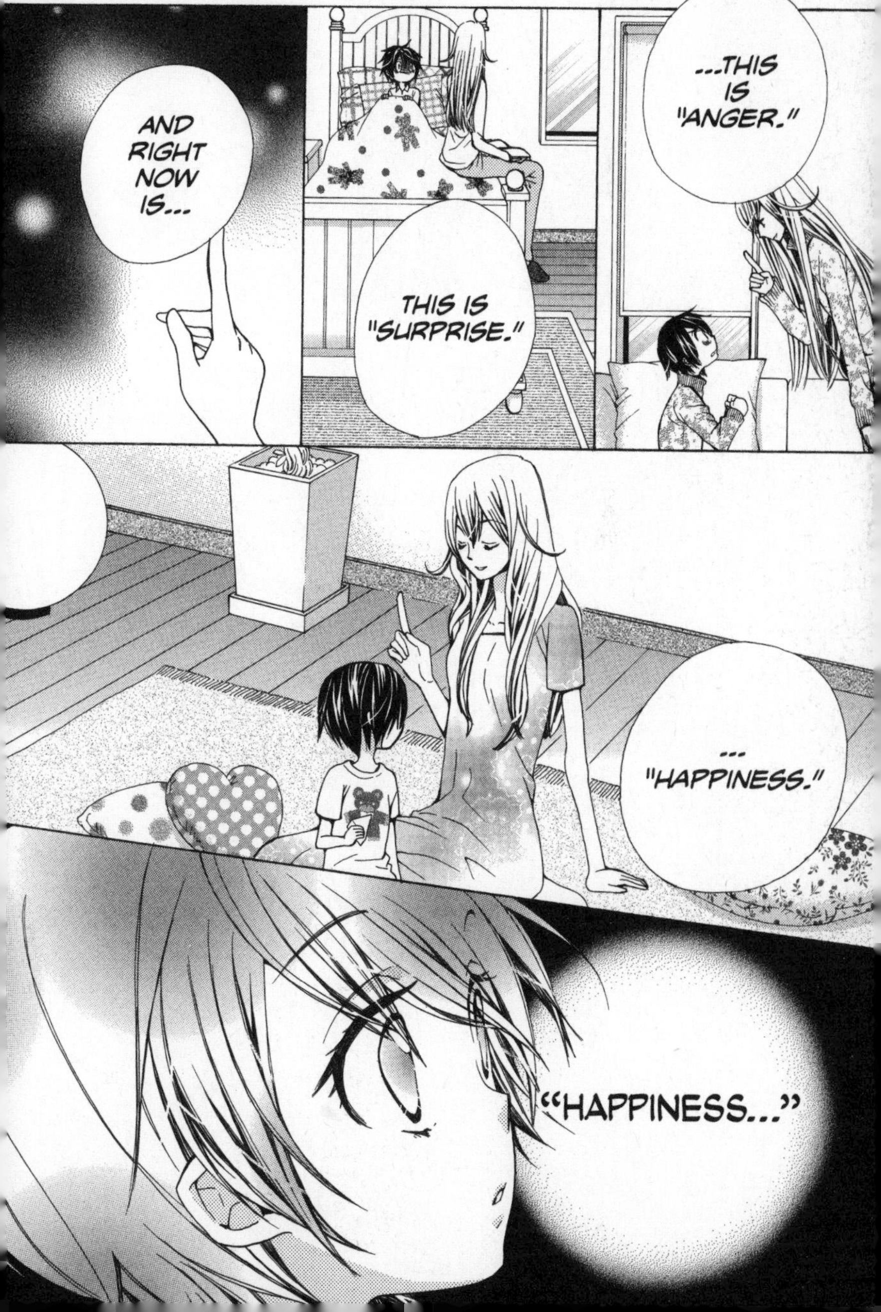
...THIS IS "ANGER."
THIS IS "SURPRISE."
AND RIGHT NOW IS...
... "HAPPINESS."
"HAPPINESS..."

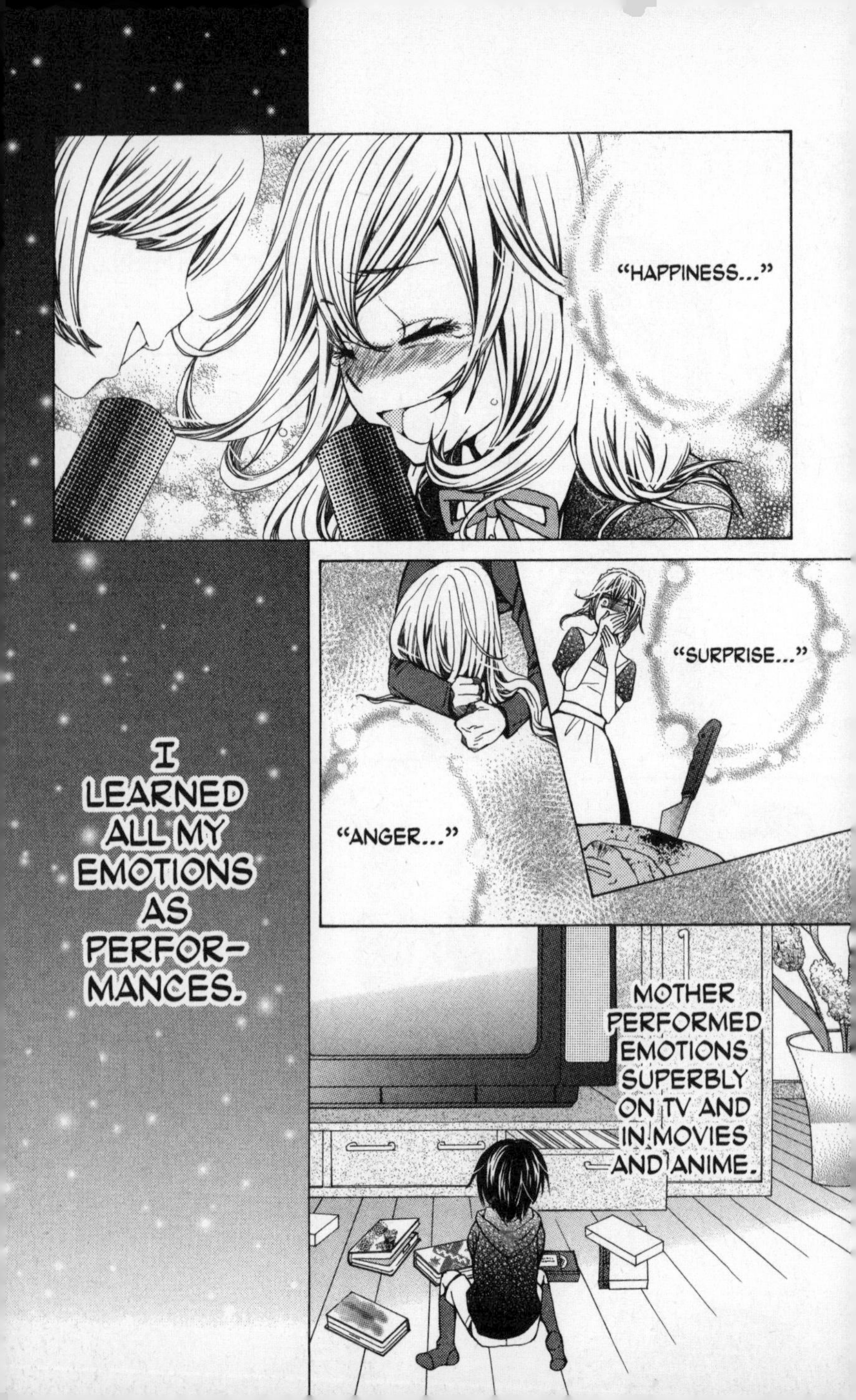
"HAPPINESS..."
"SURPRISE..."
"ANGER..."
MOTHER PERFORMED EMOTIONS SUPERBLY ON TV AND IN MOVIES AND ANIME.
I LEARNED ALL MY EMOTIONS AS PERFOR-MANCES.

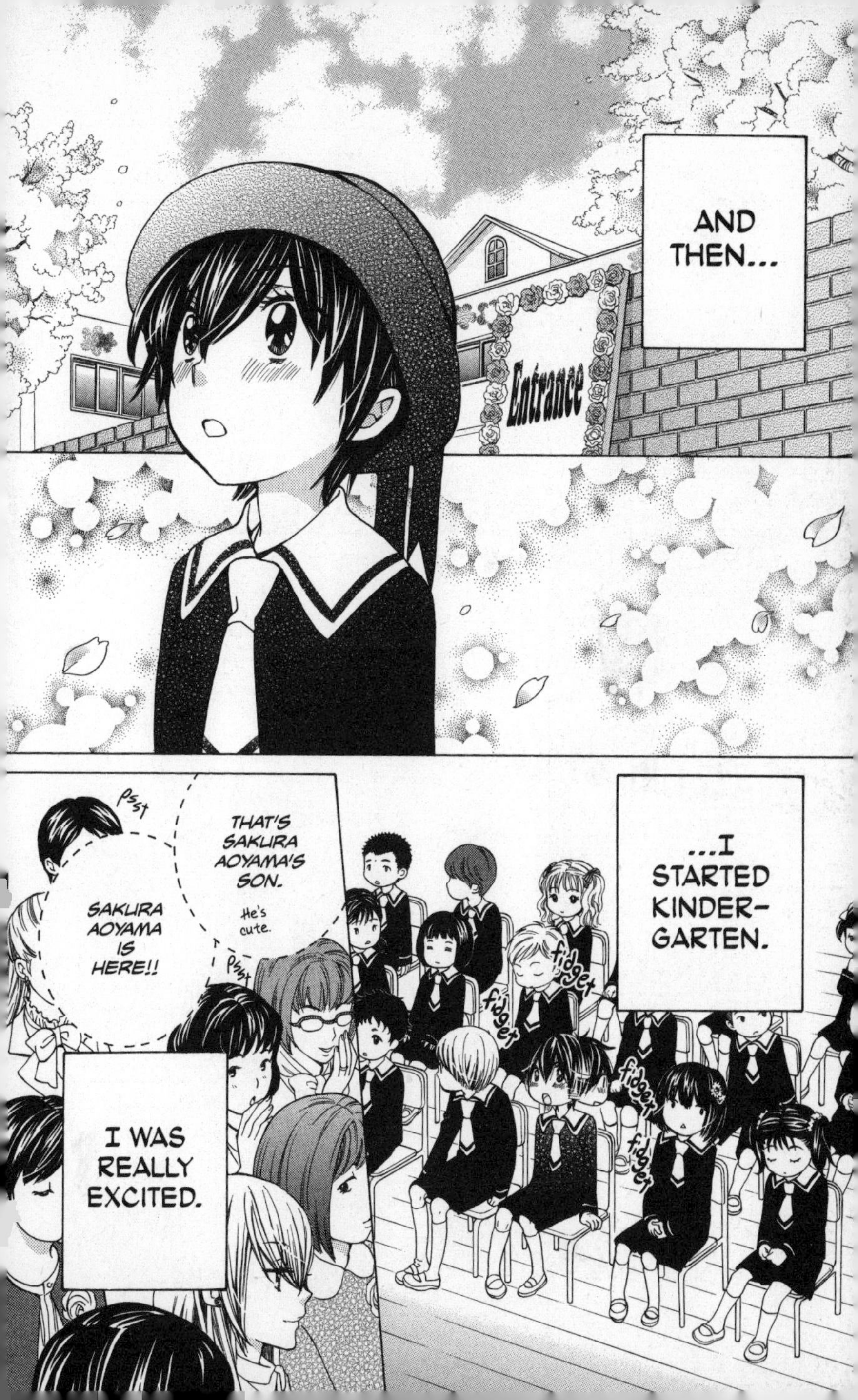
AND THEN...
Entrance
...I STARTED KINDER-GARTEN.
THAT'S SAKURA AOYAMA'S SON.
He's cute.
psst
SAKURA AOYAMA IS HERE!!
psst
fidget
fidget
fidget
fidget
I WAS REALLY EXCITED.

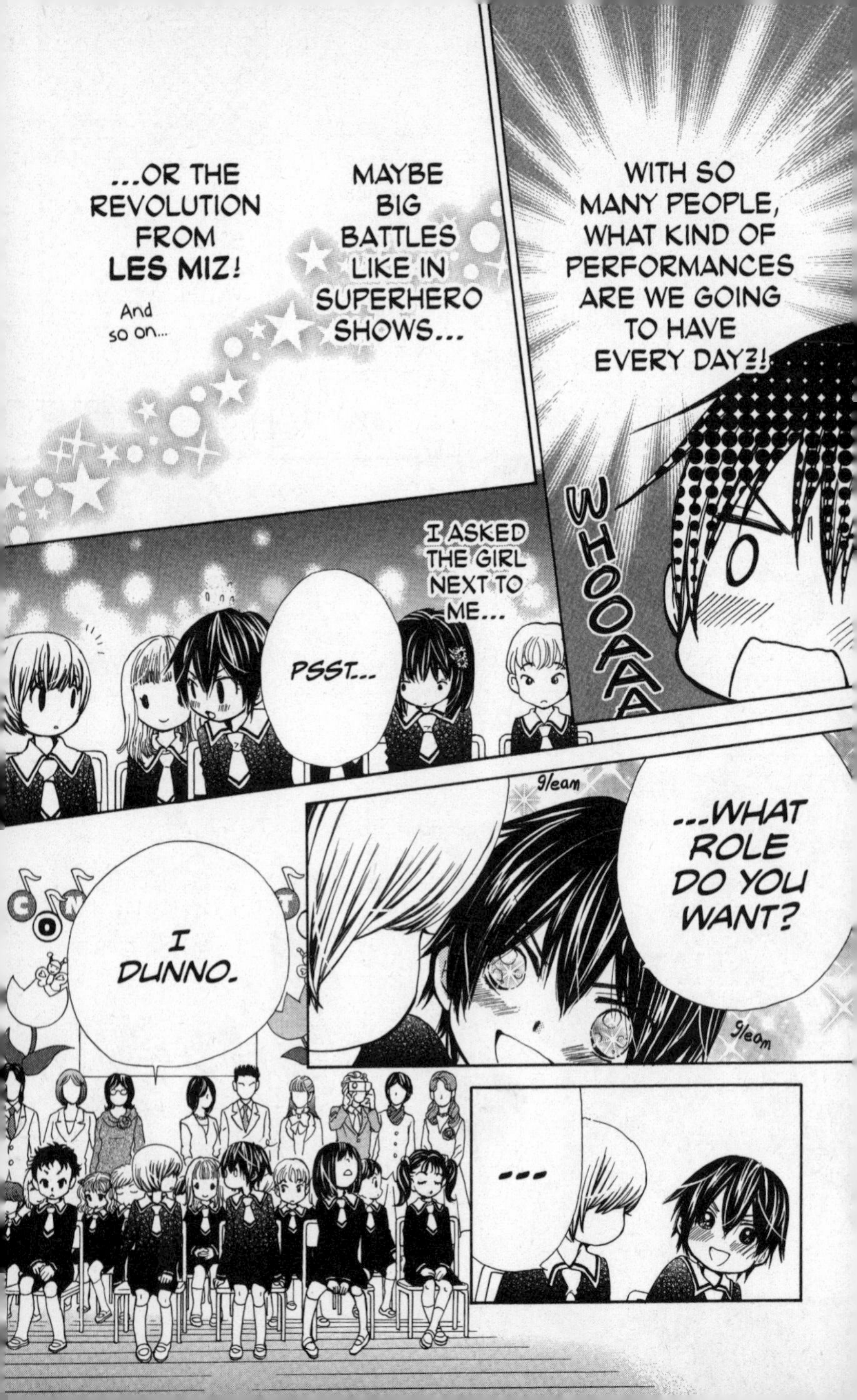
WITH SO MANY PEOPLE, WHAT KIND OF PERFORMANCES ARE WE GOING TO HAVE EVERY DAY?!
WHOOAAA
MAYBE BIG BATTLES LIKE IN SUPERHERO SHOWS...
...OR THE REVOLUTION FROM LES MIZ!
And so on...
I ASKED THE GIRL NEXT TO ME...
PSST...
gleam
...WHAT ROLE DO YOU WANT?
gleam
...
I DUNNO.

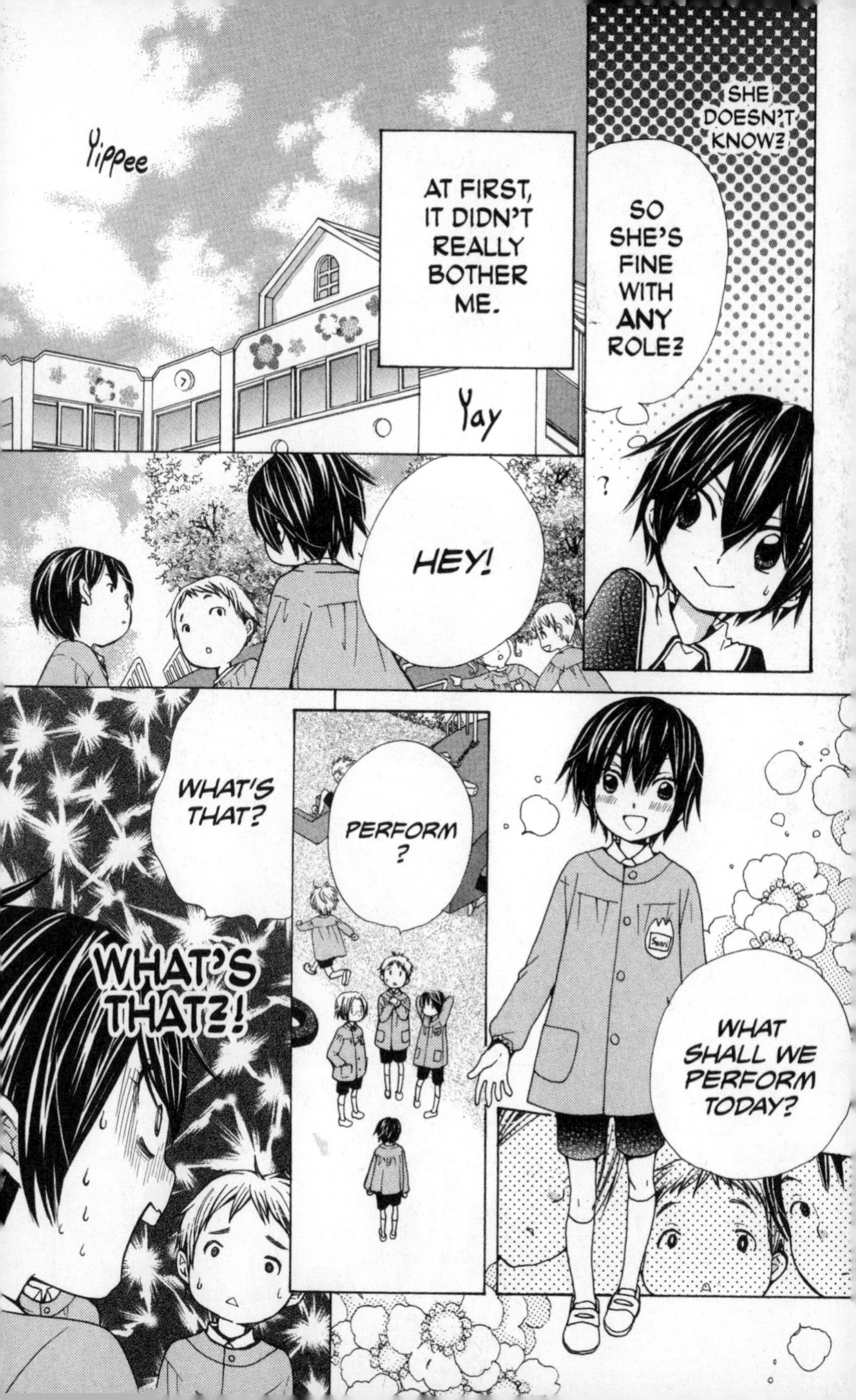
SHE DOESN'T KNOW?
SO SHE'S FINE WITH ANY ROLE?
?
AT FIRST, IT DIDN'T REALLY BOTHER ME.
Yay
Yippee
HEY!
WHAT SHALL WE PERFORM TODAY?
PERFORM?
WHAT'S THAT?
WHAT'S THAT?!

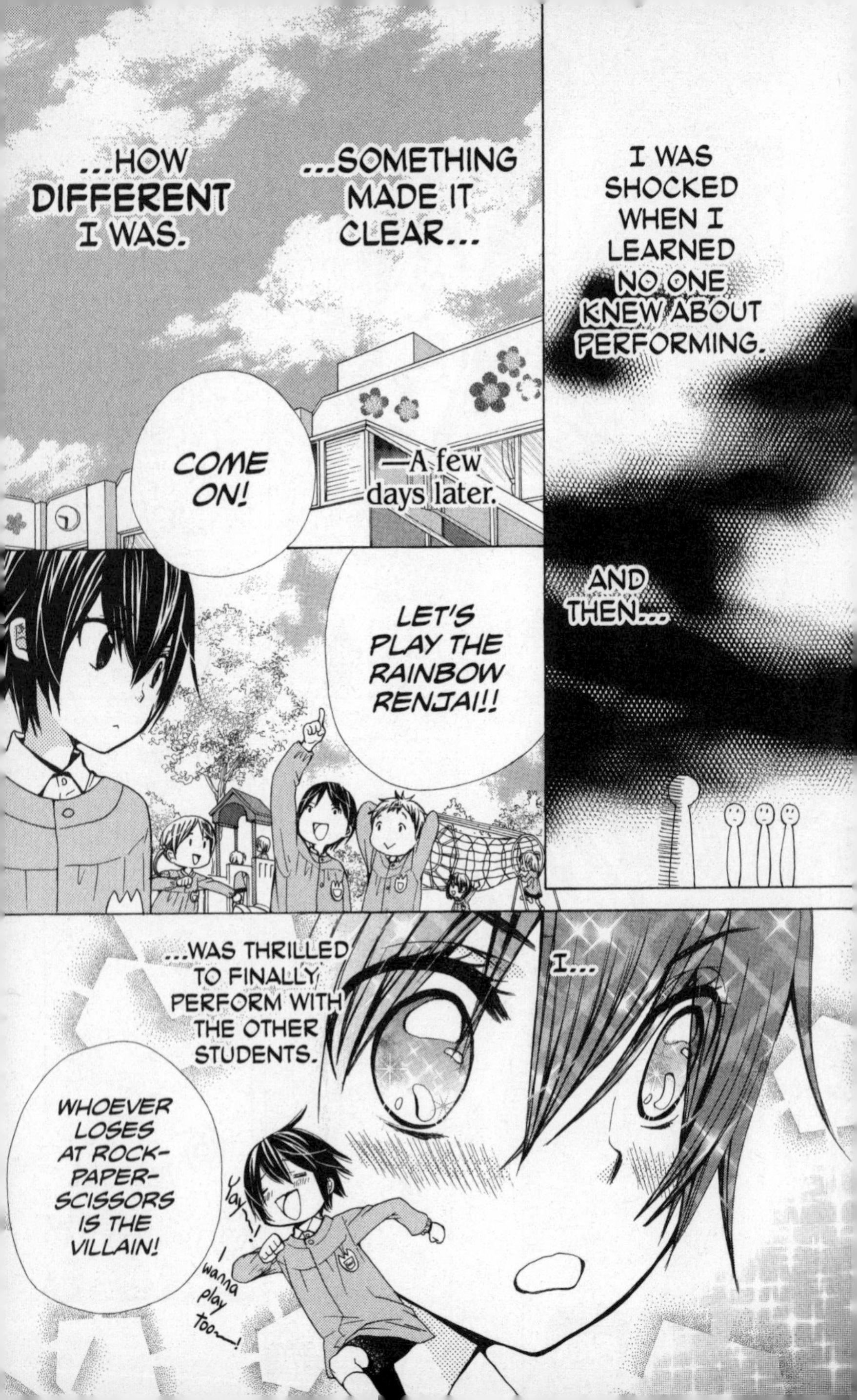
I WAS SHOCKED WHEN I LEARNED NO ONE KNEW ABOUT PERFORMING.
AND THEN...
...SOMETHING MADE IT CLEAR...
...HOW DIFFERENT I WAS.
—A few days later.
COME ON!
LET'S PLAY THE RAINBOW RENJAI!!
I...
...WAS THRILLED TO FINALLY PERFORM WITH THE OTHER STUDENTS.
WHOEVER LOSES AT ROCK-PAPER-SCISSORS IS THE VILLAIN!
Yay~!
I wanna play too~!

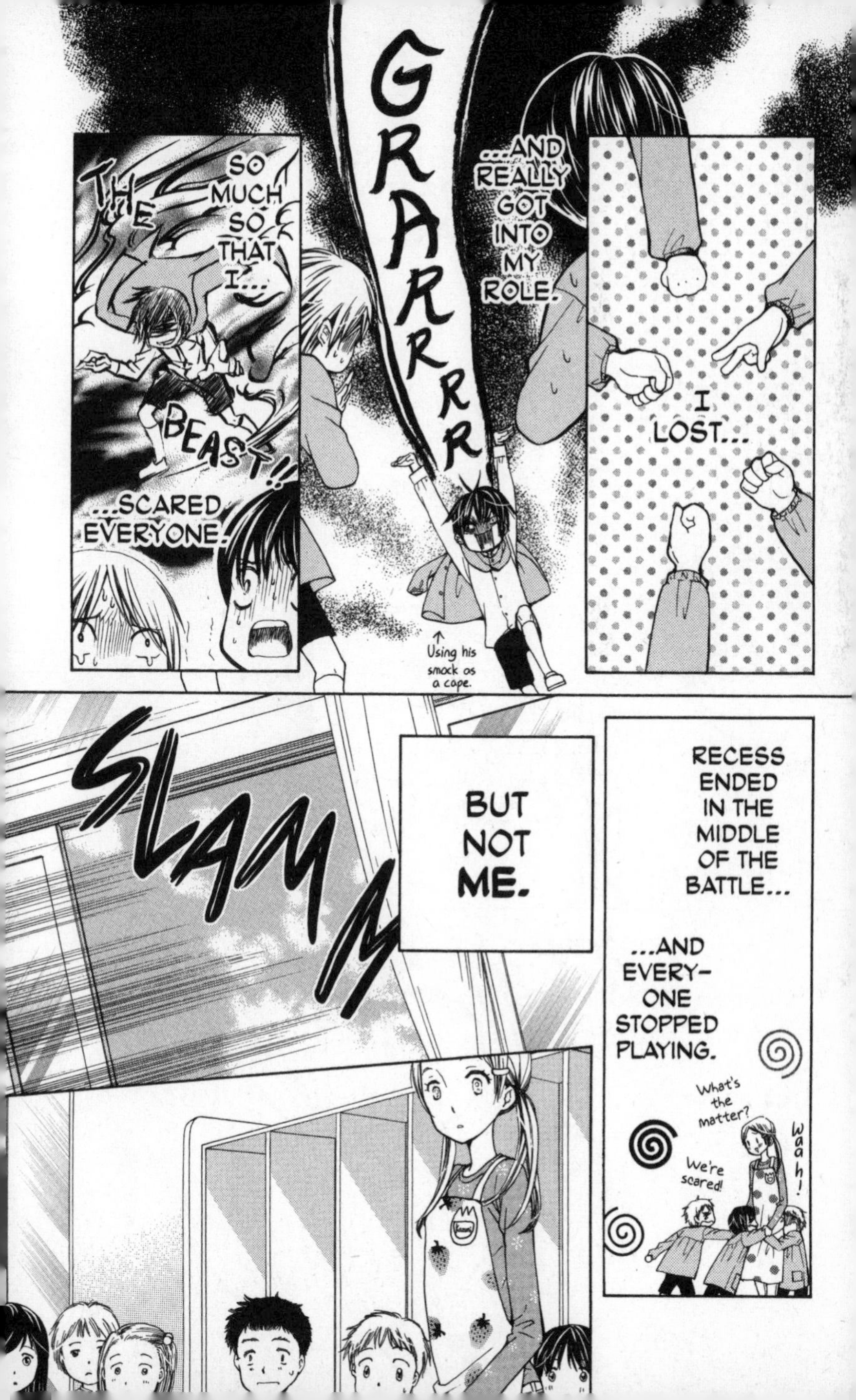
I LOST...
...AND REALLY GOT INTO MY ROLE.
GRARRRR
Using his smock as a cape.
SO MUCH SO THAT I...
THE BEAST!!
...SCARED EVERYONE.
RECESS ENDED IN THE MIDDLE OF THE BATTLE...
...AND EVERY-ONE STOPPED PLAYING.
Waah!
What's the matter?
We're scared!
BUT NOT ME.
SLAMM

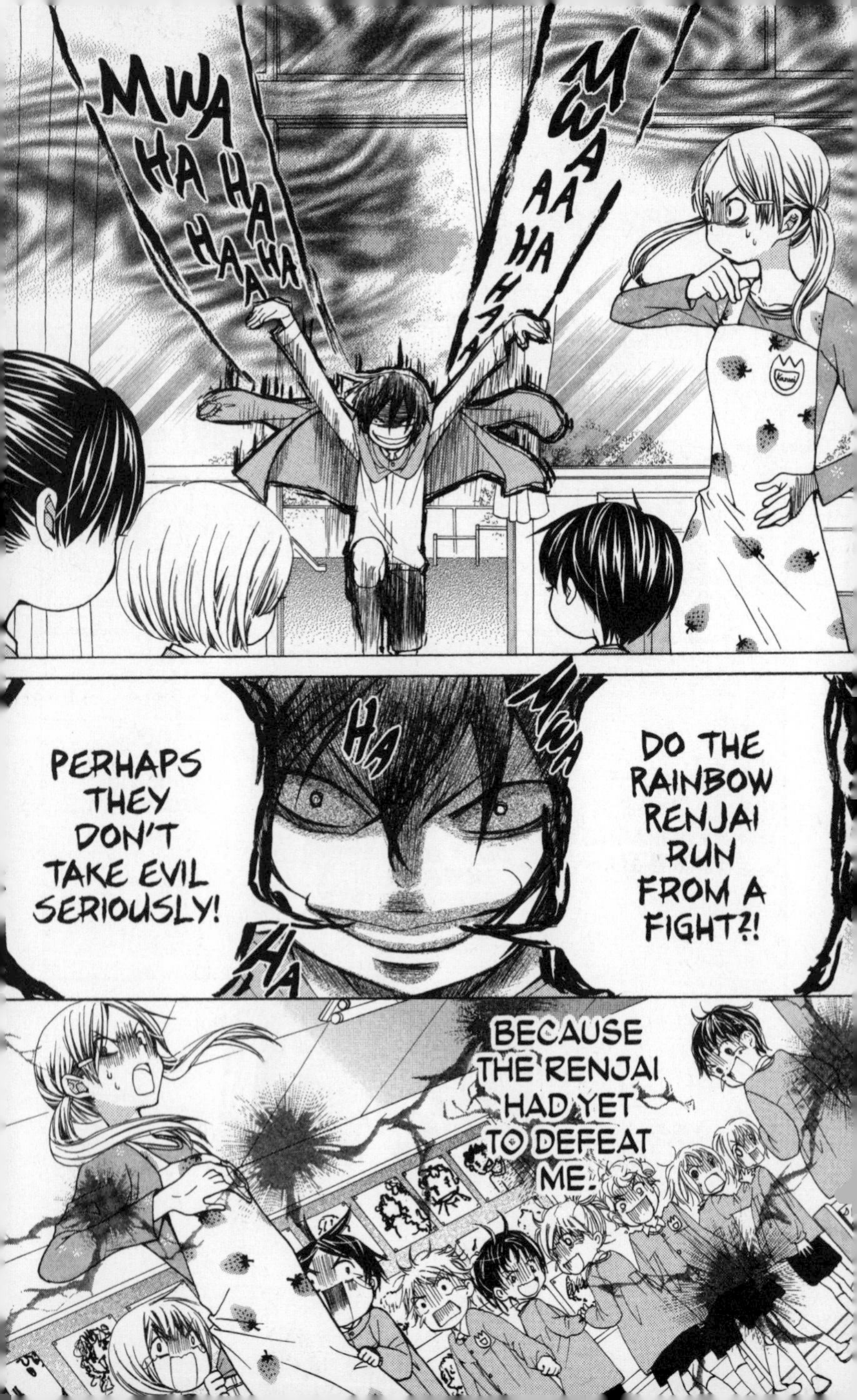
MWAAAHAHAHAA
MWAHAHAHAHAHA
DO THE RAINBOW RENJAI RUN FROM A FIGHT?!
MWA
HA
PERHAPS THEY DON'T TAKE EVIL SERIOUSLY!
HA
BECAUSE THE RENJAI HAD YET TO DEFEAT ME.

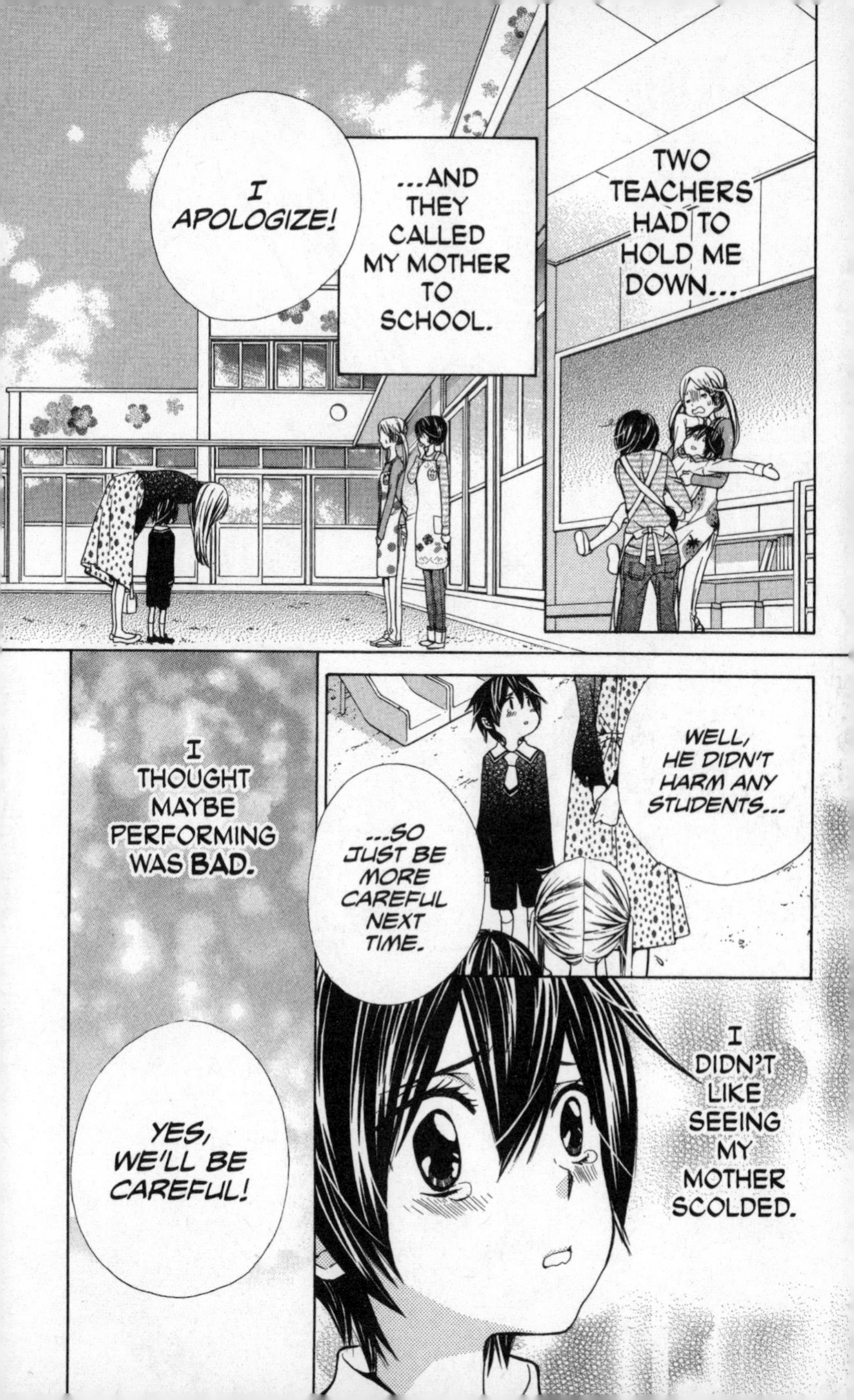
TWO TEACHERS HAD TO HOLD ME DOWN...
...AND THEY CALLED MY MOTHER TO SCHOOL.
I APOLOGIZE!
WELL, HE DIDN'T HARM ANY STUDENTS...
...SO JUST BE MORE CAREFUL NEXT TIME.
I DIDN'T LIKE SEEING MY MOTHER SCOLDED.
I THOUGHT MAYBE PERFORMING WAS BAD.
YES, WE'LL BE CAREFUL!

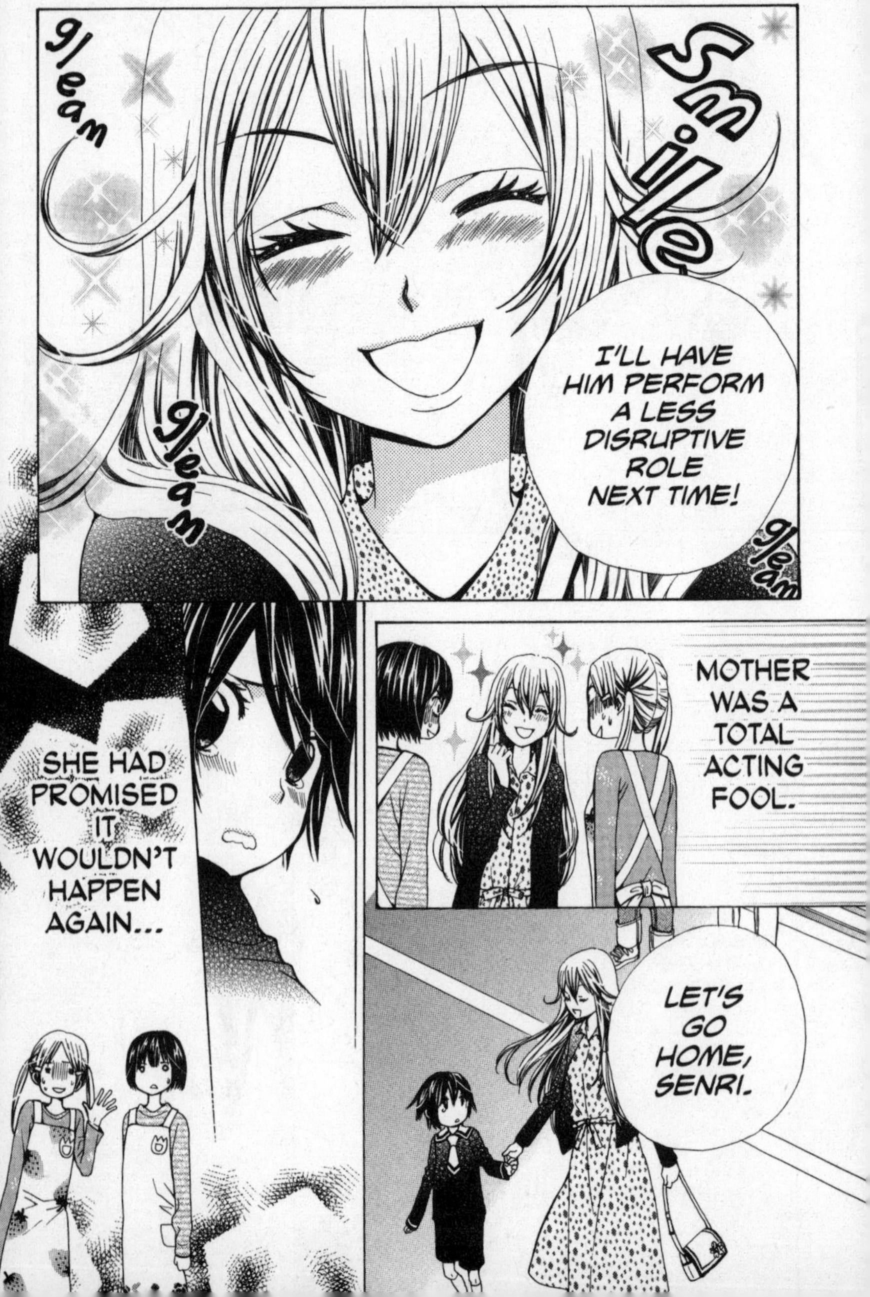
Smile
gleam
I'LL HAVE HIM PERFORM A LESS DISRUPTIVE ROLE NEXT TIME!
gleam
gleam
MOTHER WAS A TOTAL ACTING FOOL.
LET'S GO HOME, SENRI.
SHE HAD PROMISED IT WOULDN'T HAPPEN AGAIN...

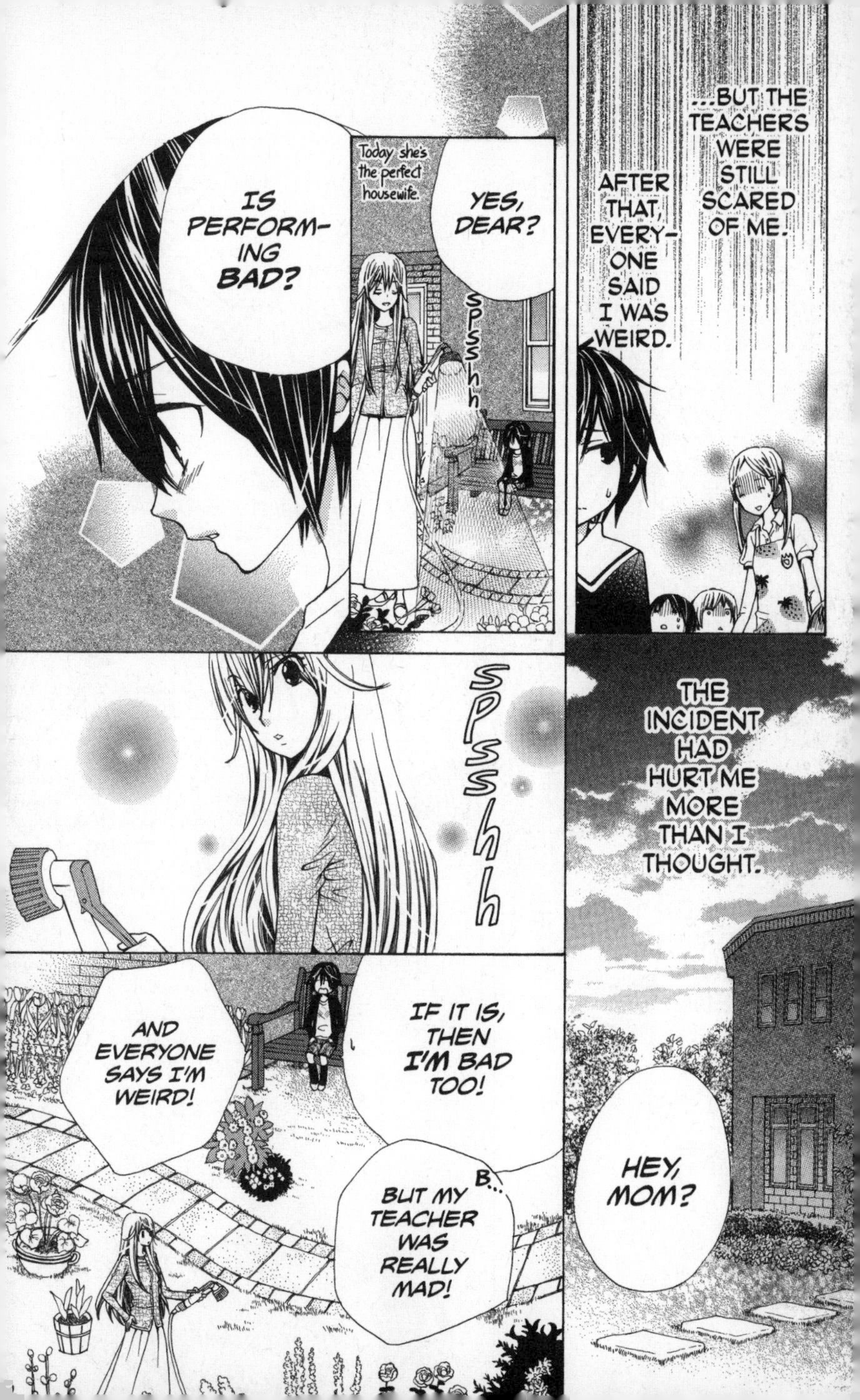
...BUT THE TEACHERS WERE STILL SCARED OF ME.
AFTER THAT, EVERYONE SAID I WAS WEIRD.
YES, DEAR?
Today she's the perfect housewife.
SPSSHH
IS PERFORMING BAD?
THE INCIDENT HAD HURT ME MORE THAN I THOUGHT.
HEY, MOM?
SPSSHH
IF IT IS, THEN I'M BAD TOO!
AND EVERYONE SAYS I'M WEIRD!
B...
BUT MY TEACHER WAS REALLY MAD!

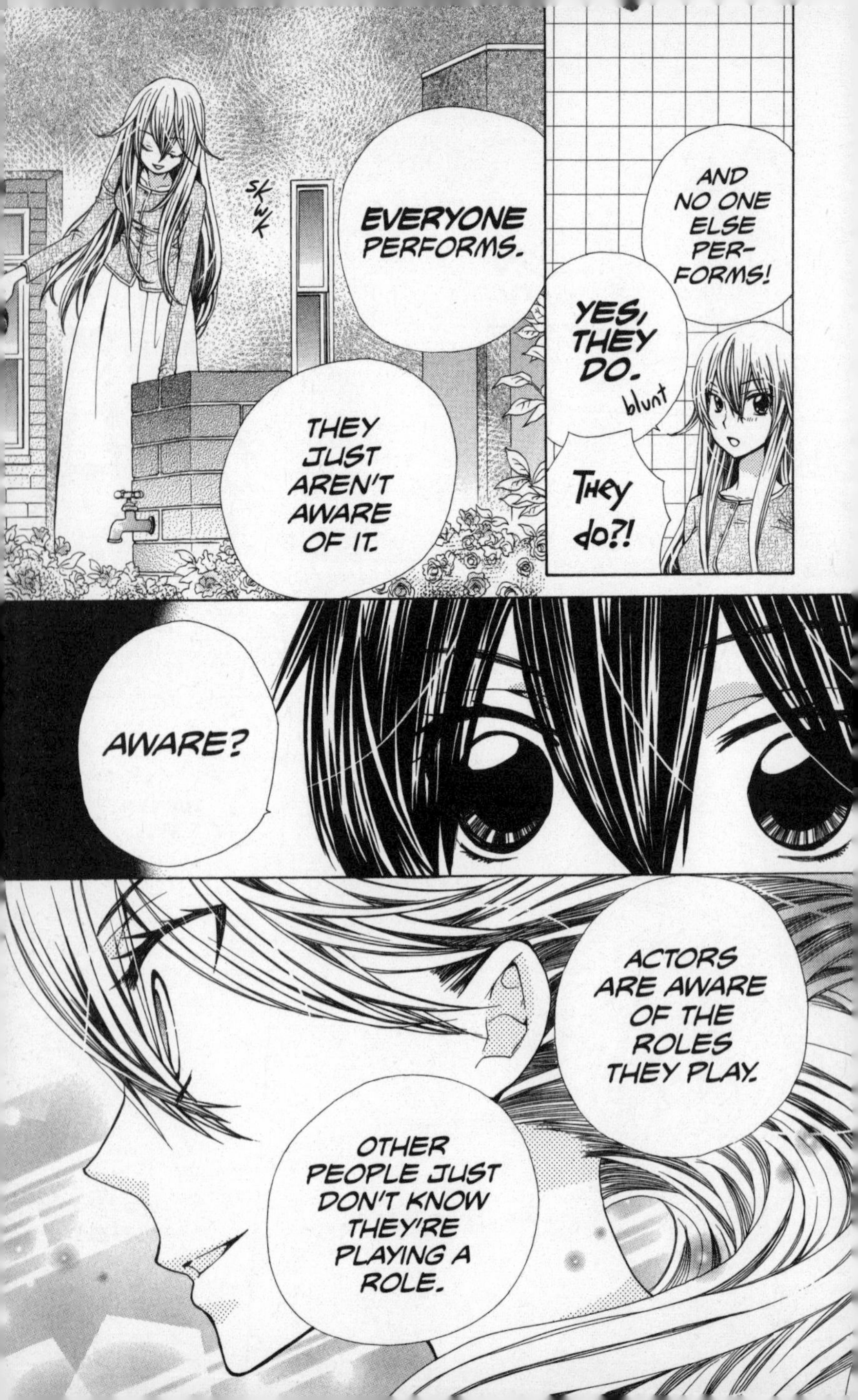
AND NO ONE ELSE PER-FORMS!
YES, THEY DO.
blunt
They do?!
EVERYONE PERFORMS.
SKWK
THEY JUST AREN'T AWARE OF IT.
AWARE?
ACTORS ARE AWARE OF THE ROLES THEY PLAY.
OTHER PEOPLE JUST DON'T KNOW THEY'RE PLAYING A ROLE.

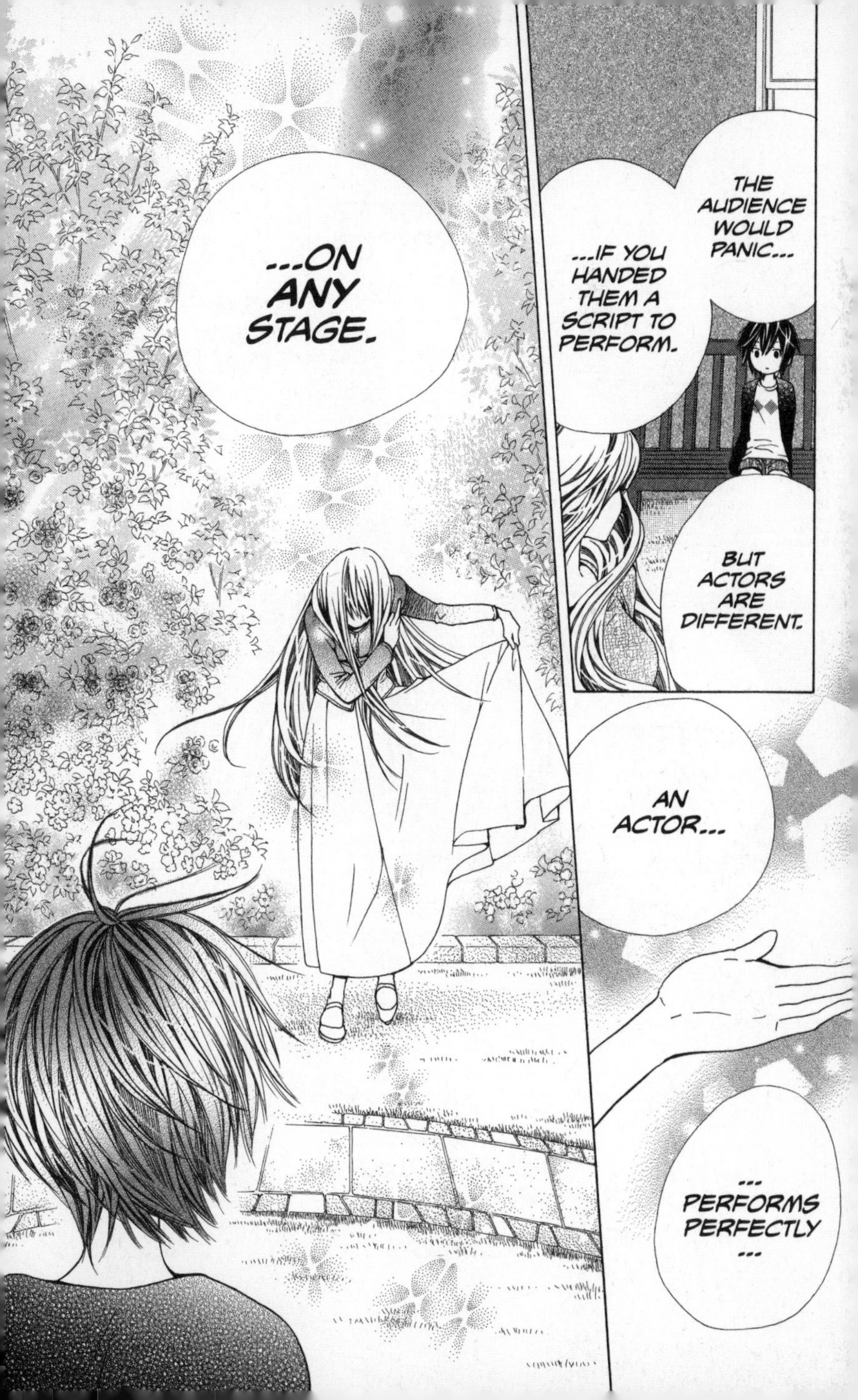
THE AUDIENCE WOULD PANIC...
...IF YOU HANDED THEM A SCRIPT TO PERFORM.
BUT ACTORS ARE DIFFERENT.
AN ACTOR...
...PERFORMS PERFECTLY...
...ON ANY STAGE.

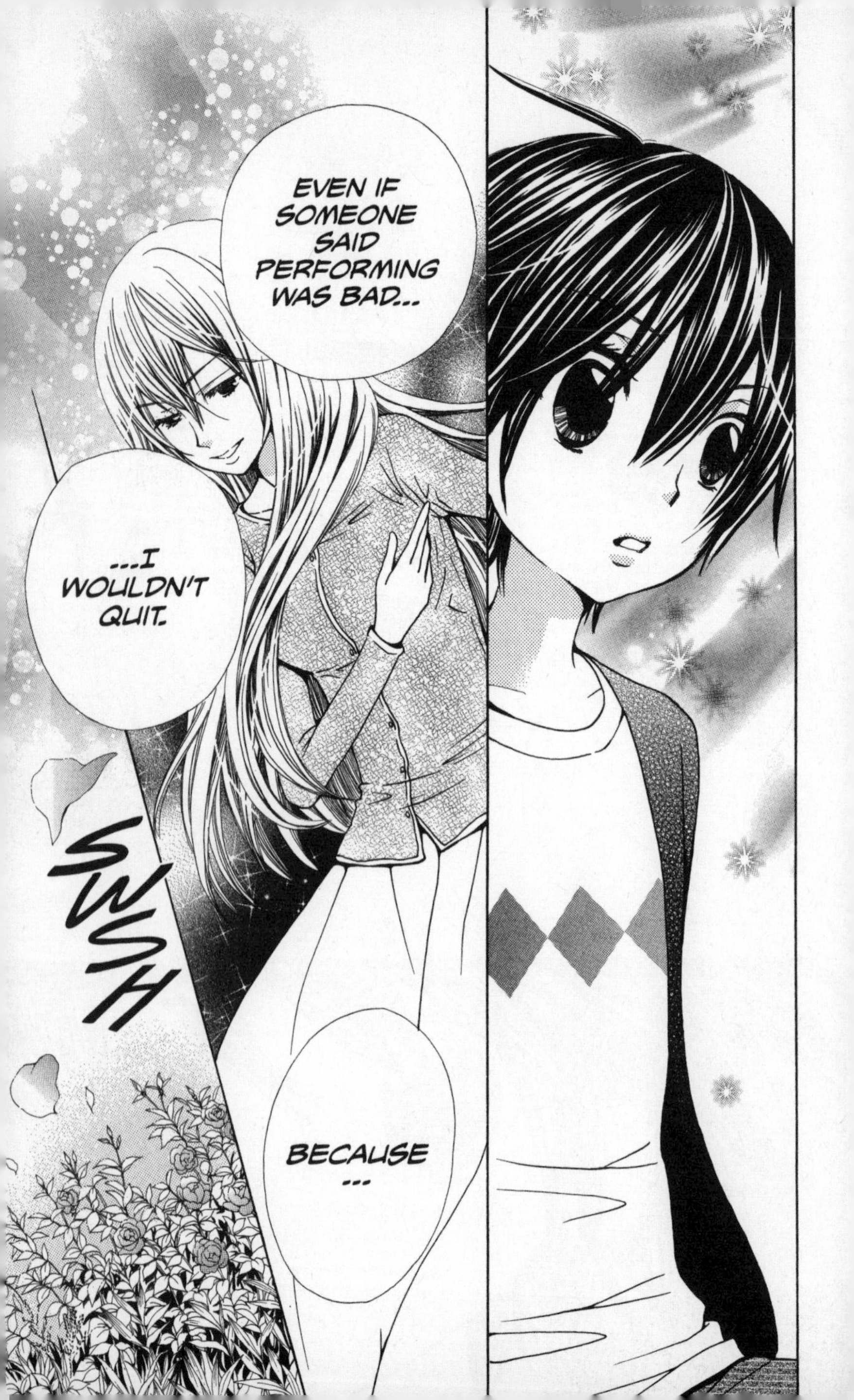
EVEN IF SOMEONE SAID PERFORMING WAS BAD...
...I WOULDN'T QUIT.
SWSH
BECAUSE ...

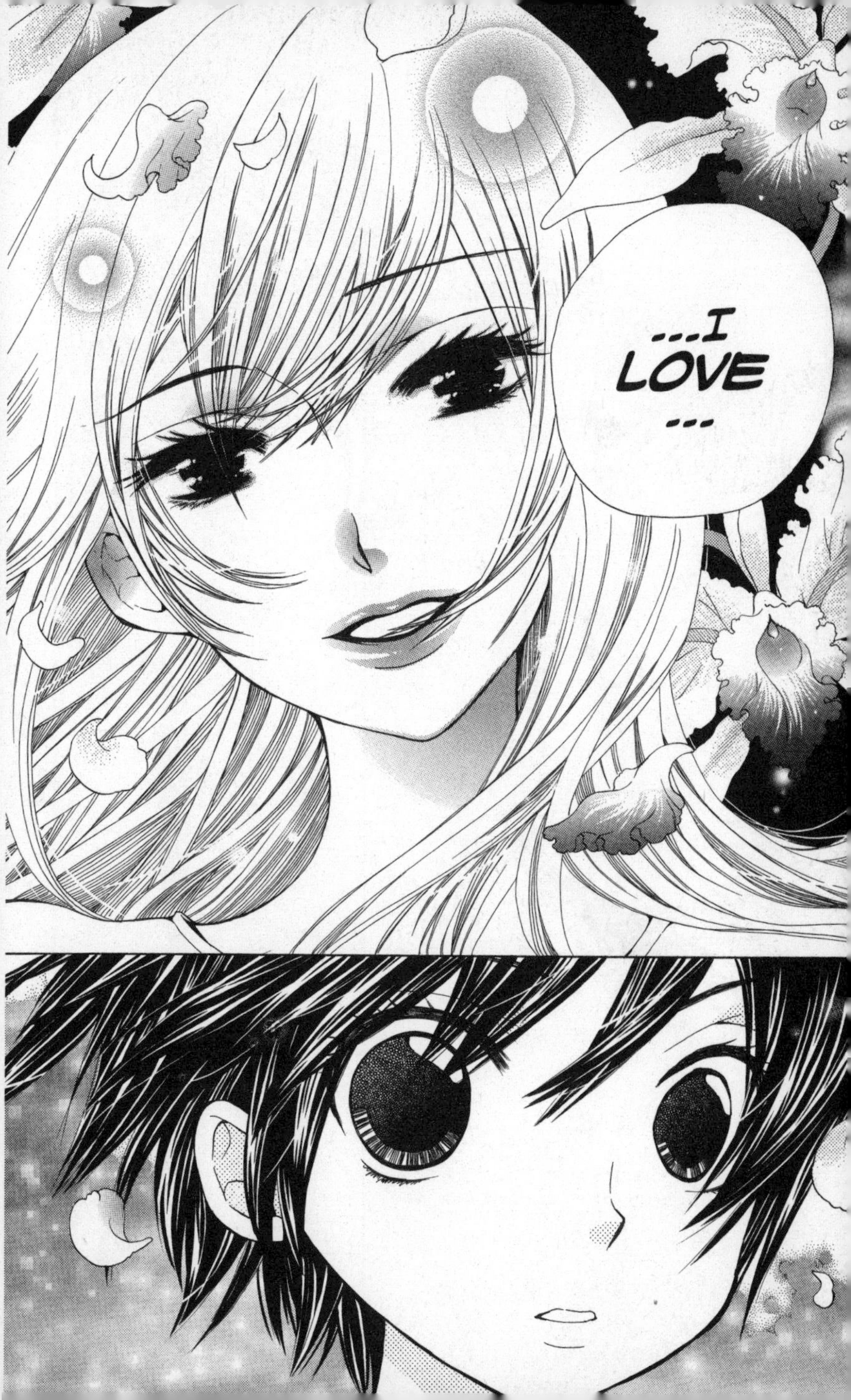
...I LOVE ...

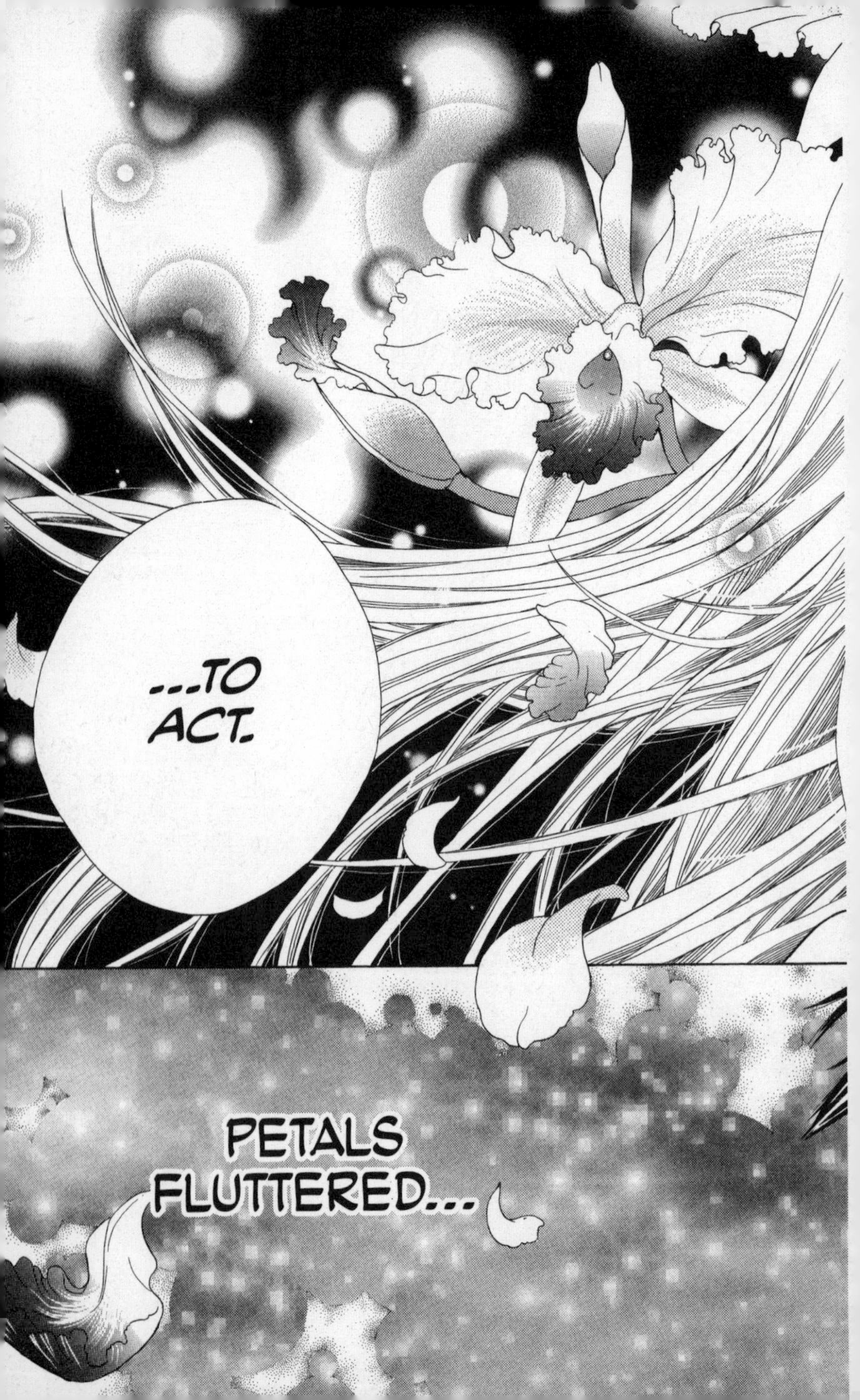
...TO ACT.
PETALS FLUTTERED...

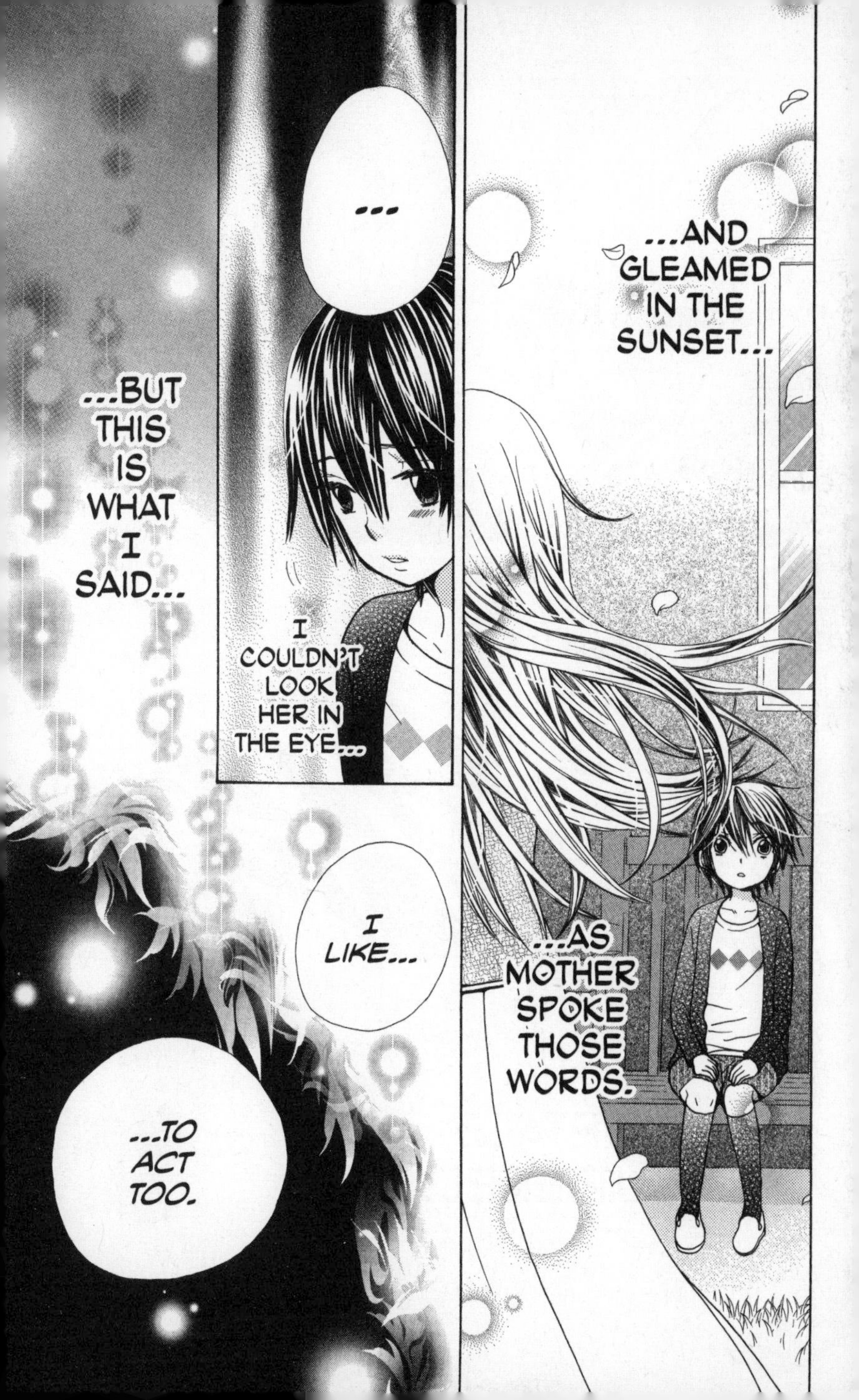
...AND GLEAMED IN THE SUNSET...
...AS MOTHER SPOKE THOSE WORDS.
...
I COULDN'T LOOK HER IN THE EYE...
...BUT THIS IS WHAT I SAID...
I LIKE...
...TO ACT TOO.

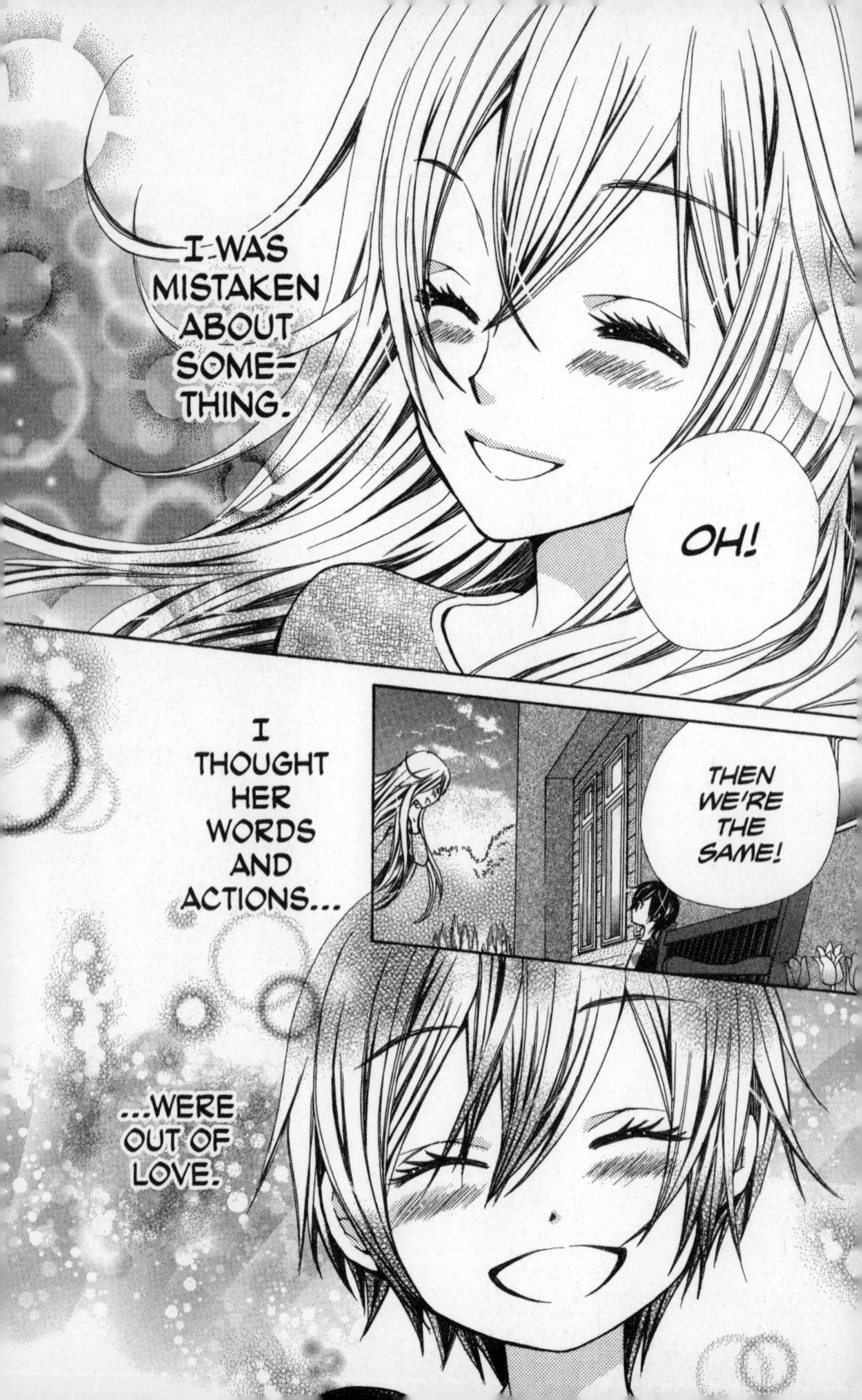
OH!
I WAS MISTAKEN ABOUT SOME-THING.
THEN WE'RE THE SAME!
I THOUGHT HER WORDS AND ACTIONS...
...WERE OUT OF LOVE.

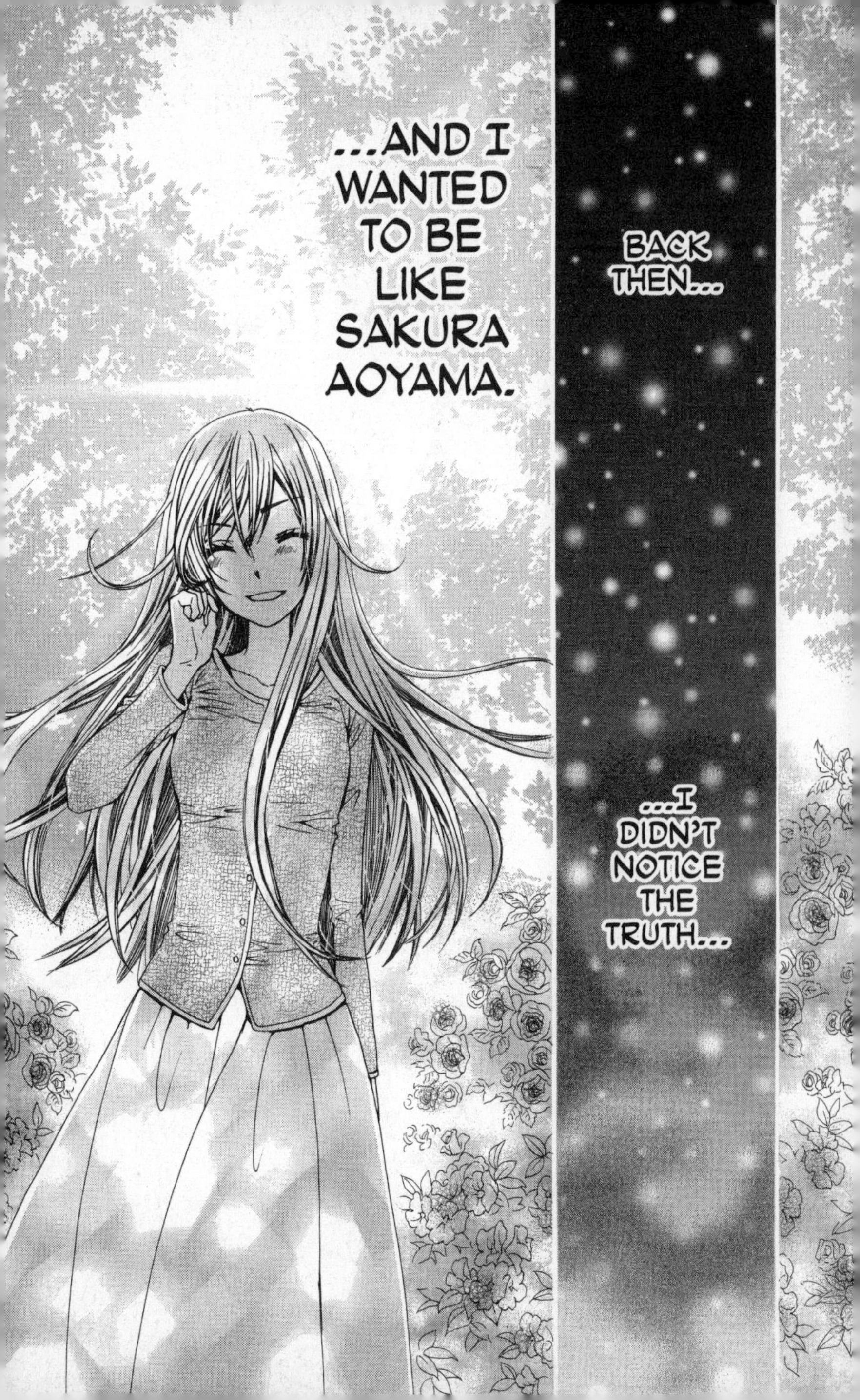
BACK THEN...
...I DIDN'T NOTICE THE TRUTH...
...AND I WANTED TO BE LIKE SAKURA AOYAMA.

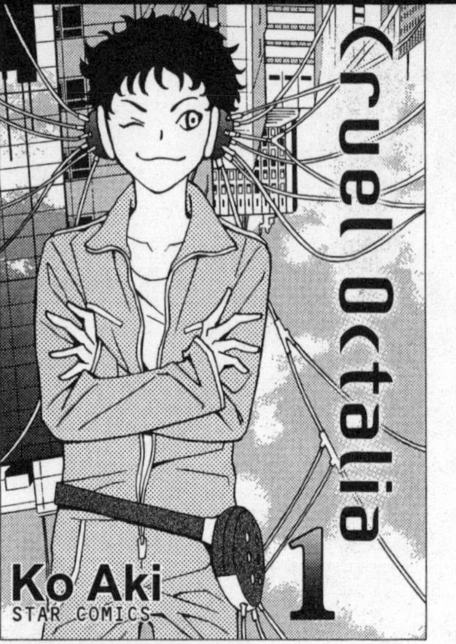
Cruel Octalia
1
Ko Aki
STAR COMICS

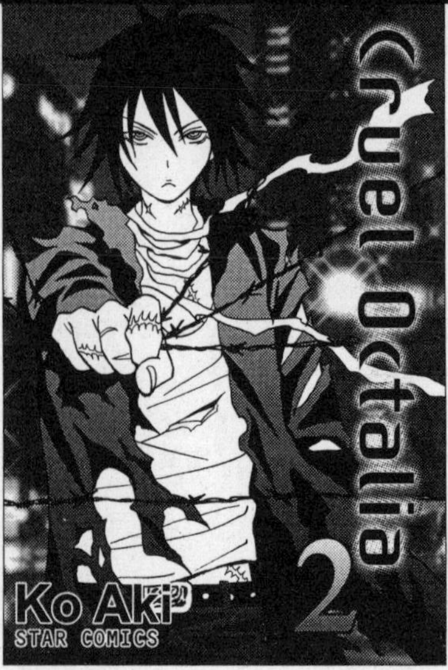
Cruel Octalia
2
Ko Aki
STAR COMICS

Sudden Bonus Content Corner ①

These are from the original manga that serves as the basis for the anime that Shiro is going to appear in. Assistant I-san drew them. They're really good! I want to read these! I thought I would have I-san complete them, but she refused. Too bad!!

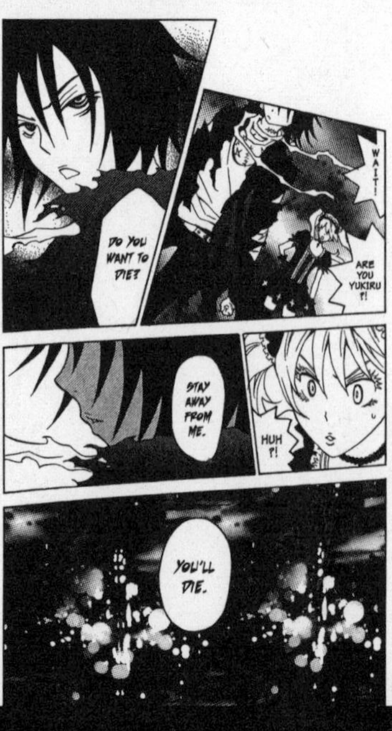
WAIT!
ARE YOU YUKIRU ?!
DO YOU WANT TO DIE?
HUH ?!
STAY AWAY FROM ME.
YOU'LL DIE.

← The character Shiro plays

Yukiru Shibuya

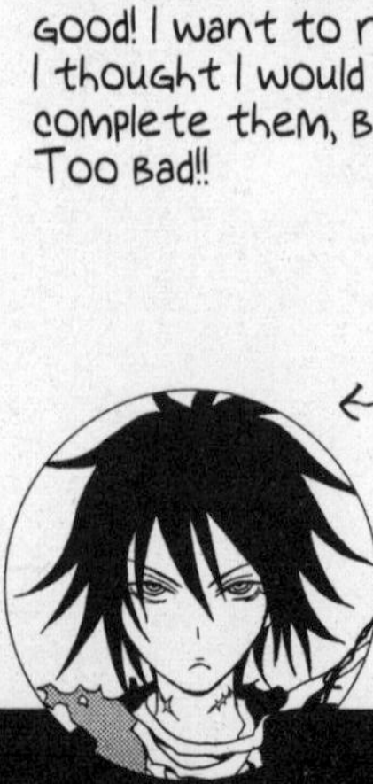

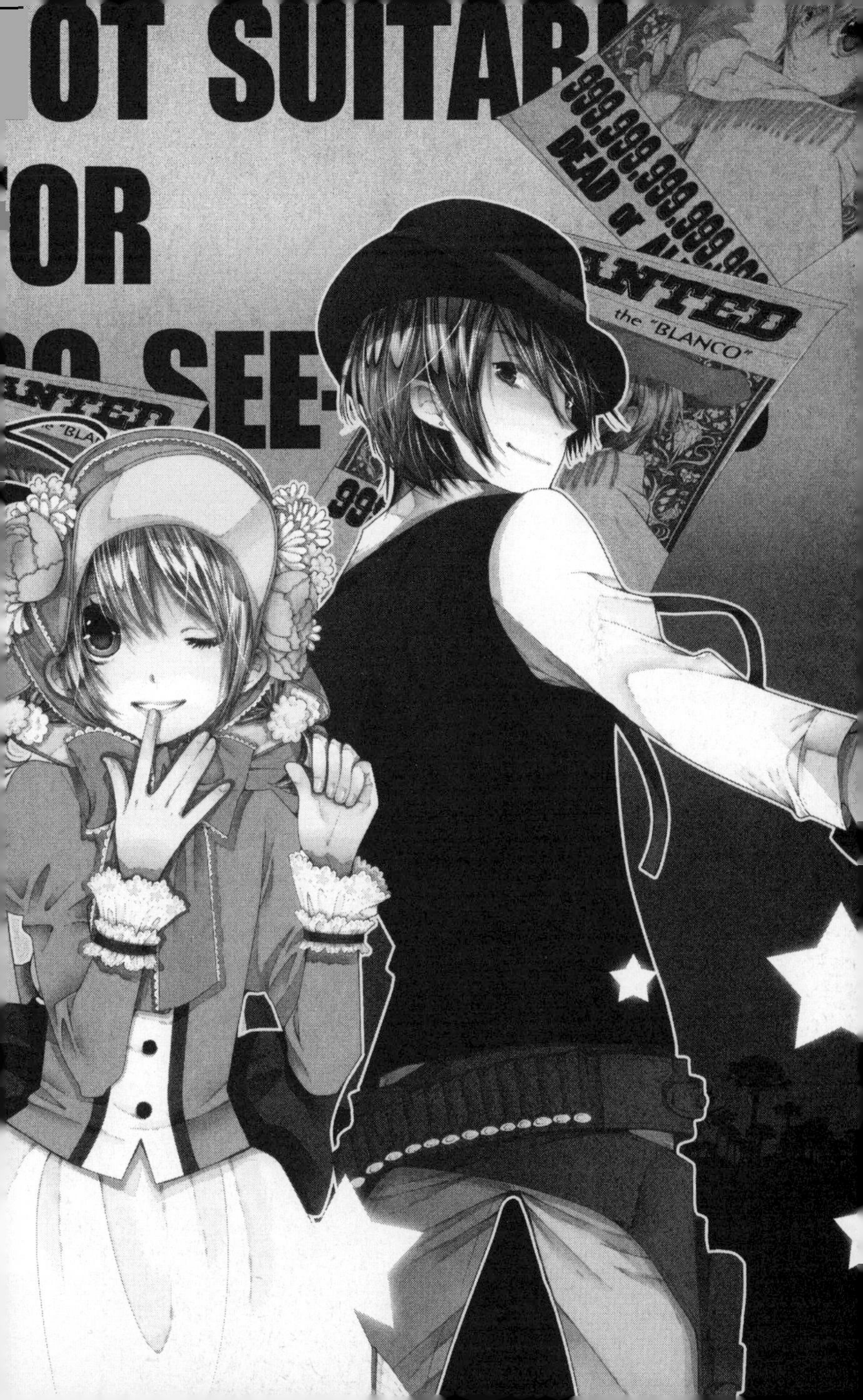
OT SUITAB
OR
SEE-
ANTED
the "BLANCO"
DEAD or

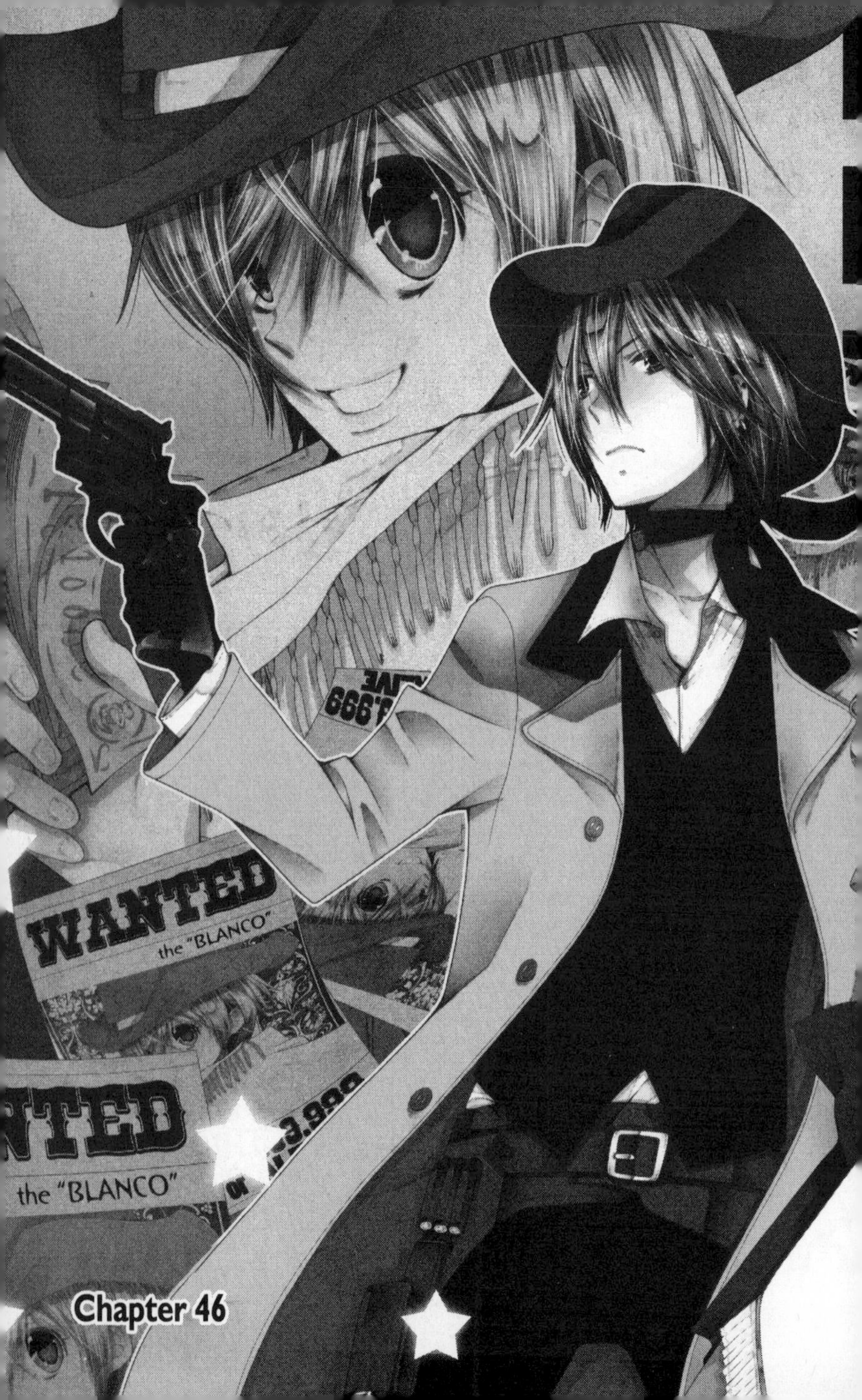
WANTED
the "BLANCO"
NTED
the "BLANCO"
Chapter 46

Sudden Bonus Content Corner ②

Cell phone lock screen

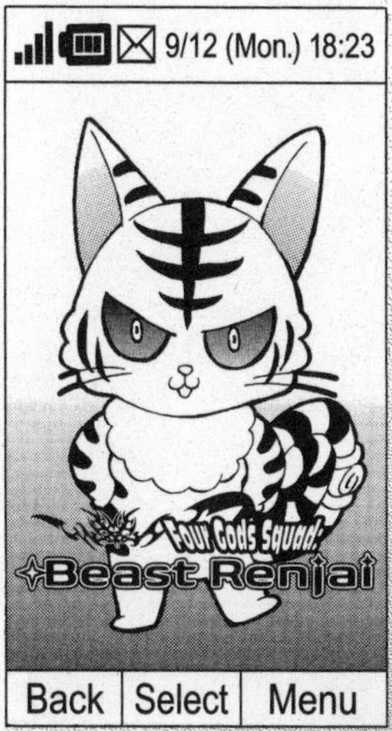
9/12 (Mon.) 18:23
Four Gods Squad!
Beast Renjai
Back
Select
Menu

★ I downloaded it as soon as it was available on the **Beast Renjai** official website! by Shiro

Assistant M-san drew this and polished it up. It's super cool!

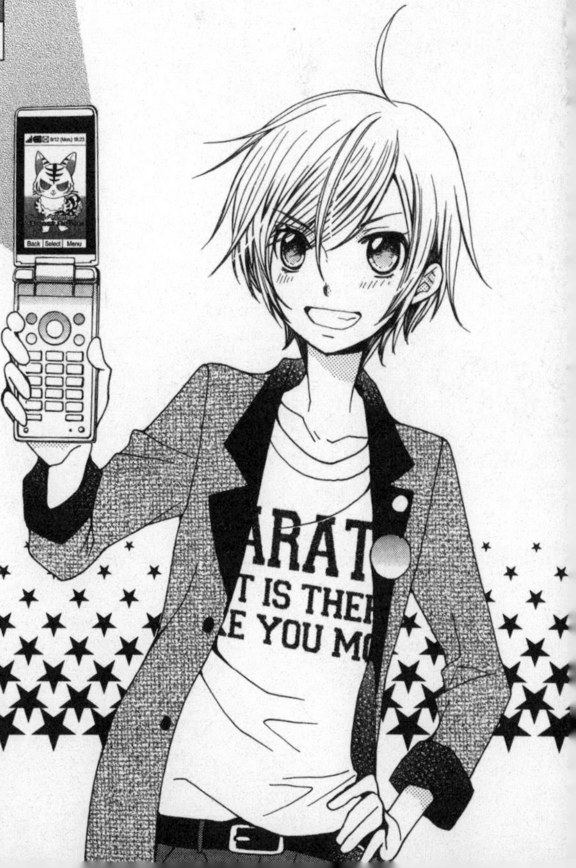
ARAT
T IS THEF
E YOU MO

M-san also designed the hero show posters in Volume 7. By mistake, I wrote in that volume that it was I-san. Sorry...

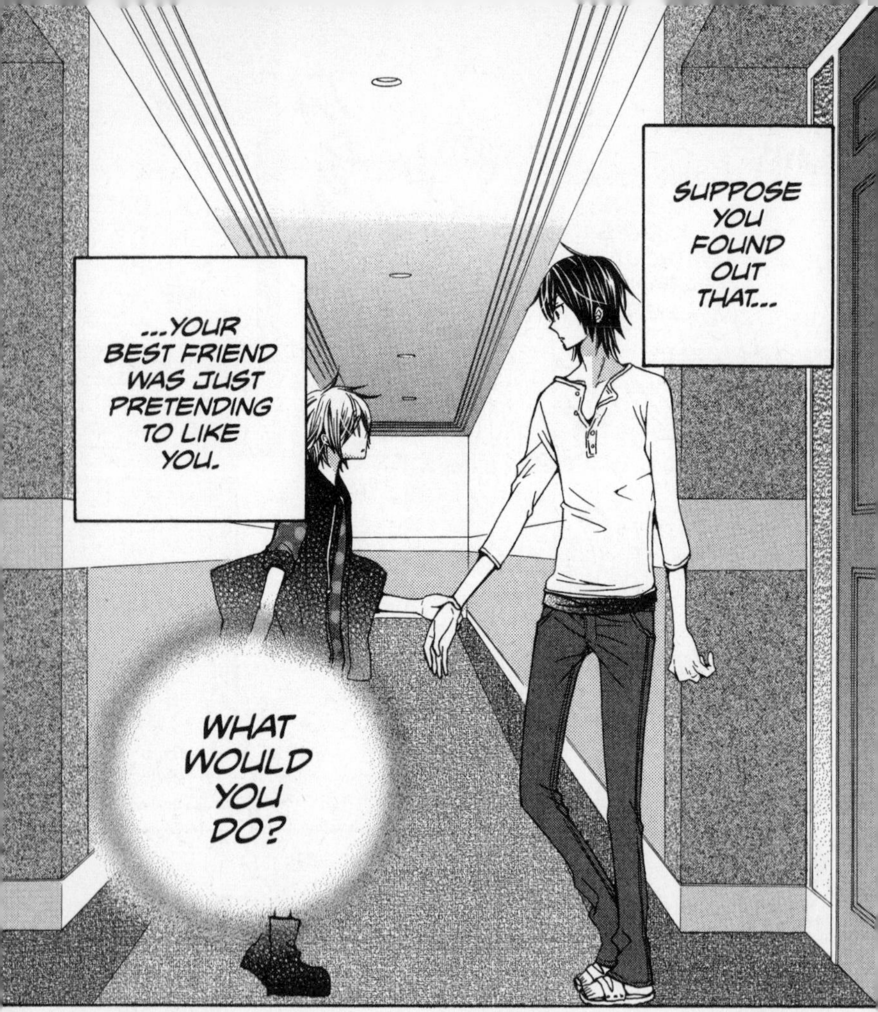
SUPPOSE YOU FOUND OUT THAT...
...YOUR BEST FRIEND WAS JUST PRETENDING TO LIKE YOU.
WHAT WOULD YOU DO?

• Various Things •

For the request!

5

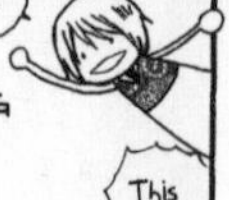

• The request this time was Mizuki as a girl. Thank you! Mizuki is showing up a lot in the bottom inserts because he doesn't appear much in this volume. That happened once before too. It's all I do!

• As I write this, 2011 is about to end, so I have to think about my 2012 New Year's cards, but 2012 is the Year of the Dragon!! It could be difficult to draw a cute dragon... Sorry. Just drawing a normal one would be hard too...

This time, the pattern on Mitchy's clothes changes!

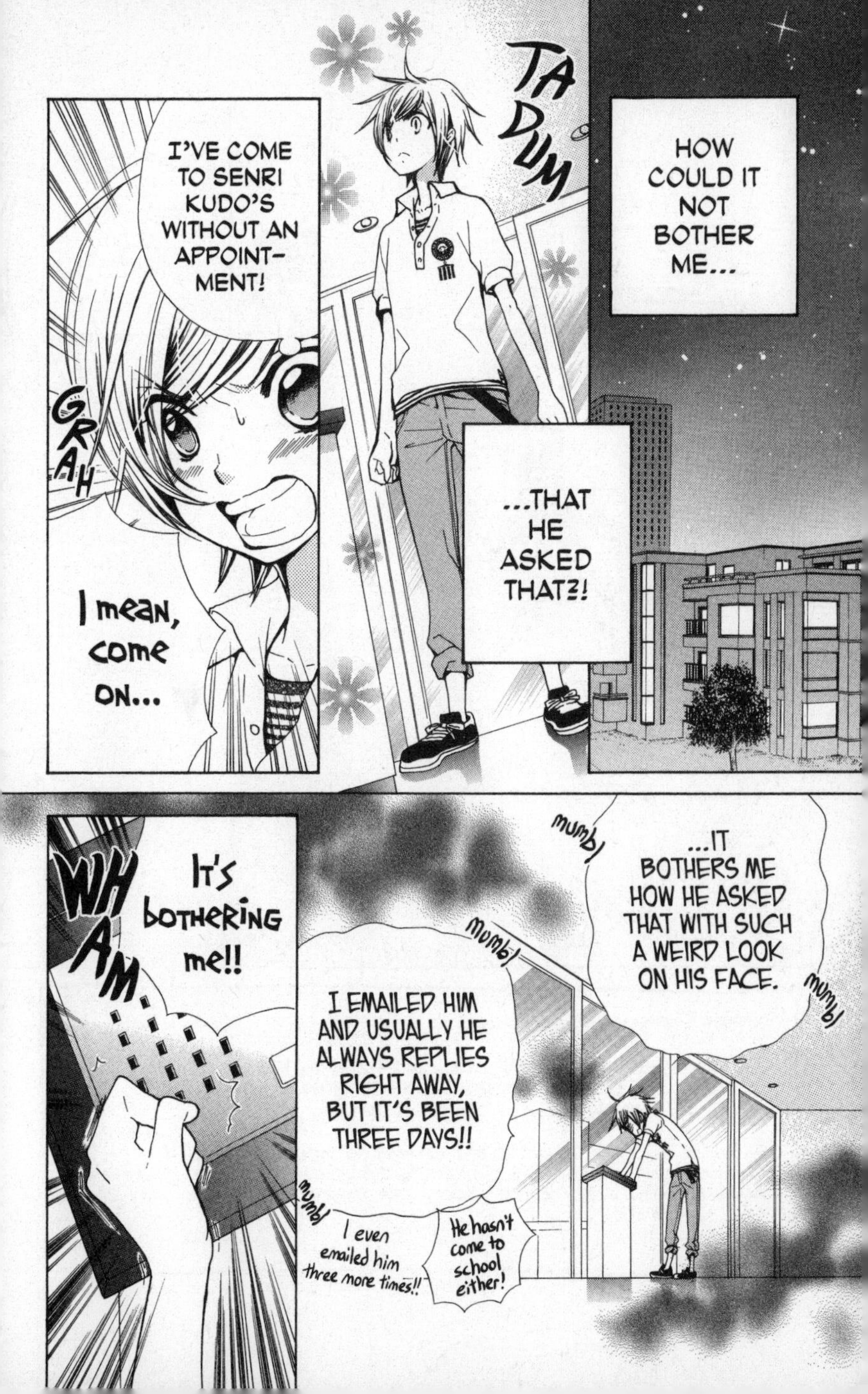
HOW COULD IT NOT BOTHER ME...
...THAT HE ASKED THAT?!
TA DUM
I'VE COME TO SENRI KUDO'S WITHOUT AN APPOINT-MENT!
GRAH
I mean, come on...
mumbl
...IT BOTHERS ME HOW HE ASKED THAT WITH SUCH A WEIRD LOOK ON HIS FACE.
mumbl
mumbl
I EMAILED HIM AND USUALLY HE ALWAYS REPLIES RIGHT AWAY, BUT IT'S BEEN THREE DAYS!!
mumbl
He hasn't come to school either!
I even emailed him three more times!!
WHAM
It's bothering me!!

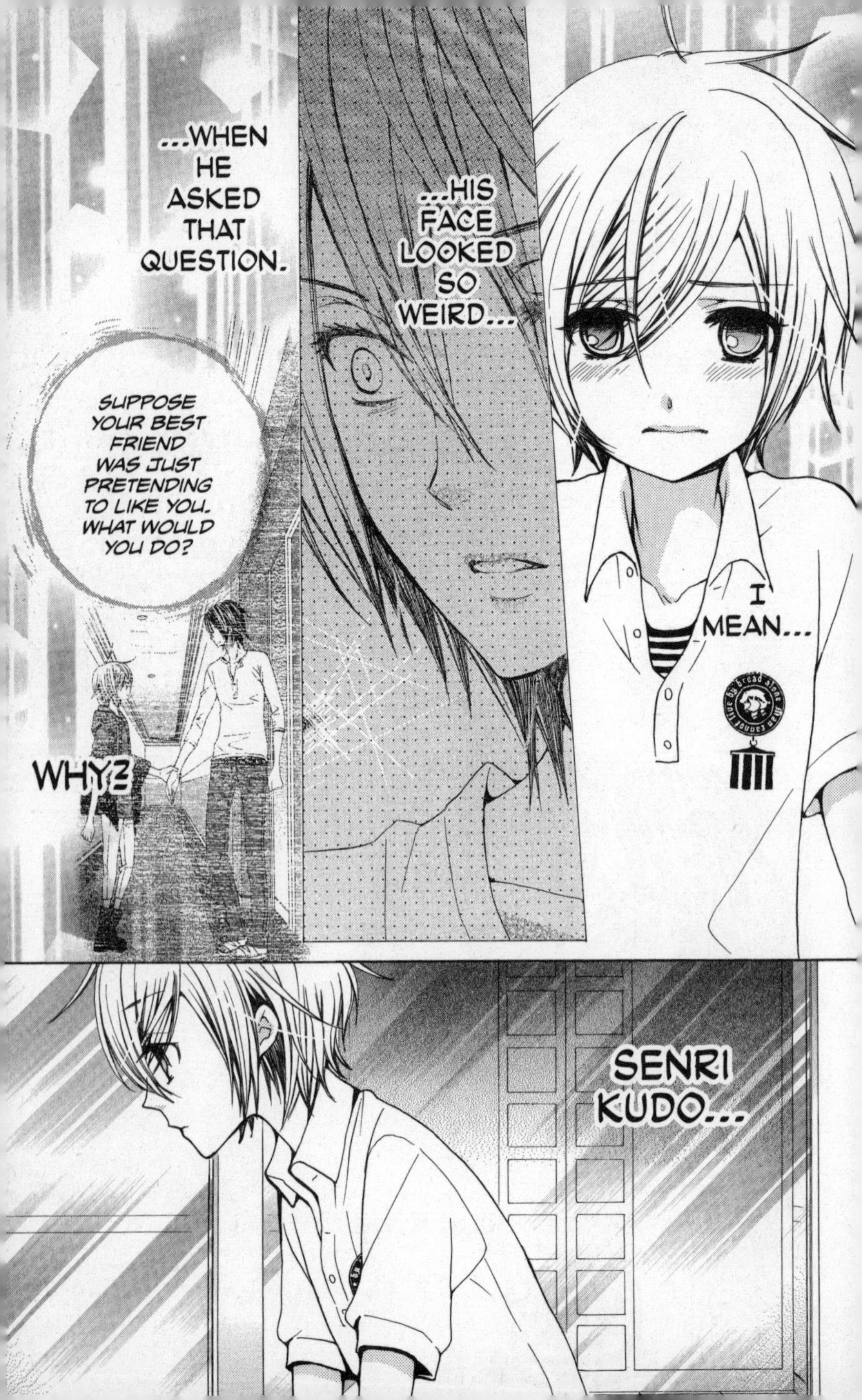
I MEAN...
...HIS FACE LOOKED SO WEIRD...
...WHEN HE ASKED THAT QUESTION.
SUPPOSE YOUR BEST FRIEND WAS JUST PRETENDING TO LIKE YOU. WHAT WOULD YOU DO?
WHY?
SENRI KUDO...

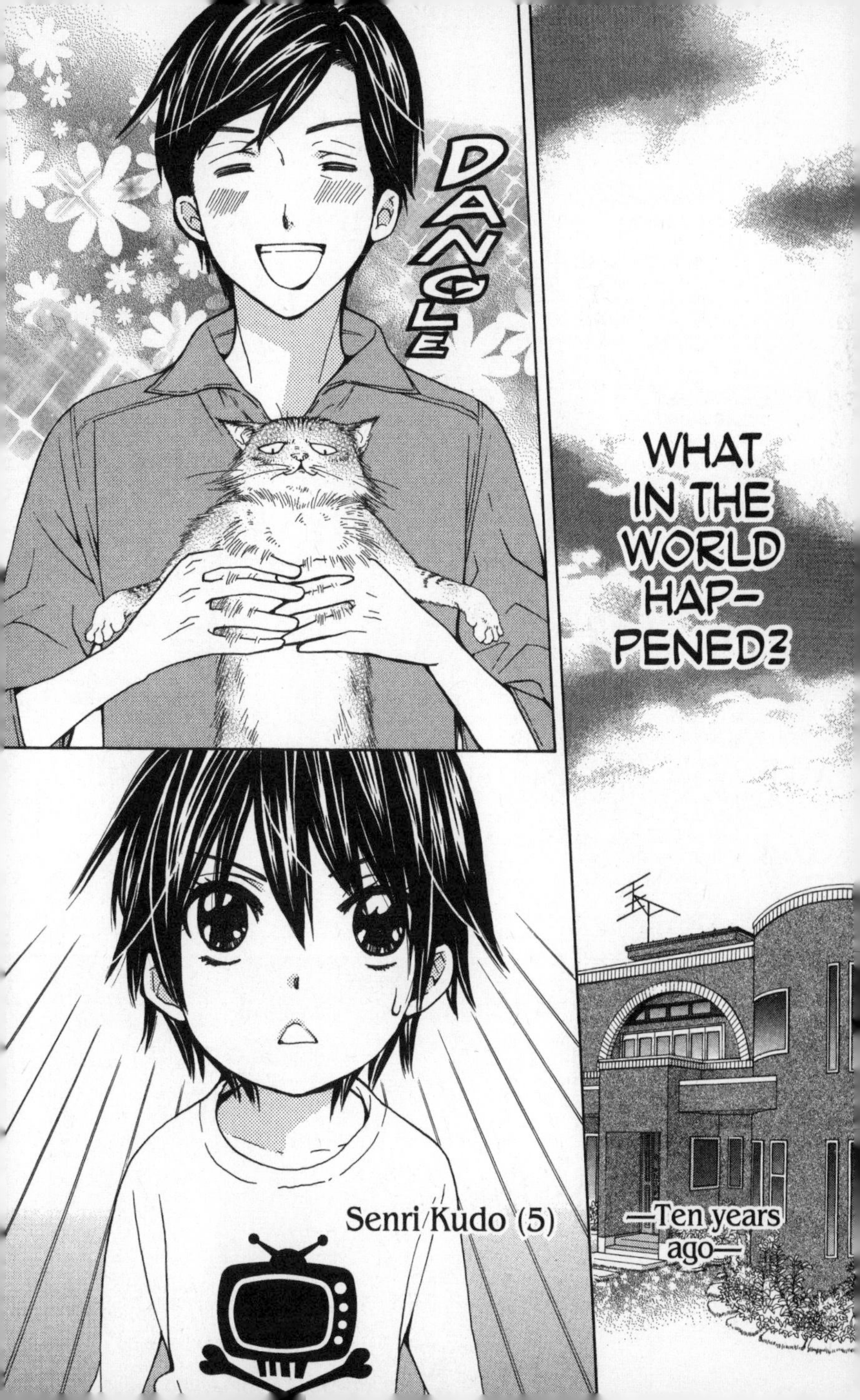
WHAT IN THE WORLD HAPPENED?
—Ten years ago—
DANGLE
Senri Kudo (5)

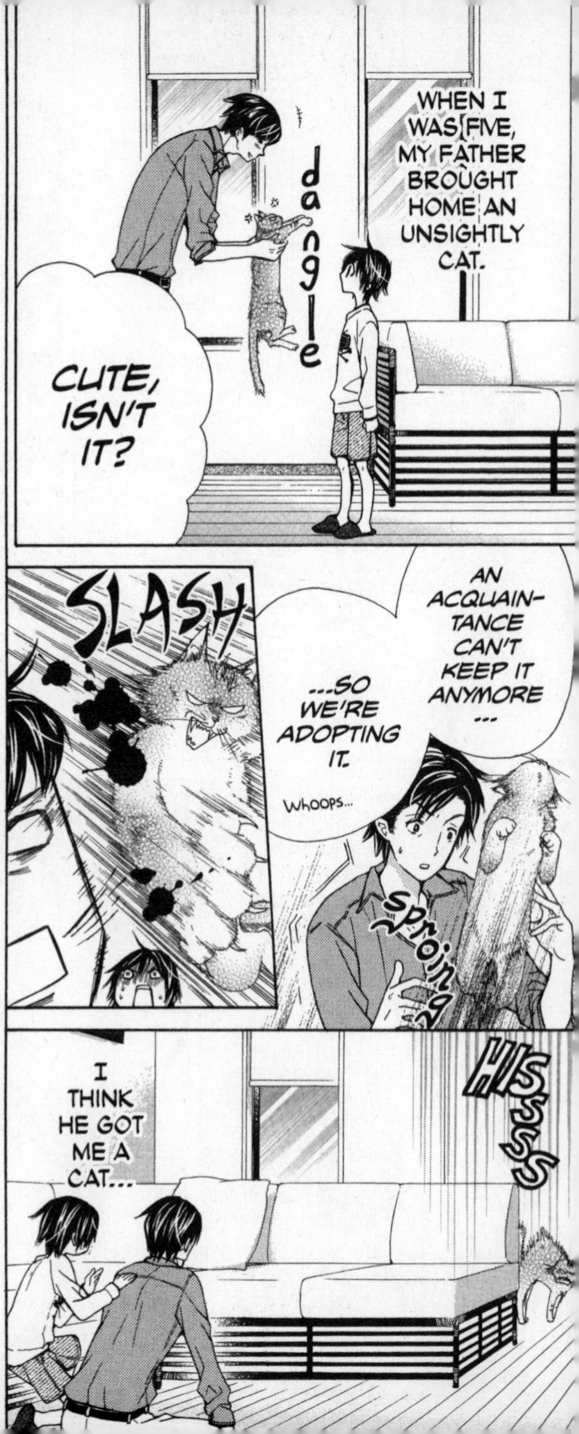
WHEN I WAS FIVE, MY FATHER BROUGHT HOME AN UNSIGHTLY CAT.
dangle
CUTE, ISN'T IT?
AN ACQUAIN-TANCE CAN'T KEEP IT ANYMORE...
...SO WE'RE ADOPTING IT.
Whoops...
sproing
SLASH
HISSSS
I THINK HE GOT ME A CAT...

• The End •

This is the last sidebar. Thanks for reading all this way! It's pretty clear I'm running out of topics for the sidebars. I'll try to go out and do something fun!

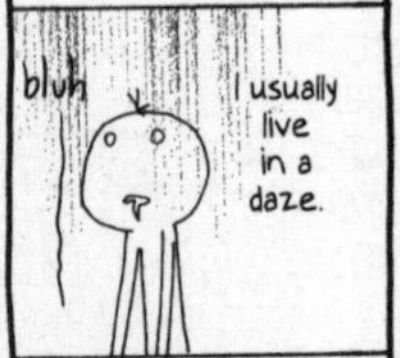
bluh
I usually live in a daze.

And much thanks to all the readers, everyone who helped with research, those who worked on the graphic novel, my editor, everyone who helped with composition, all my assistants, friends, and my family!!

♡ If you feel like it, lemme hear your thoughts! ♡

Maki Minami
c/o Shojo Beat
P.O. Box 77010
San Francisco, CA
94107

Maki Minami
南マキ

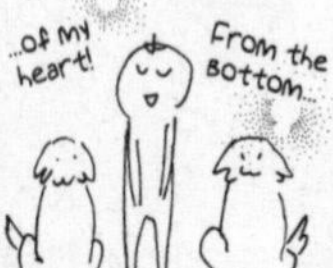
From the bottom...
...of my heart!

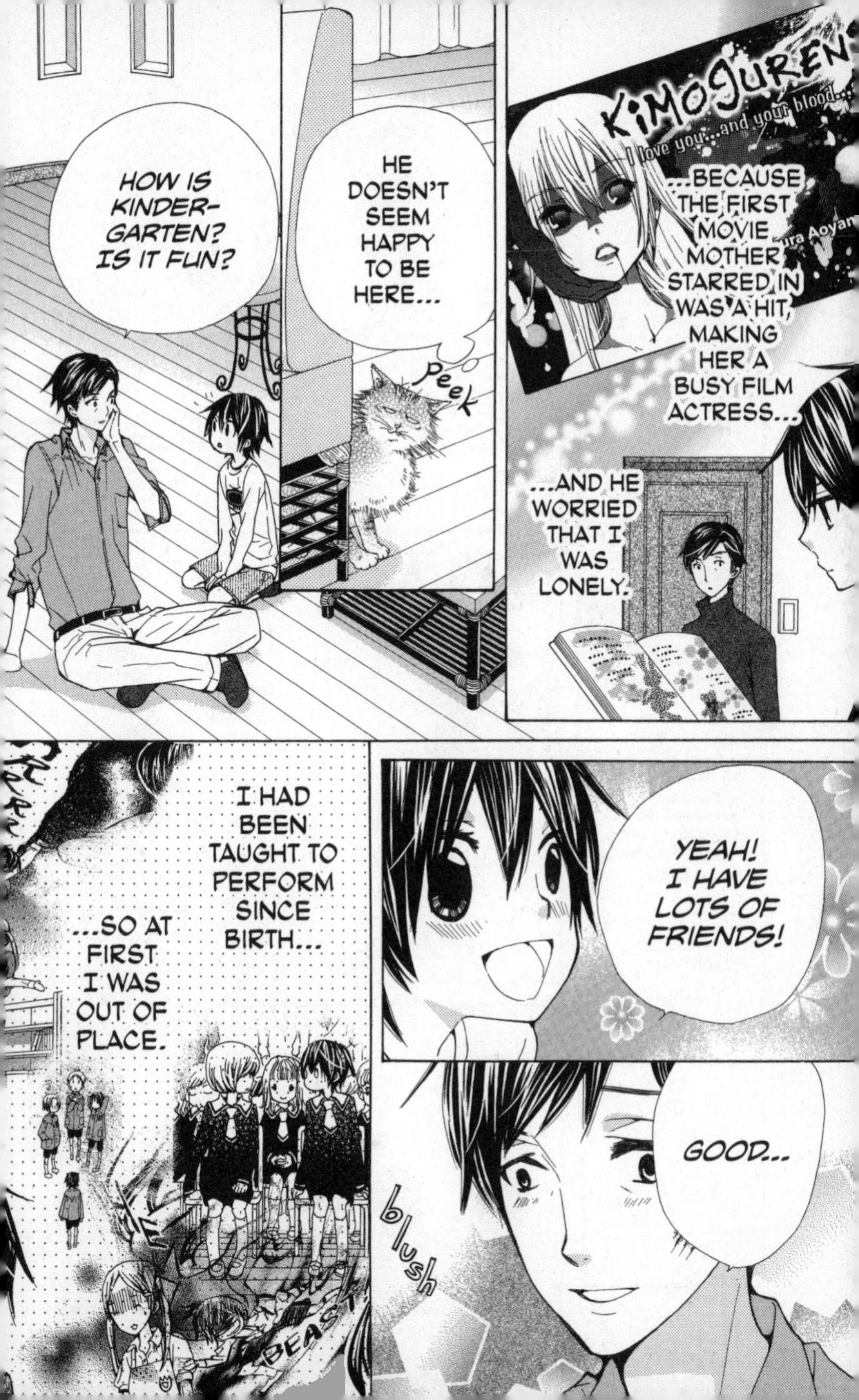
KIMOGUREN
I love you...and your blood...
...BECAUSE THE FIRST MOVIE MOTHER STARRED IN WAS A HIT, MAKING HER A BUSY FILM ACTRESS...
...AND HE WORRIED THAT I WAS LONELY.
HE DOESN'T SEEM HAPPY TO BE HERE...
Peek
HOW IS KINDER-GARTEN? IS IT FUN?
YEAH! I HAVE LOTS OF FRIENDS!
GOOD...
blush
I HAD BEEN TAUGHT TO PERFORM SINCE BIRTH...
...SO AT FIRST I WAS OUT OF PLACE.
BEAST

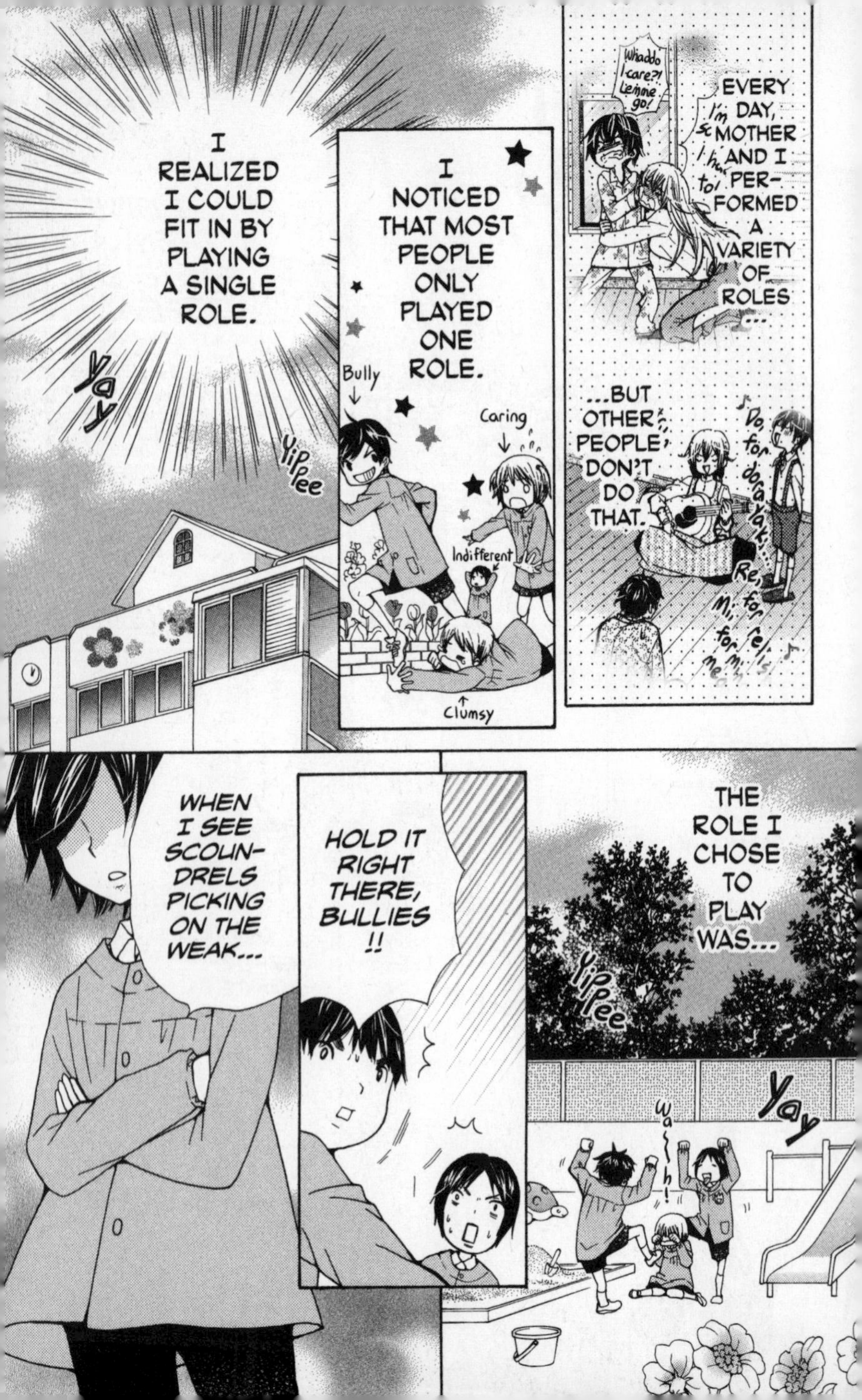
Whaddo I care?! Lemme go!
EVERY DAY, MOTHER AND I PER-FORMED A VARIETY OF ROLES...
...BUT OTHER PEOPLE DON'T DO THAT.
♪Do, for dorayaki... Re, for relish♪
I NOTICED THAT MOST PEOPLE ONLY PLAYED ONE ROLE.
Bully
Caring
Indifferent
Clumsy
I REALIZED I COULD FIT IN BY PLAYING A SINGLE ROLE.
Yay
Yippee
THE ROLE I CHOSE TO PLAY WAS...
Yippee
Yay
Wa~h!
HOLD IT RIGHT THERE, BULLIES!!
WHEN I SEE SCOUN-DRELS PICKING ON THE WEAK...

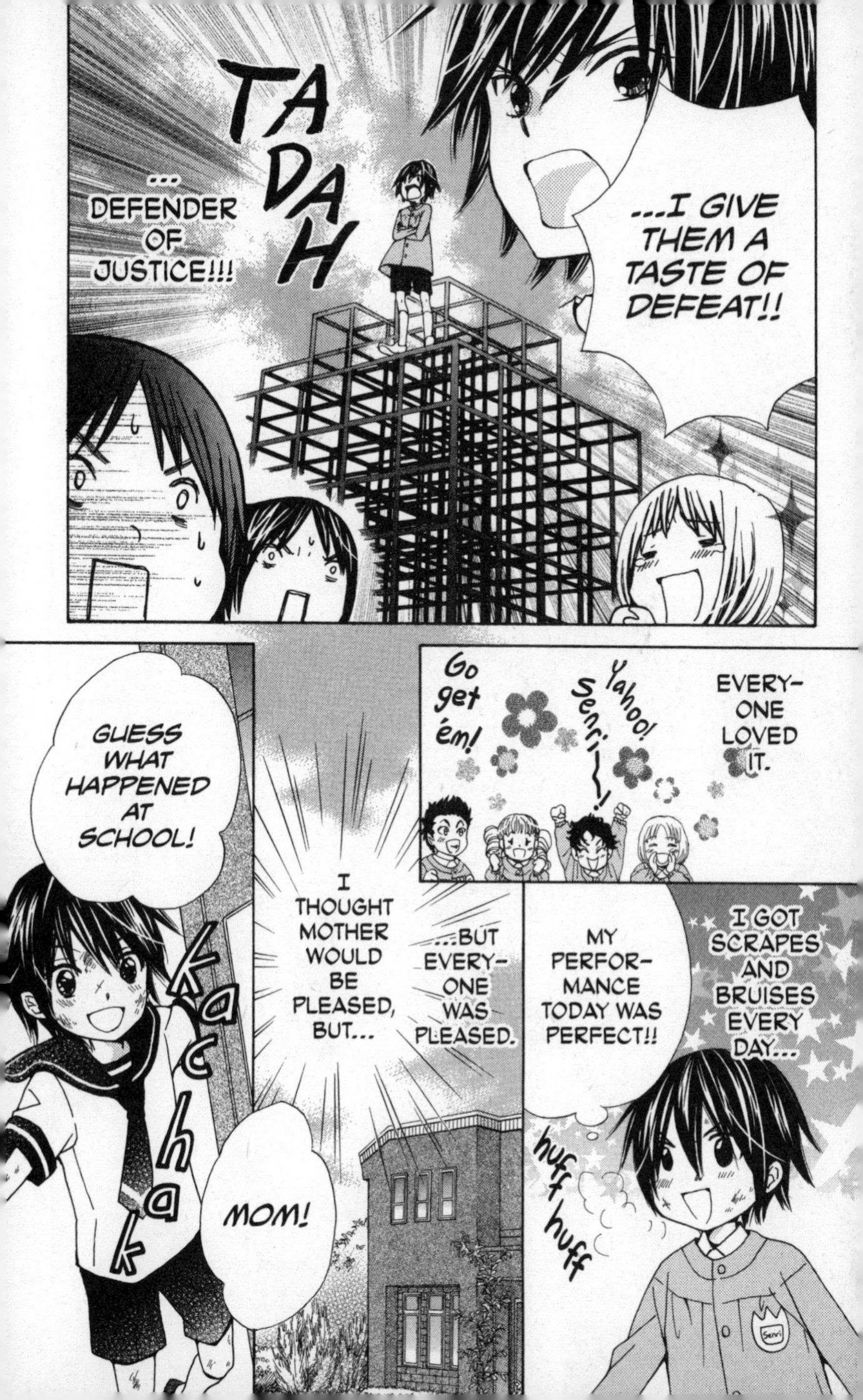
...I GIVE THEM A TASTE OF DEFEAT!!
TADAH
...DEFENDER OF JUSTICE!!!
EVERY-ONE LOVED IT.
Yahoo! Senri~~!
Go get 'em!
I GOT SCRAPES AND BRUISES EVERY DAY...
MY PERFOR-MANCE TODAY WAS PERFECT!!
huff huff
Senri
...BUT EVERY-ONE WAS PLEASED.
I THOUGHT MOTHER WOULD BE PLEASED, BUT...
GUESS WHAT HAPPENED AT SCHOOL!
kachak
MOM!

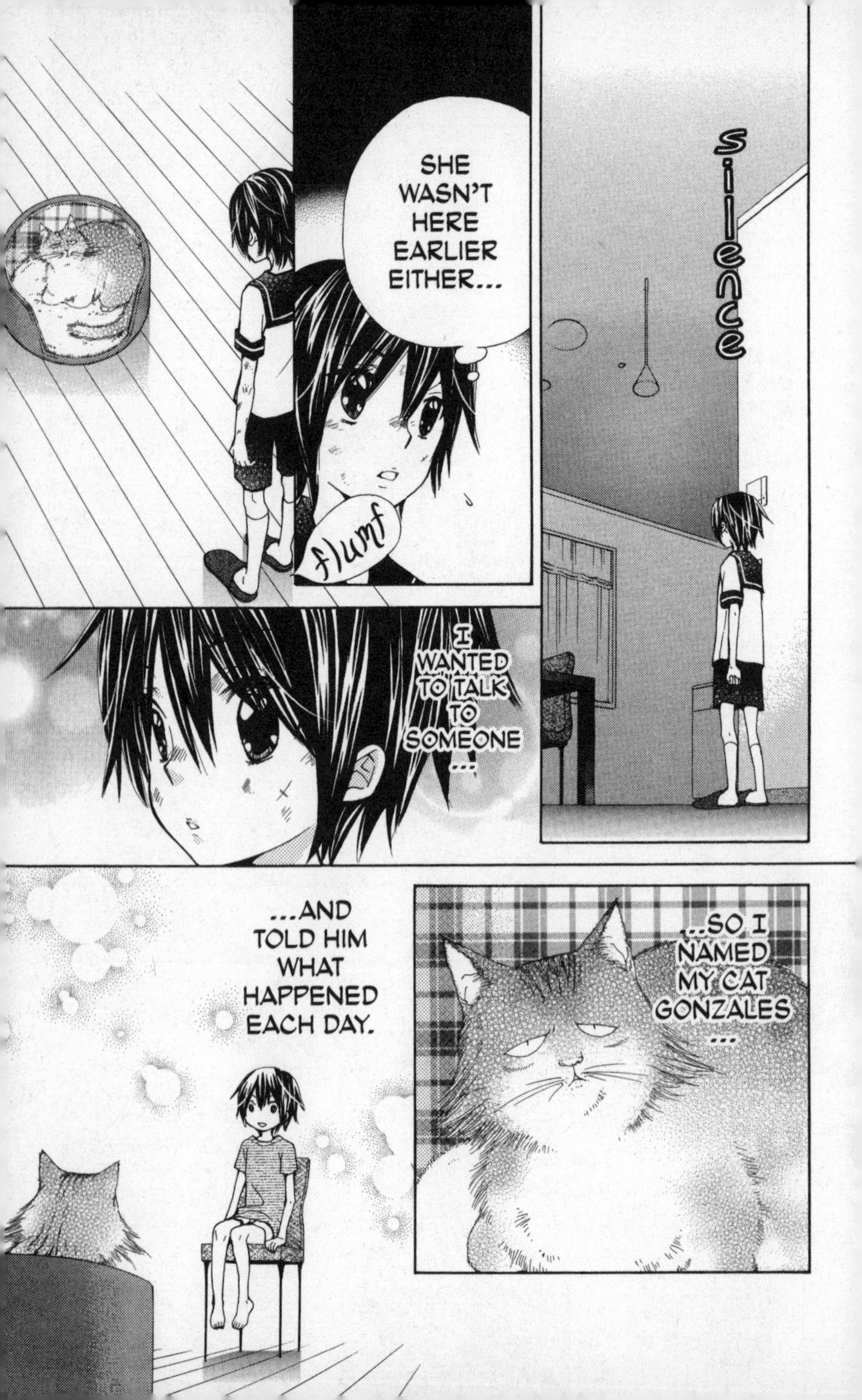
silence
SHE WASN'T HERE EARLIER EITHER...
flumf
I WANTED TO TALK TO SOMEONE...
...SO I NAMED MY CAT GONZALES...
...AND TOLD HIM WHAT HAPPENED EACH DAY.

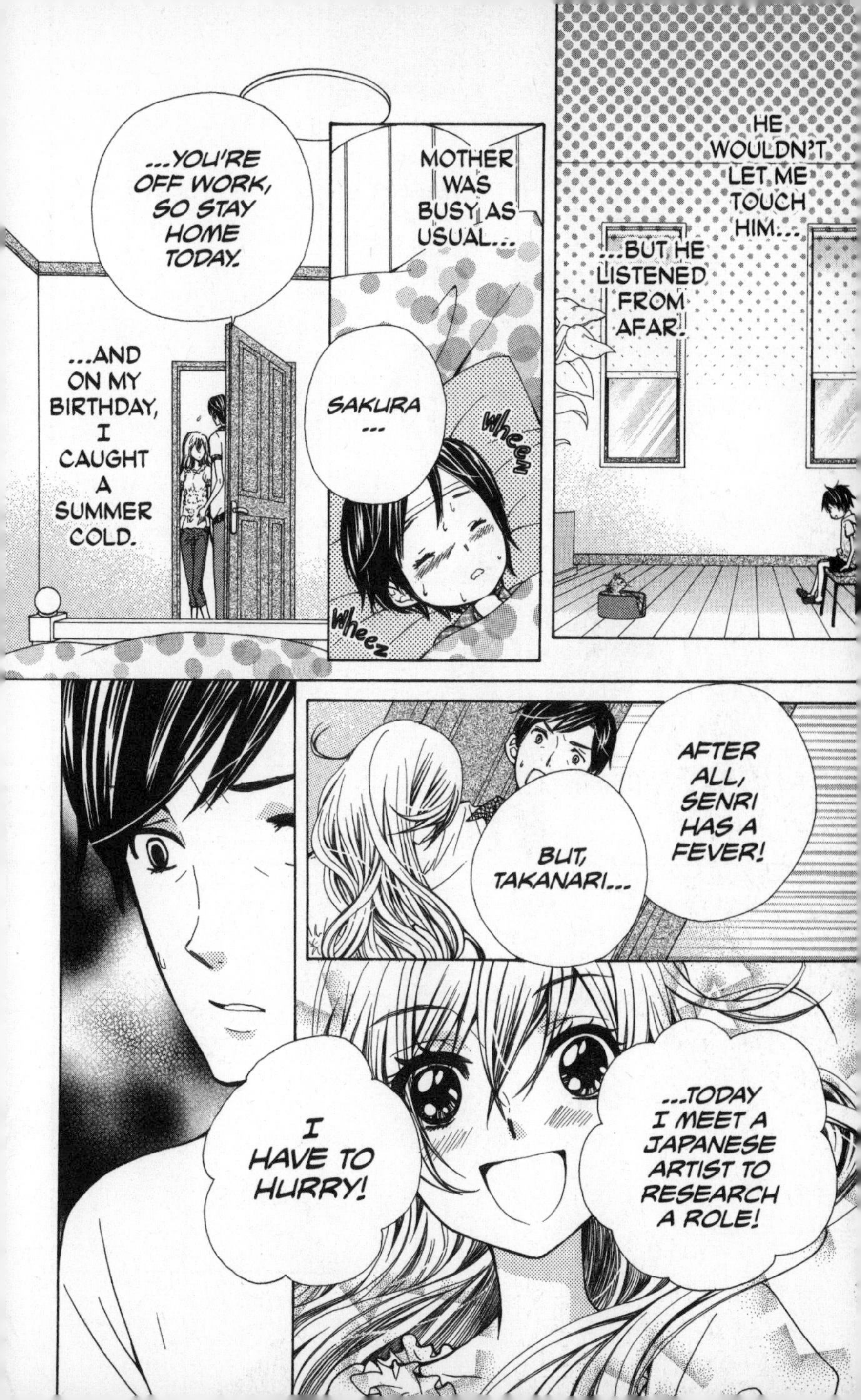

HE WOULDN'T LET ME TOUCH HIM...
...BUT HE LISTENED FROM AFAR.
MOTHER WAS BUSY AS USUAL...
SAKURA ...
wheez
wheez
...YOU'RE OFF WORK, SO STAY HOME TODAY.
...AND ON MY BIRTHDAY, I CAUGHT A SUMMER COLD.
AFTER ALL, SENRI HAS A FEVER!
BUT, TAKANARI...
...TODAY I MEET A JAPANESE ARTIST TO RESEARCH A ROLE!
I HAVE TO HURRY!

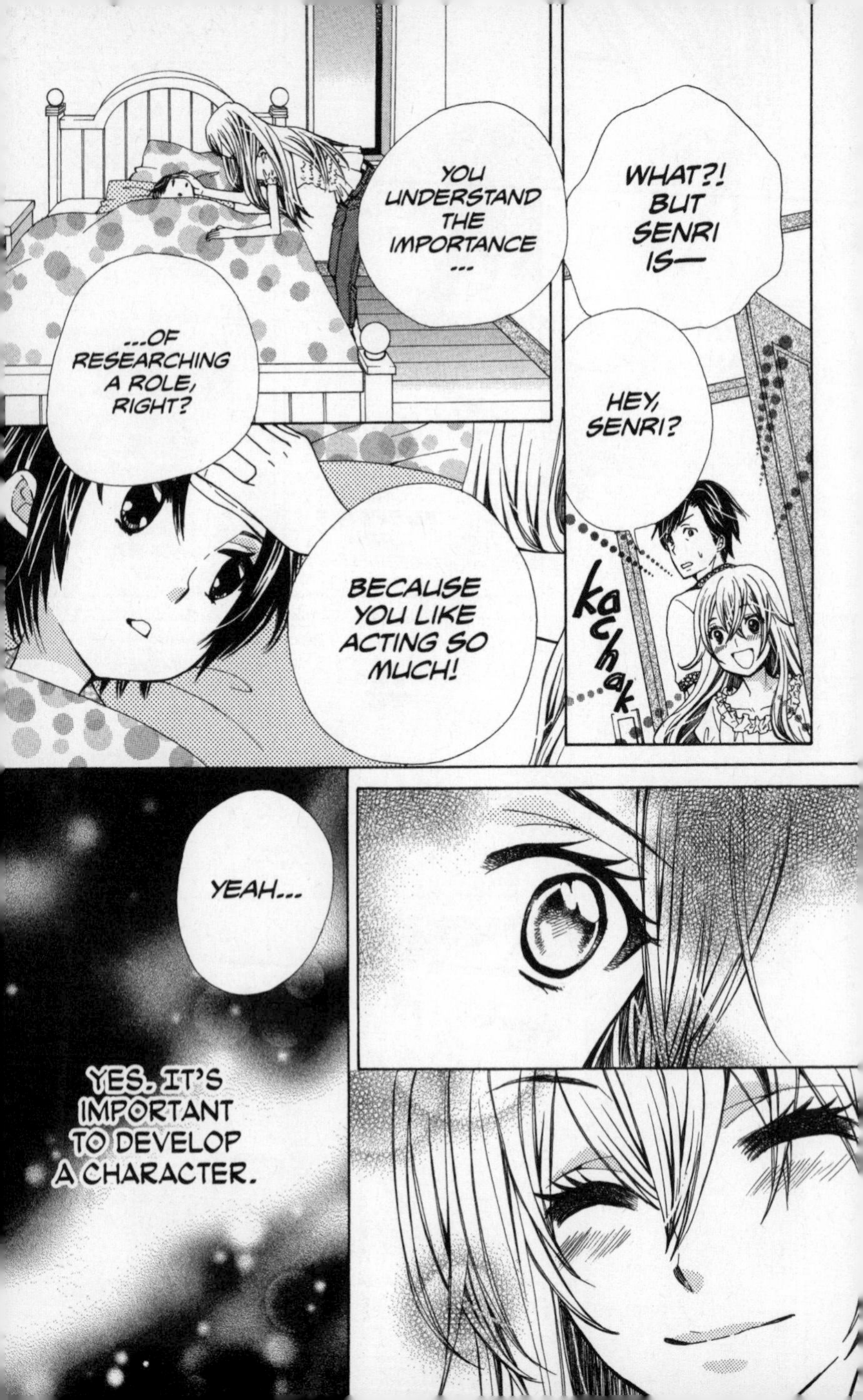
WHAT?! BUT SENRI IS—
HEY, SENRI?
kachak
YOU UNDERSTAND THE IMPORTANCE...
...OF RESEARCHING A ROLE, RIGHT?
BECAUSE YOU LIKE ACTING SO MUCH!
YEAH...
YES. IT'S IMPORTANT TO DEVELOP A CHARACTER.

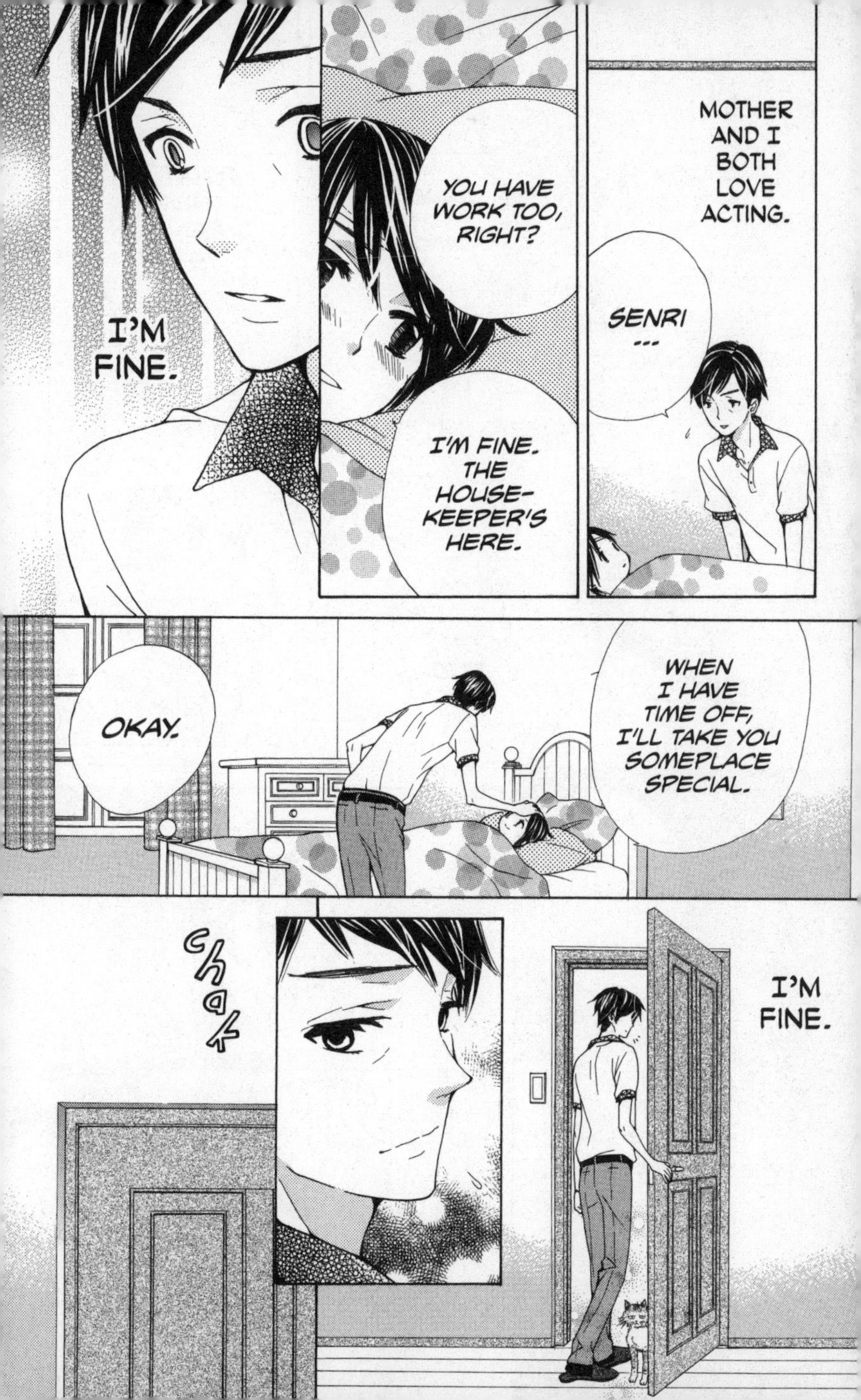
MOTHER AND I BOTH LOVE ACTING.
SENRI...
YOU HAVE WORK TOO, RIGHT?
I'M FINE. THE HOUSE-KEEPER'S HERE.
I'M FINE.
WHEN I HAVE TIME OFF, I'LL TAKE YOU SOMEPLACE SPECIAL.
OKAY.
I'M FINE.
chak

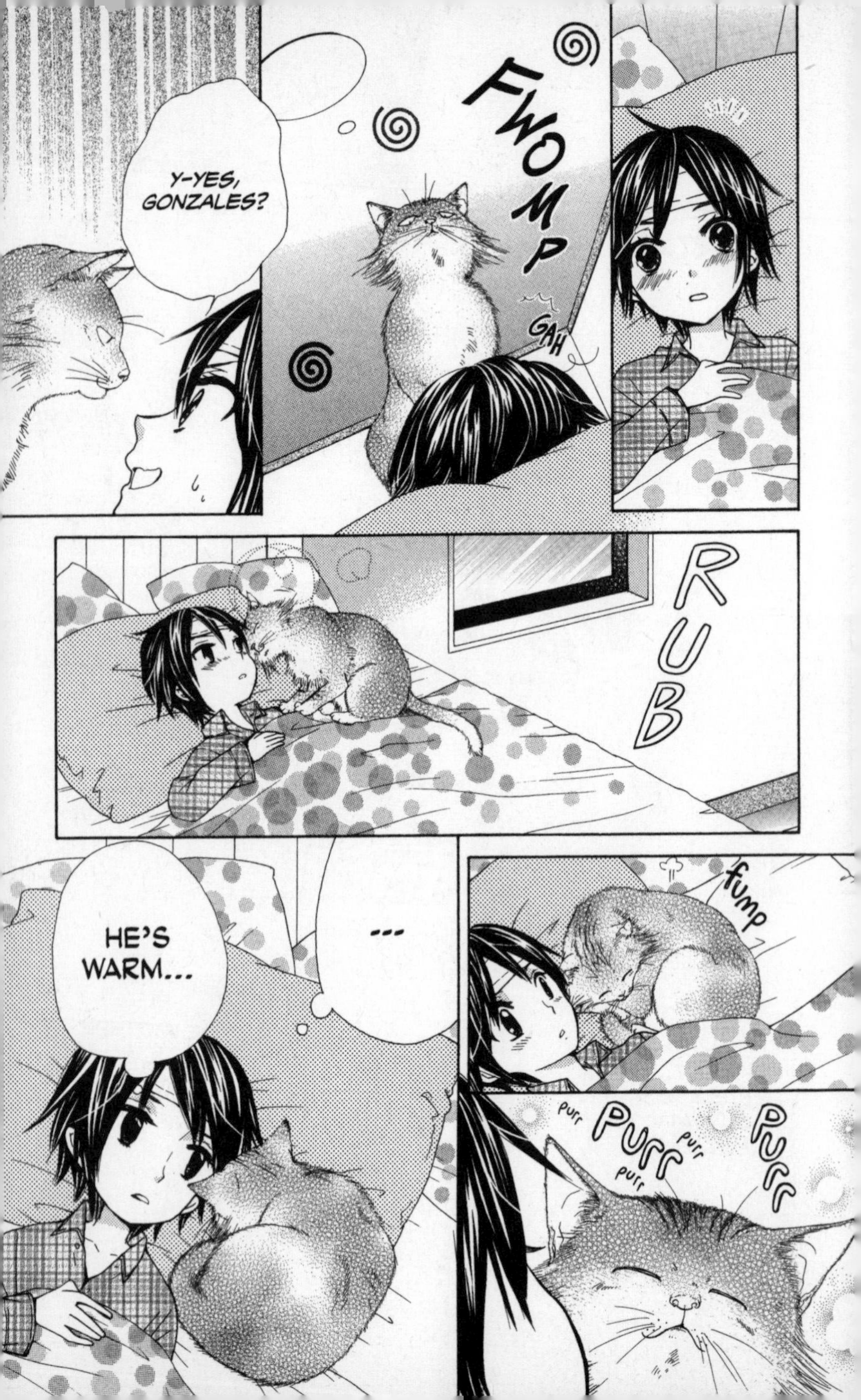
FWOMP
GAH
Y-YES, GONZALES?
RUB
fump
Purr
purr
purr
Purr
purr
purr
...
HE'S WARM...

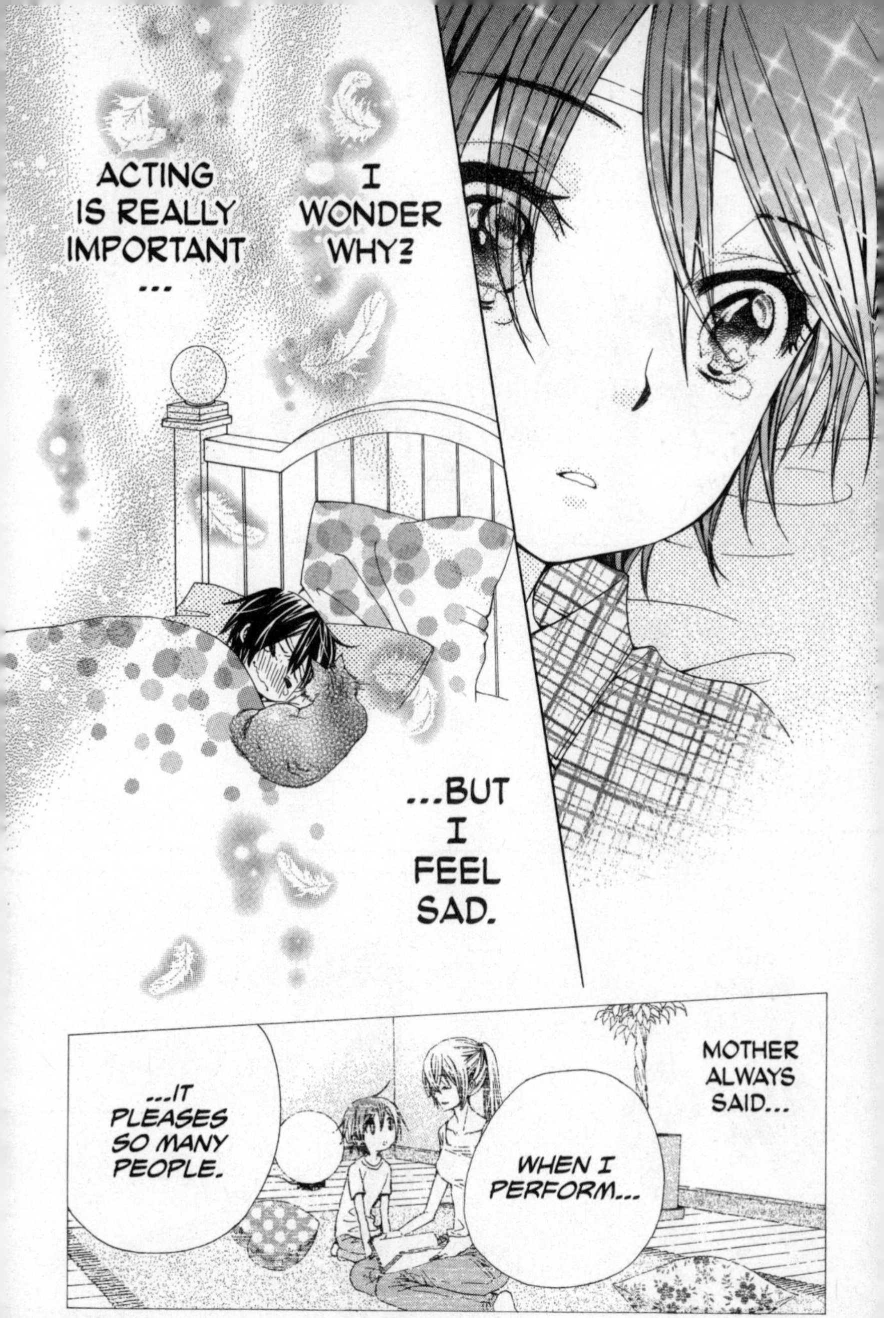
I WONDER WHY?
ACTING IS REALLY IMPORTANT ...
...BUT I FEEL SAD.
MOTHER ALWAYS SAID...
WHEN I PERFORM...
...IT PLEASES SO MANY PEOPLE.

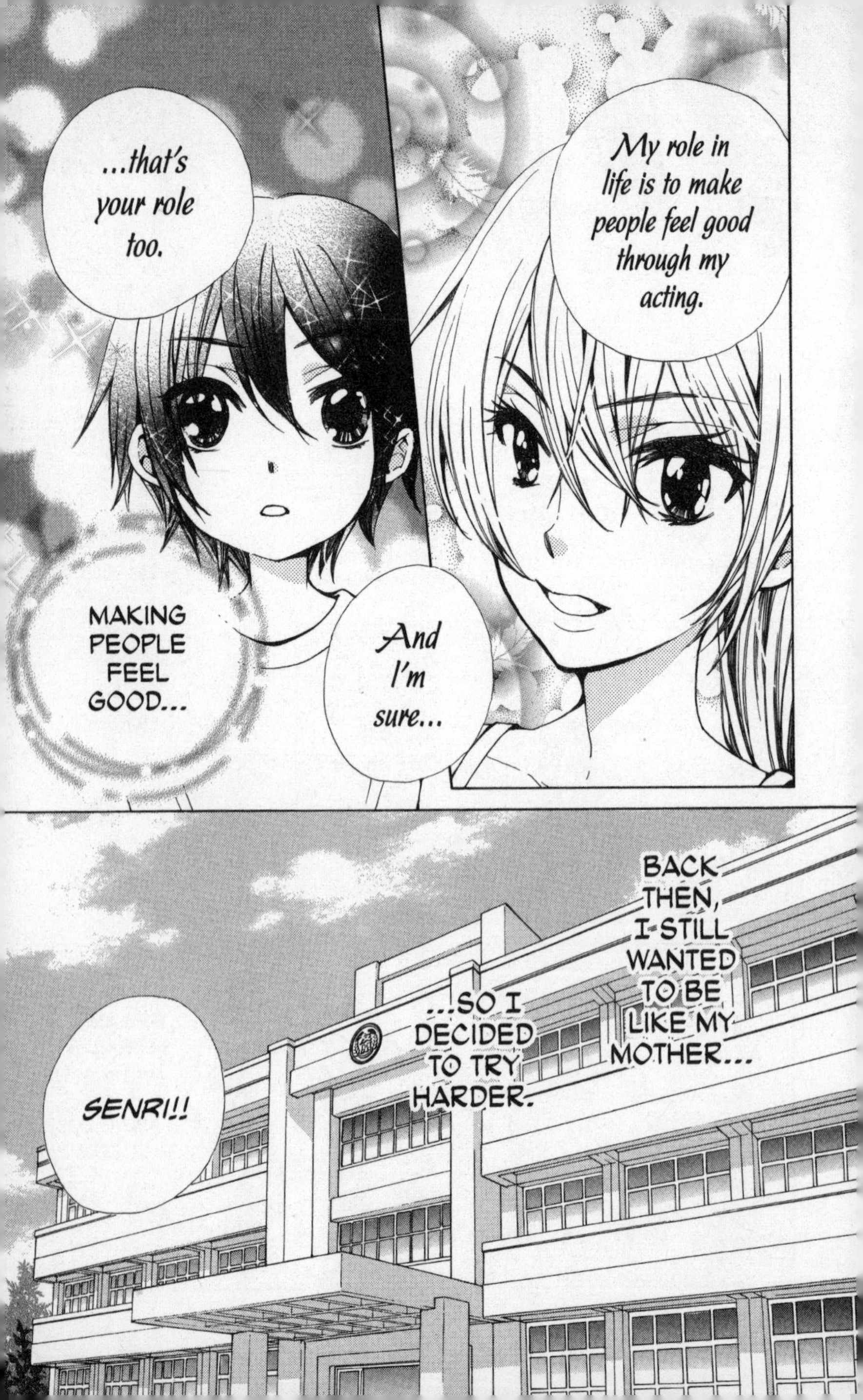
My role in life is to make people feel good through my acting.
And I'm sure...
...that's your role too.
MAKING PEOPLE FEEL GOOD...
BACK THEN, I STILL WANTED TO BE LIKE MY MOTHER...
...SO I DECIDED TO TRY HARDER.
SENRI!!

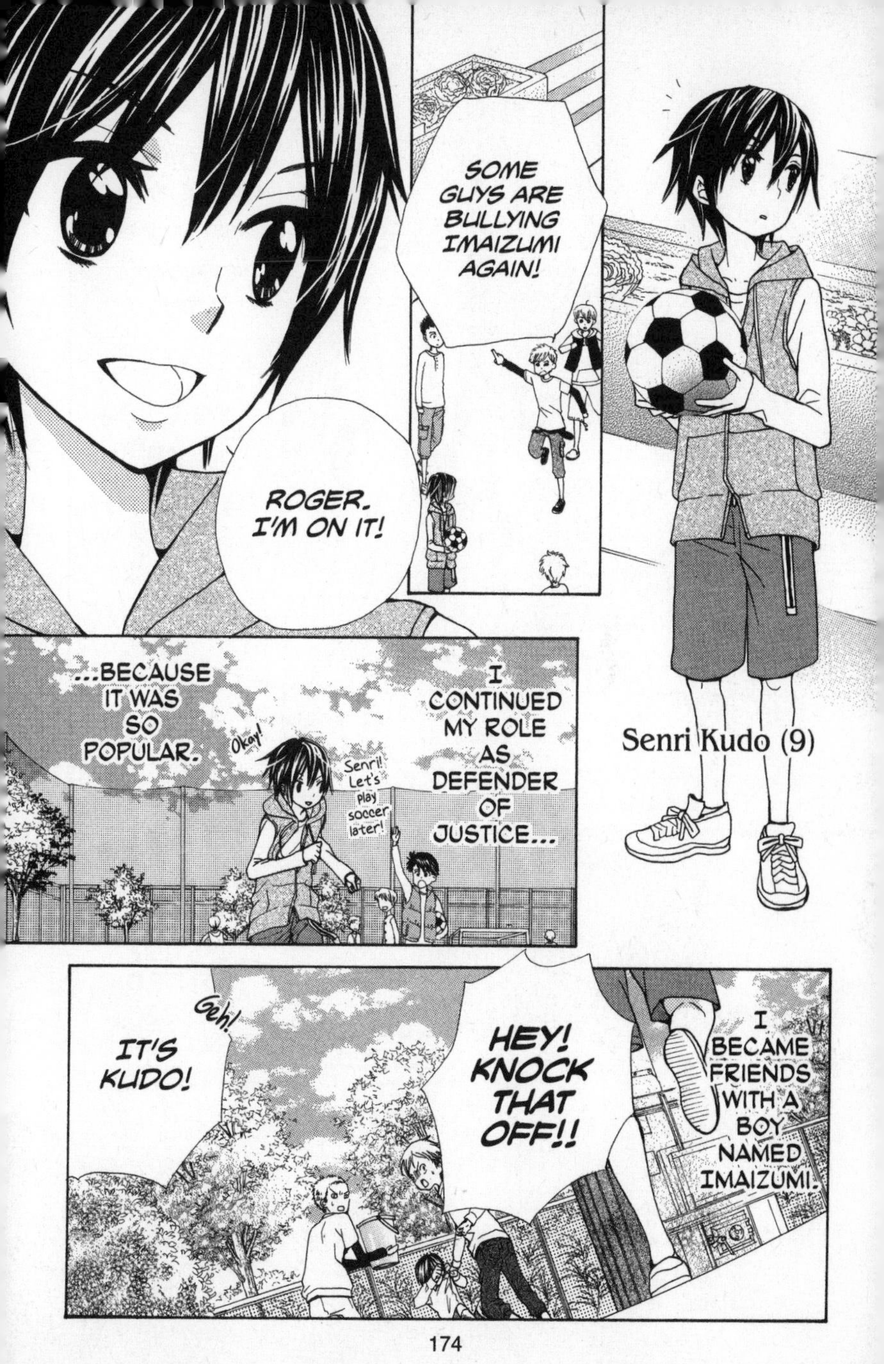
Senri Kudo (9)
SOME GUYS ARE BULLYING IMAIZUMI AGAIN!
ROGER. I'M ON IT!
I CONTINUED MY ROLE AS DEFENDER OF JUSTICE...
Senri! Let's play soccer later!
Okay!
...BECAUSE IT WAS SO POPULAR.
I BECAME FRIENDS WITH A BOY NAMED IMAIZUMI.
HEY! KNOCK THAT OFF!!
Geh!
IT'S KUDO!

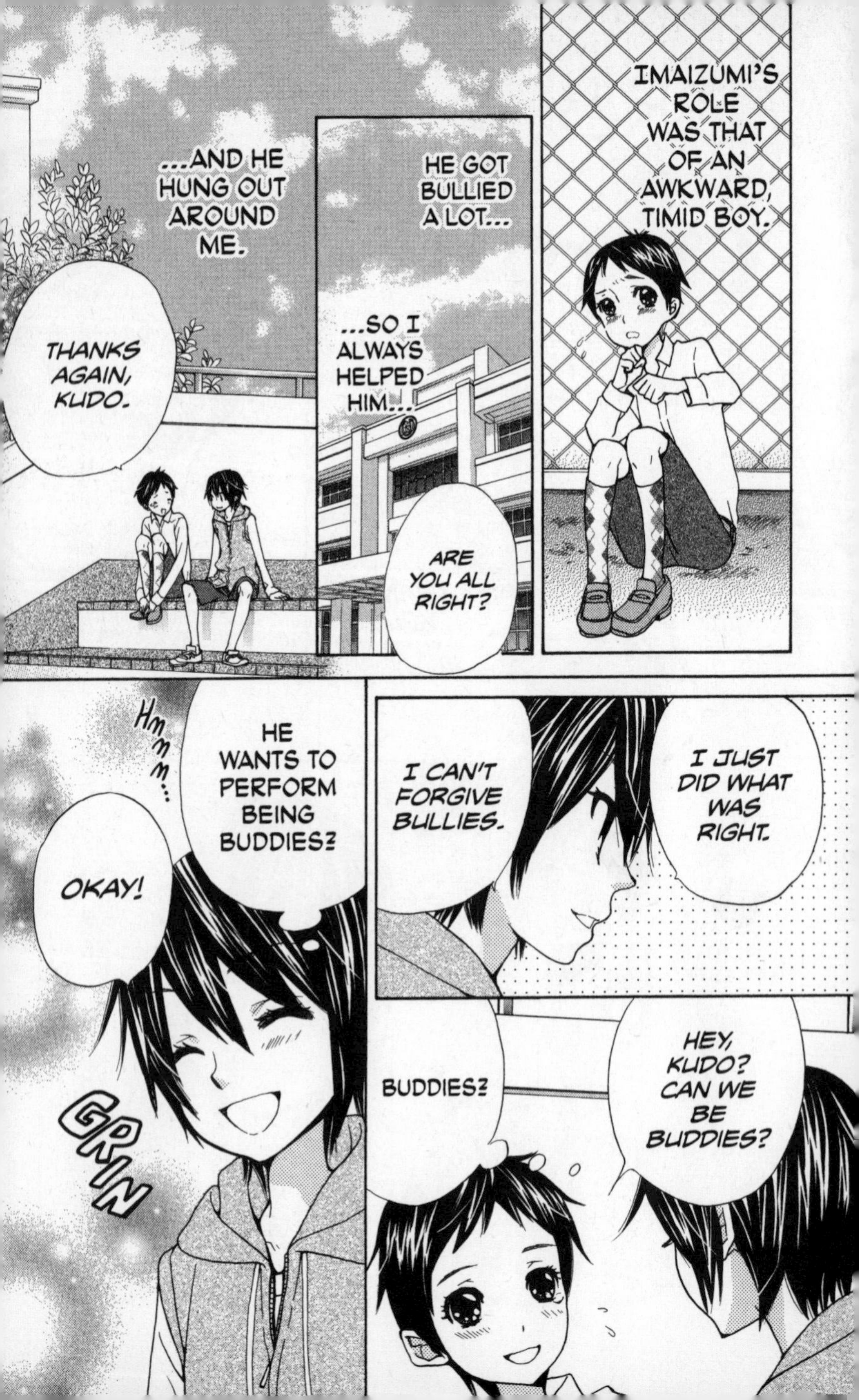
IMAIZUMI'S ROLE WAS THAT OF AN AWKWARD, TIMID BOY.
HE GOT BULLIED A LOT...
...SO I ALWAYS HELPED HIM...
ARE YOU ALL RIGHT?
...AND HE HUNG OUT AROUND ME.
THANKS AGAIN, KUDO.
I JUST DID WHAT WAS RIGHT.
I CAN'T FORGIVE BULLIES.
HEY, KUDO? CAN WE BE BUDDIES?
BUDDIES?
HE WANTS TO PERFORM BEING BUDDIES?
Hmmm...
OKAY!
GRIN

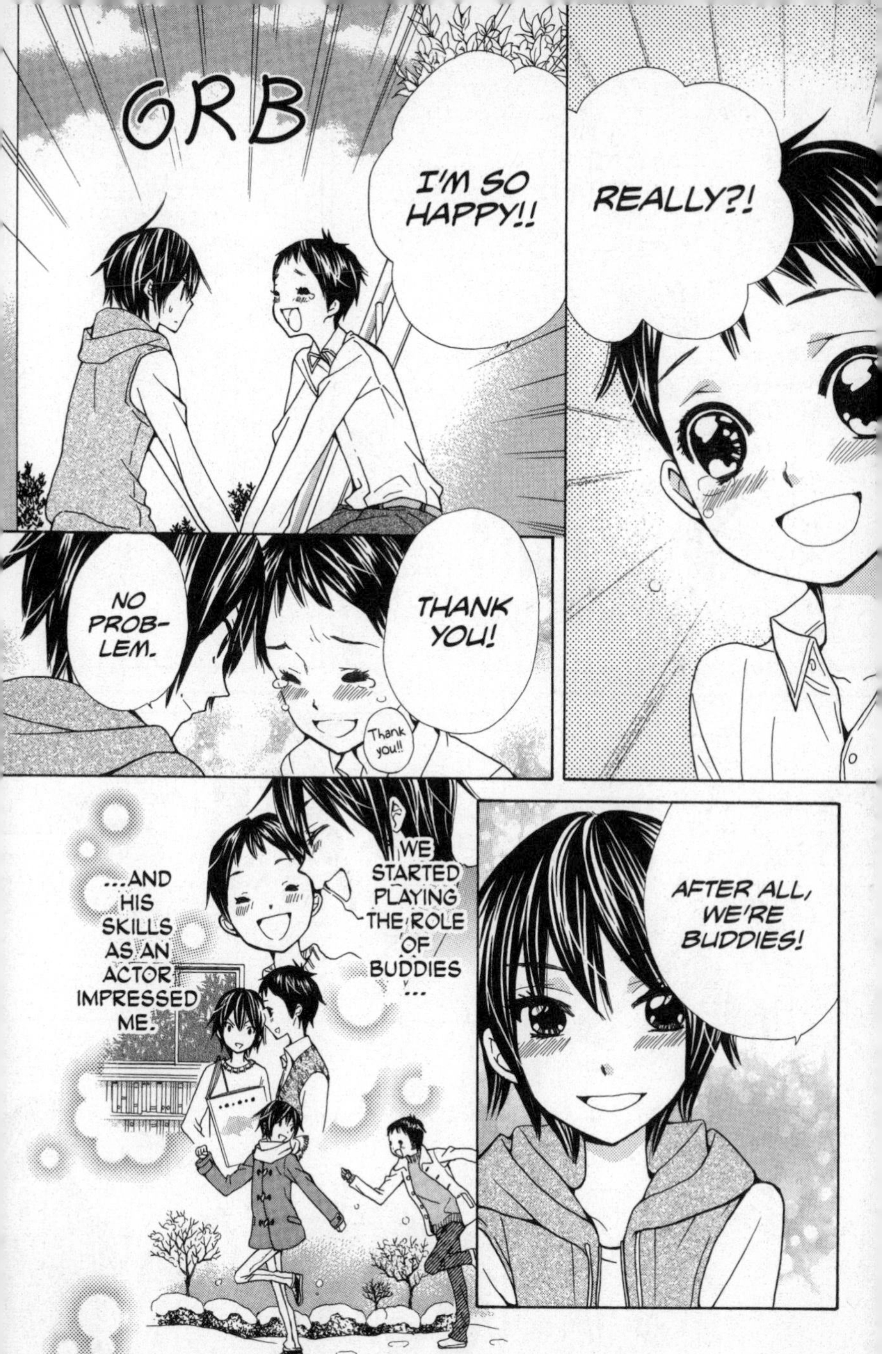
REALLY?!
GRB
I'M SO HAPPY!!
THANK YOU!
Thank you!!
NO PROBLEM.
AFTER ALL, WE'RE BUDDIES!
WE STARTED PLAYING THE ROLE OF BUDDIES...
...AND HIS SKILLS AS AN ACTOR IMPRESSED ME.

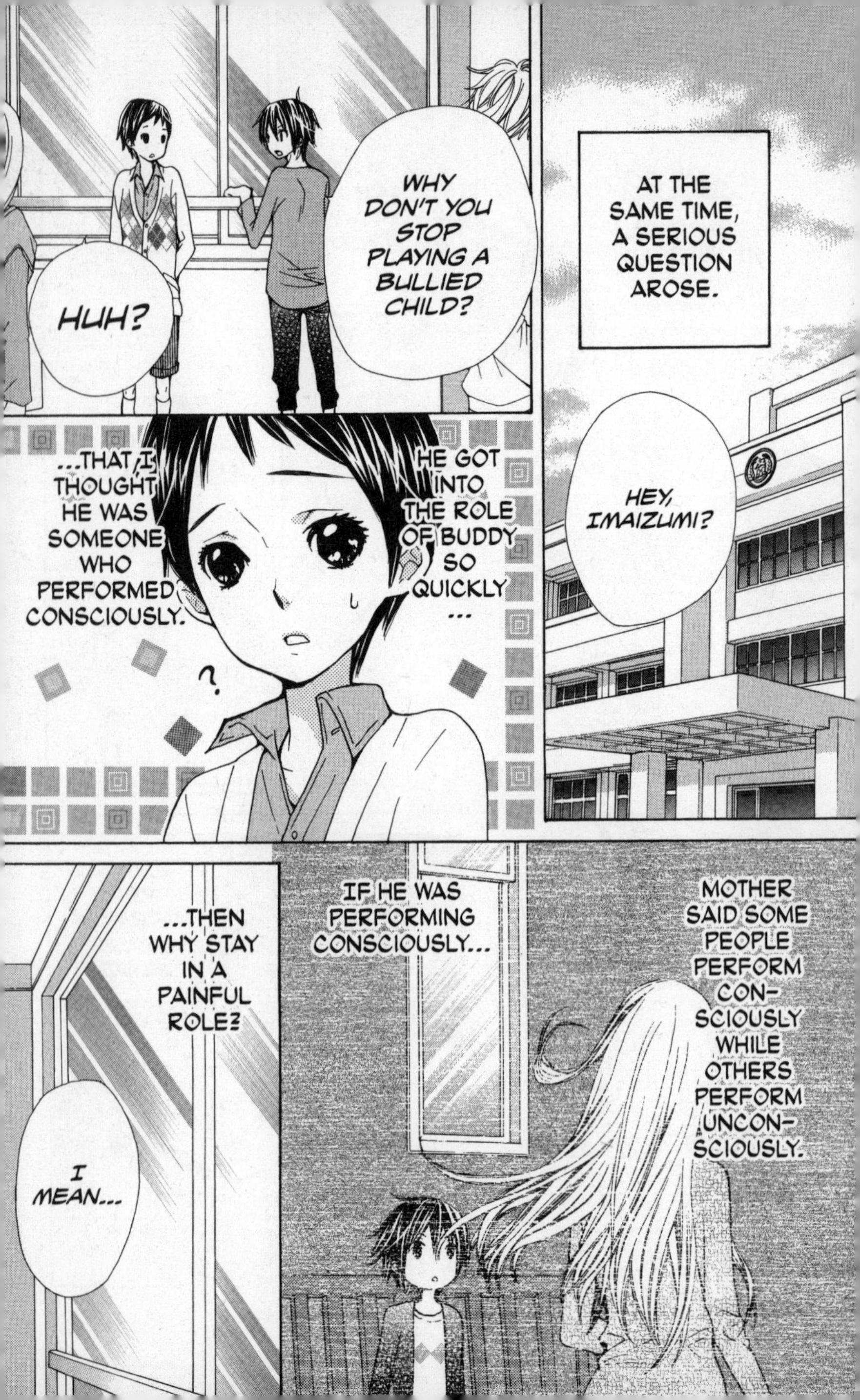
AT THE SAME TIME, A SERIOUS QUESTION AROSE.
HEY, IMAIZUMI?
WHY DON'T YOU STOP PLAYING A BULLIED CHILD?
HUH?
HE GOT INTO THE ROLE OF BUDDY SO QUICKLY...
...THAT I THOUGHT HE WAS SOMEONE WHO PERFORMED CONSCIOUSLY.
?
MOTHER SAID SOME PEOPLE PERFORM CON-SCIOUSLY WHILE OTHERS PERFORM UNCON-SCIOUSLY.
IF HE WAS PERFORMING CONSCIOUSLY...
...THEN WHY STAY IN A PAINFUL ROLE?
I MEAN...

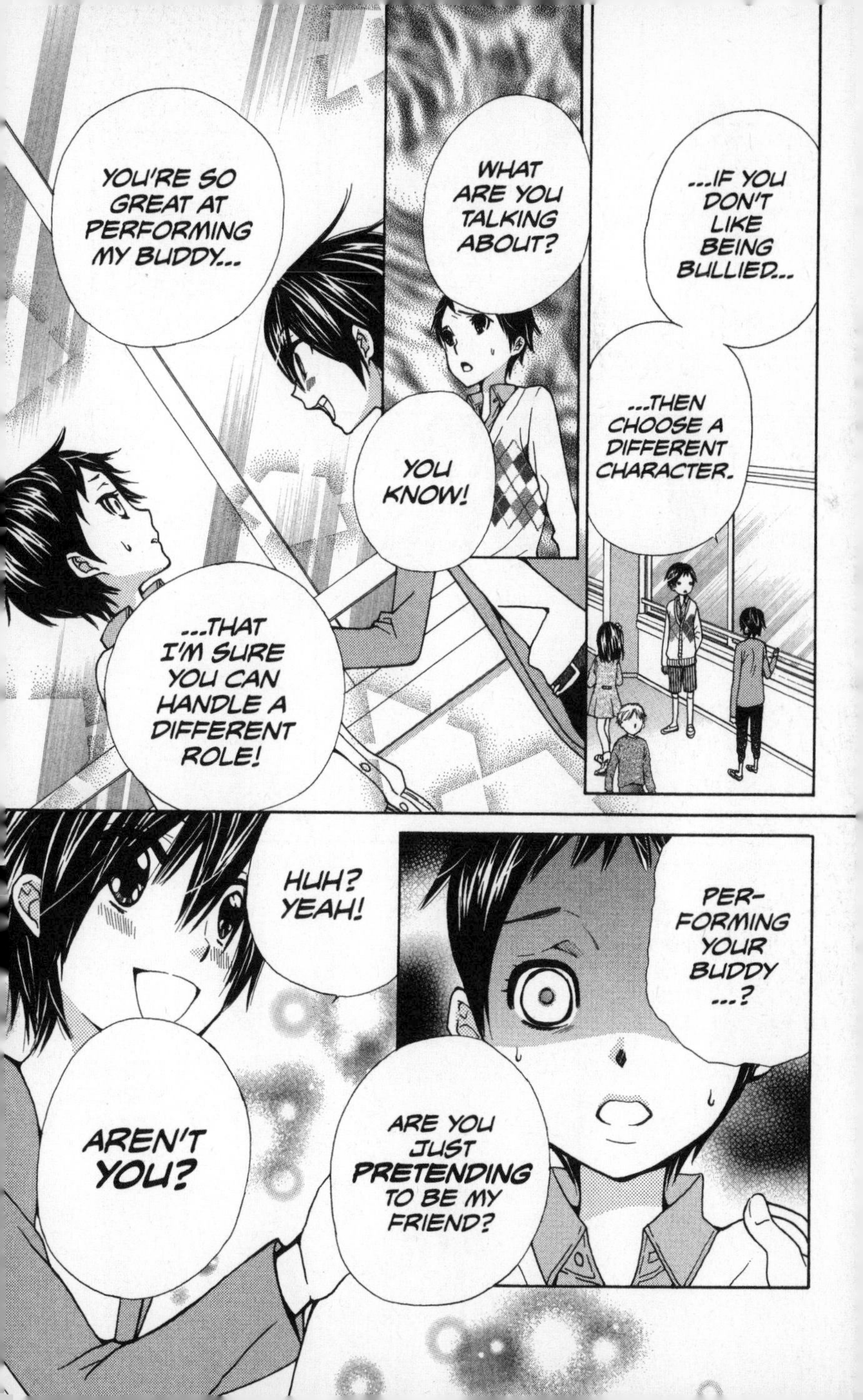
...IF YOU DON'T LIKE BEING BULLIED...
...THEN CHOOSE A DIFFERENT CHARACTER.
WHAT ARE YOU TALKING ABOUT?
YOU KNOW!
YOU'RE SO GREAT AT PERFORMING MY BUDDY...
...THAT I'M SURE YOU CAN HANDLE A DIFFERENT ROLE!
PER-FORMING YOUR BUDDY ...?
ARE YOU JUST PRETENDING TO BE MY FRIEND?
HUH? YEAH!
AREN'T YOU?

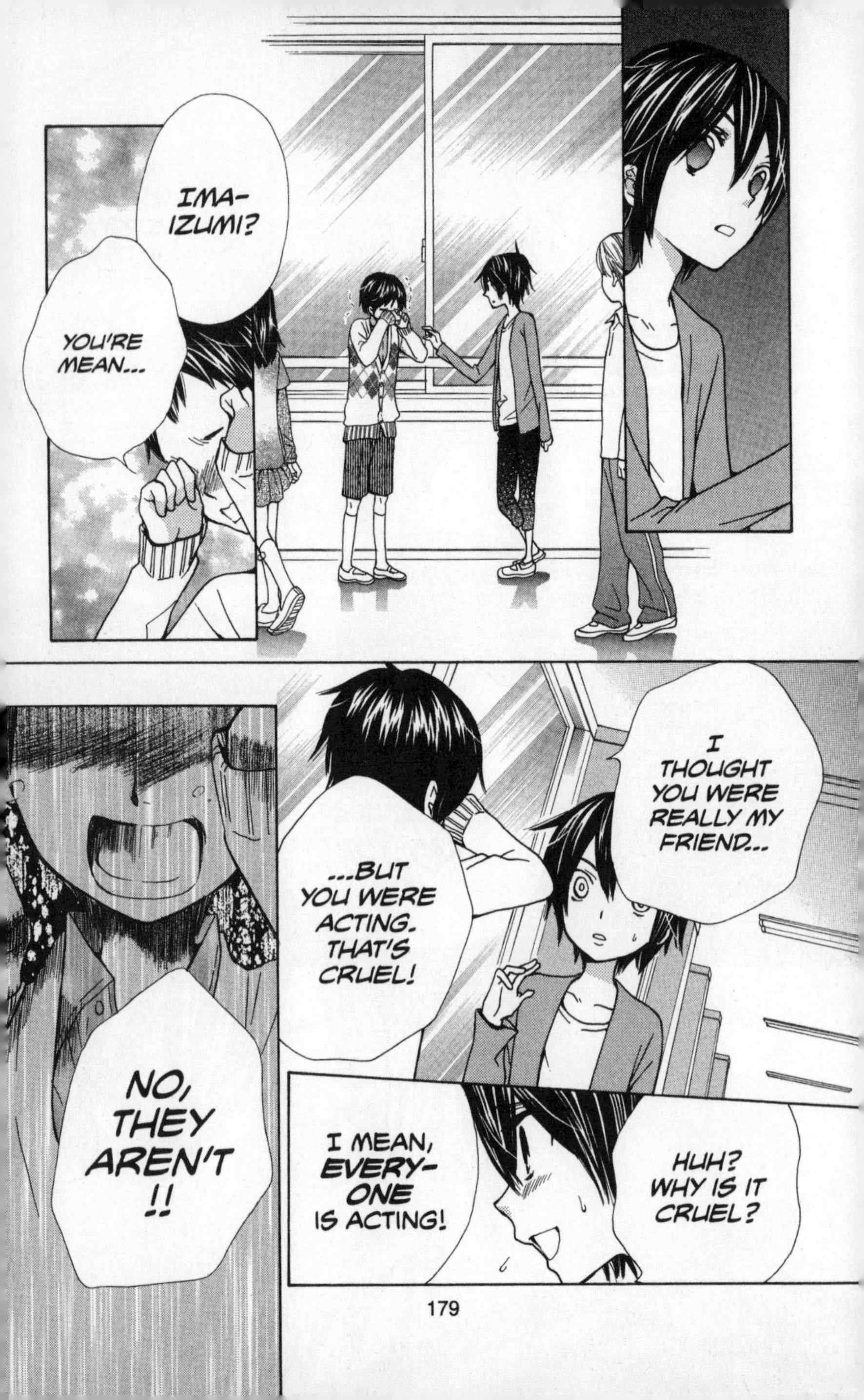
IMA-IZUMI?
YOU'RE MEAN...
I THOUGHT YOU WERE REALLY MY FRIEND...
...BUT YOU WERE ACTING. THAT'S CRUEL!
HUH? WHY IS IT CRUEL?
I MEAN, EVERY-ONE IS ACTING!
NO, THEY AREN'T!!

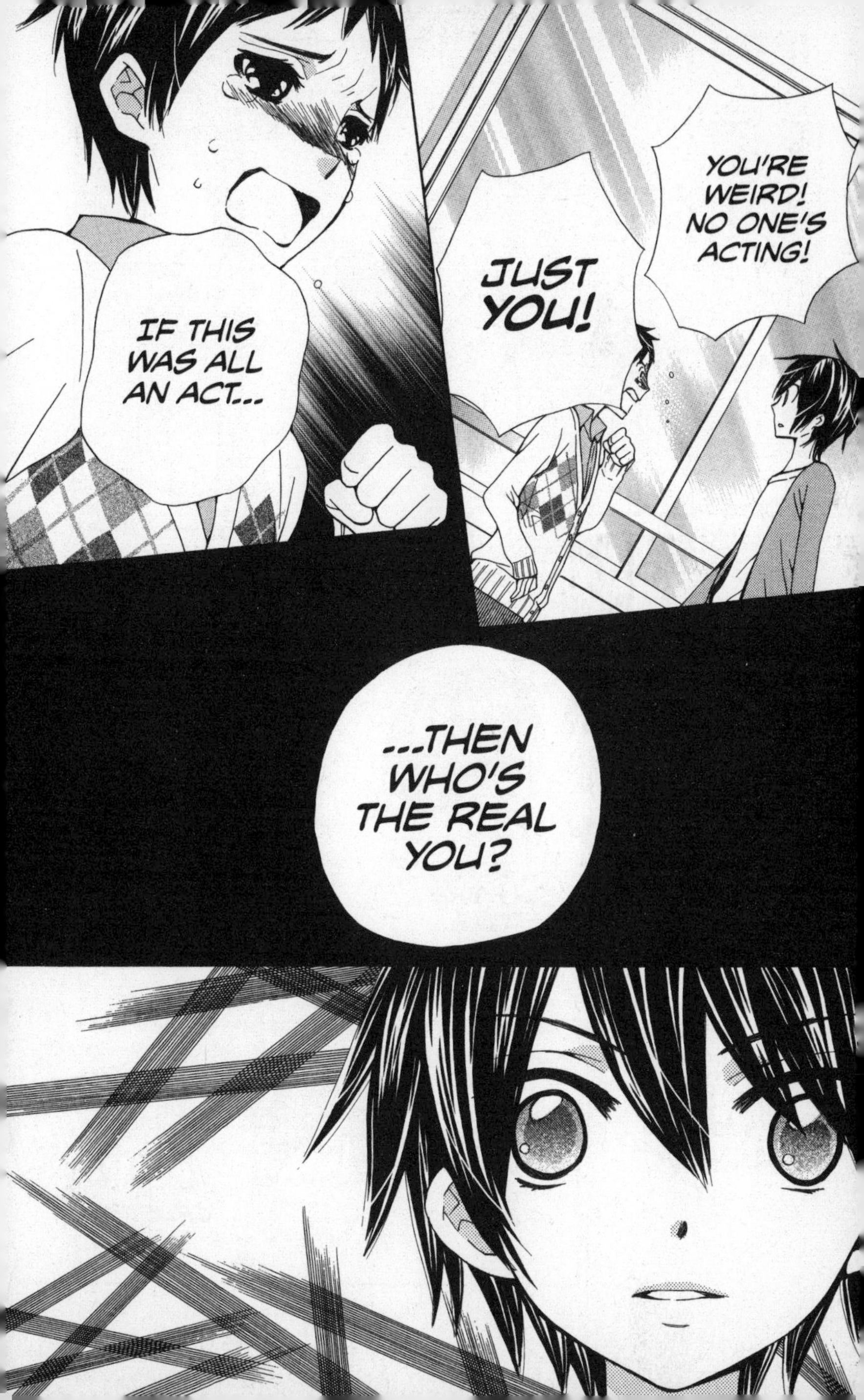
YOU'RE WEIRD! NO ONE'S ACTING!
JUST YOU!
IF THIS WAS ALL AN ACT...
...THEN WHO'S THE REAL YOU?

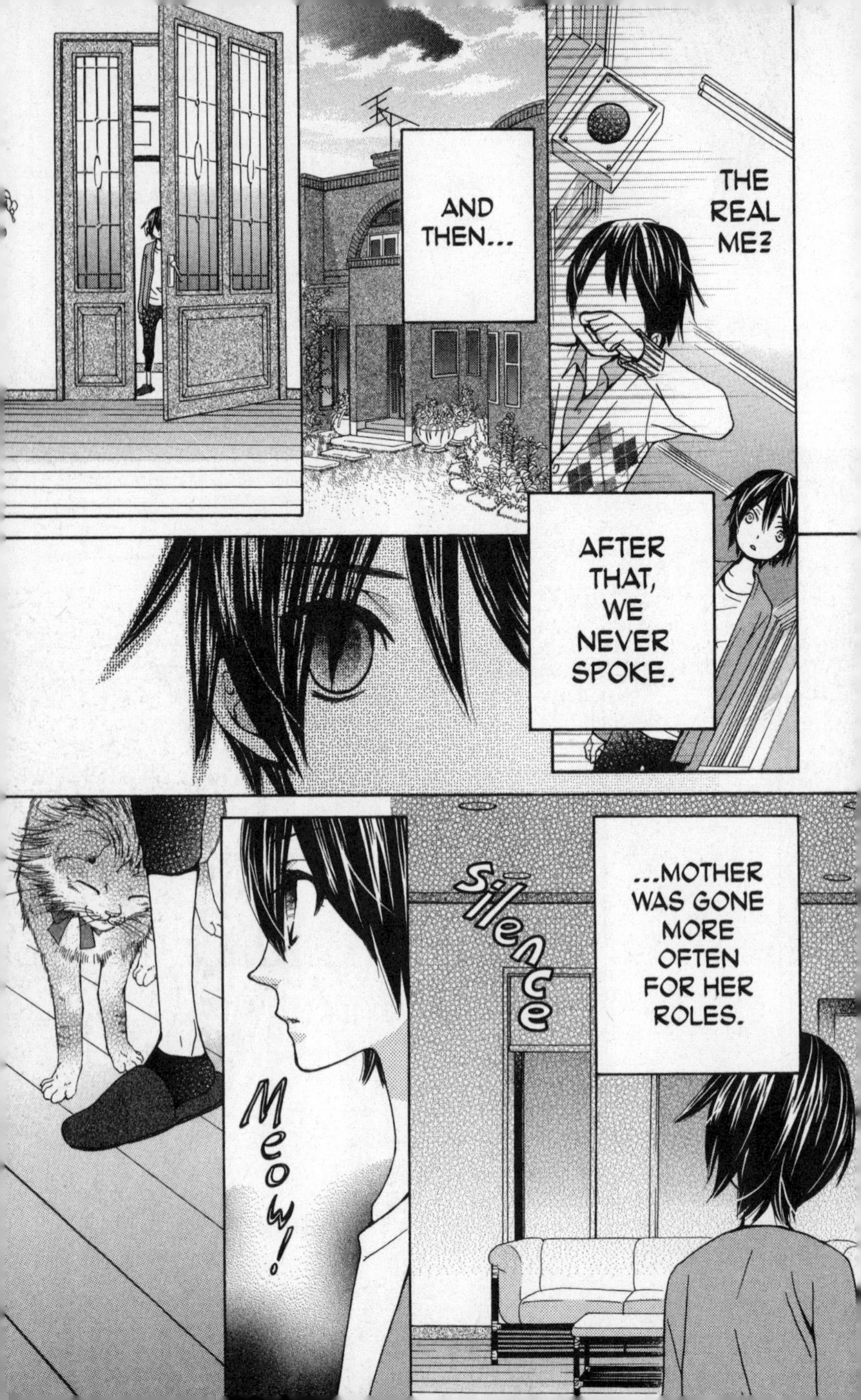
THE REAL ME?
AND THEN...
AFTER THAT, WE NEVER SPOKE.
...MOTHER WAS GONE MORE OFTEN FOR HER ROLES.
Silence
Meow!

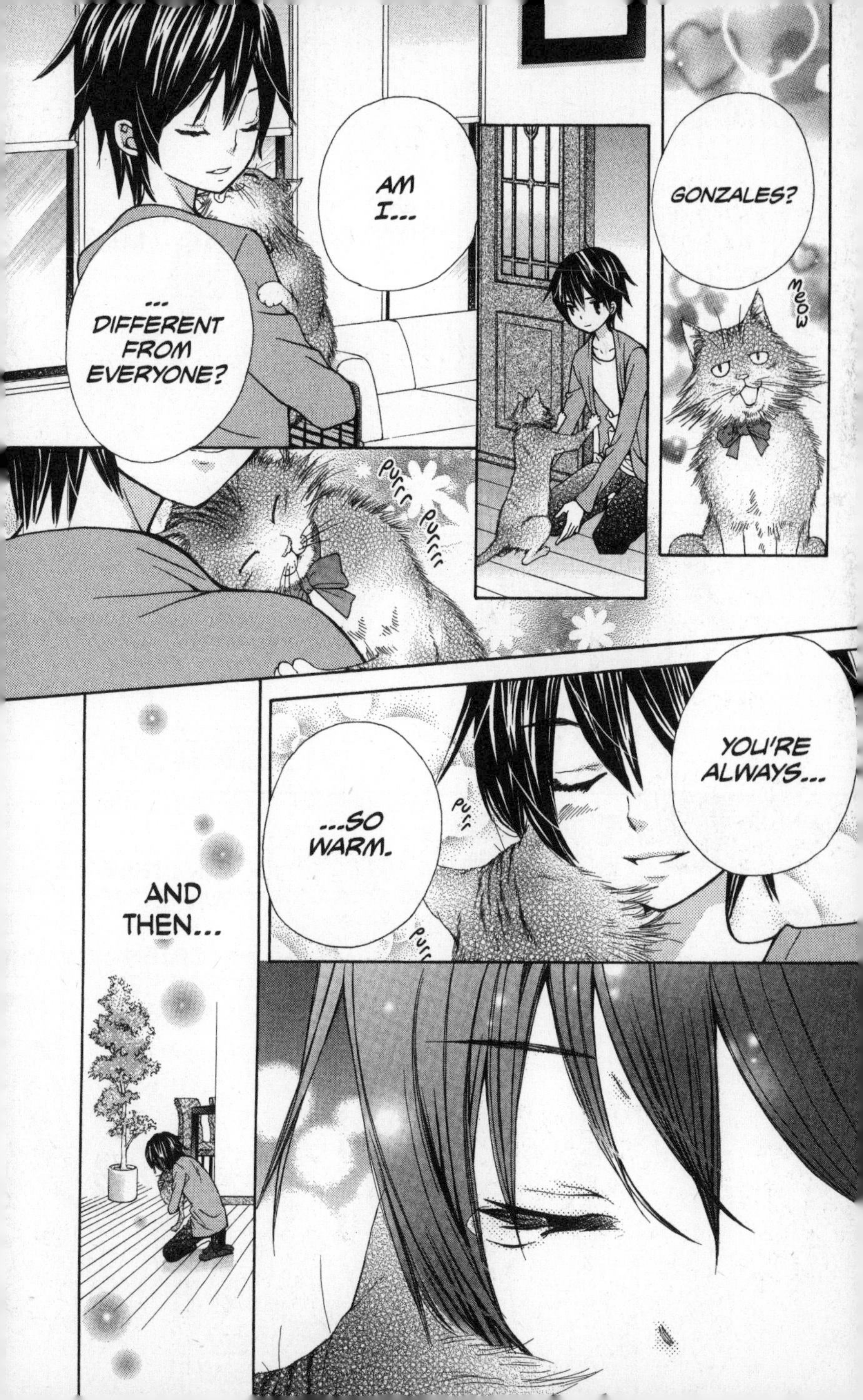
GONZALES?
MEOW
AM I...
...DIFFERENT FROM EVERYONE?
PURRR
PURRR
YOU'RE ALWAYS...
PURR
...SO WARM.
PURR
AND THEN...

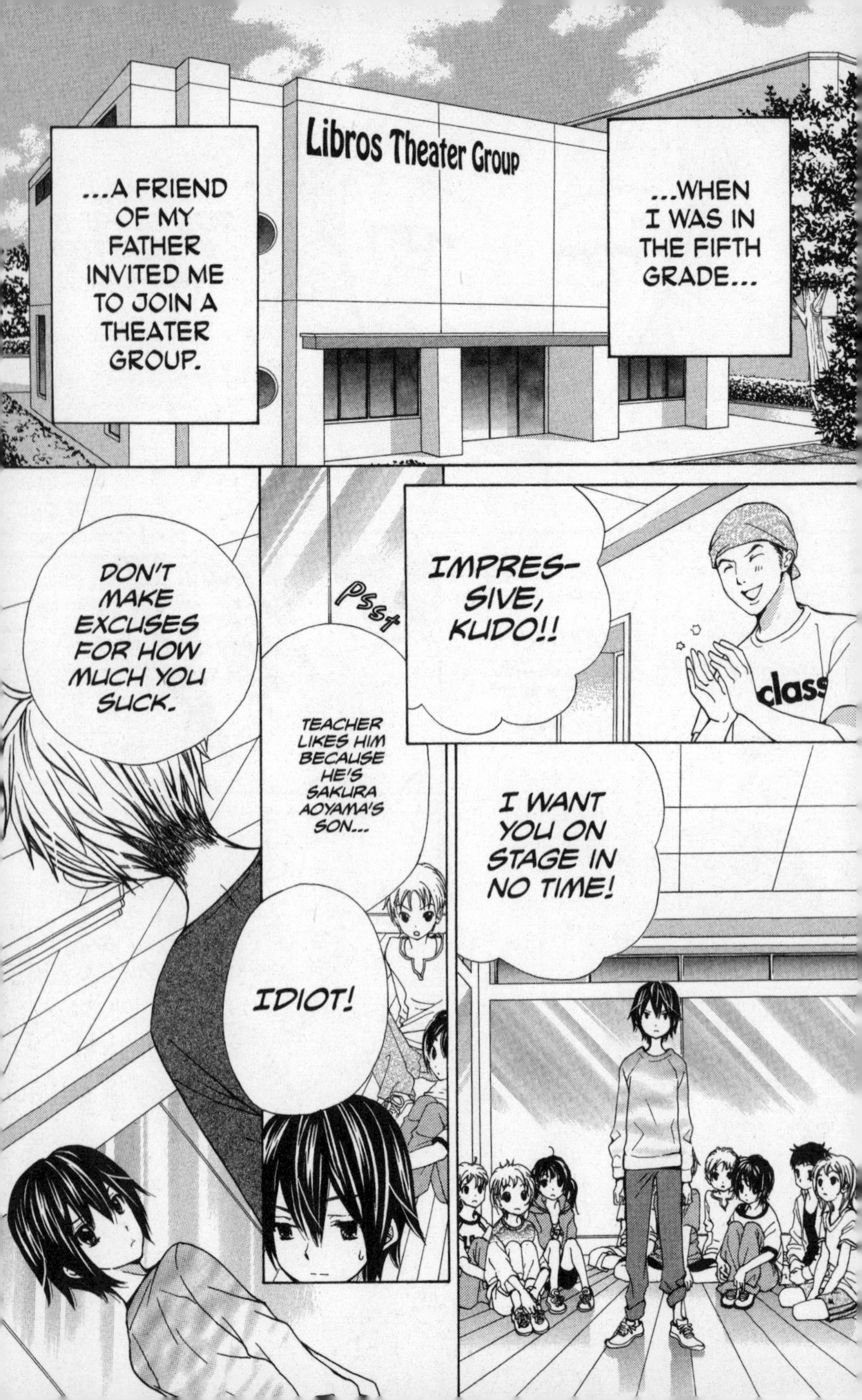

...WHEN I WAS IN THE FIFTH GRADE...
Libros Theater Group
...A FRIEND OF MY FATHER INVITED ME TO JOIN A THEATER GROUP.
IMPRES-SIVE, KUDO!!
class
I WANT YOU ON STAGE IN NO TIME!
Psst
TEACHER LIKES HIM BECAUSE HE'S SAKURA AOYAMA'S SON...
IDIOT!
DON'T MAKE EXCUSES FOR HOW MUCH YOU SUCK.

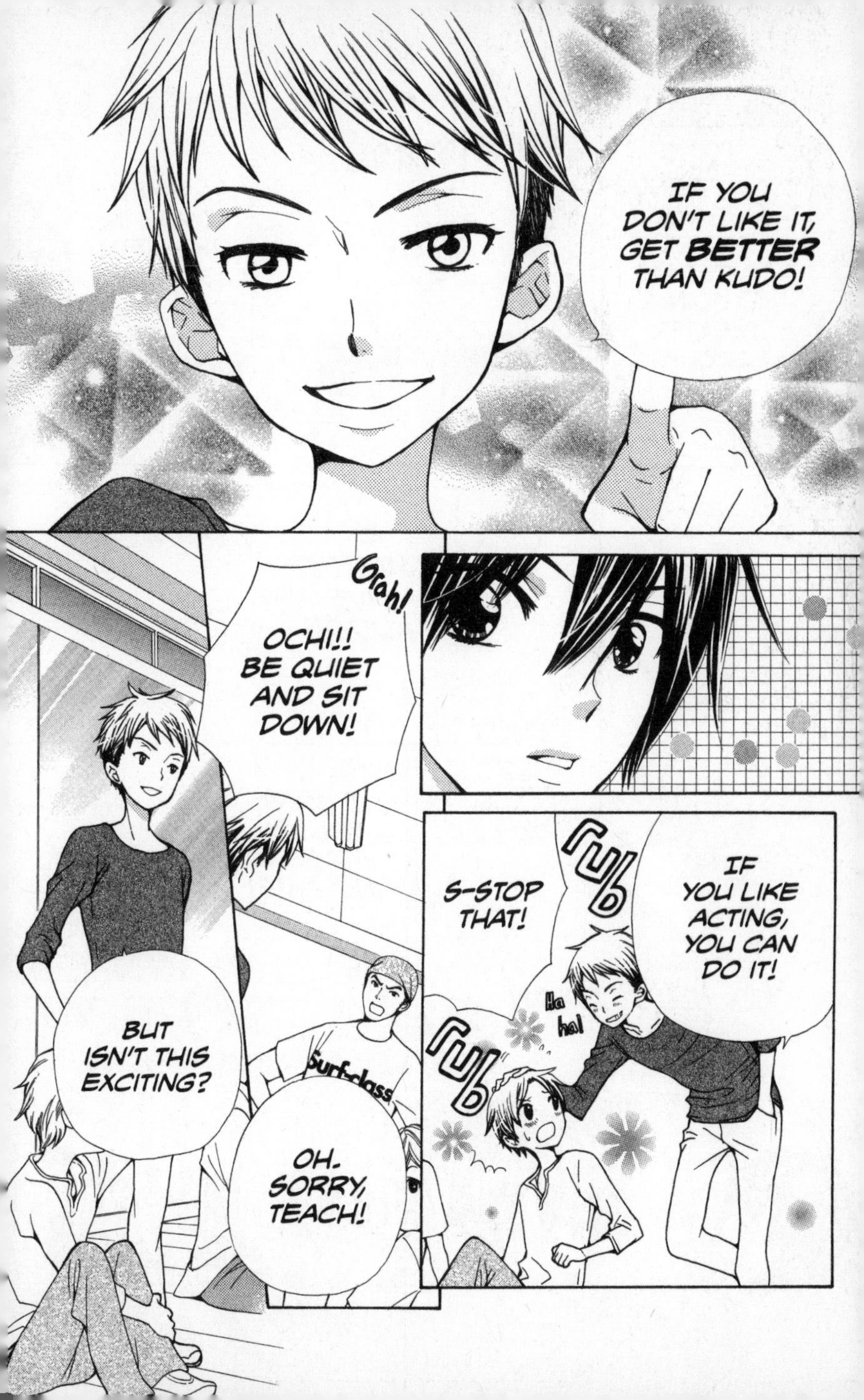
IF YOU DON'T LIKE IT, GET BETTER THAN KUDO!
IF YOU LIKE ACTING, YOU CAN DO IT!
rub
S-STOP THAT!
Ha ha!
rub
Grah!
OCHI!! BE QUIET AND SIT DOWN!
BUT ISN'T THIS EXCITING?
OH. SORRY, TEACH!
Surf-class

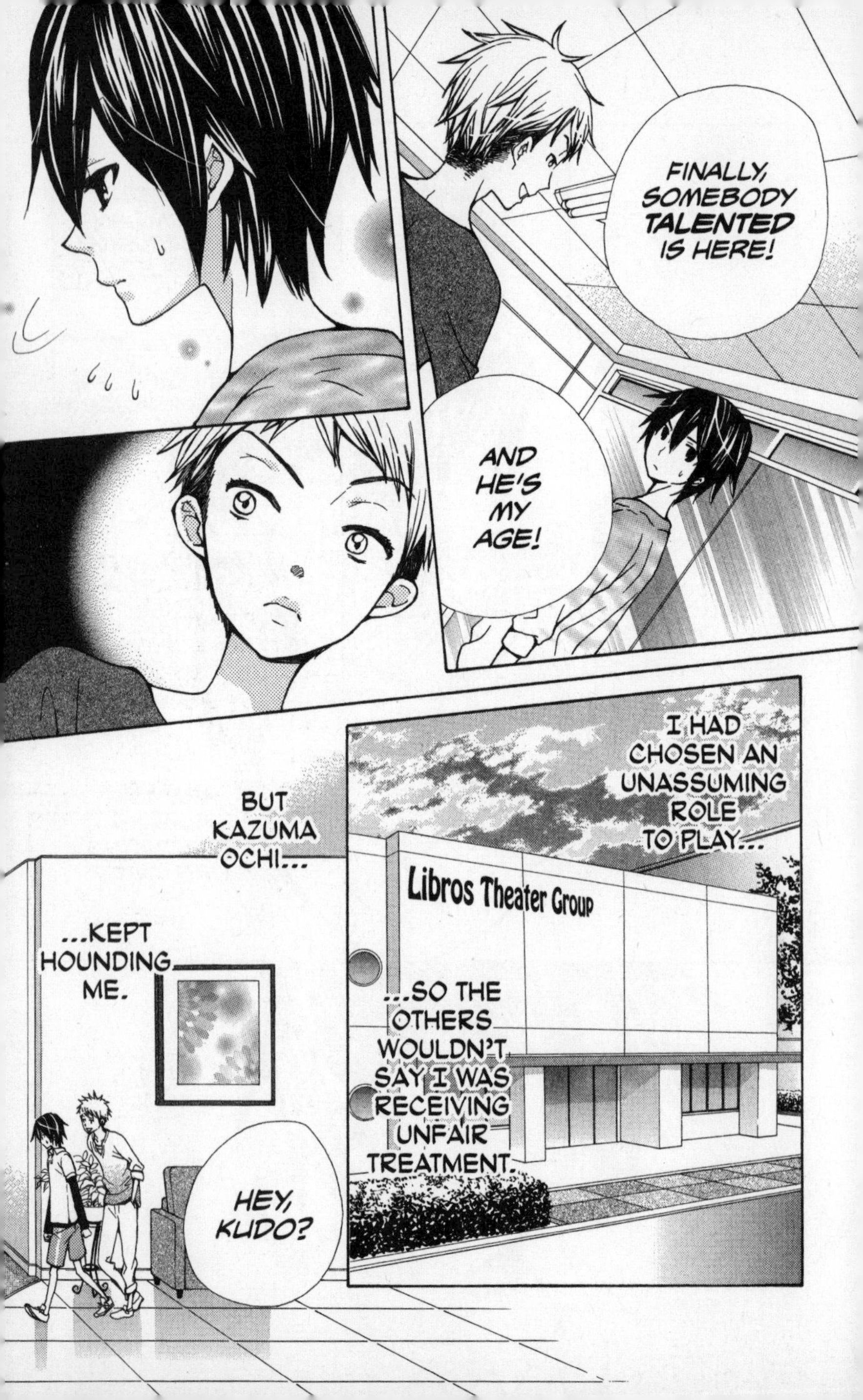
FINALLY, SOMEBODY TALENTED IS HERE!
AND HE'S MY AGE!
I HAD CHOSEN AN UNASSUMING ROLE TO PLAY...
Libros Theater Group
...SO THE OTHERS WOULDN'T SAY I WAS RECEIVING UNFAIR TREATMENT.
BUT KAZUMA OCHI...
...KEPT HOUNDING ME.
HEY, KUDO?

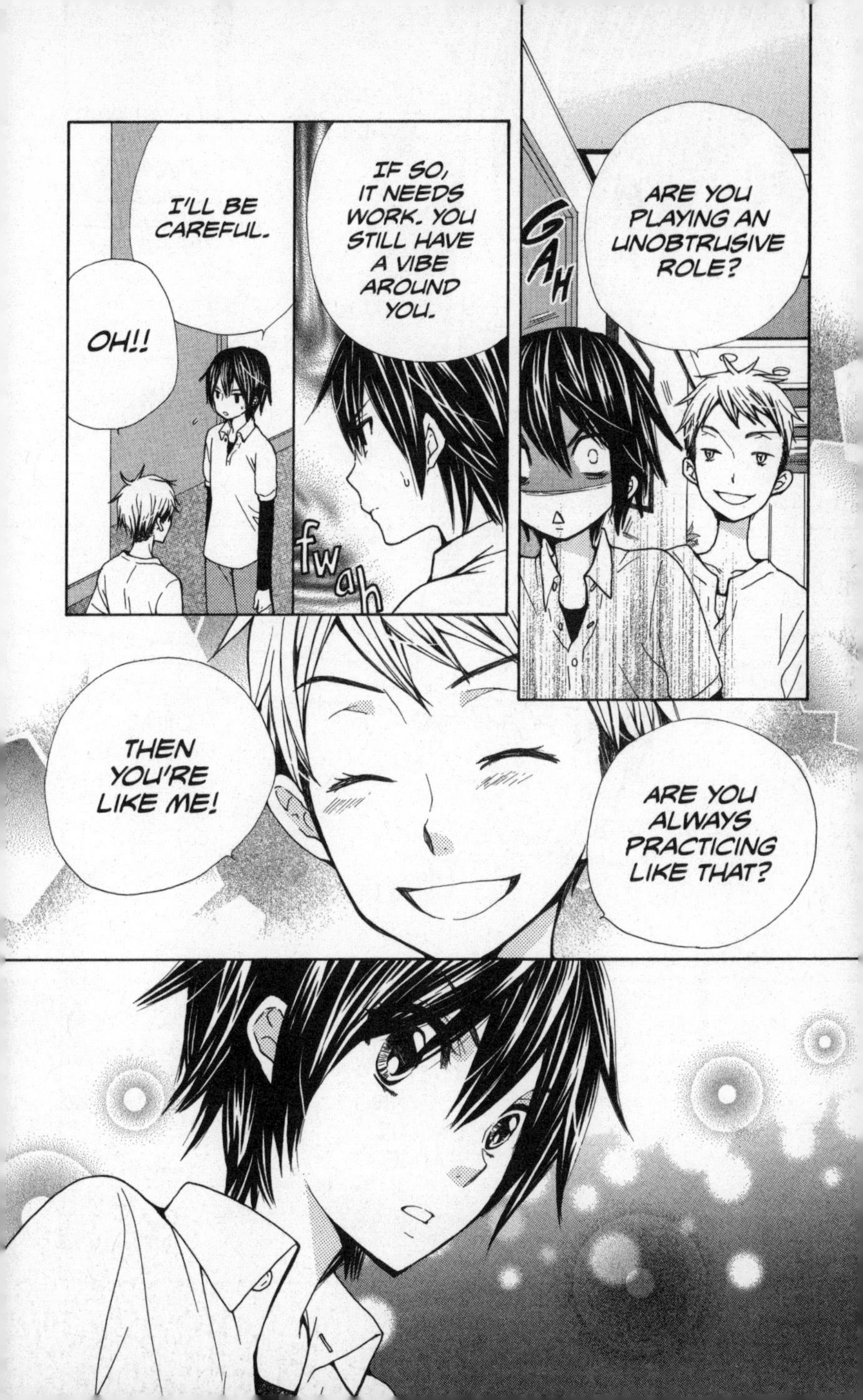
GAH
ARE YOU PLAYING AN UNOBTRUSIVE ROLE?
IF SO, IT NEEDS WORK. YOU STILL HAVE A VIBE AROUND YOU.
fwah
I'LL BE CAREFUL.
OH!!
ARE YOU ALWAYS PRACTICING LIKE THAT?
THEN YOU'RE LIKE ME!

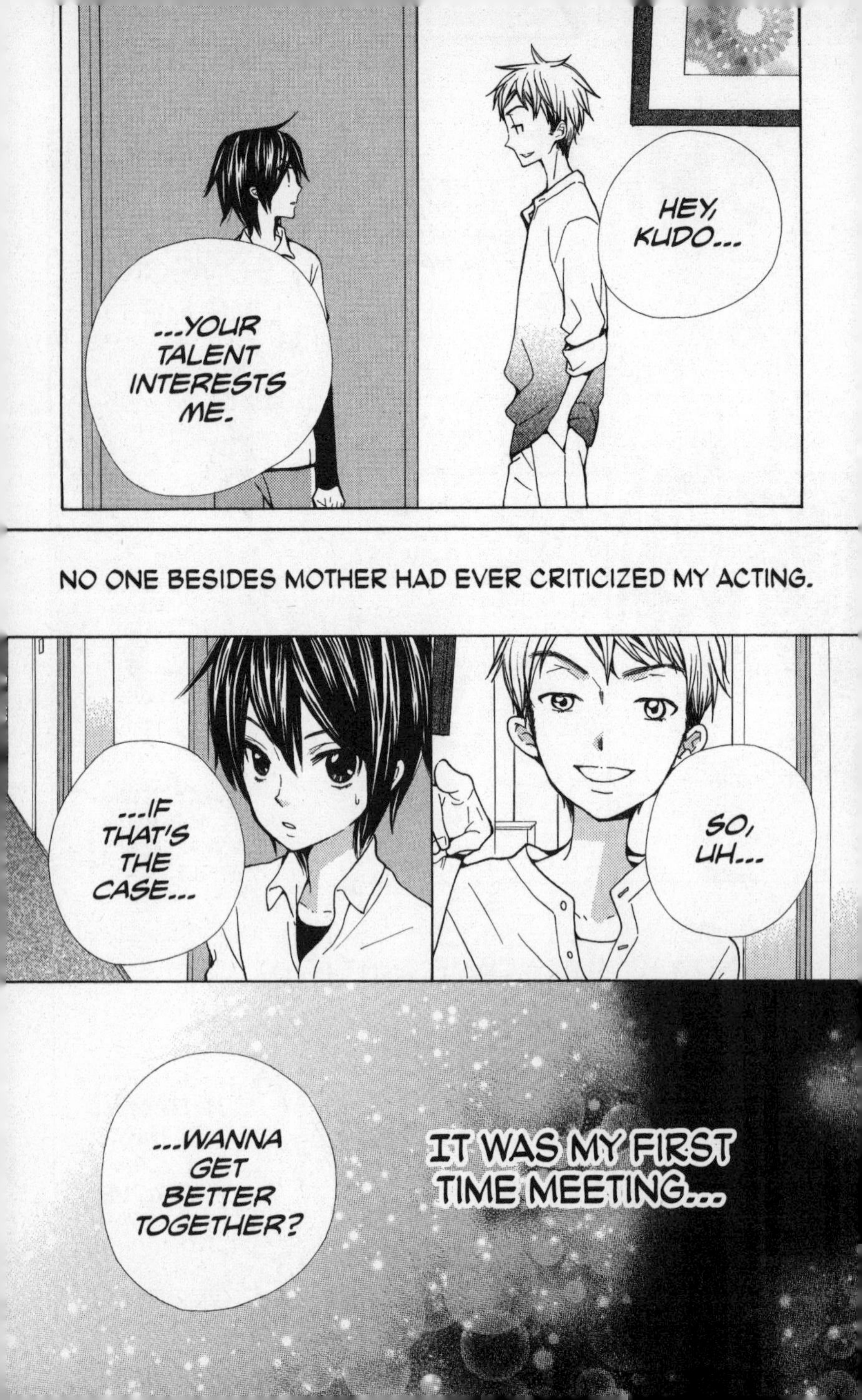
HEY, KUDO...
...YOUR TALENT INTERESTS ME.
NO ONE BESIDES MOTHER HAD EVER CRITICIZED MY ACTING.
SO, UH...
...IF THAT'S THE CASE...
...WANNA GET BETTER TOGETHER?
IT WAS MY FIRST TIME MEETING...

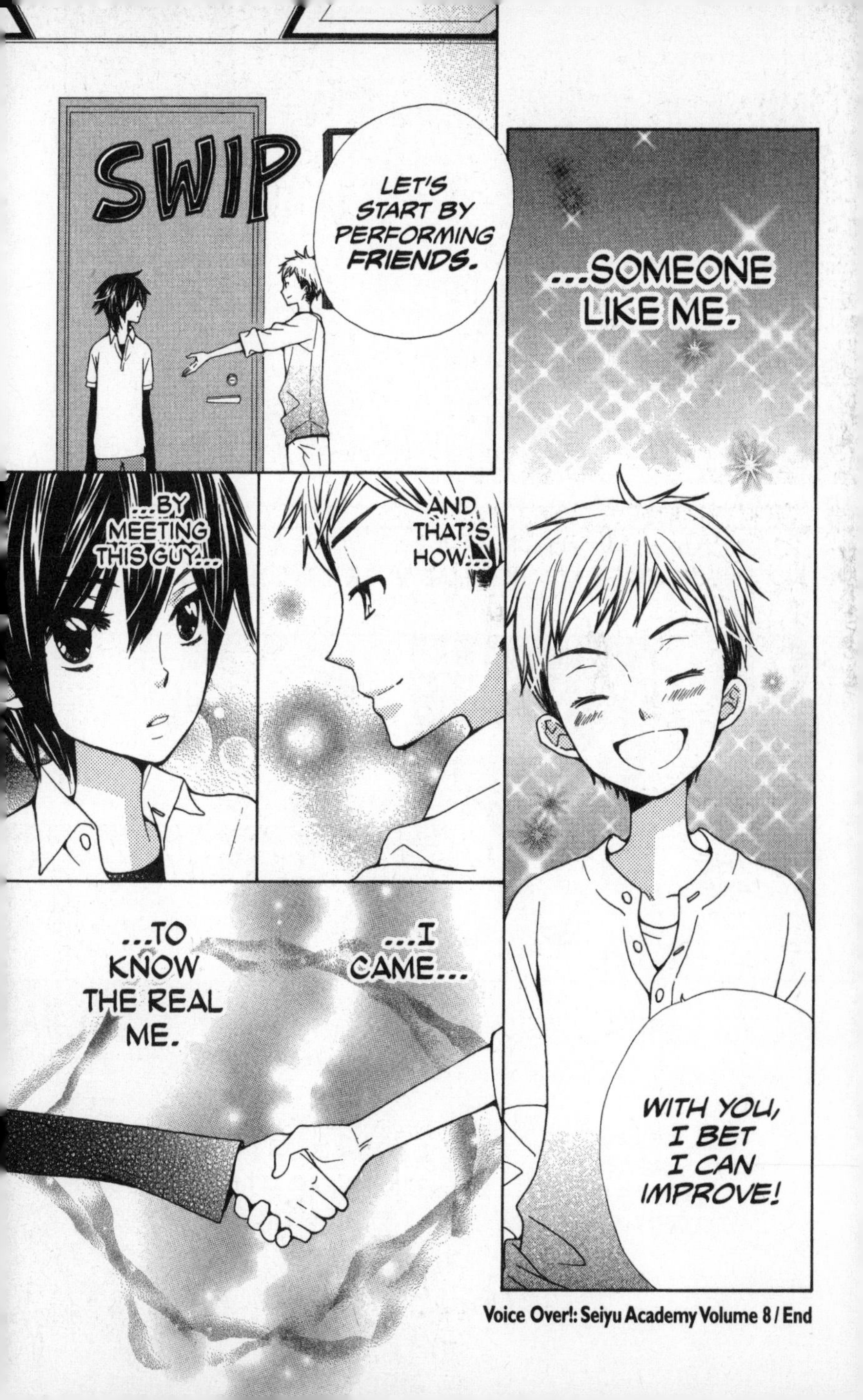
...SOMEONE LIKE ME.
WITH YOU, I BET I CAN IMPROVE!
SWIP
LET'S START BY PERFORMING FRIENDS.
AND THAT'S HOW...
...BY MEETING THIS GUY...
...I CAME...
...TO KNOW THE REAL ME.

Voice Over!: Seiyu Academy Volume 8 / End

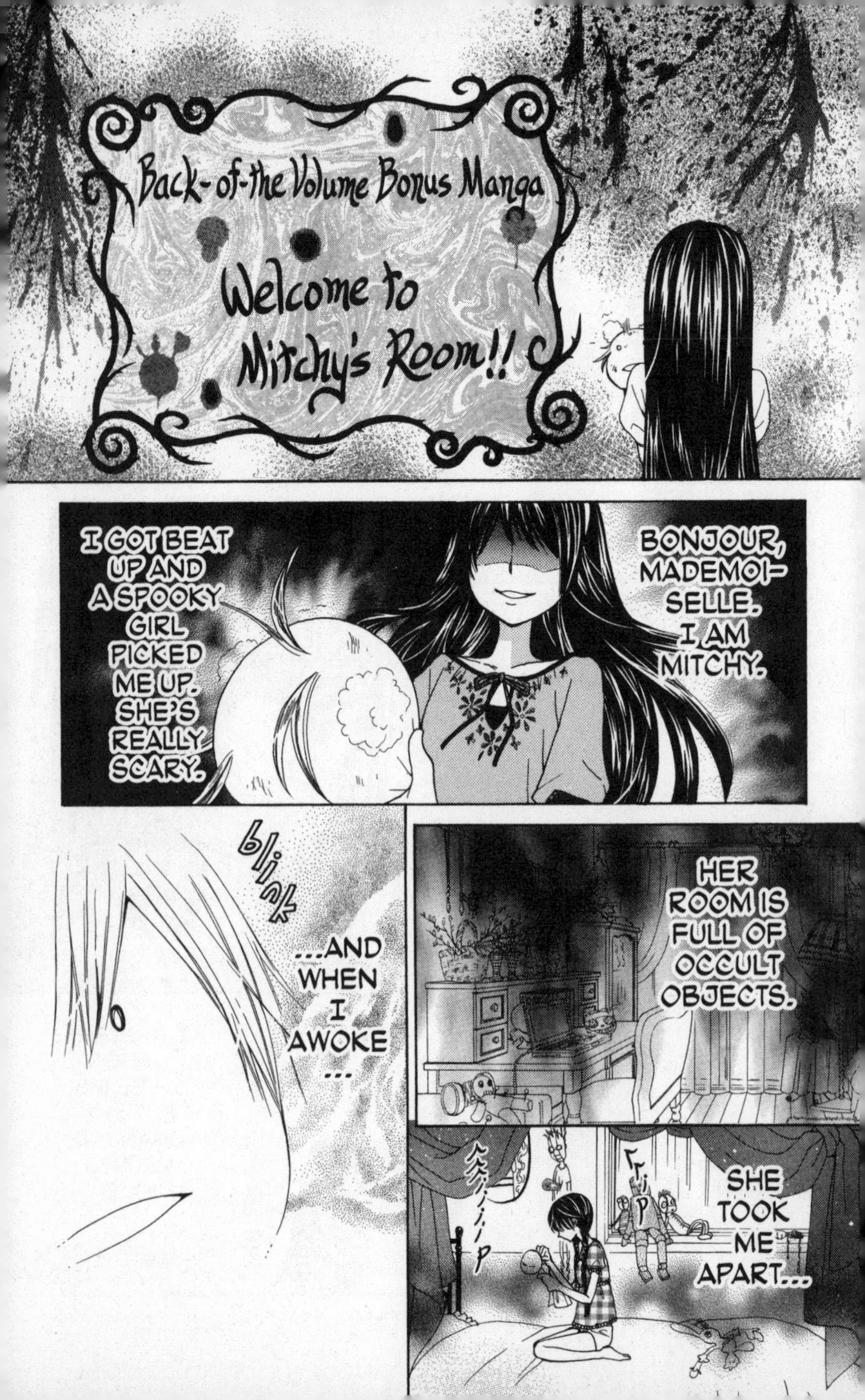
Back-of-the Volume Bonus Manga
Welcome to Mitchy's Room!!
BONJOUR, MADEMOI-SELLE. I AM MITCHY.
I GOT BEAT UP AND A SPOOKY GIRL PICKED ME UP. SHE'S REALLY SCARY.
HER ROOM IS FULL OF OCCULT OBJECTS.
SHE TOOK ME APART...
blink
...AND WHEN I AWOKE...

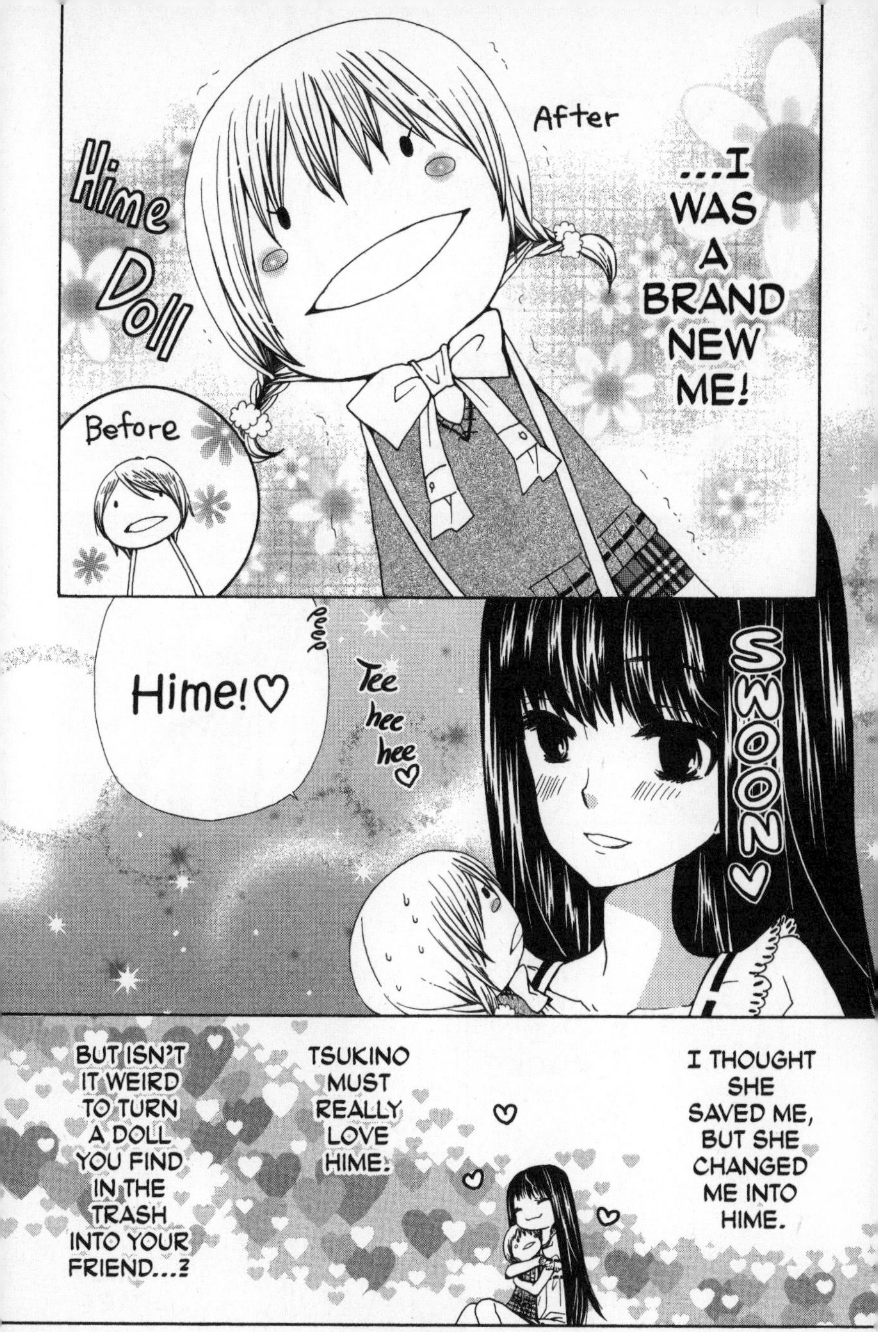
...I WAS A BRAND NEW ME!
After
Hime Doll
Before
SWOON♡
Tee hee hee♡
Hime!♡
I THOUGHT SHE SAVED ME, BUT SHE CHANGED ME INTO HIME.
TSUKINO MUST REALLY LOVE HIME.
BUT ISN'T IT WEIRD TO TURN A DOLL YOU FIND IN THE TRASH INTO YOUR FRIEND...?

Bonus Pages / End

Voice Over! Seiyu Academy

End Notes

Page 43, panel 1: Omelet rice
Omuraisu in Japanese. A traditional Japanese omelet that is filled with rice and usually topped with ketchup.

Page 132, panel 3: Dorayaki
Japanese pancakes, traditionally served sandwich fashion, with a scoop of sweet azuki bean paste between two cakes.

Page 133, sidebar: Yakisoba, kara-age
Yakisoba is a stir-fried noodle dish similar to chow mein, and *kara-age* is fried chicken. Both are classic festival foods.

Maki Minami is from Saitama Prefecture in Japan. She debuted in 2001 with *Kanata no Ao* (Faraway Blue). Her other works include *Kimi wa Girlfriend* (You're My Girlfriend), *Mainichi ga Takaramono* (Every Day Is a Treasure), *Yuki Atataka* (Warm Winter) and *S•A*, which was published in English by VIZ Media.

VOICE OVER!
SEIYU ACADEMY
VOL. 8
Shojo Beat Edition

STORY AND ART BY
MAKI MINAMI

TECHNICAL ADVISORS
Yoichi Kato, Kaori Kagami, Ayumi Hashidate,
Ayako Harino and Touko Fujitani

Special Thanks
81produce
Tokyo Animator College
Tokyo Animation College

English Translation & Adaptation/John Werry
Touch-up Art & Lettering/Sabrina Heep
Design/Yukiko Whitley
Editor/Pancha Diaz

Printed in the U.S.A.

Published by VIZ Media, LLC
P.O. Box 77010
San Francisco, CA 94107

10 9 8 7 6 5 4 3 2 1
First printing, December 2014

www.viz.com
www.shojobeat.com

PARENTAL ADVISORY
VOICE OVER!: SEIYU ACADEMY is rated T for Teen and is recommended for ages 13 and up.
RATED T FOR TEEN
ratings.viz.com

A **Publisher's Weekly** bestseller!

What happens when the hottest boy in school ...*is a girl?!?*

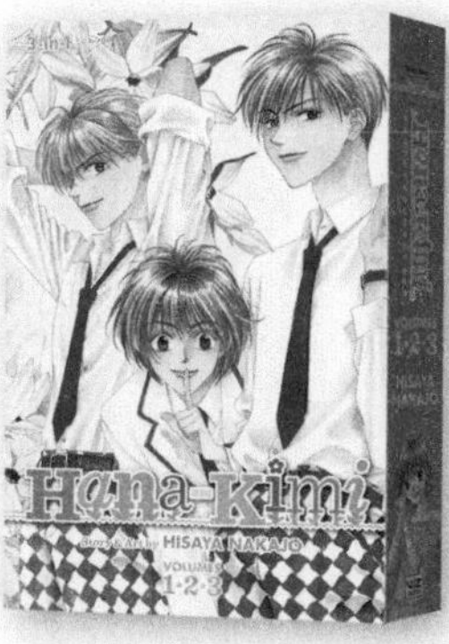
Hana-Kimi
HISAYA NAKAJO
VOLUMES 1·2·3

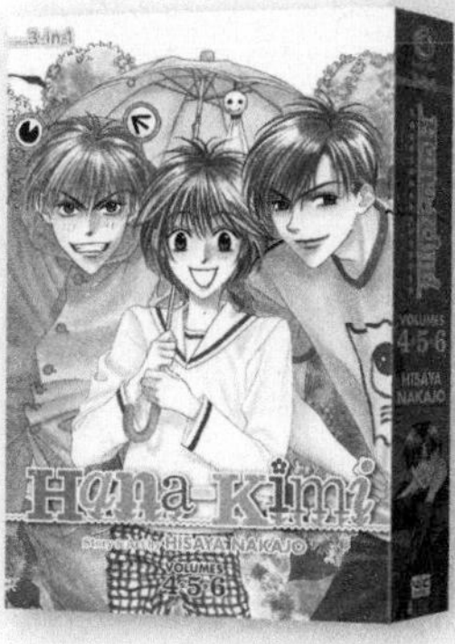
Hana-Kimi
Story & Art by HISAYA NAKAJO
VOLUMES 4·5·6

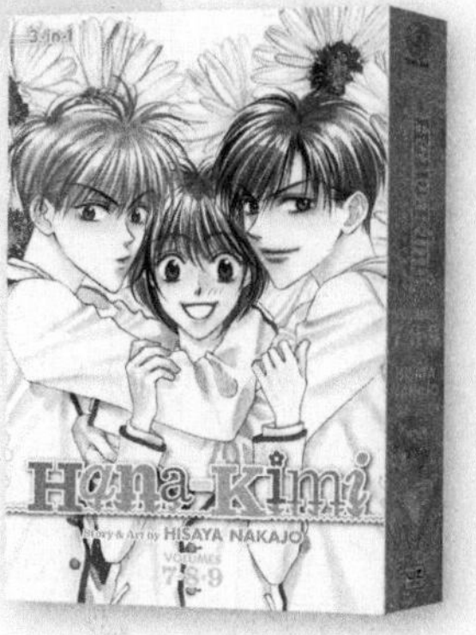
Hana-Kimi
Story & Art by HISAYA NAKAJO
VOLUMES 7·8·9

Find out in these 3-in-1 collections of the hit shojo series!

Hana-Kimi

Story & Art by HISAYA NAKAJO

Mizuki Ashiya has such a crush on a track star named Izumi Sano that she moves from the U.S. to Japan to enroll in the all-male high school he goes to! Pretending to be a boy, Mizuki becomes Sano's roommate...

...but how can she keep such a big secret when she's so close to the guy she wants?

IN STORES NOW!

3-in-1 Vol. 1 ISBN: 978-1-4215-4224-9
3-in-1 Vol. 2 ISBN: 978-1-4215-4225-6
3-in-1 Vol. 3 ISBN: 978-1-4215-4229-4

Only **$14.99 US / $16.99 CAN** each!

ratings.viz.com

www.viz.com

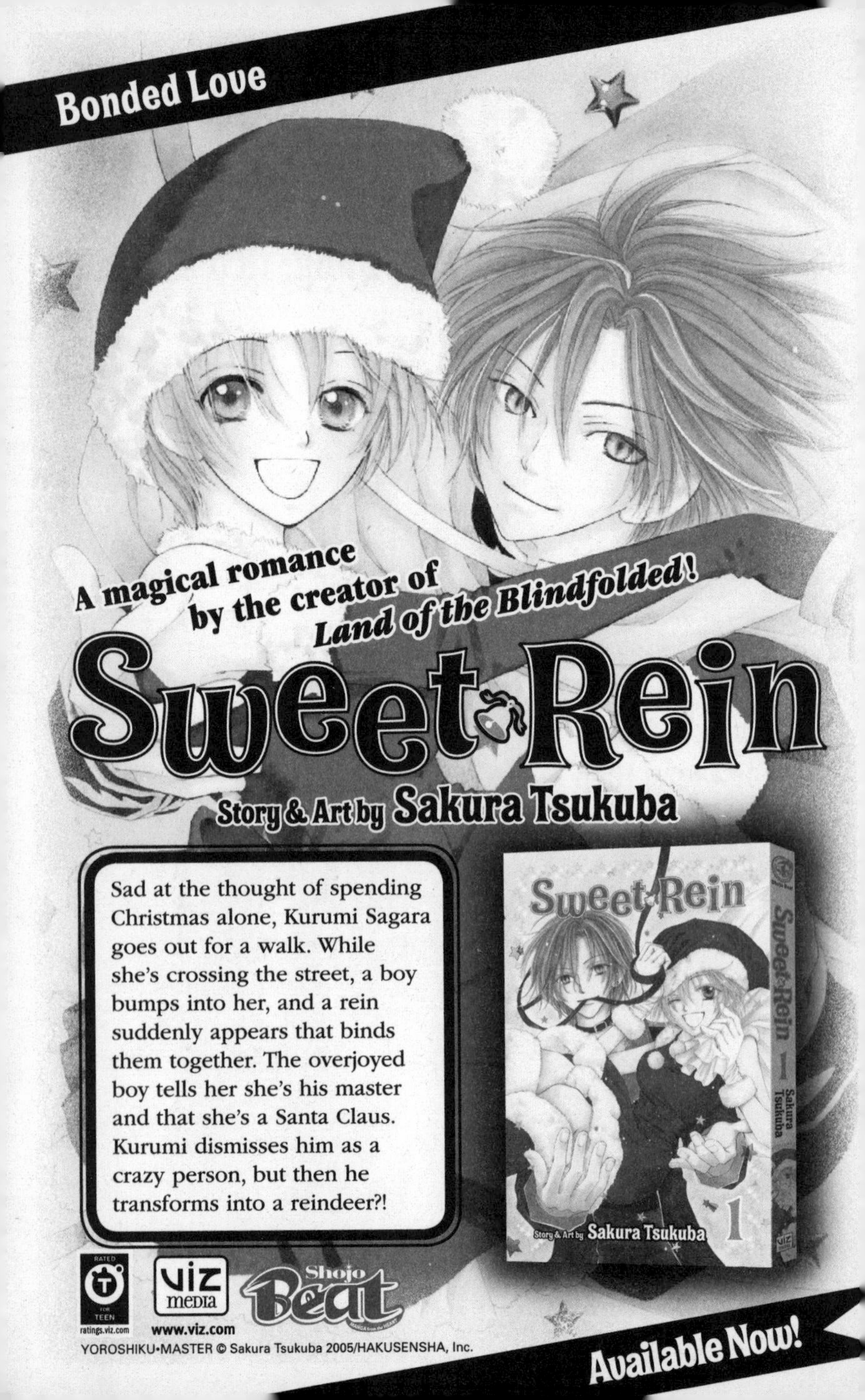
Bonded Love
A magical romance by the creator of Land of the Blindfolded!
Sweet Rein
Story & Art by Sakura Tsukuba
Sad at the thought of spending Christmas alone, Kurumi Sagara goes out for a walk. While she's crossing the street, a boy bumps into her, and a rein suddenly appears that binds them together. The overjoyed boy tells her she's his master and that she's a Santa Claus. Kurumi dismisses him as a crazy person, but then he transforms into a reindeer?!
Sweet Rein
1
Story & Art by Sakura Tsukuba
Sweet Rein
1
Sakura Tsukuba
RATED T FOR TEEN
ratings.viz.com
viz media
www.viz.com
Shojo Beat
YOROSHIKU•MASTER © Sakura Tsukuba 2005/HAKUSENSHA, Inc.
Available Now!

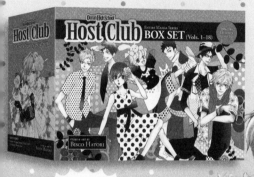

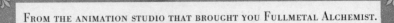
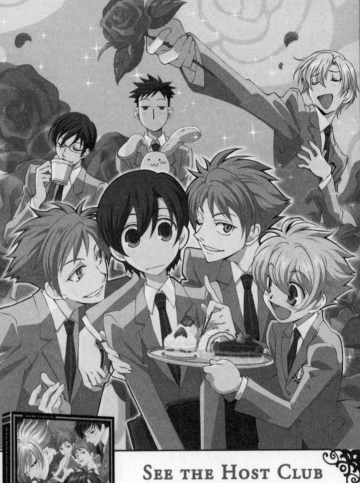

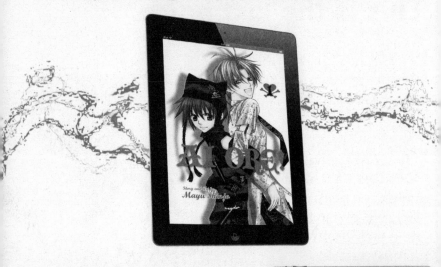
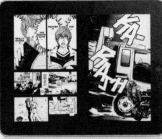
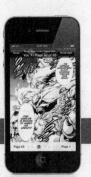

This is the last page.

In keeping with the original Japanese comic format, this book reads from right to left—so action, sound effects, and word balloons are completely reversed. This preserves the orientation of the original artwork—plus, it's fun! Check out the diagram shown here to get the hang of things, and then turn to the other side of the book to get started!

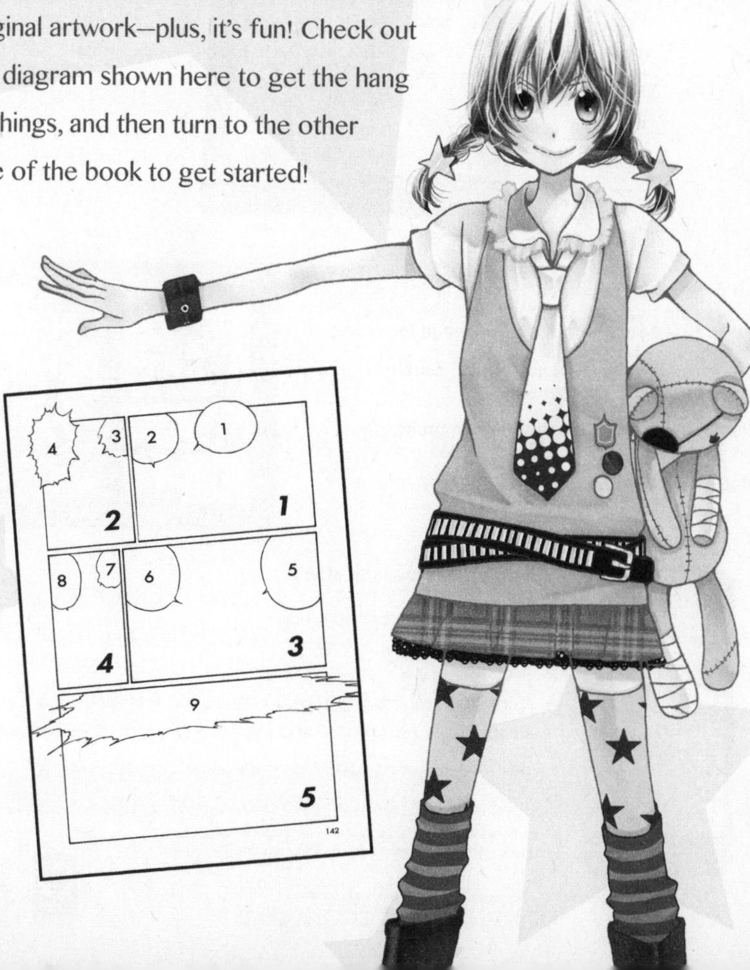
1
2
1
3
4
2
5
6
3
7
8
4
9
5
142